Bridges and Boundaries

The BCSIA Studies in International Security book series is edited at the Belfer Center for Science and International Affairs at Harvard University's John F. Kennedy School of Government and published by The MIT Press. The series publishes books on contemporary issues in international security policy, as well as their conceptual and historical foundations. Topics of particular interest to the series include the spread of weapons of mass destruction, internal conflict, the international effects of democracy and democratization, and U.S. defense policy.

A complete list of BCSIA Studies appears at the back of this volume.

Bridges and Boundaries

Historians, Political Scientists, and the Study of International Relations

Editors
Colin Elman and
Miriam Fendius Elman

BCSIA Studies in International Security

The MIT Press
Cambridge, Massachusetts
London, England

Library of Congress Cataloging-in-Publication Data

Bridges and boundaries : historians, political scientists, and the study of
international relations / Colin Elman and Miriam Fendius Elman.
p.   cm.—(BCSIA studies in international security)
Includes bibliographical references and index.
ISBN 0-262-05064-1 (hc. : alk. paper)—ISBN 0-262-55039-3 (pbk. : alk. paper)
1. History—Methodology. 2. Historiography.
3. Social sciences and history. 4. Military history—Methodology.
5. International relations—History.
I. Elman, Colin. II. Elman, Miriam Fendius. III. Series.

D16 .B84   2000
907'.2—dc21   00-056864
                                                                 CIP

10 9 8 7 6 5 4 3 2 1

Printed in the United States of America

Cover image: This print, from a collection of images of Rovereto, Italy, comes
from Rovereto nell'opera di Franz (Franciscus) Nigrinus, Giuseppe Osti, ed.
(Longo, 1997). We gratefully acknowledge the help of Museo Civico di
Rovereto, which provided this print to us free of charge.

Contents

Acknowledgments

This volume is directly descended from the papers presented and the discussions at "Diplomatic History and International Relations Theory: Respecting Differences and Crossing Boundaries," an interdisciplinary conference held in Tempe, Arizona, on January 15–18, 1998.

The conference was conceived and planned with the assistance of Edward Ingram, whose guidance, support, and gentle mid-course corrections proved invaluable. The chapter authors took time from their busy research agendas to write essays, prepare comments, and subsequently revise their contributions—more than once—for this volume. Richard Ned Lebow deserves special mention for presenting his paper, and providing commentary on others, all while coping with pneumonia. We also thank Geoffrey Parker for stepping in at unusually short notice to provide one of the best presentations at the meeting. Richard Ashley, David Dessler, Stephen Haber, Scott Sagan, and Sheldon Simon helped to shape and advance this project by their contributions to the Tempe conference. We would also like to express our gratitude to Arizona State University's President Lattie Coor and Vice Provost Jonathan Fink, who took part in the weekend activities and extended a warm welcome to the conference attendees. Finally, we thank several of our then graduate students—Cooper Drury, Kevin Ellsworth, Paul Johnson, and Greg Marfleet—for helping to prepare reports of the conference proceedings.

We are very grateful to Arizona State University's College of Liberal Arts and Sciences (CLAS), the Department of Political Science, the Graduate College, and the Arizona Foundation for jointly sponsoring the Tempe conference. In particular, we would like to express our gratitude to President Lattie Coor, Milton Glick (Senior Vice President and Provost), Gary Krahenbuhl (CLAS Dean), Milton Sommerfeld (CLAS Dean), and Stephen Walker and Robert Youngblood (the former and current Chairs of the Department of Political Science) for financing a project put together by two of their junior faculty. We hope that this book will go some way to showing that their confidence, and money, were not misplaced.

This book was completed while taking up our respective International Security Fellowships at Harvard University's Belfer Center for Science and International Affairs. We thank Graham Allison and Steven Miller for inviting us to rejoin BCSIA's intellectual community, and for their gracious encouragement. As Editor of the BCSIA Studies in International Security, Sean Lynn-Jones offered the volume a home and won an international competition to find a suitable picture for its cover. Executive Editor Karen Motley steered the book through to publication in her usual efficient manner. We are also very grateful to Miriam Avins, whose user-friendly copyediting made this a much better book.

Finally, we dedicate this book to Robert Jervis and Paul Schroeder, whose seminal work on the possibility of bridge-building between the disciplines inspired us to commence this collaborative project.

Colin Elman and
Miriam Fendius Elman

Tempe, Arizona
June 2000

Bridges and Boundaries

Introduction

Negotiating International History and Politics

Colin Elman and Miriam Fendius Elman

For this book, we asked distinguished historians and political scientists to take stock of the differences and similarities between their disciplines, to reflect on how disciplinary training influences the study of international events, and to discuss the feasibility of cross-fertilization. The resulting volume explores how scholars from the fields of history and political science can learn from one another, while recognizing some of the nontrivial obstacles that divide them.

The contributors are drawn from particular subsets of their disciplines, and the views expressed are accordingly bounded. The conversation is between what might loosely be described as methodologically traditionalist diplomatic and military historians, and international relations theorists who do qualitative case studies.[1] It would have been possible to arrange a different cross-border dialogue: a broadly conceived volume of social scientists debating humanists, for example, or one that pitted mainstream historians against formal modelers or quantitative political scientists. Although these would have been useful exercises, creating interdisciplinary dialogue is easier with groups that at least bear

We thank Elizabeth Kier for helpful comments on an earlier draft of this chapter, and for her encouragement and support. We also thank the participants at the International Security Program Seminar, Belfer Center for Science and International Affairs, Harvard University for their constructive criticism.

1. "Loosely described" because all such labels are at best approximations, and because individual scholars' work rightfully resists such simple categorizations. For example, some of the political scientists contributing to the volume have utilized quantitative approaches in their work.

some initial similarities because the likelihood for fruitful dialogue is at its highest. We believe that we have assembled two such groups here.[2]

First, the authors share an interest in a common subject matter—the state, politics, and war. This may be of particular interest to the historians, since they are likely to find few opportunities for such a dialogue within their own ranks. Their discipline now puts a premium on subjects outside the traditional purview of diplomatic and military history. Historians have moved away from analyzing statecraft, government interaction, and great political events toward the study of historically voiceless groups.[3] This decline in the study of politics and war is reflected in the diminished attention given to the topics in professional and scholarly journals, in their virtual exclusion from annual meetings of the American Historical Association, and in their falling share of university faculty appointments and curricula.[4]

Second, the political scientists and historians represented here share a number of methodological leanings. As Stephen H. Haber, David M.

---

2. See Margaret G. Hermann, "One Field, Many Perspectives: Building the Foundations for Dialogue (1998 ISA Presidential Address)," *International Studies Quarterly,* Vol. 42, No. 4 (December 1998), pp. 614–615. These are not, of course, the only two such groups that could be identified, although it should be noted that affinities between the disciplines have often been temporally displaced. For example, today's international historians might feel more affinity for the political science of the immediate post–World War II period, where multicausal analysis and the role of intentions and statesmanship figured more prominently than it does in much of the research in the international relations subfield written over the past three decades. Similarly, political scientists who study international relations today would have found more in common with historians of the nineteenth century—or the cliometricians and new economic historians of the twentieth—many of whom felt that it was not enough for historians to reconstruct the past according to original sources; historians also had to discover general laws of human behavior and development, and they had to emphasize causal explanation rather than understanding, interpretation, or moral reflection.

3. To be sure, international history never captured a monopoly position in twentieth-century historiography. The notion that "history is past politics and politics is present history" was dominant in the nineteenth century, when historical research in the United States (and also in Europe) focused on the state papers and official documents that historian Leopold von Ranke and others considered quintessential to the writing of objective historical accounts. But by the early twentieth century, with democratization and the emergence of a mass society, there was already strong support for histories that transcended politics—a "democratization of history"—by an inclusion of broader segments of the public and an extension of perspective from leading public figures to social and economic conditions. The challenge to traditional historiography—from the French *Annales* school of historians, to the new U.S. social and economic history, to Marxist class analysis—has continued unabated.

4. For example, over the past two decades, the flagship journal of the U.S. historical profession, the *American Historical Review,* has not published a single research article

Kennedy, and Stephen D. Krasner put it, "Historians who study diplomatic history and political scientists who study international politics, despite some genuine differences, have always been engaged in a similar enterprise. Both have always been committed to a positivist methodology in which claims have had to be supported by empirical data."[5] This commitment is an orthodox and dominant position in political science, but is arguably becoming less so in history. Most of the historians in this book would be unsympathetic to postmodern perspectives that tilt the balance away from an objectively knowable past toward consideration of the historian's (and reader's) particular moral, political, or ideological beliefs. While recognizing that facts and documents do not speak for themselves and that observations are theory-laden, most of the participants would agree that claims should be evaluated against empirical evidence, and that historians do not write works of fiction, where stories of the past merely reflect—and serve to perpetuate—the underlying ideologies of their authors. John Lynn puts it well:

Whereas historians in the past were prone to borrowing theoretical underpinnings from political science and sociology, today they are more likely to import much from anthropology and literary studies. Concepts generated by literary and linguistic scholars seem particularly embarrassing in the study of history because they undermine the value of evidence and conclude that documents cannot actually tell us about reality but only about the author of the document. This "linguistic turn" may be fine when approaching a novel or a poem, but it is usually malarkey when applied to the war archives.[6]

Third, just as both groups share a common commitment to attempting an objective analysis of the past, so too do they both suffer from pressures that seek to reduce their respective disciplines to communities in which qualitative research cannot find a home. In history, the popularity of postmodernist approaches has thrown traditional methods into disrepute. Diplomatic and military historians, who appeal to evidence

---

focused on the conduct of the Hundred Years' War , the Thirty Years' War, the Wars of Louis XIV, the War of American Independence, the Revolutionary and Napoleonic Wars, World War I, or World War II. See John A. Lynn, "The Embattled Future of Academic Military History," *The Journal of Military History*, Vol. 61 (October 1977), p. 780.

5. Stephen Haber, David M. Kennedy, and Stephen D. Krasner, "Brothers Under the Skin: Diplomatic History and International Relations," *International Security*, Vol. 22, No. 1 (Summer 1997), p. 34.

6. Lynn, "The Embattled Future of Academic Military History," p. 779. For another critique of the postmodern attack on objectivity, see Arthur Schlesinger, Jr., "History as Therapy: A Dangerous Idea," *New York Times*, May 3, 1996.

and share a commitment to uncovering an objectively knowable past, find themselves squeezed out of the discipline, and see themselves as one of the few remaining outposts of pre-postmodern approaches. Many traditional historians—diplomatic and military historians included—are so alienated and dissatisfied with their situation that they have formed a new professional association (the Historical Society), thereby further disassociating themselves from the discipline's mainstream.[7] For international historians the growing fear is that, among historians working in the United States at least, they are fast becoming a "dying breed," with international history dominated by political scientists who "do not do this history as historians can and should do it."[8]

In the international relations subfield of political science, by contrast, positivist approaches continue to dominate the discipline, and postmodernists are seen as minority dissidents. But international relations theorists who employ qualitative case study methods are subject to equally debilitating pressures: a large and increasing majority of effort, attention, and journal space is being given to formal modeling and quantitative research. In the flagship journal of the American Political Science Association, the *American Political Science Review,* for example, virtually none

---

7. For overviews of nineteenth- and twentieth-century trends in the study of history, see Robert William Fogel and G.R. Elton, *Which Road to the Past? Two Views of History* (New Haven, Conn.: Yale University Press, 1983); Georg G. Iggers, *Historiography in the Twentieth Century* (Hanover, N.H.: Wesleyan University Press, 1997); R.F. Atkinson, *Knowledge and Explanation in History: An Introduction to the Philosophy of History* (Ithaca: Cornell University Press, 1978), pp. 14–17; Michael Kammen, "The Historian's Vocation and the State of the Discipline in the United States," in Michael Kammen, ed., *The Past Before Us: Contemporary Historical Writing in the United States* (Ithaca: Cornell University Press, 1980), pp. 19–46. For extended discussions of the decline of diplomatic and military history in the profession, particularly in U.S. academe, see Gordon A. Craig, "The Historian and the Study of International Relations," *American Historical Review,* Vol. 88, No. 1 (February 1983), p. 2; Haber, Kennedy, and Krasner, "Brothers Under the Skin," pp. 34–43; Lynn, "The Embattled Future of Academic Military History," pp. 777–789; Charles S. Maier, "Marking Time: The Historiography of International Relations," in *The Past Before Us,* pp. 355–387; Stephen Haber, "Explaining the Methods Gap: History and the Social Sciences," paper presented at the interdisciplinary conference on Diplomatic History and International Relations Theory: Respecting Differences and Crossing Boundaries, Arizona State University, January 15–18, 1998.

8. Paul Schroeder, "The AHA and the Historical Society" reprinted in H-DIPLO@ H-NET.MSU.EDU, September 30, 1998. For more on the new Historical Society see Courtney Leatherman, "Saying Their Field Is in 'Disarray', Historians Set Up a New Society," *Chronicle of Higher Education,* May 8, 1998, p. A12; Courtney Leatherman, "The Historical Society's Own Motives Are Topic No. 1 At Its First National Convention," *Chronicle of Higher Education,* June 11, 1999, p. A16; and the debate between James Banner and Marc Trachtenberg reprinted in H-DIPLO@H-NET.MSU.EDU, September 26, 1998.

of the few articles on international relations employ qualitative methods. Qualitative international relations theorists make do with fewer funding and publishing opportunities, and are increasingly pressured to defend their status as social scientists.[9]

Viewed collectively, the authors of this book share an interest in a common subject matter, a commitment to utilizing empirical research to uncover a knowable past, and a sense that they are becoming less welcome in their own disciplines. Accordingly, addressing what international historians and political scientists who employ qualitative methods to study international relations can learn from each other may be even more important now than it has been in the past.[10] Despite their commonalities, however, there are important disagreements among the contributing political scientists and historians—both with regard to how they view their own enterprise, as well as that of the other discipline. Underlying these arguments are significant areas of difference among the disciplines, which are explored and illuminated by all of the contributors to the volume. Both groups of scholars concur that international relations theorists who do qualitative case studies are operating differently than historians who look at similar periods and events—there are real differences in approach and purpose, if not method, and the resulting works do not look or read the same.

The Roots and Organization of the Study

This volume is a subset of a larger discourse between political scientists and historians, especially between diplomatic historians and international relations theorists.[11] In particular, while acknowledging and appreciating

---

9. We are not suggesting that qualitative methodologies are inherently superior to either quantitative or formal approaches; all three approaches have much to offer, but an undue emphasis on some to the exclusion of others is harmful. For similar appeals for methodological pluralism, see Lisa L. Martin, "The Contributions of Rational Choice: A Defense of Pluralism," *International Security*, Vol. 24, No. 2 (Fall 1999), pp. 80–83; Stephen M. Walt, "Rigor or Rigor Mortis? Rational Choice and Security Studies," *International Security*, Volume 23, Number 4 (Spring 1999), pp. 7, 47–48; and Stephen M. Walt, "A Model Disagreement," *International Security*, Vol. 24, No. 2 (Fall 1999), pp. 115, 128–130.

10. On this point, see Jack S. Levy, "Too Important to Leave to the Other: History and Political Science in the Study of International Relations," *International Security*, Vol. 22, No. 1 (Summer 1997), p. 23.

11. See, for example, Christopher Thorne, *Border Crossings: Studies in International History* (Oxford: Basil Blackwell, 1988); Christopher Hill, "History and International Relations," in Steve Smith, ed., *International Relations: British and American Perspectives* (Oxford: Basil Blackwell, 1985); Rogers M. Smith, "Science, Non-science, and Politics,"

the ideas expressed in other earlier exchanges, this book builds on a 1997 symposium of historians and political scientists in *International Security*.[12]

Contributors to the symposium—political scientists Alexander George, Stephen D. Krasner, and Jack S. Levy and historians John Lewis Gaddis, Stephen H. Haber, Edward Ingram, David M. Kennedy, and Paul W. Schroeder—debated the similarities and differences in the ways that scholars from both disciplines study international war and peace and foreign policy decision-making, and identified the sort of scholarly pursuits that are respected and rewarded in the two disciplines. The near-consensus that emerged was that the differences between international historians and political scientists who study international relations through qualitative methods are not as stark as believed. Contributors noted the similarity between process tracing and historical explanation and pointed out that both sets of scholars are often just as motivated by presentist concerns—international historians and political scientists do not differ much in the view that the past can be studied to provide

---

in Terrence J. McDonald, ed., *The Historic Turn in the Human Sciences* (Ann Arbor: University of Michigan Press, 1996), pp. 119–159; Olav Njolstad, "Learning From History? Case Studies and the Limits to Theory-building," in Nils Petter Gleditsch and Olav Njolstad, eds., *Arms Races: Technological and Political Dynamics* (London: Sage, 1990), pp. 220–246; Dennis Kavanagh, "Why Political Science Needs History," *Political Studies*, Vol. 39 (1991), pp. 479–495; Kim Salomon, "What Is the Use of International History?" *Journal of Peace Research*, Vol. 30, No. 4 (1993), pp. 375–389; Donald J. Puchala, "The Pragmatics of International History," *Mershon International Studies Review*, Vol. 39, No. 1 (April 1995), pp. 1–18; David Dessler, "Empirical Research as Puzzle Solving: The Logic of Research Design in Social Science" (unpublished manuscript, Department of Government, College of William and Mary, October 1997); Paul W. Schroeder, "Quantitative Studies in the Balance of Power: An Historian's Reaction," *Journal of Conflict Resolution*, Vol. 21, No. 1 (March 1977), pp. 3–22; John Lewis Gaddis, "Expanding the Data Base: Historians, Political Scientists, and the Enrichment of Security Studies," *International Security*, Vol. 12, No. 1 (Summer 1987), pp. 3–21; Gordon Craig, "The Historian and the Study of International Relations," *American Historical Review*, Vol. 9, No. 1 (February 1983), pp. 1–11; Paul Schroeder, "Historical Reality vs. Neo-realist Theory," *International Security*, Vol. 19, No. 1 (Summer 1994), pp. 108–148; and Colin Elman and Miriam Fendius Elman, "Correspondence: History vs. Neo-realism: A Second Look," *International Security*, Vol. 20, No. 1 (Summer 1995), pp. 182–193.

12. See the seven articles in *International Security*, Vol. 22, No. 1 (Summer 1997), pp. 5–85. The debate is framed in Colin Elman and Miriam Fendius Elman, "Diplomatic History and International Relations Theory: Respecting Difference and Crossing Boundaries," *International Security*, Vol. 22, No. 1 (Summer 1997), pp. 5–21. For an overview of the symposium, see Christopher Shea, "A Journal Seeks to Be the Peacemaker in War Between Historians and Political Scientists," *Chronicle of Higher Education*, September 5, 1997, pp. A20–21.

perspectives on the present and to help solve current policy problems.[13] Both sets of scholars also agreed that, by and large, the historian's narrative need not be, and usually *is not*, atheoretical—just as international relations theories need historical facts against which they can be measured, so too do historical works offer assertions about the possible causes of the events they describe, and hence rely on causal theories. In the words of historian Edward Ingram:

The distinction between the political scientist's theory-based analysis and the historian's evidence-based description is false. The historian's description is a form of analysis (it explains); likewise, narrative (which has nothing to do with chronology) is applied theory, an analytical test of a proposition. . . . Most historians, unhappy to grope about in a fog, try to explain what did happen, as well as what their subjects thought had happened. Their work implies—and demands—a theory taken with them in their baggage.[14]

Nevertheless, participants in the symposium also addressed important differences. Each set of scholars pointed out, for instance, that political scientists are more likely to look to the past as a way of supporting or discrediting theoretical hypotheses while historians are more likely to be interested in past international events for their own sake. Although political scientists might turn to the distant past, the study of "deep" history is relevant to their research objectives only insofar as it enables them to generate, test, or refine theory. By contrast, for the historian the goal of theory-building and testing is secondary—the "past interests historians for itself."[15] Contributors noted too that political scientists tend to reward new and explicit theoretical work over a meticulous culling of archives, and are more likely to favor scholarship that is parsimonious; that is, research that demonstrates how only a few explanatory variables can account for a wide range of phenomena.[16] Historians show a greater

---

13. As Robert Jervis notes in his chapter, however, not all political scientists who study international relations are interested in real-world security issues, or want to make their work policy-relevant. On this point, see also Walt, "Rigor or Rigor Mortis?" pp. 22, 46–47; Walt, "A Model Disagreement," pp. 124–128; Frank C. Zagare, "All Mortis, No Rigor," *International Security*, Vol. 24, No. 2 (Fall 1999), pp. 113–114.

14. Edward Ingram, "The Wonderland of the Political Scientist," *International Security*, Vol. 22, No. 1 (Summer 1997), pp. 53, 55.

15. Ibid., p. 54.

16. For more on the value attached to "maximizing leverage" or explaining as much as possible with as little as possible, see Gary King, Robert O. Keohane, and Sidney Verba, *Designing Social Inquiry: Scientific Inference in Qualitative Research* (Princeton: Princeton University Press, 1994), pp. 29–31.

tolerance for overdetermined explanations and a greater affinity for scholarship that explains international and foreign policy outcomes via multiple sufficient causation or equifinality.

This book includes chapters written by several of the historians and political scientists who participated in the earlier exchange in *International Security*. But this book goes significantly beyond the symposium in three ways. First, the conversation is joined by twelve new authors. Historians (Carole K. Fink, Stephen Pelz, John A. Lynn, and Gerhard L. Weinberg) and political scientists (Andrew Bennett, Robert Jervis, Deborah Welch Larson, Richard Ned Lebow, Richard Rosecrance, Randall L. Schweller, William R. Thompson, and William R. Wohlforth) join the original contributors to the symposium, responding to the *International Security* commentaries, and discussing the impact of disciplinary guild rules on their own research. Second, the book encourages greater self-reflection. We asked authors to think about how being trained as a political scientist or historian has influenced their reading of particular international events. Third, to facilitate this introspective exercise, and to create more dialogue among the contributors than was possible in journal format, we have included three empirical pairs of chapters that juxtapose a political scientist and his or her historian counterpart, both of whom have studied the same international event.

The book is organized into three sections. In the first section, political scientists and a historian discuss the methodological differences and similarities that divide and unite them. In Chapter 1, Jack S. Levy argues that despite many similarities in approach, the criterion that best defines the difference between the two disciplines is the idiographic/nomothetic distinction. In Chapter 2, Stephen Pelz suggests ways in which historians might use the methods of political scientists—without sacrificing an interest in particular, contingent generalizations. In Chapter 3, Richard Ned Lebow says that while historians and political scientists both use theory and counterfactual reasoning, and are influenced by ideological commitment and current events, historians are less careful to posit falsifiable arguments, and frequently offer unsatisfying overdetermined explanations. In Chapter 4, Andrew Bennett and Alexander George suggest that both political scientists and historians use the "within case" method of process tracing, and that typological theory provides a middle ground between the parsimonious general theories favored by political scientists and the rich, detailed explanations of specific cases preferred by historians.

The second part of the book examines and demonstrates how the similarities and differences in method have informed the writings of historians and political scientists on specific international events: the rise and fall of British hegemony, World War II, and the Cold War. We chose these topics because it is here that political scientists and historians both have unambiguous track records, with well-established bodies of work that have been devoloped over a long period. These paired chapters directly engage the methodological issues raised in the first part of the book, address the substantive conclusions of the historian or political scientist with whom they are engaged, and illuminate the different styles of argument and presentation that historians and political scientists exhibit in their work—differences that range from language to organization. The juxtaposed empirical chapters can be viewed as representative works (see Schweller's and Weinberg's chapters in particular); direct engagements of each other (see Thompson's and Ingram's chapters in particular); and efforts to "cross over" or explicitly borrow concepts and methods from the other discipline (see Larson's and Gaddis's chapters in particular). The chapters also offer a stock-taking and self-reflective exercise in which political scientists and historians examine how their research has been guided by their respective disciplinary methodologies and guild rules. Finally, we asked commentators to provide brief postscripts on the three chapter pairs, and to weigh in on the methodological debate.

In Chapters 5 and 6, Gerhard L. Weinberg and Randall L. Schweller focus on their readings of the origins of World War II. In Chapter 5, Weinberg argues that World War II cannot be compared to previous international wars, largely because Hitler's policies represented such a radical departure from earlier great power behavior. Weinberg argues that the war must be seen as an integral component of Hitler's racial policies and his intention to demographically reorder Europe and eventually the globe. By contrast, in Chapter 6, Schweller explains the origins of World War II by first deducing how revisionist and status quo states are likely to act under tripolar international structures, and then applying this theory to great power foreign policies prior to the war. He concludes that a "structural problem," and not Hitler's war aims, was a sufficient cause of the war. In the postscript to these two chapters, Carole K. Fink uses counterfactual reasoning to poke holes in both Weinberg and Schweller's accounts, observes that both scholars ignore important factors, and questions some of the facts that each musters to bolster his argument. She concludes that combining Weinberg's actor-oriented approach with Schweller's systemic and structural approach leads to a more complete understanding of the interwar crisis and why the war broke out.

In Chapters 8 and 9, Edward Ingram and William R. Thompson reflect on their respective understandings of British hegemony. In Chapter 8, Ingram argues that Great Britain cannot be readily used as a "parable" for the U.S. experience as a world power. He shows that by relaxing the concept of sovereignty, and treating Britain as an empire rather than a nation state—or more precisely as a "dual monarchy"—the nature of British power in the nineteenth century, and the circumstances that contributed to its decline, are more accurately explained. In Chapter 9, Thompson juxtaposes historians' and political scientists' ways of thinking about Britain's role in world politics between 1816 and 1945, and suggests that there are a number of cross-cutting cleavages between the different interpretations. Directly engaging Ingram's critique of long cycle theory, he argues that Ingram's argument would also be criticized by international historians who share the political scientists' structuralist perspective. In the postscript to Ingram's and Thompson's chapters, Richard Rosecrance notes that many of the controversies between the two scholars—for example, the extent to which sea or land power is the key constituent of international power and the extent to which Britain was aided by empire—do not pit political scientists against historians; these are essentially debates that cut across the two disciplines.

In Chapters 11 and 12, John Lewis Gaddis and Deborah Welch Larson revisit the methodological underpinnings of their books on the origins of the Cold War. In Chapter 11, Gaddis discusses his notion of history as "dramatization" and shows how his conception of the historical method supports his reading of Cold War history in light of newly available archival material. In Chapter 12, Larson shows the promises of cross-fertilization between the two disciplines. On the one hand, she says that using social psychological theory to assess Cold War data has helped her uncover evidence that historians have ignored. On the other hand, because historians approach the historical record with preconceived theories of their own and advance competing explanations of the same event, she also insists that political scientists must do their own archival work, as well as assess whether documents point to a larger pattern by looking at newspapers printed during the period. In the postscript to the chapters, William C. Wohlforth points out that Gaddis and Larson both are interested in explaining a specific event; make causal statements; and agree that things could be improved in their respective disciplines by some judicious borrowing from the other. Nevertheless, he notes that each scholar argues that he or she offers a better explanation of the origins of the Cold War than the other provides.

In the last empirical chapter of the book, Chapter 14, John A. Lynn presents a military historian's overview of the study of military change. He suggests ways in which the methods and perspectives of both history and political science can shed light on the study of military change and the Revolution in Military Affairs, and briefly summarizes his own path-dependent, multicausal approach to military change as a possible avenue for future research.

In the final section of the book, Robert Jervis and Paul W. Schroeder provide two concluding chapters. In Chapter 15, Jervis highlights the areas of convergence between political scientists and historians who study international relations, offers some conjectures about why the fields grew apart, and discusses some differences in views on the value of parsimonious explanation, the priority of theory-building, the influence of moral concerns, and the centrality of time. Jervis concludes his essay by observing that, while he reads as much history as political science and learns much from both, he cannot imagine "becoming a historian." In Chapter 16, Schroeder concurs with much of Jervis's essay, but suggests that historians do not shun parsimony as much as they reject parsimonious theories that fail to integrate pertinent historical evidence, or fail to treat international relations as human conduct. Building on Jervis's observations about the moral dimension, Schroeder also elaborates on the role of moral judgment in historians' scholarship. Schroeder ends up noting that while scholars from both disciplines can be friends and even allies, he is sure that he "could never be a political scientist."

In the remainder of this chapter we take our turn from the vantage point of editors to reflect on some of the barriers between the disciplines and the opportunities for collaboration. Before proceeding, however, a few caveats are in order. First, both the boundaries and bridges that we discuss should be considered representative rather than exhaustive, and are not intended to serve as a comprehensive review. Second, it will quickly be apparent that some of the categories are very closely related, and may actually be addressing the same underlying questions. Finally, although couched in declarative language, and while the classifications may be familiar to most readers, they are by no means uncontroversial or universally accepted. Even among the small and admittedly biased sample of historians and political scientists represented in this book, these categories were contested.

International History and Politics: Boundaries

With the foregoing caveats in mind, in this section we discuss ways in which history and political science diverge. These include: different views of the purpose of theory and historical evidence; different understandings of causation; a contrasting emphasis on purposive and intentional behavior versus unintended outcomes; a related disparity in the degree to which attempts are made to attach judgments to political behavior; and a dissimilar sense of aesthetics. As we note in the next section, however, these dichotomous boundaries are increasingly challenged, and they are weakening in some important respects.

THE PURPOSE OF THEORY AND HISTORICAL EVIDENCE

While historians and political scientists apply theory to the study of international events, they use theory differently. As Richard Ned Lebow observes in his chapter, "Historians and social scientists lay claim to the same terrain with very different purposes in mind. Historians study the past as a valuable exercise in its own right. . . . Social scientists regard the past as data that might help them develop and test theories of human behavior."[17] Political scientists who study international relations from a qualitative perspective defend their research as significant and worthwhile not by demonstrating that they have helped to understand historical periods and events, but because they advance some particular research program, improve upon some existing theory, or generate new competing theories that challenge the received wisdom.[18]

Consider, by way of example, *Analytic Narratives*, a recent book by a group of distinguished political scientists. Although the chapters in the book convey an attention to historical detail and are explicitly geared to using the "narrative form, which is more commonly employed in history," the authors have a larger theoretical goal than merely explaining the "compelling" cases at hand: to further social inquiry based on the rational choice approach and game-theoretic models.[19] Randall L. Schweller's chapter in this volume provides an additional example. Schweller is explicit about why he is interested in studying the interwar period and World War II: not primarily for its own sake (i.e., not "to offer a new explanation of the war") but because of the impact his findings will have on classical realist and neorealist approaches to the study of international

---

17. See also Jack Levy's chapter. Note too Edward Ingram's "corset versus armor" metaphor for distinguishing the different ways theories are used in the two disciplines; John Lewis Gaddis's distinction between using theory to encompass narrative (political scientist) and embedding theory within narrative (historian); and Robert Jervis's and Ingram's claim that explanation and description are deeply intertwined in the historian's work, but sharply distinguished by political scientists.

18. King, Keohane, and Verba, for example, argue that good research designs in the social sciences should make an explicit contribution to the existing literature. See *Designing Social Inquiry*, pp. 15–17.

19. Robert H. Bates, Avner Greif, Margaret Levi, Jean-Laurent Rosenthal, and Barry R. Weingast, *Analytic Narratives* (Princeton: Princeton University Press, 1998).

relations. As William R. Thompson points out, and as Schweller's chapter illustrates, political scientists are rarely driven by empirical puzzles that emerge from observed events—why did the Cold War end peacefully? why did Gorbachev withdraw from Eastern Europe?—the bread and butter of the historian's enterprise. Instead, political scientists' work is puzzle- or theory-driven. Political scientists derive their puzzles from observed behavior that appears inconsistent with what existing theories would lead us to expect: how does the end of the Cold War, and Gorbachev's withdrawal from Eastern Europe, affect neorealist theories of international relations? Thus, according to Thompson, "political scientists are supposed to begin with theories and then move toward cases that can help them assess the relative utility of the theories that exist."[20]

THE NOMOTHETIC/IDIOGRAPHIC DISTINCTION. Linked to the political scientist's interest in theory-driven research is a consensus among the chapter authors that, for the most part, political scientists prefer generalizations that apply to different contexts across time and space, while historians eschew generalizations for deeper explanations and understandings of particular events—what Levy refers to as the nomothetic/ideographic distinction, or what has also been labeled narrative versus analytic explanation.[21] Instead of subordinating theory to the search for greater historical understanding of particular events and periods, political scientists are oriented to general problems and "prefer explanations of event-categories."[22] Trained in the positivist tradition,

---

20. The increasing respect for single case studies exhibited by recent proponents of qualitative methods, while further blurring the lines between history and political science in practice, has not changed the distinction between research driven by theoretical puzzles and empirical puzzles. For political scientists, single case studies are only valuable insofar as they have large theoretical implications. See Ronald Rogowski, "The Role of Theory and Anomaly in Social-Scientific Inference," *American Political Science Review*, Vol. 89, No. 2 (June 1995), pp. 467–470; and Timothy J. McKeown, "Case Studies and the Statistical Worldview: Review of King, Keohane and Verba's *Designing Social Inquiry*," *International Organization*, Vol. 53, No. 1 (Winter 1999), pp. 161–190. See also the chapter by Andrew Bennett and Alexander George in this volume.

21. See Dale H. Porter, *The Emergence of the Past: A Theory of Historical Explanation* (Chicago: University of Chicago Press, 1981); and Atkinson, *Knowledge and Explanation in History*, pp. 14, 113. As Levy notes, the nomothetic/idiographic distinction better describes contemporary differences in approach between historians and political scientists. However, it is inappropriate when considering the Hempelian tradition among historians and philosophers of history, popular in the 1940s and 1950s, which held that historians, like social scientists, explain events by subsuming them under laws governing the occurrence of like events.

22. Bruce Bueno de Mesquita, "Theory and the Advancement of Knowledge About War: A Reply," *Review of International Studies*, Vol. 10, No. 1 (January 1984), p. 67.

they explain individual events by identifying "if, then" generalizations, or covering laws, that match the pattern of the particular event. That is, an event is explained as an instance of a certain type of event, which is shown to accompany, and follow regularly from, specified initial conditions.[23] By contrast, historian Richard Hofstadter argues that "in our own time the scientific ideal no longer has quite the same plausibility for historians as it did for their predecessors in the Darwinian age, or as it now has for their colleagues in the social sciences. Most historians continue to feel that they deal with events which, though in some sense comparable, are essentially unique."[24]

Historian Clayton Roberts and political scientist Joseph Lepgold aptly observe the difference. According to Roberts: "Historians study the battle of the Marne, not battles in general; they seek the causes of the Enlightenment, not of enlightenments in general; they study the rise of Hitler, not of dictators in general. Things in general they leave to the sociologists." Says Lepgold: "A good IR [international relations] theory . . . should identify and explain patterns that transcend particular issues, actors, and historical eras. . . . Theory offers little explanatory power if it must be reinvented each time issues, actors, and eras change."[25] Similarly, John Lynn notes in his chapter that "there is some truth to the old stereotype that historians are embedded in their case studies and usually reluctant to generalize. The defining characteristic of historians may not be their dedication to the past in general, but their immersion in a *particular* past."[26]

23. Jack Snyder, "Science and Sovietology: Bridging the Methods Gap in Soviet Foreign Policy Studies," *World Politics* (1988), pp. 171–172. See also Bruce Bueno de Mesquita, "The Benefits of a Social Scientific Approach to Studying International Affairs," in Ngaire Woods, ed., *Explaining International Relations Since 1945* (Oxford: Oxford University Press, 1996), pp. 52–53.

24. Richard Hofstadter, "History and the Social Sciences," in Fritz Stern, ed., *The Varieties of History: From Voltaire to the Present* (New York: Meridian, 1957), p. 367.

25. Clayton Roberts, *The Logic of Historical Explanation* (University Park, Penn.: Pennsylvania State University Press, 1996), p. 8; Joseph Lepgold, "Is Anyone Listening? International Relations Theory and the Problem of Relevance," *Political Studies Quarterly*, Vol. 113, No. 1 (Spring 1998), p. 47.

26. Some chapter authors insist that historians *do* make generalizations (see, for example, Lynn, Pelz, Schroeder, and Gaddis), but are careful to limit these claims to specific times and places. Whereas the political scientist's scope conditions are usually analytic in nature, the historian's scope conditions are temporal and geographical. For the argument that generalizations are essential to conveying the meaning of a historical episode, and showing that it was consequential, see Raymond Martin, "Objectivity and Meaning in Historical Studies: Toward a Post-Analytic View," *History and Theory*,

Contrary to political scientists who generate causal generalizations, historians prefer to view historical cases in their entirety, and employ a holistic approach to explain complex events—effects "grow" out of "causes" by processes that cannot be broken down into identical, comparable, or discrete units.[27] Complex events such as a war, a revolution, and the rise of a parliament, are too rich in detail and too different from other members of its class to be subsumed under any covering law. Not only is the historian interested, for instance, in World War II for its own sake and not as a typical example of a great power war, but she insists that there is no such thing as a *typical* great power war. Consequently, many historians proceed, in John Gaddis's words, to "reconstruct complex events" by tracing the sequence of events that brought them about, and by showing that the connections between those events and other certain previous events "stand in an inner relationship," constitute a single process, and belong together.[28] According to Dale H. Porter, for historians

the explanation is not intended to demonstrate an invariant relationship between typical causes and typical effects, but to show that *this* particular set of events appears most intelligible if one looks at it *this* way. . . . As a pattern of events emerges, the meaning of any element in the pattern may change from what was expected at an earlier stage, and cannot be determined fully until the whole pattern has developed. Understanding events in this way requires a shift from *pre*diction to *retro*diction or reasoning from present to past . . . one has to look at the event according to its future consequences— what it meant for subsequent events. The historian does this because he senses that the significance of an event depends upon hindsight: it is really determined by what happened later.[29]

Rather than being a mere chronological sequencing of events, the historian's narrative explains an event by tracing its intrinsic relation to other

---

Vol. 32 (February 1993), pp. 44–49. According to Martin, historians make the case that we should care about the defeat of the Spanish Armada or the witch hunts of the sixteenth and seventeenth centuries by moving away "from the local and the particular and toward a larger perspective." Either the historian shows how the episode fanned out to effect aspects of subsequent history, or she shows how the event was an instance of a broader social pattern. See also Porter, *The Emergence of the Past*, pp. 35–36, 44–47.

27. Porter, *The Emergence of the Past*, p. 42.

28. Roberts, *The Logic of Historical Explanation*, pp. 16–17. Philosophers of history and historians themselves have termed this historical method in a variety of ways: narrative explanation, genetic explanation, synoptic judgment, sequential explanation, and colligation.

29. Porter, *The Emergence of the Past*, pp. 10, 14, 86–87.

events that both precede and follow it, and by seeing the same event from difference perspectives—something participants in the event could not have done. As Edward Ingram argues, "Historians live by an idiosyncratic version of clock time in which the clock may travel in both directions. . . . World War I does cause the Crimean War, for historians if not for Napoleon III and Viscount Palmerston."[30]

To be sure, we should not overstate this distinction. Many political scientists who study international relations share international historians' focus on particular, important events, and feel uncomfortable generating universally applicable law-like generalizations. They prefer contingent generalizations relevant to specific times and places. Similarly, like political scientists, many international historians appreciate that international politics can exhibit considerable continuity over time, and that within these stable periods international events can be usefully compared in generating generalizable theories.[31] Nevertheless, the nomothetic/idiographic distinction is an important one.

WHAT IS A CASE? Political scientists explain particular situations by referring to other situations of the same type. For the political scientist, historical events are discrete and clustered—they are treated as similar to the degree that they contain similar components. As Charles C. Ragin observes, "implicit in most social scientific notions of case analysis is the idea that the objects of investigation are similar enough and separate enough to permit treating them as comparable instances of the same general phenomenon."[32]

By contrast, historians are less likely to view complex historical events and processes as comparable, and resist detaching them from their "temporal moorings." For the most part, historians are unwilling to explain individual cases less fully in order to construct a grand theory that will explain the basic parameters of many cases with only a few causal factors. They also tend to view historical events as too complex to be easily classified with other events. As William C. Wohlforth puts it, "Historians' practice is a rejection of the very idea that events can be neatly coded as cases to test theories." Individual events are not simply instances, but the main theme. For example, an explanation of Louis

---

30. Ingram, "The Wonderland of the Political Scientist," p. 57.

31. On these points, see the chapters by William C. Wohlforth and William R. Thompson in this volume.

32. Ragin, "Introduction: Cases of 'What Is a Case?'" in Charles C. Ragin and Howard S. Becker, eds., *What Is a Case? Exploring the Foundation of Social Inquiry* (Cambridge: Cambridge University Press, 1992), p. 1.

Napoleon's decision to go to war with Prussia couched as "under such and such circumstances monarchs are likely to go to war" would be untenable. Even if such a statement correctly recorded that seven out of ten monarchs declared war under similar conditions, it would not explain why *Louis Napoleon* went to war.[33] In short, historians are wary of comparisons over long periods and generally reject attempts to project theories onto the future. While theories of international relations may be adequate for particular cases and periods, as time passes the assumptions on which they are based will cease to be true, and the theories will need to be revised. In the words of military historian Geoffrey Parker, "four years, let alone four centuries, can be a very long time where warfare is concerned."[34]

An example from this book nicely illustrates this difference. Historian Gerhard L. Weinberg (Chapter 5) insists that World War II cannot be compared to previous international conflicts because the German state and its war aims were unique. For Weinberg, World War II is in a class by itself. Political scientist Randall L. Schweller (Chapter 6) views Nazi Germany as a case for a generalizable theory. Instead of viewing Germany's policies as distinctive, Germany's desire for war is consistent with the foreign policy that we would expect from a revisionist state under conditions of tripolarity. For Schweller, Germany's foreign policy represents a case from a class of events—behavior encouraged by the constraints and opportunities of a tripolar international system.

Our point here is not only that Weinberg and Schweller explain the events differently, but that disciplinary norms guide the scholars in opposite directions. Political science guild rules, which reward theories that transcend time and place, encourage scholars *not* to differentiate between the world wars and compel them to treat Nazi Germany's foreign policy as an illustrative example of some larger theory of international behavior. Operating under a different set of guild rules, historians are better able to make these distinctions when the facts point in this direction. Thus, Schweller's theory-driven study forces him to "black box" Nazi Germany's domestic politics. To build a generalizable theory with Nazi Germany and World War II as illustrative cases, Germany must be treated as just another great power, and its foreign policies must be comparable to those of other states. The Holocaust as atypical genocide makes it difficult to use Germany as a case from a class of events; Schweller's

---

33. Fogel and Elton, *Which Road to the Past?* p. 43. See also Atkinson, *Knowledge and Explanation in History,* p. 35.

34. Personal correspondence, June 23, 1998.

theoretical explanation must be constructed without reference to it. By contrast, because Weinberg's guild rules allow him to consider Nazi Germany's policies as unique historical events, he is able to explain World War II by linking Germany's domestic politics with its international behavior. For Weinberg, a history of World War II that omitted the mass extermination of the Jews and the killing of other undesirables cannot be written.[35]

Another example is the difference in how Edward Ingram (Chapter 8) and William R. Thompson (Chapter 9) approach the issue of British hegemony. For political scientist Thompson, Britain can be compared to other rising and declining powers—there is nothing peculiar about its historical situation. British "hegemony" can be coded as a case covered by long cycle theory, and British ascent and decline can be seen as similar phases that other states have experienced throughout history. By contrast, historian Ingram argues that Thompson exaggerates the behavior of a particular state in constructing a general model. He insists that Thompson's emphasis on generalizable theory leads him to misperceive the nature of British power in the nineteenth century and the circumstances that contributed to its decline.[36]

ANOMALOUS EVIDENCE. The contrasting ways in which historians and political scientists regard theory and evidence leads to tendencies to respond to anomalous evidence in different ways. To be sure, as Richard Ned Lebow suggests, political scientists are aware that they "must always remain open to the possibility that there is something wrong with their premises." In fact, they frequently insist on the importance of constructing theories that clearly delineate the conditions and circumstances that will prove them false.[37] Still, political scientists tend to save theories in

---

35. Yet these two chapters also illustrate the difficulties of drawing broad conclusions about the subfields from the activities of scholars within them. Weinberg's emphasis on the importance of the individual and of intention is probably emblematic of his subfield, but his substantive interpretation of the causes of World War II is not a majority view among international historians of the interwar period. Similarly, while Schweller retains a political scientist's attention to generalization, his neoclassical realist inclusion of internally generated state differences places him on the margins of political scientists who advance theories that purport to transcend time and place.

36. For other examples of political scientists viewing the British case as one from a class of events, see Christopher Layne, "The Unipolar Illusion: Why New Great Powers Will Rise," *International Security*, Vol. 17, No. 4 (Spring 1993), pp. 5–51; and Randall L. Schweller, "Domestic Structure and Preventive War: Are Democracies More Pacific?" *World Politics*, Vol. 44, No. 2 (1992), pp. 235–269.

37. See, for example, King, Keohane, and Verba, *Designing Social Inquiry*, p. 19. According to Stephen Pelz, historians also share an interest in generating falsifiable arguments.

the face of anomalies, whether they emerge from the opening of new archives or from contemporary international events.[38] Political scientists generally believe that the route to theory advancement does not lie in amassing large numbers of disconfirming facts, but in displacing theories with better ones. Moreover, resistance to evidence that undermines a theory may be a legitimate exercise: to navigate a complex world, human beings with limited information-processing abilities must interpret new evidence based on preconceived beliefs, and thus should not discard preexisting theories whenever new evidence proves them wrong.[39] Nevertheless, this sort of activity is often portrayed as bad science, where scholars use new evidence to buttress their cherished theories, conveniently saving them from anomalies by bashing the evidence to fit the theory, and then painting it to hide the discrepancy. The result is "endless defensive moves to protect favored theories from problematic evidence."[40]

One could argue that historians are also impervious to disconfirming evidence (see Lebow's chapter). But, perhaps owing to the nature of the historical method, historians may be more willing to recognize the dynamic nature of their explanations, and may be more responsive to the possibility that new evidence will require them to revise or reject earlier

---

38. According to some views, this is a common practice among natural scientists as well as social scientists. See, for example, Imre Lakatos, "Falsification and the Methodology of Scientific Research Programmes," in Imre Lakatos and Alan Musgrave, eds., *Criticism and the Growth of Knowledge* (New York: Cambridge University Press, 1970). For a recent application of Lakatosian metatheory to international relations theory see John A. Vasquez, "The Realist Paradigm and Degenerative versus Progressive Research Programs: An Appraisal of Neotraditional Research on Waltz's Balancing Proposition," *American Political Science Review*, Vol. 91, No. 4 (December 1997), pp. 899–912. For a subsequent debate in the same journal issue, see Kenneth N. Waltz, "Evaluating Theories" (pp. 913–918); Thomas J. Christensen and Jack Snyder, "Progressive Research on Degenerate Alliances" (pp. 919–922); Colin Elman and Miriam Fendius Elman, "Lakatos and Neorealism: A Reply to Vasquez" (pp. 923–926); Randall L. Schweller, "New Realist Research on Alliances: Refining, Not Refuting, Waltz's Balancing Proposition" (pp. 927–930); and Stephen M. Walt, "The Progressive Power of Realism" (pp. 931–935).

39. See, on this point, Robert Jervis, *Perception and Misperception in International Politics* (Princeton: Princeton University Press, 1976) and Lebow's chapter in this volume.

40. William C. Wohlforth, "A Certain Idea of Science: How International Relations Theory Avoids Reviewing the Cold War," in O.A. Westad, ed., *Reviewing the Cold War: Approaches, Interpretations, Theory* (forthcoming), p. 20. Both democratic peace and balance of power theorists have been criticized, for example, for shirking anomalous empirical evidence. See, for example, David E. Spiro, "The Insignificance of the Liberal Peace," *International Security*, Vol. 19, No. 2 (Fall 1994), pp. 50–86; and John A. Vasquez, "The Realist Paradigm and Degenerative versus Progressive Research Programs."

arguments. As Gaddis notes in his chapter, a good historian treats her theory as only one from among many possible interpretations, recognizing that "there is no such thing as a definitive account of any historical episode." They necessarily view their theories as transient—"restaging" an event in light of newly discovered documentary evidence is an important component of the way historians work. Historians are always open to the possibility that some dramatic revelation in a newly opened archive can radically challenge previous explanations. Accordingly, when historians use events for theory-building, they include the reservation that new facts may compel a change of the theory. As Wohlforth suggests, because they are resigned to the provisional nature of their readings of history, historians pay more attention to fresh historical evidence discovered with the opening of archives than do political scientists, who are less likely to view anomalous evidence as having a critical bearing on their theories.[41]

CAUSES AND CAUSATION

According to Gaddis, both political scientists and historians make causal claims, but do so differently: "Historians believe in contingent, not categorical causation." Similarly, Paul W. Schroeder suggests that political scientists and historians "conceive of and deal with causes in human affairs" in different ways. Nonetheless, both sets of scholars look for the same things from an explanation—clearly assigned causes resting on evidence subject to tests and verification.[42] For political scientists, causation involves establishing a concrete and testable relationship among variables, including identifying the necessary and sufficient conditions that regularly produce a particular result. Accordingly, political scientists try to rule out, and prefer to assign weights and rank to, variables rather than resign themselves to multiple sufficient causation. They usually avoid overdetermined explanations and rule out weaker causal factors in

---

41. For an extended discussion see Wohlforth, "A Certain Idea of Science." Note, however, Deborah Welch Larson's chapter, where she discusses how newly released documentary evidence on the Cold War led her to revise previous theoretical attachments.

42. By contrast, some historians argue that historical explanation involves understanding and interpretation rather than causation. According to this view, historical events and developments are not explained by assigning specific causes for them—instead the historian attempts to explain them through a process of empathetic understanding. For a critique of this view, see Fritz K. Ringer, "Causal Analysis in Historical Reasoning," *History and Theory*, Vol. 28 (1989), pp. 154–172; and Paul W. Schroeder, "History and International Relations Theory: Not Use or Abuse, but Fit or Misfit," *International Security*, Vol. 22, No. 1 (Summer 1997), p. 67.

favor of the one cause with the greatest explanatory power, rejecting "shopping list" explanations. For example, although realists concede that domestic political pressures affected the timing and rate of British, U.S., and French rearmament against Nazi Germany and also influenced the specific strategies that these states pursued, they insist that the international-structural level of analysis provides a more parsimonious—and hence better—explanation for the inefficient balancing displayed. That is, since multipolar international distributions of power decrease the likelihood of effective balancing against rising challengers, this reading of the case should suffice.[43]

Political scientists also generally assume that causal explanation requires comparison across cases. As Andrew Bennett and Alexander George and Jack Levy observe in their chapters, the received wisdom is that causality cannot be identified within the context of a single observation. Political scientist James Lee Ray explains: "no self-respecting 'scientist' is really interested, at least while wearing his or her 'scientist's' hat, in *a* case. Single events cannot be 'explained' . . . no 'explanation' is worthy of the name unless it alludes to a pattern into which the event in question fits."[44] Political scientists devote attention to choosing appropriate cases that will afford severe—or decisive—theoretical tests. Historical cases are chosen for study if they create hard tests for preferred theories, thereby establishing greater confidence in them.[45]

Many historians find these premises suspect. Although most of the historians represented in this volume would agree that historical arguments presuppose causal statements, they would likely find the political scientist's definition of causality disturbing.

Several of the chapter authors in this book suggest that most historians attempt to establish causation by process tracing; that is, by relating events to other events in a sequence.[46] Accordingly, historians are likely to be uncomfortable with attempts to explain complex events by subsum-

---

43. See Stephen M. Walt, "Alliance, Threats, and U.S. Grand Strategy: A Response to Kaufman and Labs," *Security Studies*, Vol. 1, No. 3 (Spring 1992), pp. 448–482; and Joao Resende-Santos, "System and Agent: Comments on Labs and Kaufman," *Security Studies*, Vol. 1, No. 4 (Summer 1992), pp. 697–702.

44. James Lee Ray, *Democracy and International Conflict: An Evaluation of the Democratic Peace Proposition* (Columbia: University of South Carolina Press, 1995), pp. 133, 136.

45. On this point, see the chapter by George and Bennett in this volume. In addition to selecting crucial cases, political scientists are also often instructed to choose "nonevents," thereby allowing variation on the dependent variable. To understand great power wars, for example, cases of great power war as well as crises that did not result in war would need to be compared.

46. See, for example, the chapters by Lebow, Levy, Bennett and George, and Gaddis.

ing them under laws, and attempts to distinguish between independent and dependent variables. They would agree that some causes are more important than others, but they would resist the understanding of causation that is implicit in most international relations theory.[47] As Gaddis puts it: "Historians do not . . . accept the doctrine of immaculate causation, which seems to be implied in the idea that one can identify, without reference to all that has preceded it, such a thing as an independent variable." Since in historical explanations each part of the sequence is dependent on its predecessor, and since early events and actions are considered to have important consequences for later developments, no one causal factor can be "lifted out" of the explanation and deemed independent.[48]

Not only does this belief in historical contingency belie the notion of independent variables, but it also rejects as "irresponsible" attempts to isolate single causes for complex events.[49] For historians, causes are often things that intervene in a process that has already begun, and effects are alterations in an expected trend or chain of events that would not have occurred had the cause been absent. That is, important causes are those that depart most from the normal course of events.[50] Moreover, as Robert Jervis notes in his contribution to this volume, and as the debate between Lebow and Gaddis on the latter's treatment of the origins of the Cold War makes clear, historians are less troubled than political scientists by multiple sufficient causation or overdetermination; that is, alternative possible sequences of events such that the same outcome can be produced by different causes.

For historians, multiple sufficient causation is less worrisome partly

---

47. See the chapters by Schweller, Gaddis, Schroeder, Ingram, and Pelz in this volume. For an overview of how historians decide which causes are the most important, see Roberts, *The Logic of Historical Explanation*, chap. 5. For the argument that historians establish causation by comparing cases, usually aspects of the prior history of the actor whose fate is being explained, see Martin, "Objectivity and Meaning in Historical Studies," p. 41, and Raymond Martin, "Causes, Conditions, and Casual Importance," *History and Theory*, Vol. 21 (1982), pp. 53–74.

48. Identifying necessary or sufficient conditions might also be difficult for historians because of their tendency to view outcomes as arising through different causal paths (i.e., equifinality). For an extended discussion of equifinality, see the chapter by Bennett and George in this volume.

49. The political scientist's preference for monocausality and simplicity should not be equated with a greater concern for parsimonious explanation. Parsimonious explanations need not be monocausal, but they do seek to explain a wide range of phenomena with very few causal factors. See, on this point, Jervis's chapter in this volume.

50. See Ringer, "Causal Analysis in Historical Reasoning"; and Roberts, *The Logic of Historical Explanation*, pp. 96–99, 104, 116–117.

because international events are often considered the result of simultaneity—the interactivity among variables, which converge at a particular historical moment. It is difficult to argue that a given cause is stronger or should be given more causal weight in the analysis when causes interact with each other so as to multiply their impact. Causes often cumulate, and aggravate or amplify the effects of other causes, pushing the international system beyond some critical threshold.[51] In sum, historians find political scientists' insistence on isolating a few fundamental causes acting independently bemusing because causality is complex, and things often happen because variables are mutually reinforcing, intersecting at particular moments in space and time. For historians, history is full of these unpredictable intersections—the result of chance and accident.[52]

PURPOSIVE BEHAVIOR AND UNINTENDED CONSEQUENCES

Perhaps to compensate for their complex views of causation, historians often seem content to explain international events with particular reference to the aims of the actors involved. By contrast, while they hold more parsimonious positions on causation, international relations theorists are trained to expect and emphasize the considerable slippage between what actors want and what they get. Many of the contributors to this volume support this distinction between the historian's explanation of goal-oriented, purposive action and the political scientist's account of irrational, unintended consequences. Deborah Welch Larson argues that historians tend to adopt a "rational calculus" where actors' reasons and goals are considered explanations for their actions in response to prevailing conditions. Whereas historians focus on "human conduct," political scientists analyze "behavior," recognizing that policymakers do not always anticipate the results of their actions. Similarly, according to Paul Schroeder, historical change is explained ultimately in terms of human conduct, the purposive acts of agents, not behavior. While external, non-human factors shape historical developments, historical explanation should reveal human conduct in response to these conditions.[53] For example, Gerhard Weinberg focuses on the aims and goals motivating

---

51. See Roberts, *The Logic of Historical Explanation*, pp. 140–141.

52. For the argument that Mill's methods of difference and agreement—common procedures used by political scientists—are unhelpful when there are interaction effects and more than one cause is operating, see Stanley Lieberson, "Small N's and Big Conclusions: An Examination of the Reasoning in Comparative Studies Based on a Small Number of Cases," in Ragin and Becker, eds., *What is a Case?* pp. 105–118.

53. See also, Schroeder, "History and International Relations Theory," pp. 67–68.

Hitler's war with the allies; his chapter is less concerned with the material capabilities for carrying out these goals than with the goals themselves.

For some historians, the essence of historical explanation is the reconstruction of agents' aims, motives, and intentions. Good historical explanations are those that show how actions (not events) correspond to actors' goals and purposes; the good historian inquires about the reasons behind intentions. In other words, state behavior reflects state preferences—conflict must be provoked by an actor having a stake in the issue; cooperation will only be sought by an actor who has a reason to cooperate.[54]

By contrast, perhaps in large part due to the popularity of systems theory in general, and Kenneth N. Waltz's *Theory of International Politics* in particular, international relations theorists often label such explanations reductionist, and argue that international outcomes do not always follow from the motivations, aims, or purposes of individual policymakers. Unexpected and unwanted consequences undermine the original intent of decision-makers: cooperative international relations can emerge even when leaders are aggressive; war can result even when statesmen want peace.[55] Many international relations theorists are trained to look *first* for structural influences that generate unintended, unexpected, or ironic consequences. They believe that much of international relations can be explained without looking at actors' preferences or motivations. As Andrew Moravcsik recently notes,

"What states want is the primary determinant of what they do" may seem commonsensical, even tautological. Yet mainstream IR theory has uniformly rejected such claims for the past half-century. At the heart of the two leading contemporary IR theories, realism and institutionalism, is the belief that state behavior has *ironic* consequences. . . . What states do is primarily determined by strategic considerations—what they can get or what they know—which in turn reflect their international political environment.[56]

---

54. For an overview of the importance attached to purposive action in historical narrative, see Schroeder's chapter and Roberts, *The Logic of Historical Explanation*, chap. 8.

55. Elman and Elman, "History vs. Neo-realism," p. 189. To be fair, Waltz does recognize that motives can shape particular foreign policy choices. What he suggests is that if actors continually follow their preferences in ways that are contrary to international constraints, they will be punished for their free will—states are free to make mistakes, but those that do consistently will fall by the wayside.

56. Andrew Moravcsik, "Taking Preferences Seriously: A Liberal Theory of International Politics," *International Organization*, Vol. 51, No. 4 (Autumn 1997), pp. 521–522. In addition, many political scientists also believe that reconstructing the real motives and intentions of actors is unnecessary insofar as theories predict outcomes accurately.

These differing perspectives can affect both the explanation for particular cases (for example, the bulk of Schweller's chapter shows how
international structure intervenes between intentions and outcomes) as
well as case selection. It is not surprising, for instance, that World War I
rather than World War II has received the lion's share of interest among
political scientists. Because status quo–oriented states nevertheless went
to war, World War I is a good case for political scientists who prefer to
tease out how international constraints and opportunities can lead to
unexpected outcomes. Political scientists tend to focus greater attention
on the historical events that display a better "fit" with disciplinary guild
rules.

To be sure, all this is not to say that historians are insensitive to
unintended consequences and nonpurposive causal factors. Philosophers
of history and historians—international historians included—recognize
that outcomes can be unintended, and they have been quick to note that
historical explanations do not require purposive action.[57] As Dale H.
Porter observes, "Underlying the bulk of historical inquiries is the desire
to explain the unpredictability of human affairs, to show how things did
not turn out the way people thought or hoped they would."[58] Historians
are interested in the contrast between how things look in hindsight and
how things seemed to participants at the time. Path-dependent approaches, for example, show how events are linked to preceding events—
often in ways that were unexpected by the individuals involved in the
earlier episodes. According to this view, chance and coincidence play as
much of a role in historical explanation as do choices and decisions. In
emphasizing unexpected effects, such path-dependent explanations are
more consistent with mainstream political science than one might otherwise think.

MORALITY TALES

According to Deborah Welch Larson, historians focus on purposive action
because they are interested in rendering a moral judgment on the past.
Since human conduct is viewed as purposive attempts to achieve certain
goals, historians can hold actors morally responsible for their actions.

We can then proceed "as if" motives and intentions are fixed. For a summary of this
view, see Zagare, "All Mortis, No Rigor," pp. 108–110.

57. See, for example, Edward Hallett Carr, *What Is History?* (New York: Knopf, 1962),
pp. 55, 57, 64; and Herbert Butterfield, *History and Human Relations* (New York:
Macmillan, 1952), pp. 15–17, 19–20, 22, 77.

58. Porter, *The Emergence of the Past*, p. 34. See also Atkinson, *Knowledge and Explanation in History*, pp. 102, 127, 171, 187.

Other contributors to this book agree that historians' accounts are—
and should be—colored by moral judgment. Like Larson, Jervis notes that
it is perhaps "their greater interest in people" that lead historians to
assess the wisdom and morality of actors; Stephen Pelz comments on the
judgmental quality of history, noting that "narrative historians are often
trying to teach practical or moral lessons that their stories imply;" and
Paul Schroeder insists that moral judgments are inescapable ingredients
of historical arguments. According to Schroeder, holding actors account-
able for their actions does not mean that historians are idealists, committed to achieving a more peaceful and humane world. Rendering moral
judgment does not *require* that historians make history an instrument of
social change. Rather, Schroeder argues that in order to describe what
people do, historians need to discuss the moral dimension of their actions: "Every attempt to construct an 'objective' value-free language to
tell the story of what human beings have done and suffered not only
breaks down and denatures the narrative and analysis alike, but does so
without really avoiding moral judgments, instead masking, blurring, and
fudging them." In addition, theories and explanations of events carry
with them policy implications that can be morally suspect or ambiguous.
And to explain major events and show what the countries involved were
doing, historians must get involved in the "blame game," asking whether
the actors involved followed the rules and norms of international politics,
or whether they attempted to wreck them.[59]

By contrast, political scientists tend to address the historical record in
value-free language. As Larson puts it, "their aim is explanation, not
blame-fixing." Political scientists usually do not discuss whether actors
behaved wisely, much less morally. This may partly have to do with the
nature of their epistemology. As David Dessler argues, "generalizing
causal knowledge is typically more value-neutral with respect to the
problems it helps address than particularizing historical and interpretive
accounts are." Generalizations of the "if X, then Y" type adopt a neutral
position on the value of "X"—society may view it favorably or not; the
generalization merely produces knowledge that the different sides can

---

59. To some extent, the position adopted by Schroeder and others in this book is at
odds with dominant earlier views on the nature of historical explanation. Nineteenth-
century historians, adopting the Rankean ideal of an objective historical account—history "as it really was," independent of the historian's biases and preconceptions—eschewed casting blame or praise on historical figures, and criticized earlier
historiography for its moralizing stance. These arguments appear frequently in twentieth-century historiography as well. See, for example, Butterfield, *History and Human
Relations*, pp. 105–106, 127.

recognize as adequate.[60] As Schroeder points out, political scientists studying the democratic peace do not take a position on the relative value of democracy, as opposed to other ways of organizing the polity, when generating their causal arguments—despite the fact that the democratic peace theory entails precisely this sort of moral implication.

AESTHETICS: WHERE DO WE PUT THE PLUMBING?

The historians represented in this volume would resist the postmodern characterization of their enterprise as subjective story-telling, and would share the international relations theorists' commitment to uncovering an objectively knowable past. However, the two groups have a different sense of aesthetics. We have only to compare a few books—and the chapters in this volume—written by historians and political scientists to see that what often separates the two disciplines is not only the substance of their arguments, but also the way they organize their material. Political scientists' taste runs to separated theory and empirical sections, and to the use of flowcharts, matrices, diagrams, and figures. By contrast, historians typically find such organizational styles inelegant. They prefer to combine description with explanation (facilitated by a minimal use of headings and subheadings) and to embed theories within narratives.

This difference is noticed by the authors, several of whom refer to conspicuous differences of style and presentation. Gaddis, for example, suggests that historians prefer that form conceal function, and likens historical explanations to "dramatizations" of the past, complete with final acts, such as the end of the Cold War and the collapse of the Soviet Union, generating new productions of old plays.[61] Similarly, Ingram suggests that political scientists "want all the working shown" while historians prefer that it be "hidden and only implied."[62] Finally, echoing Ingram and Gaddis on this point, Stephen Pelz quotes David Hackett Fischer's observation that historians tend to "hide their causal models from everybody—including themselves," perhaps owing to aesthetic taste.

---

60. Dessler, "Empirical Research as Puzzle-Solving," p. 24.

61. Gaddis, "History, Theory, and Common Ground," *International Security*, Vol. 22, No. 1 (Summer 1997), p. 77. For an extended discussion of how historians use forms of plot to represent actors' goals and motives, see Porter, *The Emergence of the Past*, pp. 150–156.

62. Personal correspondence with Edward Ingram, August 21, 1998.

International History and Politics: Bridges

While the contributors to this volume identify several disciplinary cleavages, the chapters also suggest areas for cross-fertilization. This section notes how some of the disciplinary boundaries are weakening. First, political scientists increasingly acknowledge that they would benefit from a better understanding of historians' technical skills, especially by improving their own abilities to do primary research. This understanding would also provide a more nuanced awareness and a more responsible use of the historians' work they employ as secondary sources, including an appreciation of the contingent nature of historical claims and the competing historiographical debates in which they are embedded. Second, political scientists and historians have increasingly convergent understandings of process tracing, path dependence, and the importance of uncovering real causal mechanisms. Finally, there are some contemporary substantive research areas in the international relations theory subfield that may be particularly suited to the application of, and whose practitioners may have a special affinity for, historical methods.

SECONDARY SOURCES, HISTORIOGRAPHICAL DEBATES, AND TECHNICAL SKILLS

Political scientists, especially those engaging in multilingual, multistate comparative analyses, frequently rely on secondary material, which often consists of historical monographs. The problem, as Ian Lustick has observed, is that historians do not produce "an unproblematic background narrative from which theoretically neutral data can be elicited for the framing of problems and the testing of theories."[63] Lustick argues, and we agree, that political scientists should self-consciously inform themselves of the competing approaches and streams of historiography that produce the historical works on which political scientists rely.

Sometimes, even a self-conscious reading of multiple secondary sources will be insufficient. Larson suggests that Lustick's answer is incomplete, since it does not explain how a political scientist is to *judge* between the competing claims of different schools. She argues that political scientists should do primary research, since by "checking out the documents for themselves, political scientists could discriminate between competing explanations of the same event." Larson notes that "because historians and political scientists approach their topics with different sets of questions, it is all the more incumbent on political scientists to carry

---

63. Ian Lustick, "History, Historiography, and Political Science," *American Political Science Review*, Vol. 90, No. 3 (September 1996), p. 605.

out their *own* historical research. Standard historical accounts probably will not contain the kind of data that political scientists need to test a theoretical hypothesis." Some political scientists agree with Larson, and buttress their reliance on secondary sources with original archival research. International relations theorists who do primary research would gain from following historians' insistence on archival coverage and accuracy.

Even political scientists who do not do primary research would benefit from a greater awareness of historians' technical skills, and a greater understanding of how they view their findings. After investing years in the archives, historians know that there are likely to be other documents, indeed whole collections of papers, that they have not seen. Accordingly, they are inclined to view their results as the uncertain product of an incomplete evidentiary record, and are unimpressed by political scientists who mine monographs for "data points," losing along the way the qualified and contingent nature of their findings.

Just as political scientists could learn from historians' use of methods, historians could benefit from a more self-conscious definition and evaluation of their theoretical preconceptions.[64] In this volume, Gaddis, Lebow, and Pelz address how social science methodology can be of use to historians.

PROCESS TRACING, PATH DEPENDENCE, AND CAUSAL MECHANISMS
Mitigating the epistemological differences noted previously, several of the contributors to this book agree that political scientists and historians are increasingly employing similar understandings of process tracing, path dependence, and causality. This convergence helps overcome some of the boundaries described in our earlier section.

Gaddis argues that political scientists' growing interest in process tracing is not very different from the historian's construction of narratives: "It is here, I think—in a careful comparison of what our two fields mean by 'narrative' and 'process tracing'—that the most promising opportunities for cooperation between historians and international relations

---

64. Historians may leave the theories and covering laws they use implicit and unexamined because they are truisms—almost trivial. As Ian Lustick observes, "The persuasiveness of an account offered by an historian rests heavily on whether the causal effects that are claimed to be operating at every step in the story are so uncontroversial as hypotheses that arguments on their behalf are not demanded by the audience." See "Laws, Stories, and Agent-Based Modeling," *Clio: Newsletter of Politics and History*, Vol. 9, No. 1 (Fall/Winter 1998–99), p. 1. For more on the implicit use of covering laws in historical narratives, see Roberts, *The Logic of Historical Explanation*, pp. 9, 44, 54, and chap. 4.

theorists currently lie." Similarly, Andrew Bennett and Alexander George discuss at length the synergy between the "within-case" method of process tracing employed by historians and political scientists. For Bennett and George, process tracing is a special type of historical explanation that enables the analyst to identify causal links within the context of a *single* case. By identifying the "temporal and potentially causal sequences of events within a case," process tracing looks quite similar to the way many historians define, and use, narrative: explanations of outcomes that cannot be predicted a priori because a change in an early event can produce a very different sequential pattern. The difference rests primarily in the purpose behind the exercise: for political scientists, process tracing has numerous advantages for theory development and theory testing; for historians, process tracing helps historians explain what happened, and what actors at the time thought had happened. As Bennett and George point out, "Political scientists employ process tracing not only to explain specific cases but also to test and refine available theories and hypotheses, to develop new theories, and to produce generic knowledge of a given phenomenon."

A related commonality is the increasing agreement on the importance of path dependence in explanation. Process tracing can help historians and political scientists to determine whether international outcomes were sensitive to the choices made by earlier decision-makers; that is, whether the temporal sequence of events foreclosed certain paths.[65] As Gaddis points out, this notion of path dependence is central to historical explanation: historians must consider what might have been, and they must assume that history did not have to have happened in the way that it did. Narratives explain events by "casting up" a number of plausible alternative lines of development and then realizing one of them, which stands in contrast to what might have been.[66] Such conjectures about the road not taken involve counterfactual reasoning—pondering alternative scenarios to those that actually took place and assessing whether a change in some condition might have altered the outcome. Here, too, political

---

65. Path-dependent arguments can reveal self-reinforcing processes, as when small events early on have a big impact, making it difficult to conceive of alternative, previously available ways of doing things. Alternatively, events occurring at an earlier point in a sequence may affect what happens later by provoking a reaction or a "backlash" that moves patterns of behavior in new directions. For an extended discussion of these two possibilities, see Paul Pierson, "Not Just What, but *When:* Issues of Timing and Sequence in Comparative Politics," paper presented at the Annual Meeting of the American Political Science Association, Boston, September 1998.

66. Porter, *The Emergence of the Past,* pp. 20–21.

scientists and historians have another method in common than their "narcissism in minor differences" has led them to believe.[67]

A third and related convergence is the increasing agreement between political scientists and historians on the importance of identifying the causal mechanisms that connect an effect with its cause.[68] Historians have traditionally, if implicitly, favored explanations that reveal causal mechanisms. As noted in the previous section, for political scientists this has not always been the case. For example, Bennett and George note that researchers using formal models and statistical methods have long held that good scientific explanations do not require establishing intervening causal processes that link cause and effect. Rational choice theorists in particular minimize the importance of causal mechanisms, arguing that we can view decision-makers "as if" they are rational actors without suggesting that they actually calculate costs and benefits in this way. That is, rational choice assumptions are useful if the theory that employs them produces accurate predictions, regardless of whether actors actually think and speak in ways consistent with rational choice theories.[69]

However, more international relations theorists now acknowledge that mere congruence between outcomes and a theory's initial conditions

67. See Gaddis's chapter. Many of the contributors to this volume (see, for example, the essays by Gaddis, Lebow, Fink, and Pelz) agree that scholars from both disciplines employ counterfactual reasoning. For more on how counterfactual reasoning enables analysts to increase the number of cases in their research designs, see James D. Fearon, "Counterfactuals and Hypothesis Testing in Political Science," *World Politics*, Vol. 43, No. 2 (1991), pp. 169–195. For the contrary argument that the validity of historical arguments *does not* necessarily depend on counterfactual reasoning, and that historians should avoid speculating about events that did not happen, see A.J.P. Taylor, *The Struggle for Mastery in Europe, 1848–1918* (London: Oxford University Press, 1954), p. 513. For a recent comprehensive survey of counterfactual reasoning, see Philip E. Tetlock and Aaron Belkin, eds., *Counterfactual Thought Experiments in World Politics: Logical, Methodological, and Psychological Perspectives* (Princeton: Princeton University Press, 1996). Tetlock and Belkin note that historians tend to employ "idiographic case-study counterfactuals" that explore whether history had to unfold as it did and remind us that things could have easily worked out differently at particular junctures. Significantly, such counterfactual reasoning undermines deterministic forms of theory by showing how chance and factors that cannot be predicted in advance (i.e., skillful or inept leadership, and well-timed or ill-timed arguments) can decisively alter the course of events.

68. For the argument that establishing causation *requires* the specification of causal mechanisms, see, for example, Daniel Little, *Varieties of Social Explanation: An Introduction to the Philosophy of Social Science* (Boulder, Colo.: Westview, 1991), pp. 13–38. For a contrary view, although one that recognizes the value of identifying causal mechanisms, see King, Keohane, and Verba, *Designing Social Inquiry*, pp. 85–87.

69. See, for example, Christopher H. Achen and Duncan Snidal, "Rational Deterrence Theory and Comparative Case Studies," *World Politics*, Vol. 41, No. 2 (January 1989),

does not necessarily mean that the theory provides an adequate causal explanation. As James Lee Ray observes, today many international relations scholars agree that "there must be some essential core of correspondence between the actual calculations made by real decision makers and the calculations stipulated by formal models . . . a formal model, or any other theory, must in fact capture the fundamentals of real world processes if it is going to produce accurate predictions or valid explanations."[70] Some of our most influential research programs in the subfield—such as the democratic peace—explicitly reject "as if" arguments. For example, democratic peace theorists wish to determine how democratic norms and institutions affect the ways elites behave in negotiations, and how political actors justify their actions. The aim is not to show that decision-makers act "as if" they are constrained by democratic norms and principles, but that they consciously make the calculations posited by the democratic peace model.

Aimed at uncovering causal mechanisms, much international relations scholarship is becoming less antithetical to historical methods. As we have suggested elsewhere, "the recent resurgence of scientific realist understandings of social science, which mandate the search for 'real' causal mechanisms, may prove a more hospitable environment for a useful interdisciplinary conversation."[71] The flipside is that those political scientists who employ stylized facts, and who are drawn to the methods and approaches employed by economists, may be resistant to an interdisciplinary exchange with historians.

SUBSTANTIVE ARGUMENTS AND HISTORICAL METHODS

Not only are international historians and qualitative international relations theorists finding common methodological bonds, but there also new areas of convergence in substantive arguments. Increasingly, historians and political scientists mean the same thing when they talk about international relations. This convergence owes much to the end of the Cold War and the break-up of the Soviet Union. Both events motivated international relations theorists to reconsider the explanatory power of the dominant structural approaches in the field (neorealism and neoliberal

---

pp. 163–166. For more on how political scientists have relied on the "as if" assumption, eschewing investigations of causal mechanisms, see Ray, *Democracy and International Conflict*, pp. 133–134, 144.

70. Ray, *Democracy and International Conflict*, p. 151.

71. Elman and Elman, "Diplomatic History and International Relations Theory," p. 18.

institutionalism), and opened up new space for competing approaches that emphasize the role of ideas, culture, domestic politics, statesmanship, and the possibility of change.[72] Political scientists who study international relations have moved considerably closer to international historians' perspectives on the topic. Two popular strands of contemporary international relations research, constructivism and classical or neoclassical realism, are examples of this phenomenon.

Constructivists (not to be confused with the constructionist and postmodernist historians that Stephen Pelz mentions, who have more in common with critical theorists in political science) are primarily interested in how past interactions construct future patterns of behavior among states, and at how states can extricate themselves from replicating conflictual relations.[73] Rather than identify uniform state identities throughout history, recurring patterns of conflictual international relations, or the similarity of state behavior under particular structural conditions (as neorealists do), constructivists eschew notions of fixed state interests and constant international structures. Allowing for an increased role for agency, they point out that actors can often change their environment—for the better or for the worse. Alexander Wendt puts it well: "if today we find ourselves in a self-help world, this is due to process, not structure . . . structure has no existence or causal powers apart from process. . . . Anarchy is what states make of it."[74] Thus, international relations is seen as historically contingent—specific international structures are created in certain periods of history, such as the current system of sovereign states—and are potentially alterable at later periods. International structures, "although difficult to challenge, are not impregnable. Alternative actors with alternative identities, practices, and sufficient

72. For extended discussions of the end of the Cold War's impact on theorizing about international relations, see the special symposium "The End of the Cold War and Theories of International Relations," in *International Organization*, Vol. 48, No. 2 (Spring 1994), pp. 155–247; and Charles W. Kegley, Jr., "The Neoidealist Moment in International Studies? Realist Myths and the New International Realities," *International Studies Quarterly*, Vol. 37, No. 2 (June 1993).

73. For overviews of the constructivist approach, see Peter J. Katzenstein, Robert O. Keohane, and Stephen D. Krasner, "*International Organization* and the Study of World Politics," *International Organization*, Vol. 52, No. 4 (Autumn 1998), esp. pp. 674–678; Ted Hopf, "The Promise of Constructivism in International Relations Theory," *International Security*, Vol. 23, No. 1 (Summer 1998), pp. 171–200; and Dale C. Copeland, "Integrating Realism and Constructivism," paper presented at the Annual Meeting of the American Political Science Association, Boston, September 1998.

74. Alexander Wendt, "Anarchy Is What States Make of It: The Social Construction of Power Politics," *International Organization*, Vol. 46, No. 2 (Spring 1992), pp. 394–395.

material resources are theoretically capable of effecting change."[75] The explicit constructivist goal is to explain international change over time, and it is this interest that makes them far more interested in history *qua* history.

This shared interest in the study of international change provides an important link between international historians and constructivist political scientists. As Richard Rosecrance points out, "historians typically seek to explain particular turning points in international or domestic history such as the causes of the French Revolution, the origins of World Wars I and II, and the causes of the Cold War." Historical arguments about international relations involve identifying decisive changes in international relations over time—historicizing means viewing the past as constructed, recognizing that international relations' categories and identities are not given and fixed, but made and remade.[76] The historian's enterprise involves showing what led to changes in international relations, and what resulted from those changes. Like constructivists, international historians are aware of the contingent nature of their generalizations—what at first look like repetitive patterns are often only recent behaviors and thus alterable.

Not only was the end of the Cold War a catalyst for the constructivist perspective, it also raised substantial dissatisfaction among realists over the adequacy of the structural or neorealist research program. Many realists have taken a decidedly "classical realist" turn.[77] Neorealists, who dominated the security studies subfield before the end of the Cold War, did not theorize about state motives and intentions, treating them as fixed. They also focused primarily on international outcomes, stripped of any purposive element. For example, neorealists argued that balances of power emerge and reemerge automatically, and that states balance against other states' accumulations of material power regardless of these states' intentions. It is partly for these reasons that international historians have found works based on the neorealist perspective so troubling. As Schroeder notes, neorealism's "insistence on the sameness effect and on the unchanging, structurally determined nature of international politics make it unhistorical, perhaps anti-historical."[78] By contrast, classical realists—and the neoclassical realists of today—emphasize foreign policy and

---

75. Hopf, "The Promise of Constructivism," p. 180.

76. See Schroeder, "History and International Relations Theory," p. 67.

77. For an overview of recent works, see Gideon Rose, "Neoclassical Realism and Theories of Foreign Policy," *World Politics*, Vol. 51, No. 1 (October 1998), pp. 144–172.

78. Schroeder, "Historical Reality vs. Neo-realist Theory," p. 148.

decision-makers' perceptions rather than international patterns of behavior; argue that state intentions are variable instead of fixed; and suggest that international conflict can frequently be traced back to evil-minded leaders rather than to the tragedy of the situation. These are all premises that international historians would find attractive.

The central tenets of neoclassical realism—that the distribution of relative capabilities is only one factor affecting threat perceptions, and that the goals and purposes for which material power will be used are equally important—resonate well with the way many international historians understand international change and stability. As the following chapters show, for international historians war is always intended by someone and the key questions are whether power is used to manage the system and make states feel more secure, or whether its purpose is to threaten other states and undermine the rules of the game. So too for neoclassical realists, who reject the neorealist understanding of war as the result of decision-makers' misperceptions, shared situational constraints, or offensive military technologies. For both international historians and neoclassical realists in political science, war is not a tragedy but an evil. States do not go to war because of security dilemmas that arise in an anarchical international system, but because aggressor states seek to overturn the prevailing order.[79]

A Final Word

Political scientists are not historians, nor should they be. There are real and enduring epistemological and methodological differences that divide the two groups, and there is great value in recognizing, maintaining, and honoring those distinctions. It is helpful to have historical events analyzed by two groups of scholars, each trained to use distinct skills and to emphasize different aspects of a case. That being said, the chapters that follow demonstrate that despite some previous misreadings and misunderstandings, historians and political scientists have a lot to gain from continuing and deepening their dialogue.

The relationship between like-minded historians and political scientists promises to be valuable both in its own right, and as a way to offset increasing isolation within their own disciplines. In part this means a new appreciation of our comparative strengths, but it also requires transcend-

---

79. For more on the distinction between tragedy and evil in the writings of neorealists and neoclassical realists, see Michael Spirtas, "A House Divided: Tragedy and Evil in Realist Theory," *Security Studies*, Vol. 5, No. 3 (Spring 1996), pp. 385–415.

ing previous stereotypical and caricatured readings of the other subfield. We sympathize with Michael Hunt's impatience when he observes:

Those with a strong theoretical bent [have] consigned diplomatic historians to the role of the hewers-of-wood and the drawers-of-water in their world of international relations theory. The historians were to toil in the archives, constructing detailed case studies on which real social scientists were to raise grand explanatory structures that would account for enduring patterns in international relations and that would command the respect of policymakers."[80]

We have a similar impatience with historians who dismiss international relations theorists as the intellectual equivalent of Blackbeard the Pirate, pillaging their pristine histories for factual nuggets that are then collected together and buried in footnotes. If we can overcome our mutual fears of disciplinary meltdown and exploitation, the subfields have a lot to offer each other. The challenge is to chart the boundaries of a middle position that avoids either outright mimicry or rejection, and to build the institutional bridges to support it. This book suggests that such a position is both attainable and sustainable. We hope that, in demonstrating the possibilities that arise when open-minded folk from both disciplines sit down to talk, this volume will make a contribution to breaking down the parochial chauvinism that often hinders interdisciplinary cross-fertilization.

---

80. Hunt, "The Long Crisis in U.S. Diplomatic History: Coming to Closure," *Diplomatic History*, Vol. 16, No. 1 (Winter 1992), pp. 115–116.

Part I
Methods

Chapter 1

Explaining Events and Developing Theories: History, Political Science, and the Analysis of International Relations

Jack S. Levy

Historians and social scientists generally agree that although they study the same social phenomena, they do so in different ways. There is less agreement, however, on precisely what those differences are. The dialogue between historians and sociologists, which has continued for a century, is reflected in a 1994 symposium in the *British Journal of Sociology*, and the contrasting views of diplomatic historians and international relations theorists are presented in a 1997 symposium in *International Security*.[1] In this essay I focus primarily on differences in how diplomatic historians and political scientists study international relations—and my references to "historians" and "political scientists" should be interpreted in this way—although many of my arguments apply to the discipline of political science as a whole or to the social sciences more generally.[2]

I would like to thank numerous people for their helpful comments on earlier versions of this paper: Colin Elman, Miriam Fendius Elman, Scott Sagan, Hidemi Suganami, and members of the International Relations/Diplomatic History Seminar at Rutgers University—particularly Michael Adas, Martin Edwards, David Fogelsong, Lloyd Gardner, Michael Paris, and Thomas Walker.

1. See *British Journal of Sociology*, Vol. 45, No. 1 (March 1994). This responds to John H. Goldthorpe, "The Uses of History in Sociology: Reflections on Some Recent Tendencies," *British Journal of Sociology*, Vol. 42, No. 2 (June 1991), pp. 211–230. See also *International Security*, Vol. 22, No. 1 (Summer 1997).

2. Although some have argued that international relations constitutes a distinct field of study, many now argue that any gap in theory and method between international relations and other empirically oriented fields in political science—particularly American politics and comparative politics—had diminished by the late 1990s, as scholars have increasingly incorporated theories of domestic politics into theories of international relations. See Helen V. Milner, "Rationalizing Politics: The Emerging Synthesis of International, American, and Comparative Politics," *International Organization*, Vol. 52, No. 4 (Autumn 1998), pp. 759–786.

The two disciplines are said to differ in subject matter, approaches to explanation, method, and form of presentation.[3] Historians focus primarily on the past; international relations scholars, and political scientists more generally, aim to make theoretically informed and policy-relevant predictions about the future. Historians seek to understand single unique events, the *milieu et moment;* political scientists aim to generalize about classes of events and to construct theories that are valid across time and space. Historians tend to favor complex interpretations; political scientists aim for elegant and parsimonious causal explanations. Historians construct narrative-based explanations; political scientists construct theory-based explanations. Political scientists are explicit about their theoretical assumptions and causal argument; historians are more implicit.

Although scholars often treat each of these differences as polar extremes, they are best interpreted as ends of a continuum, along which many scholars would classify themselves somewhere in the middle.[4] Taken together, however, these differences between history and political science produce such sharp contrasts that it is relatively easy to identify the disciplinary affiliation of most historians and political scientists. These scholars go through very different graduate training programs, to the extent that history departments rarely hire scholars trained as political scientists and political science departments rarely hire those trained as historians.[5] Historians and political scientists generally attend different professional conferences and publish in different journals. These dissimilarities have generated distinct reward structures in the two disciplines, which in turn reinforce other differences between the disciplines.

In my own contribution to the 1997 *International Security* symposium on "History and Theory," I argued that although each discipline encompasses an enormous range of scholarship, and although the focus and methodologies of each discipline have changed significantly over time,

---

3. This summary follows Colin Elman and Miriam Fendius Elman, "Diplomatic History and International Relations Theory: Respecting Difference and Crossing Boundaries," *International Security,* Vol. 22, No. 1 (Summer 1997), pp. 5–21.

4. See William R. Thompson's chapter in this volume.

5. An interesting anecdote about these differences in graduate training is provided by Lebow's account of his efforts in graduate school to combine history and political science. Lebow wanted to explain both what was similar and unique in different political systems, to combine the construction and testing of theoretical generalizations with a sensitivity to the influence of particular historical and cultural factors. His political science professor suggested that he would feel more at home in a history department, while his history professor suggested that he return to political science. Lebow eventually moved to a different university. Richard Ned Lebow, *Between Peace and War* (Baltimore: Johns Hopkins University Press, 1981), pp. ix–x.

the criterion that best defines the different "identities" of the two disciplines is a variation of the traditional distinction between idiographic and
nomothetic orientations: the primary goal of historians is to describe,
understand, and interpret individual events or a temporally and spatially
bounded series of events, whereas the primary goal of political scientists
is to generalize about the relationships between variables and, to the
extent possible, construct law-like propositions about social behavior.[6]

In this chapter I develop this argument and show that the idio-
graphic/nomothetic distinction underlies many of the other criteria that
scholars have advanced to identify differences between the disciplines—
including the value of parsimonious explanations, the importance of
primary sources, the value of predictions and policy relevance, the feasibility of universal laws, the nature of the scope conditions that limit
theoretical generalizations, the different types of scope conditions that
define the domain of the theory, and the role of covering laws in social
explanation. Because the idiographic/nomothetic distinction subsumes
these other criteria, it is far more useful than any single criterion, and
provides a comprehensive and powerful framework for analyzing the
differences between the two disciplines. I also consider the distinction
between narrative-based explanations and theory-based explanations,
and conclude that there are too many exceptions to make this a useful
criterion for distinguishing between history and political science.

In highlighting the importance of the idiographic/nomothetic distinction, I emphasize that idiographic does not imply atheoretical, that it
is necessary to distinguish between what scholars try to explain and how
they explain it, and that the two disciplines differ in *how* they use theory,
not *whether* they use theory. To say that historians attempt to explain
events does not imply that they are atheoretical, for historians sometimes
use law-like propositions to explain those events. I also refine my earlier
argument by acknowledging that historians often generalize. Most of
these generalizations refer to particular countries or periods, whereas
political scientists' generalizations refer to certain theoretically defined
conditions. In other words, historians' generalizations are bounded by
temporal and spatial scope conditions, whereas political scientists' generalizations are bounded by analytical scope conditions.

There is a smaller set of historians who claim to generalize beyond
the spatial and temporal bounds of their historical analyses, but here too
they differ from political scientists. The difference is based on the distinc-

---

6. Jack S. Levy, "Too Important to Leave to the Other: History and Political Science
in the Study of International Relations," *International Security*, Vol. 22, No. 1 (Summer
1997), pp. 22–33.

tion between the logic of discovery and the logic of confirmation, between constructing generalizations and validating them against the empirical evidence. Political scientists not only generalize from their observed data to a more broadly defined class of phenomena; they give primacy to the question of how to test those generalizations empirically and to the task of constructing research designs for that purpose. Historians sometimes generalize but they rarely give explicit attention to the research designs and methodologies through which their generalizations might be empirically confirmed.

Before developing this argument about the differences between history and political science in their study of international relations, it is necessary to recognize that neither discipline is monolithic. There is substantial variation in the scholarship within each discipline at a given point of time, within each discipline across national boundaries, and within each discipline over time. This significantly complicates the task of identifying any single criterion that fully captures the fundamental differences between historians and political scientists in their study of international relations.

First, history and political science both incorporate an enormous range of scholarly research, to the extent that in many respects the variations in theoretical approaches and methodological orientations within each discipline may be as great as the variations between them. Diplomatic historians and international relations scholars have far more in common with each other—in terms of substance, epistemology, and methodology—than they do with many of their colleagues in other fields in their own disciplines. Diplomatic history has been less sensitive than other branches of history to changing theoretical orientations and methodological fads in the field, from the rise and fall of quantitative history to the rise of postmodernism.[7] It has consistently insisted on the empirical validation of its interpretations and in the utility of narratives and primary sources for that purpose. These considerations lead Stephen Haber, David Kennedy, and Stephen Krasner to argue that diplomatic historians and international relations scholars are really "brothers under the skin."[8]

It is important to emphasize, however, that this idea of a fraternity

---

7. The international relations field in political science has generally reflected various trends in theory and method in the discipline as a whole, from quantitative methods to rational choice and game theory to the growing influence of constructivism.

8. Stephen H. Haber, David M. Kennedy, and Stephen D. Krasner, "Brothers Under the Skin: Diplomatic History and International Relations," *International Security*, Vol. 22, No. 1 (Summer 1997), pp. 33–43. International relations scholars who use quantitative and formal methods would be less inclined to use the "brothers" metaphor.

between historians and international relations scholars is more applicable to the United States than to European countries, where disciplinary identities and the relationships between them are often different. The study of international relations in the United Kingdom, for example, is less influenced by positivistic social science and more influenced by some elements of critical theory than it is in the United States, whereas the study of diplomatic history in the two countries is characterized by few fundamental differences.[9]

In addition, a succession of "great debates" and paradigmatic battles have helped structure the international relations field as a whole in the United States. The international relations field is less cohesive in the United Kingdom, France, and Germany, where local influences are greater. Finally, the growing influence of rational choice theory in the international relations field in the United States has reinforced the field's links with other key fields within political science. European international relations scholars have been more resistant to rational choice, in part because of their disciplinary associations with sociology, anthropology, and philosophy, and perhaps also because the individualistic foundations often associated with rational choice are less appealing to Europeans.[10]

A third consideration that complicates the task of comparison across disciplines is the fact that each discipline evolves over time with the rise and fall of competing paradigms within it. Although there are some striking parallels in the evolution of history and the social sciences over the course of this century, there are important points at which they diverge, so that the differences between the disciplines as well as their distinct identities have changed over time.[11]

History and political science were much closer in the 1960s—when leading schools of thought in each discipline were quite confident in the feasibility of "scientific" knowledge and in the utility of quantitative

---

9. While the study of international relations in the United Kingdom is more historical than it is in the United States, there is in many respects a greater separation between historians and international relations scholars in Britain than in the United States. See Christopher Hill, "History and International Relations," in Steve Smith, ed., *International Relations: British and American Perspectives* (Oxford: Basil Blackwell, 1985), pp. 126–145.

10. Milner, "Rationalizing Politics;" and Ole Wæver, "The Sociology of a Not So International Discipline: American and European Developments in International Relations," *International Organization*, Vol. 52, No. 4 (Autumn 1998), pp. 687–727.

11. On parallels between history and the social sciences see Keong-il Kim, "Genealogy of the Idiographic vs. the Nomothetic Disciplines: The Case of History and Sociology in the United States," *Review*, Vol. 20, Nos. 3–4 (Summer/Fall 1997), pp. 421–464.

methods for discovering that knowledge—than in 1980s, by which time the decline of quantitative history and the "revival of narrative" had moved history further away from political science. The two disciplines are even further apart today, after the growing influence of postmodernism and the "linguistic turn" in history, and after the further spread of quantitative methods and particularly game-theoretic models in political science.[12] Comparisons between the disciplines would have looked much different in the nineteenth century, when the Rankean focus on explaining unique events contrasted sharply with the attempts by Marx, de Tocqueville, Durkheim, Weber, and other sociologists to construct historically grounded generalizations about social structures and processes.[13] Thus any comparisons between history and political science may be historically contingent.

These significant variations in the scholarship within each discipline—at any given point in time, over time, and across countries—complicate the task of identifying any essential differences between diplomatic history and international relations. Nevertheless, the central tendencies of the two disciplines differ, and most historians and political scientists agree that they differ.[14] I argue that the one criterion that best captures the differences between most leading historians and most leading international relations scholars—at least in the United States—that best reflects the scholarship that is most valued within each discipline, that involves the fewest significant exceptions, and that underlies many of the other criteria, is the idea that historians attempt to explain individual events or series of events, whereas political scientists attempt to construct generalizations (universal or contingent) about classes of events and to test those generalizations empirically. This argument represents a slight modification of the traditional distinction between idiographic and nomothetic approaches to the study of social phenomena.

The reader should understand that my generalizations about histori-

---

12. Lawrence Stone, "The Revival of Narrative: Reflections on a New Old History," in Lawrence Stone, *The Past and the Present Revisited* (London: Routledge and Kegan Paul, 1987); and John E. Toews, "Intellectual History after the Linguistic Turn: The Autonomy of Meaning and the Irreducibility of Experience," *American Historical Review*, Vol. 92, No. 4 (October 1987), pp. 879–907. On the growing gap see Kim, "Genealogy," and the chapter by Robert Jervis in this volume.

13. Leopold von Ranke, "On the Character of Historical Science," in Georg G. Iggers and Konrad von Moltke, eds., *The Theory and Practice of History* (Indianapolis: Bobbs-Merrill, 1973).

14. In other words, the scholarship in the two disciplines can be represented by overlapping distributions, each with a different mean but with substantial variation around the mean.

ans and political scientists refer to the central tendencies of the most influential "mainstream" scholars within each discipline, and that the large variances around these central tendencies mean that there will be numerous individual exceptions to my arguments. I limit my argument to the United States because of significant differences across the Atlantic.

The Idiographic/Nomothetic Distinction

In the late nineteenth century, Wilhelm Windelband and Heinrich Rickert emphasized the contrast between the idiographic method of the historical and social sciences (*Geisteswissenschaften*) and the nomothetic method of the natural sciences (*Naturwissenschaften*). The first aims to explain or understand unique sequences of events and the second seeks to develop explanatory laws. After social science diverged from history by adopting positivistic natural science as its disciplinary model, scholars began to apply the idiographic and nomothetic concepts to distinguish between history and the social sciences.[15]

Among contemporary political scientists, Joseph Nye asserts that "history is the study of events that have happened only once; political science is the effort to generalize about them." Similarly, Bruce Bueno de Mesquita argues that "the social scientist is more likely to emphasize general explanations of social phenomena, while the historian is more likely to emphasize particularistic, unique features of individual episodes of social phenomena." Stephen Van Evera argues that political scientists see the task of explaining individual cases as "the domain of historians."[16]

Sociologists make similar distinctions. Seymour Martin Lipset argues that "the task of the sociologist is to formulate general hypotheses . . . and to test them. . . . History must be concerned with the analysis of the particular set of events or processes." Edgar Kiser and Martin Hechter note that "historians' methodology stresses the accuracy and descriptive

15. Georg G. Iggers, *The German Conception of History*, rev. ed. (Middletown, Conn.: Wesleyan University Press, 1968), chap. 6. On the debate in psychology see Robert R. Holt, "Individuality and Generalization in the Psychology of Personality," *Journal of Personality*, Vol. 30, No. 3 (September 1962), pp. 377–404. See also the recent symposium on "Nomothetic vs. Idiographic Disciplines: A False Dilemma," *Review*, Vol. 20, Nos. 3–4 (Summer/Fall 1997).

16. Joseph S. Nye, "Old Wars and Future Wars: Causation and Prevention," *Journal of Interdisciplinary History*, Vol. 18, No. 4 (Spring 1988), p. 581; Bruce Bueno de Mesquita, "The Benefits of a Social Scientific Approach to Studying International Affairs," in Ngaire Woods, ed., *Explaining International Relations Since 1945* (New York: Oxford University Press, 1996), pp. 52–54; and Stephen Van Evera, *Guide to Methods for Students of Political Science* (Ithaca: Cornell University Press, 1997), p. 75.

completeness of narratives about particular events . . . the events they seek to describe and explain are both unique and complex." Robert Bierstedt notes that "history, as idiographic, is interested in the unique, the particular, the individual; sociology, as nomothetic, in the recurrent, the general, the universal."[17]

Similar views can be found among philosophers. Schopenhauer argued that "the sciences . . . speak always of kinds; history always of individuals." Isaiah Berlin explains that "in history we more often than not attach greater credence to particular facts than to general propositions" and that "the purpose of historians . . . [is] to capture the unique pattern and peculiar characteristics of its particular subject." Michael Oakeshott insists on the "absolute impossibility of deriving from history any generalization of the kind which belong to a social science," noting that "where comparison begins, as a method of generalization, history ends."[18]

This idiographic conception of what most historians do is also shared by many historians. In 1848 H.H. Vaughan stated that the first quality of a good historian was the "principle of attraction to the facts," and Leopold von Ranke argued that the aim of historians was to discover the unique in every event. For Ranke, "if generalizations were forced upon history . . . all that which is interesting about history would disappear" and "history would lose all scientific footing."[19]

Among contemporary historians, Lawrence Stone, citing Pierre Chaunu's comment that "the discipline of history is above all a discipline of context," argues that history "deals with a *particular* set of actors at a *particular* time in a *particular* place." Arthur Schlesinger, Jr., contends that

---

17. Seymour Martin Lipset, "History and Sociology: Some Methodological Considerations," in Seymour Martin Lipset and Richard Hofstadter, eds., *Sociology and History: Methods* (New York: Basic Books, 1968), pp. 22–23; Edward Kiser and Martin Hechter, "The Role of General Theory in Comparative-historical Sociology," *American Journal of Sociology* Vol. 97, No. 1 (July 1991), p. 2; and Robert Bierstedt, "Toynbee and Sociology," *The British Journal of Sociology,* Vol. 10, No. 2 (June 1959), pp. 96–97.

18. Schopenhauer is quoted in R.G. Collingwood, *The Idea of History* (Oxford: Oxford University Press, 1956), p. 167. See also Isaiah Berlin, "History and Theory: The Concept of Scientific History," *History and Theory,* Vol. 1, No. 1 (1960), pp. 9, 19; and Michael Oakeshott, *Experience and Its Modes* (New York: Cambridge University Press, 1990), p. 166, quoted in Thomas W. Smith, "Histories and the 'Science' of International Relations," paper presented at the annual meeting of the International Studies Association/South, Atlanta, Georgia, October 20–22, 1995, p. 13.

19. H.H. Vaughan, in the inaugural lecture of the Regius Professor of History at the University of Oxford, cited in Stone, *The Past and the Present Revisited,* p. 5; and von Ranke, "On the Character of Historical Science," p. 38.

Many professional historians—perhaps most—reject the idea that generalization is the goal of history. We all respond, in Marc Bloch's phrase, to "the thrill of learning singular things." Indeed, it is the commitment to concrete reconstruction as against abstract generalization—to life as against laws—which distinguishes history from sociology.[20]

Other historians recognize this as an accurate description of most historiography but argue that historians ought to be more nomothetic in orientation. In 1946, the Committee on Historiography of the Social Science Research Council concluded that for Americans "facts had become detached from any hypothesis or interpretation," and urged historians to generalize more by constructing testable hypotheses.[21] Similarly, Gordon Craig contends that historians should "overcome our congenital distrust of theory and our insistence upon the uniqueness of the historical event . . . and treat unique cases as members of a class or type of phenomenon." John Lewis Gaddis faults many historians in the security field for their lack of comparative focus and for their tendency "to preoccupy themselves with the particular."[22]

Some have interpreted the idiographic/nomothetic distinction and its application to history and social science to suggest that history, unlike the social sciences, tends to be atheoretical. This can be very misleading. We should not confuse the argument that (1) historians aim to explain particular sequences of events, whereas social scientists aim to generalize about classes of events with the assertion that (2) historians base their explanations on factors unique to an individual event or episode whereas political scientists base their explanations on theoretical models. These are two different statements. The first concerns the question of *what* we are trying to explain and the second concerns the question of *how* we explain it. I am *not* arguing that most historians are atheoretical. Rather, I am arguing that historians and political scientists tend to use theory in different ways.

---

20. Stone, *The Past and the Present Revisited*, p. 31; and Arthur Schlesinger, Jr., *The Bitter Heritage*, rev. ed. (Greenwich, Conn.: Fawcett, 1967), p. 90–91.

21. *Theory and Practice in Historical Study* (New York: Social Science Research Council, 1946), Bulletin 64, p. 31, cited in Kim, "Genealogy," p. 426. This SSRC report was followed by another, Louis Gottschalk, ed., *Generalization in the Writing of History* (Chicago: University of Chicago Press, 1963).

22. Gordon Craig, "The Historian and the Study of International Relations," *American Historical Review*, Vol. 88, No. 1 (February), pp. 1–11; and John Lewis Gaddis, "Expanding the Data Base: Historians, Political Scientists, and the Enrichment of Security Studies," *International Security*, Vol. 12, No. 1 (Summer 1987), p. 13.

THE MULTIPLE ROLES OF THEORY

Theories can be used both to explain generalized patterns of social behavior and to guide an interpretation of a particular episode or sequence
of events. Although some historians attempt to explain singular events
in terms of factors unique to those events, other historians resort to more
general theoretical propositions or "covering laws" to explain those
events.[23] The use of theory to explain singular events or sequences of
events fits Lijphart's conception of an "interpretive" case study, Eckstein's
notion of a "disciplined-configurative" case study, and Van Evera's idea
of a "case-explaining case study," as opposed to a hypothesis-generating
case study or a hypothesis-testing case study.[24]

The use of theory for explaining individual episodes or "cases" is also
common in political science, though it is not as highly valued in the
profession as theory construction and testing.[25] The highest professional
rewards in political science go to scholars who develop pathbreaking
theoretical frameworks or models. Some very influential books in the
international relations field in the past half-century have relatively little
empirical content other than illustrative material.[26] Studies that involve
rigorous empirical tests of significant theories or hypotheses are also
valued, and probably constitute the majority of articles published in the
top journals in the field, at least in the United States. These often involve

---

23. On covering laws see Carl G. Hempel, "The Function of General Laws in History," *Journal of Philosophy*, Vol. 39 (1942), pp. 35–48.

24. Arend Lijphart, "Comparative Politics and the Comparative Method," *American
Political Science Review*, Vol. 65, No. 3 (September 1971), pp. 682–693; Harry Eckstein,
"Case Study and Theory in Political Science," in Fred I. Greenstein and Nelson W.
Polsby, eds., *Handbook of Political Science*, vol. 7: *Strategies of Inquiry* (Reading, Mass.:
Addison-Wesley, 1975), pp. 79–137; and Van Evera, *Guide to Methods*, pp. 74–75. It is
interesting to note that political scientists, but not historians, often speak in terms of
"cases." Nomothetically oriented political scientists conceive of a case not in its own
terms but rather as an *instance* of a broader class of phenomena, one to which they
want to generalize. On the diverse meaning of "case" in social science see Charles C.
Ragin and Howard S. Becker, eds., *What Is a Case?* (New York: Cambridge University
Press, 1992).

25. Van Evera (*Guide to Methods*, p. 75), who believes that case-explaining case studies
are an important but neglected activity in political science, states that "political scientists seldom do case-explaining case studies, partly because they define the task of
case-explaining as the domain of historians." Van Evera understates the number of
case-explaining analyses in political science but accurately reflects the relatively low
value attached to them in the discipline.

26. The clearest examples are Kenneth N. Waltz, *Man, the State, and War* (New York:
Columbia University Press, 1959), and Waltz, *Theory of International Politics* (Reading,
Mass.: Addison-Wesley, 1979).

historical case studies, but the cases are vehicles for theory development rather than ends in themselves. Significantly fewer rewards go to those who use theory to guide historical analyses for the primary purpose of illuminating the case (which is quite common), and even less to those who do "descriptive" (atheoretical) case studies (which has become less common).

For political scientists, the worst thing that can be said of a dissertation, job talk, or article is that it is primarily descriptive or that it makes little theoretical contribution, even if it adds to our body of empirical knowledge.[27] For historians, the worst thing that can be said is that a historical study or interpretation is incorrect, that it doesn't fit the facts, tie them together, and make them comprehensible. Political scientists are less concerned about "getting the facts right," and believe that theories can be useful even if they are descriptively inaccurate.[28] Historians are less concerned about explicitly specifying the assumptions and causal propositions underlying their historical interpretations.[29]

Just as political scientists complain that historians are not theoretical enough, or at least not explicit enough about their underlying assumptions and causal propositions, historians complain about political scientists' use (or abuse) of history. They argue that political scientists allow their theories to take priority over the evidence, focus on those historical

---

27. The notable exception is in area studies in the field of comparative politics, where "thick description" of the politics and culture of a country long dominated the field. The influence of area specialists has declined since its peak thirty years ago, however, and there has been a strong shift toward a more nomothetic orientation in the study of comparative politics in the 1990s. Robert H. Bates, "Area Studies and the Discipline: A Useful Controversy?" *PS: Political Science and Politics*, Vol. 30, No. 2 (June 1997), pp. 166–178.

28. The priority given to theory over historical accuracy is suggested by the fact that international relations theorists continued to assign Graham Allison's original treatment of alternative explanations of the Cuban Missile Crisis (*Essence of Decision: Explaining the Cuban Missile Crisis* [Boston: Little Brown, 1971]) in their graduate and undergraduate courses until the late 1990s, long after the release of new information left Allison's historical analysis badly out of date, and, in numerous places, simply inaccurate. These empirical problems have been corrected in Graham Allison and Philip Zelikow, *Essence of Decision: Explaining the Cuban Missile Crisis*, 2nd ed. (New York: Longman, 1999).

29. Some political scientists even emphasize the "heuristic value" of theory over its explanatory power. A theory can be useful if it generates new research questions and stimulates new approaches, even if it is weak on other grounds. James Rosenau once argued (in a talk at the University of Wisconsin in the early 1970s) that "bad theory is better than no theory." Although political scientists might debate this point, they would probably see more merit in Rosenau's argument than historians would find in an argument that "a bad interpretation is better than no interpretation."

events that confirm their theories, and ignore the larger context in which events occur and in the absence of which those events cannot be fully understood. This is closely related to the charge by historians that the emphasis on constructing and testing theories in political science, reinforced by the reward structure in the discipline, leads political scientists to try so hard to confirm their theories that they are unreceptive to contrary evidence.

Historians contrast what they regard as the rigid use of "theory" in political science with their own preference for more flexible "hypotheses" (or theoretical "hunches") that guide historical research but that can be abandoned in the face of conflicting evidence.[30] Historians' conceptions of the rigid or dogmatic use of theory in political science are reflected in Isaiah Berlin's comment that an "addiction to theory—being doctrinaire—is a term of abuse when applied to historians; yet it is not an insult if applied to a natural scientist."[31]

One can undoubtedly find many cases in which political scientists cling rigidly to their theories in the face of substantial contrary evidence, or in which they focus only on those historical cases that fit their theories. But one can also find many examples of historians guilty of the same rigidities and biases in their case selection and interpretations.[32] Good scholars in each discipline, however, are sensitive to disconfirming evidence and critical of their colleagues who are not, and the question of whether one discipline is more guilty than the other of ignoring inconsistent evidence is less important than questions relating to the different criteria for disconfirmation in the two disciplines given their different scholarly purposes, methodologies, and data.

THE ISSUE OF OBJECTIVITY

Interdisciplinary debates about the proper role of theory are often unproductive because scholars use "theory" to mean many different things, ranging from a logically connected set of propositions deduced from

---

30. I thank David Fogelsong (private correspondence) for emphasizing this line of argument.

31. Berlin, "History and Theory," p. 9.

32. A.J.P. Taylor begins his study of the origins of modern wars since 1789 with an arbitrary exclusion of cases that do not fit his argument: "Two major wars—the American civil war of 1861 to 1865 and the Russo-Japanese war of 1904 to 1905, being fought entirely outside Europe, do not fall into the pattern of the others and I have therefore omitted them from my survey of how modern wars begin." A.J.P. Taylor, *How Wars Begin* (New York: Atheneum, 1979), p. 1. Noted in Thomas C. Walker, "Peace, Rivalry, and War: A Theoretical and Empirical Study of International Conflict" (Ph.D. dissertation, Rutgers University, chap. 8).

axiomatic assumptions to the implicit analytical assumptions that guide scholars' worldviews and interpretations. With regard to the latter, it is clear that it is now the conventional wisdom in both history and political science that all empirical observations are filtered through a priori mental frameworks, that all facts are "theory laden." This is accepted by both practitioners and philosophers of social science and history. As Goethe wrote, "every fact is already a theory."[33]

Political scientists and historians agree in principle that one's theoretical preconceptions affect the question one asks, the data one selects to study, and the explanations that one constructs—of singular events as well as of more general patterns. J. David Singer, who constructed the most widely used data set in the study of international conflict, has repeatedly emphasized that data are "made" rather than simply collected. The historian E.H. Carr argues that facts are like "fish swimming about in a vast and sometimes inaccessible ocean; and what the fisherman catches will depend, partly on chance, but mainly on what part of the ocean he chooses to fish in and what tackle he chooses to use—these two factors being determined by the kind of fish that he wants to catch."[34] The disagreement between historians and social scientists is not so much over the influence of theoretical preconceptions, but rather in how explicit scholars should be about the analytic assumptions and causal propositions upon which their explanations of social phenomena are based. Political scientists are far more concerned than historians about making their assumptions and causal propositions explicit.

Historians have not always believed that empirical facts are interpreted through intervening mental frameworks. The leading school of historiography by the later part of the nineteenth century was the "scientific history" of Leopold von Ranke and his followers. Ranke insisted that the aim of the historian was to show history "as it really was," to recreate the past that exists independently of the preconceptions and prejudices of the historian, and to achieve value-free, scientific certainty. The aim was not just to get the facts right, but to understand how discrete facts were interconnected. For Ranke this involved the hermeneutic method, the critical analysis of texts with particular emphasis on primary sources, including diplomatic documents, memoirs, diaries, letters, and the like.[35]

---

33. Goethe is cited in Kenneth N. Waltz, "Evaluating Theories," *American Political Science Review*, Vol. 91, No. 4 (December 1997), p. 913.

34. J. David Singer, "Data-Making in International Relations," *Behavioral Science*, Vol. 10, No. 1 (January 1965), pp. 68–80; and E.H. Carr, *What Is History?* (Harmondsworth, UK: Penguin, 1964), p. 23.

35. Ranke, "The Character of Historical Science"; Georg G. Iggers, "The Image of

This view of understanding history "as it really was" is implicit in John Goldthorpe's argument that the distinctive difference between history and sociology (and by implication the social sciences more generally) is that historians *discover* evidence while sociologists *invent* evidence.[36] We might call this the "Dragnet" conception of history: "Just the facts, ma'am, just the facts."[37]

Historians soon reacted against the Rankean idea of an objective, value-free history.[38] Critics pointed out that Rankean history assumed the centrality of the state and focused narrowly on political history to the exclusion of social, economic, and cultural history. Its methodology utilized national archives as its main sources. The substance of Rankean historiography varied from country to country, primarily in a way that reflected their separate political cultures, mythical national pasts, and perceived threats to the state. In Germany, for example, the opposition to social history was clearly linked to the fear of democratization.[39]

Historical "idealists" have long argued that the study of history reflects the preconceptions of the historian and the social context in which she writes rather than any objective reality.[40] Oakeshott, reflecting the

---

Ranke in American and German Historical Thought," *History and Theory,* Vol. 2, No. 1 (1962), pp. 17–40; and Georg G. Iggers, *New Directions in European Historiography,* rev. ed. (Middletown, Conn.: Wesleyan University Press, 1984). See also Richard J. Evans, *In Defense of History* (New York: W.W. Norton, 1999), chap. 8.

36. Goldthorpe, "The Uses of History in Sociology," p. 214.

37. The same charge—of underestimating the role of theoretical preconceptions underlying all observation and believing in the possiblity of a value-free science—could be leveled against some strands of political science, particularly during the behavioral revolution in the 1960s. But just as Rankean epistemology has gone out of favor, so has the atheoretical "number-crunching" that characterized cruder forms of quantitative analysis.

38. The theoretical ideas subsumed in Ranke's *Aussenpolitik* are still quite influential, both among realist international theorists and their counterparts in diplomatic history.

39. Iggers, *New Directions,* chap. 1.

40. For example, "progressive historians" in the United States reflected the democratic values of the progressive era. See, for example, Charles A. Beard and Mary R. Beard, *America in Midpassage* (New York: Macmillan, 1939). Most contemporary cultural and postmodern historians study the past "from the bottom up," from the perspective of the powerless, the voiceless, the marginalized, and with a clear normative bias in favor of these groups. For an argument on why the study of the "voiceless" lends itself to a postmodern orientation, see Haber, Kennedy, and Krasner, "Brothers Under the Skin," pp. 38–40. But this link is far from perfect. Some postmodernists study elites, and though it is true that it is difficult to apply Rankean methods in the absence of "documents," one can certainly study the powerless from a more positivistic orientation.

historical idealist perspective, argued that "history is a historian's experience. It is 'made' by nobody save the historian; to write history is the only way of making it." Similarly, Carl Becker wrote that "the facts of history do not exist for any historian till he creates them."[41]

Contemporary "constructivists" share this idealist perspective. So do postmodernists, but in a more extreme way. Postmodernists reject the possibility of objective knowledge because the very concepts the analyst uses to describe the world are fundamentally shaped by their cultural context, by power relationships, and by language. For postmodernists, language is a self-contained system that exists independently of its relation to the external world. The text does not reflect reality but instead constructs that reality. In Jacques Derrida's words, "there is nothing outside of the text." As Hayden White argues, "historical narratives are verbal fictions, the contents of which are as much *invented* as *found* and the forms of which have more in common with their counterparts in literature than they have with those in the sciences."[42] Postmodernists reject the distinction between fact and fiction, between history and rhetoric, and thus reject empirical accuracy as a criterion for the evaluation of theories.[43]

E.H. Carr offered a powerful but balanced statement of the theory-laden character of all empirical observation, rejecting the extremes of both Rankeans and historical idealists. Carr criticized the "fetishism of facts" in Rankean historiography and emphasized that all observation involves the "selective filtering of the facts." He also criticized the exclusive reliance on the documents, "the Ark of the Covenant in the temple of facts" in Rankean historiography. At the same time, however, Carr rejected the idealists' argument that empirical observations were entirely determined

---

41. Oakeshott, *Experience and Its Modes*, p. 99; Carl Becker, writing in *Atlantic Monthly* (October 1910), p. 528, cited in Carr, *What Is History?* (London: Macmillan, 1961) p. 21. See also Collingwood, *The Idea of History*.

42. Derrida and White are each cited in Georg C. Iggers, *Historiography in the Twentieth Century: From Scientific Objectivity to the Postmodern Challenge* (Hanover, N.H.: Wesleyan University Press, 1997), pp. 9, 118–119.

43. This distinguishes postmodernists from "softer" constructivists, who recognize limitations on the transhistorical and transcultural validity of theoretical concepts but who are more open to the empirical validation of particular historical interpretations. The possibility of generalizing across cases is contested territory among constructivists (or interpretivists). Ted Hopf argues that "interpretivists are most hesitant to ever generalize across cases, and see even within-case generalizations to be problematic," but then goes on to emphasize the limits of particularism as well as universalism. See Ted Hopf, "The Limits of Interpreting Evidence" (Ohio State University, unpublished manuscript, 2000).

by theoretical preconceptions. Carr argued that "the historian is neither the humble slave nor the tyrannical master of his facts," and that history is "a continuous process of interaction between the historian and his facts, an unending dialogue between the present and the past."[44]

This middle ground between a Rankean positivist and historical idealist viewpoint is one with which many contemporary diplomatic historians and political scientists would feel quite comfortable. Haber, Kennedy, and Krasner argue that "the interplay of fact and theory has been the defining characteristic of the study of international politics. . . . Social behavior can be objectively observed even if it is based on inter-subjectively shared understanding." James Lee Ray and Bruce Russett argue that although "observations are inevitably theory-*laden* they are not theory-*determined*." Most political scientists would accept Carr's argument that the scholar engages in a "continuous process of molding his facts to his interpretation and his interpretation to his facts," that there is an unending dialogue between theory and evidence.[45]

The idiographic/nomothetic distinction—defined in terms of what is to be explained rather than how to explain it—underlies the logic of several of the other criteria of demarcation between the disciplines, including the relative preferences for parsimony, the role of primary and secondary sources, the importance of prediction and policy relevance, beliefs in the feasibility of universal laws, the nature of scope conditions of generalizations, and the role of covering laws. By linking these other criteria within an overarching framework, the idiographic/nomothetic distinction gains considerable analytic power.

PREFERENCES FOR PARSIMONY

Few would disagree that political scientists are far more interested than are historians in "parsimonious" theories and explanations. By this I mean that political scientists attempt to explain as much as possible with as little theoretical apparatus as possible. They prefer one theory to another if the first explains as much empirical phenomena as the second but with fewer assumptions.[46] Historians prefer "total" explanations that

---

44. Carr, *What Is History?* pp. 20–21, 26–30.

45. Haber, Kennedy, and Krasner, "Brothers Under the Skin," pp. 36–37; and James Lee Ray and Bruce Russett, "The Future as Arbiter of Theoretical Controversies: Predictions, Explanations, and the End of the Cold War," *British Journal of Political Science,* Vol. 26, No. 4 (October 1996), pp. 441–470. Carr, *What Is History?* p. 29.

46. This is the conventional use of parsimony in political science. A theory is not parsimonious in the abstract but only relative to other theories that purport to explain the same phenomenon. Preferences for parsimonious theories go back to Occam's

recognize the complexity in the world and attempt to explain much of that complexity in their interpretations in order to account for a set of events in their entirety.[47]

The nature of total explanations varies by historical school. For idealists, it involves *verstehen*, an empathetic understanding of the beliefs, emotions, intentions, reasoning, and very personality of the actors themselves in an attempt to understand the meanings individuals attached to their own actions.[48] This is associated with the idea that the historian aims at understanding and interpretation rather than causal explanation.[49] The concepts of total explanation and "understanding" take us far from the more parsimonious theorizing of most political science.[50]

Many political scientists also recognize complexity in the world, but attempt to abstract from that complexity to explain the most fundamental features of social phenomena. The preference for parsimony derives from the goal of theorizing about relationships between classes of events rather than explaining individual events, and the belief that theoretical generalization must be based on models that are considerably less complex than the world they aim to represent. The more complex and nuanced an explanation, the less likely that it will "travel well" across cases. No two cases are exactly alike, and the more one explains what is unique to a

---

Razor from the fourteenth century and to Karl Popper's argument that simpler theories are easier to falsify and consequently they contain more explanatory power. See Karl Popper, *The Logic of Scientific Discovery* (New York: Harper Torchbacks, 1965). In this view parsimony relates to theories that one constructs to explain the world, not to beliefs about the simplicity of the world itself, which is an alternative conceptualization of parsimony. This alternative view is adopted by Gary King, Robert O. Keohane, and Sidney Verba, *Designing Social Inquiry: Scientific Inquiry in Qualitative Research* (Princeton: Princeton University Press, 1994), who refer to the first conception of parsimony as "maximizing leverage." See also the chapter by Jervis in this volume.

47. As Eric Hobsbawm argues, in *On History* (New York: The New Press, 1997), p. 109, "basically all history aspires to what the French call 'total history'." By this he means that "history . . . cannot decide to leave out *any* aspect of human history *a priori* . . . ," that ideally all aspects of an episode must be included in a historical explanation.

48. Collingwood, *The Idea of History*; Benedetto Croce, *History: Its Theory and Practice* (New York: Russell and Russell, 1960); and William Dilthey, *Meaning in History* (London: Allen & Unwin, 1961).

49. Historians themselves debate the utility of this distinction. See Roberts, *Historical Explanation*, chap. 11.

50. An important exception is constructivism, which shares an interest in the complex social contexts of human behavior and the meanings individuals attach to their actions. See Martin Hollis and Steve Smith, *Explaining and Understanding International Relations* (Oxford: Clarendon Press, 1990); and Hopf, "The Limits of Interpreting Evidence."

particular case, the less one can use the same conceptual apparatus to explain the essential features of another case.

This difference between historians and political scientists in their treatment of complexity has begun to narrow in some important respects. By the mid-1990s international relations theorists had begun to build more complexity into their models, with greater emphasis on interaction effects between variables at different levels of analysis; on uncertainty, unanticipated consequences, and nonlinear relationships; and on selection effects, reciprocal causation, and other forms of endogeneity, where the dependent variable has some impact on the independent variable.[51]

Although historians rarely refer explicitly to the concept of endogeneity, in some respects they have been more likely than political scientists to incorporate the role of endogeneity into their historical explanations. Historians have long argued that "everything is connected to everything else." They have repeatedly criticized the simplistic tendencies of political scientists to speak in terms of "independent" and "dependent variables," and to assume that historical "cases" are independent. Historians generally trace the historical roots of behavior further back in time, and they emphasize the non-independence of discrete events.[52] On the other hand, political scientists have made important contributions by constructing models to deal with endogeneity effects in a more systematic way.[53]

Given their interest in constructing parsimonious theories and explanations, political scientists often complain that the nonparsimonious explanations of historians, area specialists, and others tend to be overdeter-

---

51. The quantitative international relations literature has begun to give more attention to context. See Gary Goertz, *Contexts of International Politics* (Cambridge: Cambridge University Press, 1994). Both game-theoretic models and the statistical models used to test them have incorporated more complexity in order to deal with endogeneity. See Robert Powell, *In the Shadow of Power* (Princeton: Princeton University Press, 1999); and Curtis S. Signorino, "Strategic Interaction and the Statistical Analysis of International Conflict," *American Political Science Review,* Vol. 93, No. 2 (June 1999), pp. 279–297. For a nonformal treatment see Robert Jervis, *System Effects: Complexity in Political and Social Life* (Princeton: Princeton University Press, 1997). On increasing complexity in theories of war, see Jack S. Levy, "The Causes of War and the Conditions of Peace," *Annual Review of Political Science,* Vol. 1 (1998), pp. 160–161.

52. This implies that the standard assumptions underlying the statistical methods that political scientists commonly use are frequently violated. Political scientists have begun to devote increasing attention to this problem. On the issue of independent and dependent variables, see John Lewis Gaddis's essay in this volume.

53. James D. Fearon, "Signaling versus the Balance of Power and Interests: An Empirical Test of a Crisis Bargaining Model," *Journal of Conflict Resolution,* Vol. 38, No. 2 (June 1994), pp. 236–269.

mined—in that the analyst advances more causes for an outcome than are needed to explain it. To the political scientist, this represents a failure to differentiate primary from secondary causal factors and diminishes the analytical power of the argument and the ability to generalize to other cases. Historians, on the other hand, often complain that the so-called parsimonious explanations of political scientists are underdetermined— they fail to capture the nuances of individual events or periods, and they also fail to explain the variation across historical episodes.[54]

It is important to note that overdetermined explanations are not equivalent to multicausal explanations.[55] In overdetermined explanations, there are several factors, or sets of factors, that are individually sufficient for an outcome. In multicausal explanations, a set of factors may be jointly sufficient for a particular outcome. The two are not the same. In the first situation, but not the second, the absence of one causal factor would leave the outcome unchanged. In fact, political scientists would be quite pleased with explanations that specify jointly sufficient conditions. They seek parsimony but not necessarily monocausal explanations, for they have gradually come to conclude that there are few causal variables that are individually necessary or sufficient for explaining outcomes.[56]

I will return to the role of theory in historical explanation, but it is useful to note here that to the extent that historians are explicit in their use of theory in their explanations, they reject the idea that a single theory can provide a total explanation and prefer to draw on many different theories. As Melvyn Leffler argues in explaining how he uses theories from all levels of analysis in his study of the Cold War, "I applied no single theory. . . . if reality is too complex to be captured by a single

---

54. Criticisms of excessively or inadequately parsimonious explanations can be found within each discipline. Many political scientists have criticized neorealist theory for being too parsimonious and for generating underdetermined outcomes. See Waltz, *Theory of International Politics;* and Robert O. Keohane, ed., *Neorealism and Its Critics* (New York: Columbia University Press, 1986).

55. Compare this treatment with the one in Richard Ned Lebow's chapter in this volume.

56. An important exception here is the proposition that joint democracy is a sufficient condition for peace (defined as the absence of war), which "comes as close as anything we have to an empirical law in international relations." See Jack S. Levy, "Domestic Politics and War," *Journal of Interdisciplinary History,* Vol. 18, No. 4 (Spring 1988), p. 662; and James Lee Ray, *Democracy and International Conflict* (Columbia: University of South Carolina Press, 1995). The absence of variables that are either necessary or sufficient to explain variations in outcomes in a theoretical sense does not imply that there cannot be necessary or sufficient conditions for outcomes in particular cases, though strict proponents of covering-law explanations would probably dissent from this view.

theory, different theories may help the historian to make sense of different parts of the phenomenon or event or process under scrutiny."[57]

Leffler implies that theory is like a toolbox, a set of instruments from which to draw, with the assumption that a different set of tools will be used in different cases depending on what needs to be explained. This view may be helpful in providing total explanations of individual phenomena. It does not facilitate the formulation or testing of theoretical generalizations, at least in the eyes of the political scientist.[58] This task requires a single, well-specified, and integrated theoretical structure, the derivation of a set of propositions, and their empirical validation through an appropriate research design. The use of multiple theories without integrating them into an overarching theoretical structure increases the likelihood of logical inconsistencies and contradictions among different theoretical propositions, and is an important line of criticism that deductively-oriented theorists make of both historians and inductively-oriented political scientists.[59]

It is useful to contrast the "toolbox" conception of theory with the norm that has developed in political science for scholars to analytically distinguish their own theories (or explanations of individual cases) from competing theories or explanations and to explicitly test their theory against the leading alternatives. Many case studies in political science, for example, are organized around competing theories rather than a single narrative. To the extent that historians deal with competing theories in their narratives, this is much less explicit and rarely serves as an organizing device. The political scientist's preference for pitting theory against competing theory rather than integrating elements from different perspectives into a single, more complex theory is consistent with the goal

---

57. Melvyn P. Leffler, "New Approaches, Old Interpretations, and Prospective Reconfigurations," *Diplomatic History*, Vol. 19, No. 2 (Spring 1995), p. 179.

58. The "toolbox" metaphor comes from Edgar Kiser, "The Revival of Narrative in Historical Sociology: What Rational Choice Theory Can Contribute," *Politics and Society*, Vol. 24, No. 3 (September 1996), p. 258.

59. Isaiah Berlin makes a similar argument (in "History and Theory," p. 9) when he says that the "crucial difference" between history and the natural sciences is that "the generalizations of history, like those of ordinary thought, are largely unconnected." Waltz has something like this in mind when he describes the evidence that Paul Schroeder compiles against neorealist theory as "a melange of irrelevant diplomatic lore," though Schroeder's work has been quite influential in political science, and rightfully so. See Paul W. Schroeder, "Historical Reality vs. Neo-Realist Theory," *International Security*, Vol. 19, No. 1 (Summer 1994), pp. 108–148; and Waltz, "Evaluating Theories," p. 914.

of making theories as parsimonious as possible. One can debate, however, whether this increases our understandings of individual cases.

Political scientists agree with historians that no single theory can provide a complete explanation of a set of events. Unlike historians, however, political scientists have no interest in providing complete explanations. They only want to explain theoretically relevant aspects of the case, as determined by their own conceptual framework, and to generalize to the broader universe of all comparable cases.[60]

This difference between attempting to maximize descriptive accuracy in a particular case and insisting upon a more parsimonious theory to facilitate generalization reflects the basic tradeoff between internal validity and external validity—between providing an exact and precise explanation of a particular "case" or set of events or data, and providing a reasonable basis for generalizing beyond the data to other similar instances of the same class of events. Historians give primacy to internal validity, while political scientists are willing to sacrifice some internal validity in order to increase external validity.[61]

PRIMARY AND SECONDARY SOURCES

The different tradeoffs historians and political scientists make between internal and external validity, which derive from their respective idiographic and nomothetic aims, helps explain the emphasis each places on primary sources. Historians have traditionally insisted on the central importance of primary sources, while political scientists have been more willing to rely on secondary sources based on the work of historians.

One problem that political scientists must confront in their use of secondary sources is that the implicit (or explicit) theoretical questions that guided the historian's study may have been quite different from the questions the political scientist wants to answer, and this may limit the utility of particular secondary sources for the political scientist. This mismatch between theory and data, along with other considerations, leads Deborah Larson to call for political scientists to rely less on histo-

---

60. Area specialists constitute an important exception.

61. On different conceptions of validity, see Thomas D. Cook and Donald T. Campbell, *Quasi-Experimentation* (Chicago: Rand McNally, 1979), chap. 2. This discussion of tradeoffs suggests the potential utility of multi-method approaches to social and political analysis, in which the combination of two or more methods can help to compensate for the limitations of any single method. The combination of case study and statistical or game-theoretic methods (or both) has become more common in political science, and its potential utility is demonstrated by research on the democratic peace.

rians' secondary sources and to do more archival work themselves in the construction and testing of their theories.[62]

This may be good advice in principle, assuming that the types of data that one's theory calls for are available in the archives. But an important practical problem arises from the kinds of research designs that political scientists construct for the purposes of theoretical generalization, which require a test of the theory either against a large number of cases in a quantitative study, or against a more modest number of cases for the purposes of controlled comparison. Either way, it is simply not possible for a single scholar to engage in a thorough investigation of all available primary sources for each case. This is particularly true given diplomatic historians' recent emphasis on the use of multi-archival sources from different countries. As Theda Skocpol notes with respect to historical sociology, "a dogmatic insistence on redoing primary research for every investigation would be disastrous; it would rule out most comparative-historical research."[63]

A second problem in the use of secondary sources is the potential for selection biases. Given the large number of secondary sources from which to choose, how does the analyst select which to use or to rely upon most heavily? The analyst may be drawn to precisely those sources that reflect her own theoretical preconceptions, which precludes a fair test of the author's theory against alternative explanations.[64] It may be possible, however, for the comparative researcher to minimize these selection biases by securing advice from several leading historians regarding the

---

62. See Deborah Welch Larson's chapter in this volume. See also Gaddis, "Expanding the Data Base." Political scientists often use some primary sources in doing historical case studies. Quantitative studies based on content analysis also rely heavily on primary sources. One example of the latter is the Stanford 1914 Project, directed by Robert North in the 1960s and 1970s. For a review see Francis W. Hoole and Dina A. Zinnes, eds., *Quantitative International Politics: An Appraisal* (New York: Praeger, 1976), part V.

63. Theda Skocpol, "Emerging Agendas and Recurrent Strategies in Historical Sociology," in Theda Skocpol, ed., *Vision and Method in Historical Sociology* (New York: Cambridge University Press, 1984), p. 382.

64. Ian S. Lustick, "History, Historiography, and Political Science: Multiple Historical Records and the Problem of Selection Bias," *American Political Science Review*, Vol. 90, No. 3 (September 1996), pp. 605–618; and Paul W. Schroeder, "History and International Relations Theory: Not Use or Abuse, but Fit or Misfit," *International Security*, Vol. 22, No. 1 (Summer 1997), p. 71. The general problem, as Skocpol ("Emerging Agendas," p. 382) has noted, is that "comparative historical sociologists have not so far worked out clear, consensual rules and procedures or the valid use of secondary sources as evidence."

major debates among historians, the best secondary sources, and the analytical biases of particular historians.

It is not clear that the problem of selection bias in the use of secondary sources is any more serious than the potential biases that affect the analyst who works alone in the archives. There is no perfect solution here. Insisting that the political scientist work the archives and in addition read all relevant secondary sources, and do this for enough cases to facilitate the ability to generalize, is impractical. Insisting that researchers using both primary and secondary sources be more sensitive to the potential biases in their sources and in their own minds, and more cognizant of the wide range of interpretations in various secondary sources, while helpful, does not fully eliminate the problem.

PREDICTION AND POLICY IMPLICATIONS

The nomothetic/idiographic distinction also helps explain why political scientists are generally more interested than historians in prediction and possibly also in the utility of scholarship for statecraft.[65] Gaddis argues that with respect to prediction (or at least policy implications), "most historians shy from these priorities like vampires confronted with crosses. Many political scientists embrace them enthusiastically."[66] Edward Ingram argues that "political scientists are interested in the past only as it affects the present. The past interests historians for itself." He also maintains that "for political scientists, what matters is not what mattered at the time but what contributes to what will matter later on."[67]

Arthur Schlesinger, Jr., has a more ambivalent view of historians'

---

65. These differences over the importance of policy relevance may have deep historical roots. Once the natural sciences had become associated with technological progress, the social sciences, struggling to establish a disciplinary identity distinct from history, sought legitimation by emphasizing its pragmatic and policy-relevant side. See Kim, "Genealogy," pp. 423–428.

66. John Lewis Gaddis, "History, Theory, and Common Ground," *International Security*, Vol. 22, No. 1 (Summer 1997), p. 84. Gaddis argues, however, that while we cannot predict the future, we can prepare for it (pp. 84–85), and that an understanding of the past is one form of training that helps us prepare for the future. The implication is that we can better understand which events are more likely to occur than others. While Gaddis clearly rejects the idea of making "point predictions" about the future, his comment about preparing for the future is not dissimilar to political science predictions based on statistical probabilities.

67. Edward Ingram, "The Wonderland of the Political Scientist," *International Security*, Vol. 22, No. 1 (Summer 1997), pp. 54–55. In contrast to Ingram, however, it has also been said that "History is the use the present makes of the past for the sake of the future." Cited in *New York Times*, January 1, 2000, p. A1.

attitudes toward prediction. He states that historians "privately regard history as its own reward; they study it for the intellectual and aesthetic fulfillment . . . but for no more utilitarian reason. They understand better than outsiders that historical training confers no automatic wisdom in the realm of public affairs." Yet a page later he argues that generalizations, however defective, are possible, and that they "can strengthen the capacity of statesmen to deal with the future."[68]

It is probably true that political scientists are more interested in prediction than are historians. Some people undoubtedly choose to become political scientists rather than historians precisely because they want to influence policy and because the generalizing aims of political science are more conducive to prediction than the particularizing tendencies of history. This does not necessarily imply, however, that political scientists are always more influenced by contemporary policy concerns than are historians. All historiography involves, to some extent, seeing the past through the eyes of the present. As Benedetto Croce argued, "all history is contemporary history." Similarly, Frederick Jackson Turner wrote that "each age writes the history of the past anew with reference to the conditions uppermost in its own time."[69]

In fact, it is often more difficult to identify the social, political, and cultural biases in theoretical models in contemporary social science, which often prides itself on its "objectivity," than in the work of historians, which can be quite evaluative. As Ingram argues, historical narratives tell a story, and a morality play is often part of the story.[70] The influence of these analytic and normative biases on historical studies does not necessarily imply, however, that these studies are conducted or written in such a way that might generate specific future predictions or policy prescriptions that are well grounded in either theoretical logic or historical evidence.[71]

There is another reason why political scientists are interested in

---

68. Schlesinger, *Bitter Heritage*, pp. 90–91.

69. Croce cited in Carr, *What Is History?* pp. 20–21; and Frederick Jackson Turner, "The Significance of History," in *The Early Writings of Frederick Jackson Turner* (Madison: University of Wisconsin Press, 1891/1938), p. 52.

70. See Edward Ingram's chapter in this volume; Robert Jervis and Paul W. Schroeder also make similar points in their chapters.

71. It is interesting that some of the historical studies with the greatest policy relevance have had greater impact on international relations scholars than on historians. One example might be Paul M. Kennedy, *The Rise and Fall of the Great Powers: Economic Change and Military Conflict from 1500 to 2000* (New York: Random House, 1987).

prediction.[72] By using a theory to make predictions and then testing the accuracy of those predictions, one can ensure that a theory is tested against data that played no direct role in the generation of the theory.[73] The aim is to avoid the common error of using the data to generate a theory and then using that same data to test the theory. For this purpose prediction refers not only to forecasts about future events, but also to "predictions" of past events that are unknown to the analyst, or at least that played no direct role in the formulation of his theories. Such predictions are often referred to as postdictions or retrodictions.[74] The importance of postdictions springs from the scientific imperative to derive from a theory as many testable implications as possible, in as many varied temporal and spatial domains as possible, and to subject those predictions to multiple empirical tests.[75]

The methodological mandate to avoid testing a theory with the same data that were used to construct the theory raises a particular problem for historical interpretation. Historical narratives are always written with a knowledge of the outcome of the story, but this raises the danger that the known outcome influences the interpretation of chronologically earlier events. As C.V. Wedgwood wrote, "History is lived forward, but it is written in retrospect. . . . We know the end before we consider the begin-

---

72. An important exception here is evolutionary theory, which emphasizes the difficulty of making predictions because of path dependence, uncertainty, and nonlinear complexity. See the special issue of *International Studies Quarterly* on "Evolutionary Paradigms in the Social Sciences," Vol. 40, No. 3 (September 1996).

73. This is Milton Friedman's argument for the importance of prediction in "The Methodology of Positive Economics," in Milton Friedman, *Essays in Positive Economics* (Chicago: University of Chicago Press, 1953). It is also the basis of Imre Lakatos's argument that the prediction and confirmation of "novel facts" is a central component of scientific progress. See Imre Lakatos, "Falsification and the Methodology of Scientific Research Programmes," in Imre Lakatos and Alan Musgrave, eds., *Criticism and the Growth of Knowledge* (New York: Cambridge University Press, 1970), pp. 91–196. For a review of debates regarding exactly what constitutes a "novel fact" see Colin Elman and Miriam Fendius Elman, "Appraising Progress in International Relations Theory: How Not to Be Lakatos Intolerant," unpublished manuscript, 1999.

74. See Ray and Russett, "The Future as Arbiter," p. 447.

75. King, Keohane, and Verba, *Designing Social Inquiry*; and Van Evera, *Guide to Methods*. The need to make predictions in unfamiliar domains is emphasized by Nobel Prize–winning physicist Richard Feynman: "If you will never say that a law is true in a region you have not already looked you do not know anything. If the only laws that you find are those which you have just finished observing then you can never make any predictions." See Richard Feynman, *The Character of Physical Law* (Cambridge, Mass.: MIT Press, 1965), p. 76.

ning and we can never wholly recapture what it was to know the beginning only."[76]

THE FEASIBILITY OF UNIVERSAL LAWS

Those who test theories over different historical periods necessarily assume that these periods are sufficiently comparable that cross-temporal theoretical generalizations are meaningful. This raises questions of the continuity of history and the feasibility of universal laws as opposed to contingent generalizations. Political scientists are more willing than historians to assume a continuity or commensurability in history and to seek transhistorically valid theoretical generalizations. Historians are more likely to argue that each historical era has its own culture and "character" and that any historical "laws" are consequently temporally bound. This is expressed in Ranke's dictum that "every epoch is immediate unto God." Terrence Ball argues that it is history's reliance on temporally bound rather than universal laws that makes a historical explanation historical. From a different perspective, John Gaddis emphasizes the nonreplicable nature of the phenomena that we try to explain.[77]

We must be careful not to push this distinction too far. The historian Marc Bloch argued that "the only true history . . . is universal history," and some schools of historiography do aim for universal generalizations.[78] One example would be the "New Economic History" in the United States, which utilizes general deductive models of the economy to generate predictions, including counterfactual predictions of what would have occurred under a different set of circumstances.[79]

Other scientific schools of historiography reject the possibility of universal laws but are willing to make generalizations about phenomena

---

76. C.V. Wedgwood, *William the Silent* (New York: Norton, 1968), cited in *New York Times*, March 19, 1995. Political scientists' interpretations of historical cases are also frequently informed by a knowledge of the outcome, though the methodological emphasis on selecting cases based on values of the independent variable, not the outcome, reduces this tendency. See King, Keohane, and Verba, *Designing Social Inquiry*.

77. Von Ranke, "On Progress in History," in Iggers and von Moltke, eds., *The Theory and Practice of History*, p. 53; Terrence Ball, "On 'Historical' Explanation," *Philosophy of the Social Sciences*, Vol. 2, No. 3 (September 1972), pp. 183–184; and Gaddis, "History, Theory, and Common Ground," pp. 81–82.

78. Marc Bloch, *The Historian's Craft* (New York: Vintage, 1964), p. 47.

79. Key works include Robert William Fogel, *Railroads and American Economic Growth* (Baltimore: Johns Hopkins University Press, 1964); and Robert William Fogel and Stanley L. Engerman, *Time on the Cross: The Economics of American Negro Slavery* (Boston: Little Brown, 1974). This approach has declined from its strong influence in the 1960s.

in more restricted times and places. Many Marxists, for example, assert that social behavior is governed by laws, but these laws are limited to specific points of historical development and are "counteracted" by concrete historical circumstances.[80] Similarly, the French *Annales* school, which was quite influential in the 1950s, 1960s, and 1970s, emphasized middle-range generalizations based on an emphasis on both broad structural patterns and the "total" character of each historical setting.[81]

Many political scientists are also much more comfortable with middle-range theory and contingent generalizations than with universal generalizations.[82] Alexander George, for example, who works within a decision-making framework, has long argued for the value of contingent generalizations and for the role of "typological theory" to generate such generalizations.[83] Some structural theorists are willing to make broad generalizations about recurrent patterns within historical systems spanning many centuries (the Westphalian system since 1648, for example) but make no claim that such patterns characterize other historical systems. At some point, however, historical systems may be defined so broadly that generalizations about them take on a near-universal character.[84]

---

80. As Iggers (*New Directions,* p. 40) argues, "a great deal of Marxist historical research has combined Marxist questions and social critique with rigorous empirical-analytical and text-critical methods" and has "struck a balance between quantitative analytical and qualitative hermeneutical methods."

81. The classic study of the *Annales* school is Fernand Braudel, *The Mediterranean and the Mediterranean World in the Age of Philip II,* trans. Sian Reynolds, 2 vols. (New York: Harper & Row, 1972). For a useful review see Iggers, *New Directions,* chap. 2.

82. The middle-range character of theoretical generalizations is determined not only by their contingent as opposed to universal scope, but also by how broadly the dependent variable is defined. One example might be the analysis of the conditions for international cooperation, as opposed to the narrower question of the conditions for the ratification of agreements.

83. Alexander L. George and Richard Smoke, *Deterrence in American Foreign Policy* (New York: Columbia University Press, 1974). On typological theory see Andrew Bennett and Alexander L. George, *Case Studies and Theory Development* (Cambridge, Mass.: MIT Press, forthcoming).

84. George Modelski and William Thompson find recurrent patterns of concentration and deconcentration in the global distribution of power and wealth over the past ten centuries of "modern economic growth," and are willing to make other qualified generalizations back to 4000 B.C. See Modelski and Thompson, *Leading Sectors and World Politics: The Coevolution of Global Economics and Politics* (Columbia: University of South Carolina Press, 1996), and "Pulsations in the World System: Hinterland-to-Center Incursions and Migrations, 4000 B.C. to 1500 A.D.," in Nicholas Kardulias, ed., *Leadership, Production, and Exchange: World Systems Theory and Anthropology* (Boulder, Colo.: Rowman & Littlefield, 1998).

SCOPE CONDITIONS

I have argued that to the extent that historians attempt to generalize, their generalizations are usually restricted to a well-defined period.[85] The conditional nature of the historian's generalizations does not differentiate her from the social scientist, because many social science generalizations are conditional rather than universal, so that the social scientist must specify the "scope conditions" under which her generalizations or theory is valid. The difference lies in how the limiting conditions on generalizations are specified. Historians use temporal and spatial criteria whereas social scientists use analytical criteria, as contained in the explicit assumptions underlying their theories. The social science emphasis on analytical scope conditions is expressed in the injunction that in their theoretical propositions scholars should replace the identity of countries, places, and dates with conceptual variables.[86]

While most political scientists conceive of generalizations in terms of relationships between conceptual variables, many historians do not. They are willing to speak of "generalizations" about particular periods, particular countries, or even particular individuals, and treat these generalizations as fully valid and law-like within particular spatial and temporal bounds.[87] Such generalizations are based on knowledge of the period (or country or individual) rather than on universal or contingent covering laws.

This is the argument advanced by N. Rescher and O. Helmer for the role of explanatory laws in historical cases. They argue that statements like "heretics were persecuted in seventeenth-century Spain" are law-like generalizations.[88] An even more restricted form of generalization would be what Gilbert Ryle calls "dispositional explanations" of the behavior of

---

85. This is reflected in some historians' response to questions about other countries or other periods: "It's not my period." Comparative history provides significant exceptions.

86. Adam Przeworski and Henry Tuene, *The Logic of Comparative Social Inquiry* (New York: Wiley, 1970). Kiser ("Revival of Narrative," pp. 256–259) differentiates between historical and abstract scope conditions.

87. This discussion builds on William Dray, "The Historical Explanation of Actions Reconsidered," in Patrick Gardner, ed. *The Philosophy of History* (London: Oxford University Press, 1974), pp. 66–89, especially pp. 80–83.

88. N. Rescher and O. Helmer, "On the Epistemology of the Inexact Sciences," *Management Science*, Vol. 5 (October 1959), pp. 25–40; see also N. Rescher and C. B. Joynt, "The Problem of Uniqueness in History," *History and Theory*, Vol. 1, No. 2 (1961), pp. 150–162.

a particular individual, which he claims are law-like in nature. Ryle gives the example of the statement "Disraeli was ambitious."[89]

While philosophers of history debate whether statements like this are restricted law-like generalizations,[90] political scientists would generally reject such arguments. They generalize not about particular countries or individuals, but rather about *kinds* of countries or individuals. They might generalize about countries *like* seventeenth-century Spain, defined in terms of certain political, social, or cultural characteristics. They might generalize about the motivations of individuals *like* Disraeli, and say that individuals with certain personalities, social backgrounds, or belief systems tend to behave in predictable ways. But political scientists prefer not to generalize about particular countries or individuals, and they would not claim that such statements were law-like generalizations.[91] These different meanings that historians and political scientists attach to the notion of generalization helps to explain their strong differences regarding their respective answers to the question of how much historians generalize.

This difference in the specification of scope conditions in history and in political science is revealed in the titles of some of the more influential recent books in peace, war, and security in the two disciplines. The inclusion or noninclusion of spatial and temporal scope conditions in the title provides a strong indicator of the author's disciplinary affiliation.[92]

There are some historians who seek to construct universal theoretical generalizations and who are exceptions to my distinction between history

---

89. Gilbert Ryle, *The Concept of Mind* (London: Hutchinson, 1966), chap. 6.

90. Dray, "Historical Explanations of Actions Reconsidered," pp. 80–84.

91. An interesting exception is James N. Rosenau's argument that we can have "single-country" theories of foreign policy, in "Toward a Single-Country Theory: The USSR as an Adaptive System," paper presented at the Conference on Domestic Sources of Soviet Foreign and Defense Policies, University of California at Los Angeles, 1985.

92. Consider the following books by historians contributing to this volume: Carole Fink, *The Genoa Conference: European Diplomacy, 1921–1922* (Chapel Hill: University of North Carolina Press, 1984); Edward Ingram, *The Beginning of the Great Game in Asia, 1828–1834* (New York: Oxford University Press, 1979; John A. Lynn, *Giant of the Grand Siècle: The French Army, 1610–1715* (Cambridge: Cambridge University Press, 1997); Stephen E. Pelz, *Race to Pearl Harbor: The Failure of the Second London Naval Conference and the Onset of World War II* (Cambridge, Mass.: Harvard University Press, 1974); Schroeder, *The Transformation of European Politics, 1763–1848;* and Gerhard L. Weinberg, *A World at Arms: A Global History of World War II* (Cambridge: Cambridge University Press, 1994). Books by political scientists contributing to this volume include Miriam Fendius Elman, ed., *Paths to Peace: Is Democracy the Answer?* (Cambridge, Mass.: MIT Press, 1997); Robert Jervis, *Perception and Misperception in International Politics*; Richard

and political science. The clearest example is Arnold Toynbee, who aimed to discover the laws driving the life-cycles of twenty-one civilizations in the past in his multivolume *A Study of History*.[93] But this is the exception that proves the rule. Historians and philosophers of science have responded quite critically to Toynbee and to "speculative history" more generally.[94] In terms of the distinction between history and social science, one scholar asserts that Toynbee's work "is not, in fact, a history of anything at all. It is . . . a search for sociological principles of a most general and universal kind." The question is "not whether *A Study of History* belongs to history or to sociology, but only whether it is good sociology or bad sociology."[95]

THE ROLE OF COVERING LAWS

I have argued that some historians explain singular events or episodes in terms of unique contextual factors, and other historians explain those events in terms of more general theoretical propositions. There is a substantial consensus among most political scientists (with the important exception of many constructivists), but not among historians, that only the latter is a valid form of explanation. That is, as a discipline political science is far more likely than history to accept Hempel's covering law (or nomological) model of explanation, in which an explanation of a concrete event requires the subsumption of that event under general laws of behavior. Given general laws (deterministic or probabilistic) and initial

---

Ned Lebow, *Between Peace and War* (Baltimore: Johns Hopkins University Press, 1981); Jack S. Levy, *War in the Modern Great Power System, 1495–1975* (Lexington: University Press of Kentucky, 1983); Richard Rosecrance, *The Rise of the Trading State: Commerce and Conquest in the Modern World* (New York: Basic Books, 1986); and William R. Thompson, *On Global War* (Columbia: University of South Carolina Press, 1988). Book titles are less revealing for Cold War history, where the differences between the disciplines begin to blur. One non–Cold War title that does not fit this distinction is Randall L. Schweller, *Deadly Imbalances: Tripolarity and Hitler's Strategy of World Conquest* (New York: Columbia University Press, 1998).

93. Arnold Toynbee, *A Study of History*, 12 vols. (London: Oxford University Press, 1948–61).

94. See Pieter Geyl, *Debates with Historians* (London: Fontana, 1962). See also Clayton Roberts, *The Logic of Historical Explanation* (University Park: Penn State University Press, 1996). It is also significant, as Roberts argues (p. 13), that "Historians today do not cite or quote from *A Study of History*."

95. Bierstedt, "Toynbee and Sociology," pp. 95–96. After reading an earlier version of this essay, Matthew Melko wrote (private correspondence, October 7, 1999) that in the early 1960s he asked Toynbee how he would categorize himself, Spengler, the sociologist Pitirim Sorokin, and the anthropologist A.L. Kroeber, who are all now regarded as founders of the civilizational paradigm. Toynbee replied, "We are all sociologists."

conditions, a particular event is certain or likely to occur. These general laws may be implicit in the historian's narrative, but without general laws explanation is not possible.[96] As Jeffrey Issac argues, "deductive nomological explanation is "the dominant view of causality and scientific explanation in political science."[97]

In contrast, most historians formally reject the covering law model.[98] Many implicitly accept some version of Oakeshott's view that "the relation between events is always other events."[99] This is inherent in the idea of "genetic" or "sequential" explanation based on a fine-tuned description or process tracing of how one event leads to another.[100] But (following Hume) how can we be certain that one observed event *causes* another? Hempel's response, implicitly accepted by most political scientists, is that each link in the causal chain must be based on empirically validated theoretical propositions.[101] In the absence of deterministic laws we must settle for probabilistic laws and hence a causal chain with a series of probabilistic linkages.

96. Hempel, "The Function of General Laws in History;" Popper, *The Logic of Scientific Discovery;* and Arthur C. Danto, *Analytical Philosophy of History* (Cambridge: Cambridge University Press, 1965). Hempel refers to explanations in which assumptions are not explicit as "incomplete explanations."

97. Jeffrey C. Isaac, "After Empiricism: The Realist Alternative," in Terrence Ball, ed., *Idioms of Inquiry* (Albany: State University of New York Press, 1987), p. 189.

98. For critiques, see William H. Dray, *Laws and Explanation in History* (London: Oxford University Press, 1957); Alan Ryan, *The Philosophy of the Social Sciences* (New York: Pantheon, 1970); and Maurice Mandelbaum, "The Problem of 'Covering Laws'," in Patrick Gardiner, ed., *The Philosophy of History* (London: Oxford University Press, 1974), pp. 51–65. Dray argues that theory-driven explanation (in the form of covering laws) "sets up a kind of *conceptual barrier* to a humanistically oriented historiography." Dray, "The Historical Explanation of Actions Reconsidered," p. 89. This suggests that there may be a fundamental difference in the way that most historians and political scientists conceive of causation, but I save a more detailed discussion of this for another time. See Hidemi Suganami, *On the Causes of War* (Oxford: Clarendon Press, 1996), chaps. 4–5.

99. Michael Oakeshott, *Experience and Its Modes* (Cambridge: Cambridge University Press, 1933), p. 141, cited in Smith, "Histories," p. 13.

100. See Ernest Nagel, *The Structure of Science* (Indianapolis: Hackett, 1979), pp. 564–568; W.B. Gallie, "The Historical Understanding," *History and Theory*, Vol. 3, No. 2 (1963), pp. 149–202; Louis O. Mink, *Historical Understanding*, eds. Brian Fay, Eugene O. Golob, and Richard T. Vann (Ithaca: Cornell University Press, 1987).

101. Roberts, *Historical Explanation*. This requires both a theoretical explanation and demonstrated empirical regularity. The belief that much positivistic political science has emphasized the latter at the expense of the former has led some to adopt a "scientific realist" epistemology because of its emphasis on causal mechanisms. David Dessler, "Beyond Correlations: Toward a Causal Theory of War," *International Studies*

One important implication of this argument is that it is necessary to go beyond the set of events one wants to explain in order to explain them, because the validation of general laws (whether deterministic or probabilistic) requires the confirmation of observable regularities over a broader empirical domain. As Ray argues, "single events cannot be 'explained' in isolation" and that "*comparison* of an event to be understood and explained with other events is logically impossible to avoid."[102] The widespread acceptance of this argument by political scientists and its rejection by many historians is reflected in the tendency of the former but not the latter to shun single case studies in favor of comparative case studies or large-*n* statistical studies.[103] Political scientists focus on the general rather than the particular because they believe that theory construction is both an end in itself and a necessary means to explain particular events by subsuming them under covering laws.

SYNOPTIC JUDGMENT

In his discussion of the essence of historical analysis, Paul Schroeder argues that Louis Mink's concept of "synoptic judgment" best captures the task of the historian. Mink claimed that historians attempt to "understand an event as unique rather than as typical." He argued that the "distinctive characteristic of historical understanding consists of comprehending a complex event by 'seeing things together' in a total and synoptic judgment which cannot be replaced by any analytic technique." Schroeder writes that "a synoptic judgment means a broad interpretation of a development based on examining it from different angles to determine how it came to be, what it means, and what understanding of it best integrates the available evidence." For Schroeder, the more synoptic judgments are guided by theory, the better.[104] Similarly, W.H. Walsh

---

Quarterly, Vol. 35, No. 3 (September 1991), pp. 337–355; Alexander E. Wendt, "The Agent-Structure Problem in International Relations Theory," *International Organization*, Vol. 41, No. 3 (Summer 1987), pp. 335–370; and Ruth Lane, "Positivism, Scientific Realism and Political Science," *Journal of Theoretical Politics*, Vol 8, No. 3 (July 1996), pp. 361–382.

102. Ray, *Democracy and International Conflict*, pp. 134, 148. Ray's discussion of the role of covering laws in case study explanations (chap. 4) is quite useful and fairly representative of the view of most political scientists.

103. An important exception in history is comparative history. In political science, single case studies can be justified in the context of larger research programs that are more comparative in orientation. Single case studies can also involve within-case comparisons over time.

104. Schroeder, "History and International Relations Theory," pp. 66–69; and Mink, *Historical Understanding*, pp. 81–87.

argues that "different historical events can be regarded as going together to constitute a single process, a whole of which they are all parts and in which they belong together in a special intimate way." The "first aim of the historian" is to see an event "as part of a process, to locate it in its context."[105]

This conceptualization nicely captures what a lot of historians do. It is also perfectly consistent with my argument that most historiography aims to explain a series of discrete events rather than construct general propositions about relationships between variables. Mink's focus is still on events, not classes of events or theoretical categories; the same is true of Walsh. It is also significant that Schroeder illustrates the synoptic judgment concept with his own work on the single case of World War I, and by his use of the metaphor of the physician's diagnosis—which includes theoretical knowledge and "skill in seeing which interpretation of the evidence works best in a *particular* case."[106]

Narrative-Based Explanation and Theory-Based Explanation

It is often said that a key difference between historians and political scientists is that historians tend to construct narrative-based explanations while political scientists (and social scientists more generally) tend to construct theory-based explanations.[107] This argument implies that narrative-based explanations and theory-based explanations are analytically distinct, that historians' narratives are not theory-based, and that political scientists' explanations do not involve narratives. Each of these points is problematic, depending on precisely how one defines both "narrative" and "theory." After elaborating what I mean by narrative, I consider the role of narrative in political science and the role of theory in history.

I follow the historian Lawrence Stone and define narrative as "the organization of material in a chronologically sequential order, and the focusing of the content into a single coherent story, albeit with subplots." In narrative history, as distinct from structural history, Stone argues, "the arrangement is descriptive rather than analytical," and "its central focus is on man not circumstances. It therefore deals with the particular and specific rather than the collective and statistical. Narrative is a mode of historical writing, but it is a mode which also affects and is affected by

---

105. W.H. Walsh, *Philosophy of History,* rev. ed. (New York: Harper Torchbacks, 1967), pp. 24–25.

106. Schroeder, "History and International Relations Theory," p. 69. My emphasis.

107. Elman and Elman, "Diplomatic History and International Relations Theory," p. 7; and Kiser and Hechter, "The Role of General Theory," p. 2.

the content and the method." Stone goes on to say that a narrative is guided by a "pregnant principle" and includes "a theme and an argument."[108]

Stone's conception of narrative is generally useful, but I see no reason to separate narrative history from structural history and to focus narrowly on "man not circumstances." Historical narrative can easily combine both the evolution of international and domestic structures within which human agents act as well as agents' beliefs, goals, motivations, and personalities. Indeed, narrative explanation, just like any explanation, must do so. On theoretical grounds neither an agent-based nor a structure-based explanation is complete without the other, and both should be integrated into our explanations, whether they be theoretical models or historical narratives. We can ignore neither the preferences of actors nor the structural or informational environments in which they act.[109]

Paul Schroeder makes an argument similar to Stone's when he suggests that historians, unlike political scientists, "explain historical change primarily or ultimately in terms of human conduct, that is, purposive acts of agency, not behavior." But Schroeder follows with a rather nuanced discussion, and a paragraph later refers to his own interpretation of World War I as "the result of systemic breakdown." Similarly, Schroeder's analysis of the Vienna settlement of 1815 and the Concert of Europe emphasizes both the autonomous beliefs of political leaders and structural factors such as the impact of the "shared hegemony" of Britain and Russia and certain "subhegemonies" on the continent.[110] Schroeder's

---

108. Stone, *The Past and the Present Revisited*, p. 74. There is a substantial debate among historians regarding the meaning of narrative. See W.H. Dray, "On the Nature and Role of Narrative in Historiography," *History and Theory*, Vol. 10 (1971), pp. 153–171; and Louis Mink, "Narrative Form as a Cognitive Instrument," in Robert H. Canary and Henry Kozicki, eds., *The Writing of History* (Madison: University of Wisconsin Press, 1978). See also Molly Patterson and Kristen Renwick Monroe, "Narrative in Political Science," *Annual Review of Political Science*, Vol. 1 (1998), pp. 313–331; and Suganami, *Causes of War*. Edward Ingram, in his chapter in this volume, argues that narrative does not necessarily have to follow a chronological sequence; it can also be a "collage."

109. James D. Morrow, "Social Choice and System Structure in World Politics," *World Politics*, Vol. 41, No. 1 (October 1988), pp. 45–97; and David A. Lake and Robert Powell, "International Relations: A Strategic Choice Approach," in David A. Lake and Robert Powell, eds., *Strategic Choice and International Relations* (Princeton: Princeton University Press, 1999), chap. 1.

110. Schroeder, "History and International Relations Theory, " pp. 67–68. See also Paul W. Schroeder, "World War I as Galloping Gertie," *Journal of Modern History*, Vol. 44, No. 3 (September 1972), pp. 319–345; Paul W. Schroeder, *The Transformation of European Politics, 1763–1848* (Oxford: Oxford University Press, 1994); and Jack S. Levy,

interpretations are powerful precisely because they focus both on purposive acts of agency and the structures within which agents act.

THE ROLE OF THEORY IN HISTORY

The hypothesized dichotomy between narrative and theory implies that historians mainly write narratives and that these narratives are atheoretical. This is misleading, as many narratives are guided by a well-defined theoretical perspective, and several important schools of historiography do not utilize narratives.

Although political scientists are generally more explicit about their analytical assumptions than historians are, there are many important historical paradigms that are quite explicit in the assumptions and causal laws upon which their frameworks and interpretations are based. Some of the best examples can be found in Marxist economic history, the *Annales* school in France, or the "New Economic History" in the United States.[111] These approaches clearly reject the view of history as narrative containing its own explanation and seek to base historical explanations on theories and causal laws from the social sciences and to demonstrate their validity through methods that most social scientists would find acceptable. *Annales* historians, for example, are explicit in their conception of a causal hierarchy that consists of a fundamental level of geographic, climatic, biological, and economic factors; a second level of enduring social structures; and a ephemeral level of political events, religion, culture, and intellectual developments.[112] There are numerous other examples of historical studies that are more nomothetic than idiographic.[113]

Although these historical paradigms have for the most part focused on social and economic history, one can find a number of studies of diplomatic history that organize their historical data around analytic categories instead of (or perhaps in conjunction with) chronological narratives. Gaddis's analysis of the long peace since World War II focuses on several alternative theoretical explanations. In form it is indistinguishable

---

"The Theoretical Foundations of Paul W. Schroeder's International System," *International History Review*, Vol. 16, No. 4 (November 1994), pp. 715–744.

111.   For a good review of these schools of thought see Iggers, *New Directions*. American cliometricians are defined more by their quantitative methodology than by any particular substantive theory of history, though they have been particularly influential in economic history.

112.   Braudel, *The Mediterranean and the Mediterranean World*.

113.   Two that come to mind are William Hardy McNeill, *Plagues and Peoples* (New York: Anchor, 1989), and *Keeping Together in Time: Dance and Drill in Human History* (Cambridge: Cambridge University Press, 1995).

from the work of political scientists, and in substance it was the first good theoretical study of that topic in either discipline. James Joll begins his study of the origins of World War I with a brief discussion of alternative interpretations, follows with a narrative overview of events of the July crisis, and then organizes the bulk of the book around theoretical variables. Jeremy Black organizes his study of British foreign policy in the early eighteenth century around chapters on the Crown, the Foreign Ministry, trade, religion, the press, and other theoretical variables, and Michael Hogan and Thomas Patterson organize their volume of essays on U.S. foreign relations around analytic categories that are quite familiar to international relations scholars.[114]

Some diplomatic historians organize their material chronologically but are quite explicit about the theoretical themes underlying their studies. A.J.P. Taylor, for example, begins his study of European diplomacy from 1848 to 1918 with an analysis of the changing balance of power over this period. Some historians are conversant with international relations theory and incorporate some of its key concepts into their own frameworks, and some have made important contributions to international relations theory. Prime examples of the latter include Schroeder's analysis of balancing in neorealist theory and his analysis of alliances as instruments of management and control within an alliance. Other examples include Paul Kennedy's study of imperial overextension and the rise and fall of great powers, and Arno Mayer's work on the domestic sources of war.[115]

The role of theory is also quite explicit and quite influential in postmodernist history, but here theory takes on a different form. History after

---

114. John Lewis Gaddis, "The Long Peace: Elements of Stability in the Postwar International System," *International Security*, Vol. 10, No. 4 (Spring 1986), pp. 99–142; James Joll, *The Origins of the First World War* (London: Longman, 1984); Jeremy Black, *British Foreign Policy in the Age of Walpole* (Edinburgh: John Donald, 1985); and Michael J. Hogan and Thomas G. Patterson, eds., *Explaining the History of American Foreign Relations* (Cambridge: Cambridge University Press, 1991). Other examples of historical studies in which narratives are organized around analytic categories include Hans-Ulrich Wehler, *The German Empire, 1871–1918* (Dover, N.H.: Berg, 1985); and P.M.H. Bell, *The Origins of the Second World War in Europe* (New York: Longman, 1986).

115. A.J.P. Taylor, *The Struggle for Mastery in Europe, 1848–1918* (Oxford: Oxford University Press, 1954); Schroeder, "Historical Reality vs. Neo-Realist Theory;" Paul W. Schroeder, "Alliances, 1815–1945: Weapons of Power and Tools of Management," in Klaus Knorr, ed., *Historical Dimensions of National Security Problems* (Lawrence: University Press of Kansas, 1986), pp. 227–262; Kennedy, *The Rise and Fall of the Great Powers;* and Arno J. Mayer, "Internal Crisis and War Since 1870," in Charles L. Bertrand, ed., *Revolutionary Situations in Europe, 1917–1922* (Montreal: Interuniversity Centre for European Studies, 1977), pp. 201–233.

the "linguistic turn" is theoretical,[116] but it a theory influenced by literary criticism and symbolic anthropology and not by theories of social science.[117] Although postmodernism has had a substantial influence on the philosophy of history, it has had less influence on the actual writing of history. There are relatively few postmodern diplomatic histories, for postmodern historians have shifted the focus from political, diplomatic, and even economic history to questions of culture, *mentalité,* and subalternity.[118] Many diplomatic historians argue, however, that the rise of postmodernism in history has contributed to the declining influence of diplomatic history within the discipline, at least in the United States.[119]

The influence of postmodernism on political science has been much more limited, though "softer" forms of constructivism that are open to an empirical research agenda are growing in influence. Unlike their colleagues in history, however, critical theorists, feminists, and constructivists in political science have given considerable attention to international relations. The early focus was on metatheoretical and methodological issues, but that has begun to change, and empirically oriented studies are now more common.[120]

---

116. See Toews, "Intellectual History after the Linguistic Turn."

117. An interesting anecdote on the influence of "theory" on history is provided by Gordon Schochet. On meeting a good friend who had returned from a summer of research in London, Schochet said, "it must have been very difficult and crowded at the British Library. I hate doing research in London in the summer, what with all those Americans climbing all over one another." His friend, an intellectual historian, replied: "No, it wasn't bad at all; there was hardly anyone there. No one's using books any more. They're all doing theory." Gordon Schochet, "Where Have All the Historians Gone?" Presented at the Annual Meeting of the American Society for Eighteenth-Century Studies, Austin, Texas, 1996.

118. This is slowly beginning to change. For recent constructivist or postmodern approaches to diplomatic history, see the symposium on "Culture, Gender, and Foreign Policy," *Diplomatic History,* Vol. 18, No. 1 (Winter 1994); and Frank Costigliola, "Unceasing Pressure for Penetration: Gender, Pathology, and Emotion in George Kennan's Formation of the Cold War," *Journal of American History,* Vol. 83, No. 4 (March 1997), pp. 1309–1339.

119. Haber, Kennedy, and Krasner, "Brothers Under the Skin." See also Ernest R. May, "The Decline of Diplomatic History," in George Athan Billias and Gerald N. Grob, eds., *American History: Retrospect and Prospect* (New York: Free Press, 1971), pp. 399–430; and John A. Lynn, "The Embattled Future of Academic Military History," *Journal of Military History,* Vol. 61 (October 1997), pp. 777–789. This trend is much less pronounced in Europe.

120. Important works include Nicholas Onuf, *World of Our Making* (Columbia: University of South Carolina Press, 1989); Friedrich Kratochwil, *Rules, Norms, and Decisions* (Cambridge: Cambridge University Press, 1989); Suganami, *Causes of War;* Alexander E. Wendt, *Social Theory of International Politics* (Cambridge: Cambridge University

NARRATIVES IN POLITICAL SCIENCE

A significant percentage of books and even journal articles in political science incorporate historical case studies. These are usually preceded by a section on theory and method, which includes a discussion of the author's theory or hypotheses, usually one or two alternative theories against which they will be tested, criteria for case selection, the empirical indicators to tap one's general theoretical concepts, and other elements of the research design. The historical material is sometimes organized around explicitly analytical criteria and sometimes in an approximately chronological manner, though one that is often couched in a theoretically relevant language. Many of these narratives look quite comparable to historians' narratives, but political scientists usually do comparative studies of two or more cases and explicitly address the question of whether the historical evidence is consistent with the predictions of the theory and perhaps those of alternative theories.

Recent work on qualitative methodology has led to considerable improvements in comparative case studies in international relations. The goal is to increase the relevance of case studies for the construction and validation of theories, to help transform descriptive historical accounts into analytic accounts. Alexander George's methodology of structured focused comparison, in which each case is structured by a single set of questions and focused on those aspects of each case that the theory defines as relevant, has been particularly important in this regard. George emphasizes the role of process tracing, a within-case method that involves an attempt to explain outcomes by tracing the sequence of events that brings them about. This is quite similar to the form of explanation adopted by most historians and labeled "genetic explanation" (Ernest Nagel and W. B. Gallie), "sequential explanation" (Louis Mink), or "colligation" (Clayton Roberts).[121]

Press, 1999); David Dessler, "Constructivism within a Positivist Social Science," *Review of International Studies,* Vol. 25, No. 1 (January 1999), pp. 123–137; Emmaneul Adler, "Seizing the Middle Ground: Constructivism in World Politics," *European Journal of International Relations,* Vol. 3 (1997), pp. 319–363; V. Spike Peterson, *Gendered States: Feminist (Re)Visions of International Relations Theory* (Boulder, Colo.: Lynne Rienner, 1992); and Christine Sylvester, *Feminist Theory and International Relations in a Postmodern Era* (New York: Cambridge University Press, 1994). More empirically oriented studies include Jeffrey Legro, *Cooperation under Fire: Anglo-German Restraint during World War II* (Ithaca: Cornell University Press, 1995); Peter J. Katzenstein, ed., *The Culture of National Security: Norms and Identity in World Politics* (New York: Columbia University Press, 1996); and Elizabeth Kier, *Imagining War: French and British Military Doctrine between the Wars* (Ithaca: Cornell University Press, 1997).

121. Alexander L. George, "Case Studies and Theory Development," paper presented to the Second Annual Symposium on Information Processing in Organizations,

In both his earlier work and his more recent work with Andrew Bennett, George emphasizes the potential utility of the "congruence method," which is more correlational in structure and which plays a more ambiguous role in structured focused comparison.[122] The congruence method builds on the comparative method formalized by John Stuart Mill, and parallels the logic underlying historical sociology and comparative history.[123] It is often difficult to differentiate between comparative history, historical sociology, and comparative work in political science. Although comparative historians are relatively few in number, they constitute an important exception to my argument that most historians are primarily interested in explaining particular historical episodes or periods.

I should emphasize that process tracing, like many methods, can be utilized with a variety of theoretical orientations. Although some advocates of process tracing in political science seek a sophisticated methodological alternative to the growing influence of rational choice approaches in the discipline, there is no inherent incompatibility between rational choice as a theoretical orientation and process tracing as a methodology. Many historians' narratives are consistent with a rational choice orienta-

---

Carnegie-Mellon University, Pittsburgh, October 15–16, 1982; Nagel, *The Structure of Science*, pp. 564–568; Gallie, "The Historical Understanding;" Louis O. Mink, *Historical Understanding*; and Roberts, *Historical Explanation*.

122. Bennett and George, *Case Studies and Theory Development*.

123. Mill's "method of agreement" attempts to control for extraneous variables and establish causation by focusing on cases that are similar on the dependent variable and different on all but one of the independent variables. Mill's "method of difference" focuses on cases that are different on the dependent variable and similar on all but one of the independent variables. Mill acknowledged the limitations of these methods for the social sciences. See John Stuart Mill, *A System of Logic*, 9th ed. (London: Longmans, Green, Reader, and Dyer, 1875). See also Neil J. Smelser, *Comparative Methods in the Social Sciences* (Englewood Cliffs, N.J.: Prentice-Hall, 1976); and Charles Ragin, *The Comparative Method* (Berkeley: University of California Press, 1987). On historical sociology see Skocpol, ed., *Vision and Method in Historical Sociology*. On comparative history see Charles Tilly, *As Sociology Meets History* (New York: Academic Press, 1981); Tilly, *Big Structures, Large Processes, Huge Comparisons* (New York: Russell Sage, 1984); Bloch, *The Historian's Craft*; William H. Sewell, Jr., "Marc Bloch and the Logic of Comparative History," *History and Theory*, Vol. 6, No. 2 (1967), pp. 208–218; George M. Frederickson, "Comparative History," in Michael Kammen, ed., *The Past Before Us* (Ithaca: Cornell University Press, 1980), pp. 457–473; and Michael Adas, "Imperialism and Colonialism in Comparative Perspective," *International History Review*, Vol. 20, No. 2 (June 1998), pp. 371–388. On the problems involved in applying Mill's methods to a relatively small number of cases, see Stanley Lieberson, "Small N's and Big Conclusions: An Examination of the Reasoning in Comparative Studies based on a Small Number of Cases," in Ragin and Becker, eds., *What Is a Case?* chap. 4.

tion, and one can find historical case studies by historians and political scientists that are self-consciously guided by a rational choice frame-work.[124]

The compatibility of a narrative methodology with a rational choice theoretical orientation is developed more systematically by Kiser in response to "the revival of narrative" in historical sociology. He argues that "rational choice narrativism" can incorporate human agency, particular events, temporality, and path dependence (and, I might add, important informational considerations) in a way that overcomes some limitations in current applications of narratives in historical sociology.[125]

A similar development is underway in political science. Some leading rational choice theorists have developed the methodology of "analytic narratives." The approach is analytic in that it involves explicit and formal lines of reasoning based on rational choice and game-theoretic models, but it organizes much of the material in a narrative manner, pays close attention to context, and involves the continuous interplay between theory and data. This approach, like George's structured focused comparison, constitutes a potential point of convergence with the narrative methodology of many historians.[126]

It is clear, then, that the argument that historians use narrative-based explanations whereas political scientists adopt theory-based explanations is both analytically flawed and a significant distortion of the work done by influential scholars in both disciplines.

---

124.   L.L. Farrar, Jr., "The Limits of Choice: July 1914 Reconsidered," *Journal of Conflict Resolution*, Vol. 16, No. 1 (March 1972), pp. 1–24; Jack S. Levy, "Preferences, Constraints, and Choices in July 1914," *International Security*, Vol. 15, No. 3 (Winter 1990/91), pp. 151–186; and Bruce Bueno de Mesquita and David Lalman, *War and Reason: Domestic and International Imperatives* (New Haven: Yale University Press, 1992), chap. 7.

125.   Kiser, "The Revival of Narrative."

126.   Robert H. Bates et al., *Analytic Narratives* (Princeton: Princeton University Press, 1998); Bennett and George, *Case Studies and Theory Development*. There have also been calls for a greater dialogue between rational choice theory and constructivist or interpretist approaches, even critical theory approaches. See John Ferejohn, "Rationality and Interpretation: Parliamentary Elections in Early Stuart England," in Kristen Renwick Monroe, ed., *The Economic Approach to Politics: A Critical Assessment of the Theory of Rational Action* (New York: HarperCollins, 1991), pp. 279–305; James Johnson, "Is Talk Really Cheap? Prompting Conversation Between Critical Theory and Rational Choice," *American Political Science Review*, Vol. 87, No. 1 (March 1993), pp. 74–86; and John W. Schiemann, "Meeting Halfway Between Rochester and Frankfurt: Generative Salience, Focal Points and Strategic Interaction," *American Journal of Political Science*, Vol. 44, No. 1 (January 2000), pp. 1–16.

The Logic of Discovery and the Logic of Confirmation

I have argued that the nomothetic/idiographic distinction—defined in terms of what scholars aim to explain rather than how they explain it—provides the single best criterion for differentiating between history and political science in general and diplomatic history and international relations theory in particular: historians aim to explain sequences of events, while political scientists aim to construct generalizations about the relationships between theoretical variables. I have emphasized, however, that to say that historians are idiographic does not necessarily imply that they are atheoretical; they just use theory in different ways than political scientists. I have focused on the central tendencies of the most influential scholars within each discipline, with particular attention to the United States. There are substantial variations around these central tendencies, and the distributions of scholarship in the two disciplines are overlapping, so that there will be numerous exceptions to my argument.

I suspect that political scientists are more likely than historians to accept my argument. Historians will insist not only that their narratives are guided by theoretical assumptions and perhaps more fully developed causal hypotheses, but also that their analyses of particular historical events or periods is suggestive of more general theoretical relationships. Many follow Marc Bloch and argue that the idiographic method can be used for nomothetic purposes, that by focusing on the particular the historian can understand the general. Edward Ingram, for example, argues that "rarely do historians who write about politics and international relations deal with particular instances . . . even microhistorians claim to see the entire world in their grains of sand." He goes on to say that political and diplomatic historians examine political systems, including the international system, "as vehicles or signifiers, opportunities to explain something else."[127]

It is true that historians often generalize, but those generalizations usually apply to a particular country or period, based on the common belief that each historical era has its own character. Occasionally, however, historians generalize beyond the data they observe. This brings us to a more fundamental difference between historians and political scientists, one that derives from differences between the logic of discovery and the logic of confirmation, between theory construction and theory testing.[128] Historians may generalize beyond their data, but they rarely share politi-

127. Bloch, *The Historian's Craft*; and Ingram, "The Wonderland of the Political Scientist," pp. 53–54.

128. Popper, *Logic of Scientific Discovery*.

cal scientists' concern with the process of *validating* those generalizations empirically, with developing methodologies that permit inferences from an observed sample to an analytically defined universe.[129]

Most graduate training programs in political science require a course (or sequence of courses) on research design and statistics, and in the past decade courses on qualitative methods or qualitative research design have become more common. The fundamental problem for the case study researcher in political science is how to generalize from her data to a broader domain of behavior, how to rule out the causal influences of extraneous variables, and how to select cases in a way that facilitates the empirical test of theoretical propositions.[130] In contrast, graduate training programs in history are much less likely to offer courses devoted primarily to methodology. While political science conventions almost always include some panels devoted primarily to methodology, it is rare that history meetings and workshops include panels devoted primarily to methodology.[131] Just as historians' theoretical assumptions and propositions are embedded in their historical narratives, their discussions of methodology are embedded in their discussions of concrete subject matter.[132]

---

129. Two important exceptions come to mind. First, some applied game theorists place primary emphasis on theory construction and give very little attention to the systematic testing of those theories, though they may use historical examples to *illustrate* the theory. See Powell, *In the Shadow of Power.* Similarly, some social constructivists show little interest in demonstrating their theoretical arguments with detailed empirical research. See Wendt, "The Agent-Structure Debate." Note that although Powell and Wendt are among the most influential scholars in their respective research communities (and that neither would object to others doing the empirical work), most applied game theorists and social constructivists now emphasize the need to couple theoretical argument with empirical research. In fact, both the rising influence of decision-theoretic and game-theoretic modeling in the 1980s and 1990s, and the rising influence of constructivism in the 1990s, owe much to the development of empirical research agendas during these periods.

130. Political scientists are trained to base their case selection on theoretical and methodological criteria, and they criticize what they see as historians' tendencies to pick their subject of inquiry because of its intrinsic historical interest and because that episode has yet to be adequately explained. This relates to Jervis's notion (in his chapter in this volume) that historians focus on empirical puzzles while political scientists focus on theoretical puzzles.

131. On the second point see Robert Jervis's chapter in this volume. Although political scientists often deviate from this methodological norm, in doing so they open themselves up to considerable criticism.

132. One of the most obvious exceptions is John Lewis Gaddis, whose essays on methodology have contributed significantly to methodological debates in the international relations field. See Gaddis, "Expanding the Data Base;" "History, Theory, and

Because they believe that theoretical considerations must inform all aspects of empirical inquiry, political scientists are troubled by the failure of historians to be explicit about their theoretical assumptions and propositions. Political scientists argue that this undercuts the ability of other researchers to validate the historian's interpretations, causal inferences, and claims of generalizability to other historical periods.

Consider the case of Thucydides, who believed that the events of the Peloponnesian War would repeat themselves and who was convinced that he was writing "for all time." Thucydides' *History of the Peloponnesian War* may have been driven by a clear set of theoretical assumptions, but he was not explicit about what they were.[133] Scholarly debate continues, for example, about whether or not Thucydides was a realist and about numerous other aspects of his historical interpretation. Thucydides may have been correct that the patterns of the Peloponnesian War would repeat themselves, that his interpretation of the war between Athens and Sparta could be generalized to other times and other places. Before accepting this, however, most political scientists would insist on an explicit specification of Thucydides' hypotheses and the construction of a research design that permitted a systematic empirical test of those hypotheses over a wider range of historical systems and theoretical conditions.

Conclusions

I have argued that the primary distinction between history and political science—or at least between the most influential scholarship in each discipline—is that historians attempt to understand and explain sequences of events within a given period while political scientists attempt to explain relationships among variables. This does not imply that historians are necessarily atheoretical. All historical interpretations are guided by underlying analytic assumptions and causal propositions, implicit or otherwise. Some historians are more explicit than others about those assumptions, some take time to organize their research explicitly around theoretical categories, and some give explicit attention to the causal

Common Ground;" and "History, Science, and the Study of International Relations," in Ngaire Woods, ed., *Explaining International Relations Since 1945* (New York: Oxford University Press, 1996), pp. 32–48.

133. Thucydides, *History of the Peloponnesian War*, in Robert B. Strassler, ed., *The Landmark Thucydides* (New York: Free Press, 1996), p. 16. As Stanley Hoffmann notes in *Janus and Minerva: Essays in the Theory and Practice of International Politics* (Boulder, Colo.: Westview, 1987), p. 3, Thucydides' *History* contained neither explicit generalizations of an "if . . . then" nature or analytic categories.

mechanisms driving the behavior they observe. A smaller number of historians attempt to generalize beyond their observed data to other times and other places. But very few historians give much attention to the methodologies through which their theoretical generalizations might be empirically validated. Political scientists, on the other hand, are consumed by the question of how to generalize beyond their data to the larger universe from which their data were selected. It is this concern for the empirical validation of theoretical generalizations that in the end best distinguishes political science from history.

This is not to say that international relations theorists have been particularly successful in their task of empirically validating their theoretical generalizations. We have relatively few law-like generalizations in the field, the closest being the proposition that democracies rarely if ever fight each other. But even this proposition is contested, and even its supporters concede that this is an empirical "law" for which a convincing theoretical explanation has yet to be found.[134] This seems to support the argument of most historians that the context-dependent nature of international behavior makes it extraordinarily difficult if not impossible to identify transhistorically valid, law-like patterns of international relations. But it is equally true that few historical interpretations of particular events or particular eras are uncontested. Debates about the validity of historical interpretations are as commonplace and animated as debates about the validity of international relations theories.

Implicit in this discussion is the argument that although historians and political scientists generally have different objectives, they can better achieve those objectives if they make a greater effort to learn from each other and build on each other's accomplishments. Research on international relations can be cumulative across disciplines as well as between disciplines. Greater attention to the analytic assumptions and causal propositions underlying their interpretations would help historians to sharpen the theoretical coherence of those interpretations and eliminate logical contradictions in their arguments. Similarly, greater attention to historical context would help political scientists construct more valid indicators for their theoretical concepts, recognize the spatial and temporal domains over which their generalizations are valid (which would help them better specify the analytical scope conditions for their theories), and facilitate the task of developing contingent generalizations. Just as a

134.   Ray, *Democracy and International Conflict;* Michael E. Brown, Sean M. Lynn-Jones, and Steven E. Miller, eds., *Debating the Democratic Peace* (Cambridge, Mass.: MIT Press, 1996).

complete description of the connections between events is not sufficient for good history in the absence of a specification of underlying causal mechanisms, a rigorous formulation of a logically coherent theoretical structure is insufficient for good theory in the absence of the empirical validation of the testable implications of the theory over a wide range of conditions. As I concluded in my earlier essay on this issue, history is too important to leave to the historians, and theory is too important to leave to the theorists.[135]

---

135. Levy, "Too Important to Leave to the Other," p. 33.

Chapter 2

Toward a New Diplomatic History: Two and a Half Cheers for International Relations Methods

Stephen Pelz

Historians of international relations have been living through somewhat trying times due to the fragmentation of their field in subject matter, method, and normative approach.[1] In addition to the traditional deep splits among economic determinists, realists, and eclectics, it has recently

Parts of this chapter first appeared in *The International History Review,* and the author thanks Edward Ingram and the *Review* for permission to reprint them here. The author also wishes to acknowledge the aid provided by the following organizations: the National Fellows Program, Hoover Institution, Stanford, California; the International Security Studies Program of the Woodrow Wilson International Center for Scholars, Washington, D.C.; and the East Asian Institute, Columbia University. I have benefited a great deal from the comments of Andrew Bennett, David Dessler, Colin Elman, Miriam Fendius Elman, and Stephen Haber. None of the institutions or individuals mentioned here can be held responsible for the contents of the chapter.

1. For critical appraisals, see Ernest R. May, "The Decline of Diplomatic History," in George Athan Billias and Gerald N. Grob, eds., *American History: Retrospect and Prospect* (New York: Free Press, 1971), pp. 399–430; and Charles Maier, "Marking Time: The Historiography of International Relations," in Michael Kammen, ed., *The Past Before Us: Contemporary Historical Writing in the United States* (Ithaca: Cornell University Press, 1980), pp. 355–387. For a more optimistic discussion of the widening horizons of the field, see Richard W. Leopold, "The History of United States Foreign Policy: Past, Present, and Future," in Charles F. Delzell, ed., *The Future of History: Essays in the Vanderbilt University Centennial Symposium* (Nashville, Tenn.: Vanderbilt University Press, 1977), pp. 231–246; Alexander DeConde, "On the Nature of International History," *International History Review,* Vol. 10, No. 2 (May 1988), pp. 282–301; and Alexander DeConde, "What's Wrong With American Diplomatic History," *SHAFR Newsletter,* Vol. 1, No. 2 (May 1970), pp. 1–16. For an earlier article that suggests using political science approaches, see John Lewis Gaddis, "New Conceptual Approaches to the Study of American Foreign Relations: Interdisciplinary Perspectives," *Diplomatic History,* Vol. 14, No. 3 (Summer 1990), pp. 403–425. For a much more optimistic review of the field that rejects international relations theories and celebrates ideological and cultural analysis, see Michael H. Hunt, "The Long Crisis in U.S. Diplomatic History: Coming to Closure," *Diplomatic History,* Vol. 16, No. 1 (Winter 1992), pp. 115–140.

been suggested that we adopt social, cultural, or postmodern linguistic approaches.[2] One practical danger in using such disparate methods is that international historians will lose their analytical focus and produce a series of studies on a variety of worthy but unconnected topics. As Bernard Bailyn has pointed out, unrelated research reports that duck questions of causation do not consititute analytical history.[3] Stephen H. Haber, David M. Kennedy, and Stephen D. Krasner have shown in depressing detail the decline of historical positivism and the parallel retreat of analytical diplomatic history before the tide of postmodernist, cultural, political, and social history.[4] In this chapter I argue that political science methods are much more likely to yield progress toward a better diplomatic history than are social, cultural, linguistic, or narrative approaches.

As a first step toward understanding what is required for productive dialogue between our disciplines, I try to make explicit how analytical historians explain the past. This formal review of explanation also shows how much many diplomatic historians have in common with some international relations specialists. Later, I suggest that diplomatic historians should test hypotheses derived from social science theories against carefully selected cases. Historians can benefit from testing midrange generalizations and exploring causal mechanisms for subjects that crop up repeatedly in their work. These improved and validated analytical tools can then contribute to writing better analytical history and better pure narratives. The chapter also suggests more tentatively that historians can

---

2. On the deep splits in the U.S. field, see, for example, Jerald A. Combs, *American Diplomatic History: Two Centuries of Changing Interpretations* (Berkeley: University of California Press, 1983), pp. 180–181, 220–257; Akira Iriye, "Culture and Power: International Relations as Intercultural Relations," *Diplomatic History*, Vol. 3, No. 2 (Spring 1979), pp. 115–128; Akira Iriye, "Responses to Charles S. Maier," *Diplomatic History*, Vol. 5, No. 4 (Fall 1981), pp. 359–361; Charles Lilly and Michael H. Hunt, "On Social History, the State, and Foreign Relations: Commentary on 'The Cosmopolitan Connection,'" *Diplomatic History*, Vol. 11, No. 3 (Summer 1987), pp. 243–250; William O. Walker III, "Drug Control and the Issue of Culture in American Foreign Relations," *Diplomatic History*, Vol. 12, No. 4 (Fall 1988), pp. 365–382; and Frank Ninkovich, "Interests and Discourse in Diplomatic History," *Diplomatic History*, Vol. 13, No. 2 (Spring 1989), pp. 135–161. For a review of new methods, see Michael J. Hogan and Thomas G. Paterson, eds., *Explaining the History of American Foreign Relations* (New York: Cambridge University Press, 1991).

3. Bailyn is quoted by Stephen G. Rabe, who has other interesting things to say about social history approaches. See "Marching Ahead (Slowly): The Historiography of Inter-American Relations," *Diplomatic History*, Vol. 13, No. 3 (Summer 1989), pp. 301–304.

4. Stephen H. Haber, David M. Kennedy, and Stephen D. Krasner, "Brothers Under the Skin: Diplomatic History and International Relations," *International Security*, Vol. 22, No. 1 (Summer 1997), pp. 35, 42–43.

lend helpful perspective to the efforts of international relations specialists by reminding them that the operation of causal variables may operate differently in different historical eras, in different cultural areas, and with different decision-makers in power.

Postmodernism and Narrativism vs. Analytical History

Most analytical international historians use generalizations and theories to explain events, even if they are reluctant to admit to the practice. When summarizing the approaches of historians as diverse as M.I. Finley, Arthur Wright, Robert R. Palmer, William O. Aydelotte, and Thomas C. Cochrane, Louis Gottschalk concluded:

[these] historians . . . all agree that the historian willy-nilly uses generalizations at different levels and of different kinds. They all agree, too, that some good purpose is served when he does so, if only to present a thesis for debate. . . . A few maintain even that, whether borrowed or independently derived, historical generalizations can in some persuasive manner be tested.[5]

Diplomatic historians will write better history if they define, evaluate, and use their explanatory generalizations more consciously. Unfortunately, unlike political science departments, most history departments do not require their first-year graduate students to take a course in theory building and testing. The result is that each historian is her own methodologist.[6] Serious diplomatic historians need to produce competing, testable models of explanation for their traditional main subjects—the political, military, and economic relations among nations.

International historians use many different types of historical explanation: sequential explanations, which use a continuous series of events to explain the origins of an action or condition; positivist arguments, which use either law-like statements or hypotheses, which are first and incomplete drafts of law-like explanations; decision-making explanations, which require the historian to discover the decision-maker's thought processes; functional explanations, which use positive and negative feedback to explain changes in systems and outcomes; and the linguistic

---

5. Louis Gottschalk, ed., *Generalization in the Writing of History: A Report of the Committee on Historical Analysis of the Social Science Research Council* (Chicago: University of Chicago Press, 1963), pp. 208–209; and Robert Brown, *Explanation in Social Science* (Chicago: Aldine, 1963), pp. 165–171.

6. Stephen Haber, "Explaining the Methods Gap: History and the Social Sciences," paper presented at the Diplomatic History and International Relations Theory Conference, Tempe, Arizona, January 16–18, 1998.

approach, which is sensitive to shifts in underlying structures of thought.[7] As David Hackett Fischer points out, "the specific kind of causal explanation a historian employs must be selected according to the nature of the effect to be explained. . . . Most of the trouble historians get themselves into . . . consists in a stubborn determination to locate the cause. And . . . these problems are aggravated by the unfortunate tendency of historians to hide their causal models from everybody—including themselves."[8] All but the linguistic mode of explanation fall into the category of philosophical realism, because they assume that we can recover and explain large parts of a past that really happened. By contrast, the linguistic turn to postmodernism is characteristic of what philosophers of history term constructionism.

Constructionism presents a major challenge to the traditional assumptions of most international historians. Constructionists believe that historians "have no superior standpoint from which to render the objective judgement of history." Words are impossibly complex and do not correspond directly to reality, and historians arrange words in patterns according to irrational and deeply held cultural and psychological constructs that are shaped by the historians' time, gender, generation, place, and class.[9] These cultural and psychological constructs fundamentally distort the way that historians select their evidence, and consequently each generation rewrites history from its own ideological perspective. There is no true history. In short, constructionists believe that historical writing is a form of fiction. While such an approach to the problem of knowledge may appear to be logically defensible, it is not particularly fruitful for most practicing historians, other than those who are studying the effects of cultural values on behavior. In fact, the constructionists'

---

7. Brown, *Explanation in Social Science*, pp. 40–164; and David Hackett Fischer, *Historians' Fallacies: Toward a Logic of Historical Thought* (New York: Harper & Row, 1970), pp. 183–186.

8. Fischer, *Historians' Fallacies*, p. 186.

9. Ninkovich, "Interests and Discourse in Diplomatic History," pp. 138–141, 154–155, 157–158. For an introduction to the postmodern approach, see Peter Berger and Thomas Luckman, *The Social Construction of Reality* (New York: Anchor, 1966); see also Frank Ninkovich, "No Post-Mortems for Postmodernism, Please," *Diplomatic History*, Vol. 22, No. 3 (Summer 1998), pp. 451–466. For a brief defense of the philosophical position of historical realism, see Adrian Kuzminski, "Defending Historical Realism," *History and Theory*, Vol. 13, No. 3 (1979), pp. 316–349; for the constructionist position, see W.B. Gallie, *Philosophy and the Historical Understanding* (New York: Schocken, 1964), pp. 72–104, 124–125; on the rise of historical relativism, see Peter Novick, *That Noble Dream: The "Objectivity Question" and the American Historical Profession* (Cambridge: Cambridge University Press, 1988), pp. 111–249, 415–537.

argument is not even logically defensible, because it commits the self-exceptionalist fallacy: Since all knowledge is constructed and therefore untrue, then not only their own stories about the past, but also their epistomological approaches, are equally constructed and untrue, unless they exempt themselves from their own argument.[10]

The major problem with constructionism, however, is that constructionists misconstrue what neopositivist historians do.[11] Historians do not merely deal with words. They use hard evidence that is a logical part of the case they are studying. They deal with past events that had material results and left tangible evidence—verified sets of written and physical remains that historians can check against each other to recreate what happened. Historians then use this evidence, which is external to their story, to establish the truth of their narrative. Indeed, modern international historians are blessed, sometimes cursed, with massive documentary records, which often lead to agreement about what happened and when, and occasionally why. A good historian can not omit relevant evidence in order to improve her tale or to make her explanation more plausible. And a good historian who is doing multiple case studies to investigate a causal theory will choose hard cases as well as ones that easily confirm her theories. In sum, international historians do not write fiction.[12]

In fact, analytical history is quite different from fiction. There is widespread agreement among historians on the chronology of what happened, as well as on the importance of certain events. In addition, historians corroborate, supplement, and correct each other's work. In this way, some debates about the past are resolved among professional historians. Most professional historians do not believe that Franklin D. Roosevelt invited the Pearl Harbor attack; the debate has ended. Historians of international relations tell stories, whose beginnings and middles help to explain the endings. And the better historians analyze why things turned out as they did. In the end, then, most practicing diplomatic historians would agree with the philosophical realists: Historians study a past that is knowable in considerable part through research, narrative organization, and generalizations drawn from logical and empirical models.

---

10. Michael E. Hobart, "The Paradox of Historical Constructionism," *History and Theory*, Vol. 28, No. 1 (1989), pp. 43–46, 49.

11. Fischer, *Historians' Fallacies*, pp. 131–132.

12. For the assertion that history is fiction, see Hayden White, *Metahistory* (Baltimore: Johns Hopkins University Press, 1973); for an effective realist reply, see Maurice Mandelbaum, *The Anatomy of Historical Knowledge* (Baltimore: Johns Hopkins University Press, 1977), pp. 7–8, 14–15, 187, 192–193.

To say that most serious diplomatic historians believe in the primacy of hard evidence does not mean that all of them are radical positivists. Many of them do a better job treating changing ideas than postmodernists do. Good diplomatic historians recognize that: the reigning assumptions and ideas of an era may change, usually along with changes in international and domestic systems; common norms held by a majority of the decision-makers in the system may similarly evolve; different generations and different cultures may draw different lessons from the past and adopt different expectations about the future; and leaders of revolutionary states may operate on very different assumptions than conservative decision-makers do. Historians can find evidence of these different ideas in governmental records, private papers, and public statements of the leaders and in media sources and opinion surveys, where available. Such sources will be much less clear than evidence about events, because such ideas are often filled with ambiguity and are open to textual and contextual interpretation. Nevertheless, Akira Iriye has made the role of elite ideas concerning the international system a major theme in his work, and Paul Schroeder has shown the effects of changing norms on the European international system.[13]

In political science, analysts of changing ideas and norms have emerged who also treat their subject matter in a positivistic manner. They are known as constructivists (not constructionists), and their work ties changing ideas and norms not only to textual evidence, but also to changes in the institutions that embody them. There is considerable debate about the relationship between ideas and norms and their institutional bases, but the constructivists offer useful methods for international historians who work at the cognitive and regime levels of analysis.[14]

In the end, international historians must make a leap of faith that they have done their best to expunge their biases and to consider all the relevant arguments and evidence fairly. Such leaps cross much narrower ditches than postmodernists claim in their quest to justify their own suspect methods.

---

13. For the effects of changing ideas and norms, see Paul W. Schroeder, *The Transformation of European Politics, 1763–1848* (Oxford: Clarendon Press, 1994); and Akira Iriye, *After Imperialism: The Search for a New Order in the Far East, 1921–1931* (Cambridge, Mass.: Harvard University Press, 1965).

14. For an introduction to the constructivist approach, see Alexander Wendt, "Constructing International Politics," *International Security*, Vol. 20, No. 1 (Summer 1995); and Alexander Wendt, "Anarchy is What States Make of It: The Social Construction of Power Politics," *International Organization*, Vol. 46, No. 2 (Spring 1992), pp. 391–427. See also Scott D. Sagan, "Culture, Strategy, and Selection in International Security," forthcoming; I am indebted to Scott Sagan for sharing this with me.

In addition to the assault from social, cultural, and postmodern historians, there has been a revival of traditional narrative history, with assertions that narrative comprises the closest simulation to the past that historians can muster. Despite John Lewis Gaddis's earlier endorsement of some political science methods, recently he has asserted the superiority of narrative (see Chapter 11). Gaddis argues that narratives are superior to social scientific accounts of the past because they include the effects of unpredictable human actions and accidents in their stories. And because historians have the ability to see complex events whole, they can compare these events intuitively and analogically to other events in the past. He also claims that narrative is a powerful tool for understanding complex events, because it uses embedded and implicit theories of contingent causation. "Any historical narrative," he writes, "cannot help but combine the general with the particular: revolutions, for example, have certain common characteristics; but the details of each one differ. Historians could hardly write about revolutions without some prior assumptions as to what these are and what we need to know about them: in this sense, they depend upon theory."[15]

There are many problems with these assertions. First, narratives often deal with single cases, and the cases that interest historians are often the colorful, aberrant ones. To understand the causal factors that operate through a period of history, however, the analytical historian must analyze several fairly normal cases. Second, Gaddis's assertion that narrative historians embed good theories in their narratives is doubtful at best. Embedded theory is unexamined theory. It does not specify independent and dependent variables and the causal relations between them. Third, by exalting the importance of individuals and accidents, narrativists downplay the importance of structural factors, such as the balance of power, resource distributions, and arms races. Academic historians frequently break from their narratives to engage in such analysis.[16] Fourth,

---

15. See John Lewis Gaddis's chapter in this volume. For the revival of narrative, see Lawrence Stone, *The Past and the Present Revisited* (London: Routledge and Kegan Paul, 1987), pp. 74–96. For Gaddis's earlier approval of some political science methods, see "New Conceptual Approaches," *Diplomatic History*, pp. 403–425; for his disappointment with political scientists' inability to predict how the Cold War would end, see his "International Relations Theory and the End of the Cold War," *International Security*, Vol. 17, No. 3 (Winter 1992/93), pp. 18, 28, 55–56.

16. Much of Gaddis's recent work is more analytical than narrative in form; see, among others, *We Now Know: Rethinking Cold War History* (Oxford: Clarendon, 1997); for excellent traditional narrative see Gaddis's *Russia, the Soviet Union, and the United States: An Interpretive History*, 2nd ed. (New York: McGraw-Hill, 1990). I am indebted to David Dessler for his comments on the problems of traditional narrative history.

narrative historians are often trying to teach the practical or moral lessons which their stories imply, but another analyst has no empirical method by which to evaluate the narrativist's normative judgments.[17]

In spite of the rise of these new approaches and the recrudescence of pure narrative, some diplomatic historians have turned to methods drawn from their cousins in the social sciences. In doing so, they have followed the positivist examples set by such leaders as Robert Fogel and Douglass North in the New Economic History and Joel Silby and Alan Bogue in the New Political History.[18] We need to follow their examples.

What Is Analytical History?

Analytical historians have a common set of positivist methods for establishing the truth. They believe that propositions about the past are true if those propositions fit the evidence and all the available and relevant evidence has been considered; if the historian can specify what evidence would prove the proposition untrue, and if he searches for such falsifying evidence and does not find it; if the historian states his hypotheses in language which is as neutral as possible; if he quantifies those relevant pieces of evidence that can be counted as units of one, as opposed to data that the analyst must estimate or metricize; if he tries to use propositions about which there is substantial agreement, such as the pricing mechanisms of the international commodities markets; and if his work survives the criticism of colleagues who are experts in the subject.[19] Historians share these methods with international relations specialists.

These methods are too general to tell us about the specific modes of explanation in international history. Consequently we must examine in more detail what neopositivist philosophers of history have to tell us about historical knowledge and explanation. These philosophical realists tell us that both particular events and some classes of events are not matters of chance, but are to be expected because of certain antecedent and simultaneous conditions.[20] These conditions explain how and why

---

17. I am grateful to John Gaddis and Paul Schroeder for their comments on the judgmental quality of much history; and I am indebted to David Dessler for the point that such normative judgments, as qualitative judgments, are nonfalsifiable.

18. Haber, "Explaining the Methods Gap."

19. Robert A. Packenham, *The Dependency Movement: Scholarship and Politics in Development Studies* (Cambridge, Mass: Harvard University Press, 1992), p. 41. See Novick, *That Noble Dream*, pp. 51–60, 299, 383–385, 393–399, 597–598, 625–626 for an account of the struggle to create an empirical history in the face of recurrent relativism.

20. Novick, *That Noble Dream*, p. 393.

an event was both possible and probable. The modern philosophy of history distinguishes between the conditions responsible for a class of events and the causes of the particular event by calling the first the necessary conditions, and the second the sufficient conditions.[21]

Philosophical realists argue that you can explain with great confidence why an event did or did not occur if you know its prior and sufficient conditions and its causal mechanisms.[22] Changes in prior standing conditions can point the way toward a cause, if they are frequently associated with a certain type of result. The change creates a new condition necessary to the result. The initial set of conditions would have led to one outcome, but a change in the condition caused a change in the expected outcome. For example, a shift in the naval balance against a leading power may require that power to withdraw from less valuable regions in order to defend more valuable ones. Thus Great Britain withdrew from its deployments in the Caribbean in 1900–10 to concentrate its forces against the rising German fleet in the North Sea. The British Cabinet's decision to redeploy its fleet then becomes the proximate, or sufficent cause of the action. Thus both historians and political scientists can use balance of power theory to predict what rational policymakers would probably do under conditions of conventional multipolarity.

By balance of power theory I do not mean Kenneth Waltz's structural theory, which is pitched at too high a level of generalization and which is too ahistorical to explain much that is of use to historians.[23] I refer instead to the traditional realist theories of Hans Morgenthau, as modified by a number of writers to take into account the changing nature of the international system in different eras. The balance operates under different norms and poses different incentives and disincentives depend-

---

21. For the distinction, see Mandelbaum, *Anatomy of Historical Knowledge*, p. 81.

22. Louis O. Mink, "Philosophy and Theory of History," in Georg G. Iggers and Harold T. Parker, eds., *International Handbook of Historical Studies: Contemporary Research and Theory* (Westport, Conn.: Greenwood Press, 1979), pp. 17–27. See also David Dessler, "Beyond Correlations: Toward a Causal Theory of War," *International Studies Quarterly*, Vol. 35, No. 3 (September 1991), pp. 345–353.

23. Kenneth N. Waltz, *Theory of International Politics* (Reading, Mass.: Addison-Wesley, 1979). For a critique of Waltz's approach, see Paul Schroeder, "Historical Reality vs. Neo-realist Theory," *International Security*, Vol. 19, No. 1 (Summer 1994), pp. 108–148. Schroeder's critique of balance of power theory goes too far in casting doubt on the utility of the approach; can generations of historians be that wrong about the operation of the international system in the eighteenth and nineteenth centuries? For an effective defense of realism, see Colin Elman and Miriam Fendius Elman, "Correspondence: History vs. Neo-realism: A Second Look," *International Security*, Vol. 20, No. 1 (Summer 1995), pp. 182–193.

ing on whether the period has a traditional multipolar, nonnuclear bipolar, revolutionary, or nuclear bipolar structure.[24]

Explanations from necessary and sufficient conditions take the form: If there is a change in a necessary or sufficient condition from (C1) to (C2), then this kind of event (E1) will probably occur. In other words, given the change from (C1) to (C2), then we could have probably predicted the occurrence of (E1). Similarly, without the change from (C1) to (C2), there probably would have been no (E1). Thus, the historian or political scientist starts with an historical scene that contains (C1)–(Cn) as a baseline and then indicates which (C) or (Cs) change to produce (E1).[25] Historians can even explain some of these changes in deductive, law-like ways: for example, as trade becomes freer, competition and resource consumption tends to equalize factor costs for firms over time.

Unchanged necessary or sufficient conditions, on the other hand, may lead to repeated international actions. Both of these explanations may require induction from a variety of cases. For example, the historian induces Hitler's self-defeating tendency to take extreme risks from his behavior in the beer hall putsch attempt, the invasion of the Rhineland, the attacks on Poland and the Soviet Union, his declaration of war on the United States, and his occasional orders that his armies not retreat in the face of heavy Russian offensives.[26] Hitler's unchanging personality structure and his tight grip on power explain much of the aggressive and irrational nature of Nazi foreign policy.

At one time, some philosophers of history proposed that all proper historical explanation should be law-like. In 1942, Hempel proposed that the course of history was explainable in terms of general laws. Hempel's models for historical laws were laws from the physical sciences, in which

---

24. Hans J. Morgenthau, *Politics Among Nations: The Struggle for Power and Peace*, 3rd ed. (New York, 1961). For an example, see Stephen M. Walt, *The Origins of Alliances* (Ithaca: Cornell University Press, 1987). For an attempt to understand how balancing works differently in different eras, see Stephen Pelz, "Changing International Systems, the World Balance of Power, and the United States, 1776–1976," *Diplomatic History*, Vol. 15, No. 1 (Winter 1991), pp. 47–81.

25. Mandelbaum, *Anatomy of Historical Knowledge*, pp. 28–30. There are special cases in which different antecedents can produce the same result; for the basic form of the argument and a critique, see R.F. Atkinson, *Knowledge and Explanation in History: An Introduction to the Philosophy of History* (Ithaca: Cornell University Press, 1978), pp. 102–111.

26. For the combination of deduction and induction, see Fischer, *Historians' Fallacies*, pp. xii, xvii; for Hitler's approach to risk, see James H. McRandle, *The Track of the Wolf: Essays on National Socialism and its Leader, Adolf Hitler* (Evanston, Ill.: Northwestern University Press, 1965), pp. 146–248.

one type of event invariably follows another.[27] Such laws take the form, whenever A, then B. Thus in chemical experiments, the results of changes from (C1) to (C2) can be predicted with great certainty, because chemists deal with only a few variables, which are measurable in units of one and which exist in a closed environment.[28]

Economists live in a less certain world than chemists do, and they find it difficult to quantify all of the independent, intervening, and boundary variables that are in operation in the economy.[29] They can still validate their laws statistically, however; such validation takes the form, whenever A, *x* probability of B. Thus, economists' laws have less certainty than scientific laws. Some political scientists aspire to achieve probabilistic laws of the level that economics has achieved, but most political scientists and historians have even more difficulty quantifying many of their important variables than economists do. Consequently, the analyses of historians and political scientists take the form, whenever A, then often B.[30] Thus their explanations are more like those of meteorologists, rather than chemists.[31] In sum, historical explanations use probabilistic law-like propositions, but rarely use laws in the scientific sense. In Chapter 1 Jack Levy also makes the point that historians often use generalizations that are probabilistic and contingent on the conditions prevailing during a certain period.

International history requires other types of explanation as well. Functional explanations explain persisting phenomena. Whenever a historian encounters an important persisting system, she may also find the regulating mechanisms that help maintain the system. For example, the conference system of the great powers worked fairly well and preserved the monarchical balance of power system for much of the eighteenth and nineteenth centuries. In this case the system persisted because it compen-

---

27. Mandelbaum, *Anatomy of Historical Knowledge*, p. 49.

28. Fischer, *Historians' Fallacies*, pp. 103, 128–130.

29. For boundary variables, see Mandelbaum, *Anatomy of Historical Knowledge*, pp. 179–180; for explanation by law-like generalization, see Atkinson, *Knowledge and Explanation in History*, pp. 104, 179.

30. See Atkinson, *Knowledge and Explanation in History*, pp. 151–154; Fischer, *Historians' Fallacies*, pp. 103, 128–130; Fritz K. Ringer, "Causal Analysis in Historical Reasoning," *History and Theory*, Vol. 28, No. 2 (1989), pp. 154–159; and Harold and Margaret Sprout, *An Ecological Paradigm for the Study of International Politics* (Princeton: Princeton University Press, 1968), pp. 144–148, 158–161.

31. The characterization of political science as being more akin to meteorology, rather than chemistry, comes from my colleague, Eric Einhorn, Chairman of the Department of Political Science, University of Massachusetts, Amherst.

sated for tendencies toward hegemony by adjusting alliances and redistributing territories. Such explanations help to account for stability and peace and for the fact that international changes occurred within certain ranges. These functional explanations are a subset of explanation based on necessary conditions.[32]

Functional explanations can also help to account for large changes. Most often, these explanations point to positive feedback spirals as the cause of a system's collapse.[33] In such cases, apparently rational short-term decisions can lead to unanticipated systemic breakdown. Power A might seek more security by building additional armaments. Power B will then exceed A's program to preserve its margin of security, thereby setting off a spiral of ever greater programs and counterprograms. Finally, one of the powers will approach the financial breaking point and choose to surrender or attack the other while it still has the military lead. Meanwhile, powers C and D have stayed on the sideline, spending more on their industrial plants than A or B. At the end of the war, they emerge as the superior powers. Thus A's rational intentions and the positive feedback spiral of the arms race ended in less, rather than more safety for A. And the system in which A and B were the dominant powers has changed drastically. One of my favorite examples for such an arms race is Japan's drive for naval superiority in the western Pacific in 1931–41. Japan sought a qualitative lead over the U.S. Navy in airpower, torpedo platforms, and superbattleships between 1937 and 1940. When the United States responded with an unmatchable naval construction program in 1940, the Japanese Naval General Staff pressed for war, while it still had a chance for victory.[34]

Other types of explanation are more particularistic, in that they seek to explain a particular phenomenon during a shorter but still lengthy period. These generalizations and historical theories do not attempt to explain history in general, or even long periods of history, but are more limited in time and extent. The most typical form that these more limited generalizations take is the narrative form, which seeks to explain the

---

32. Mandelbaum, *Anatomy of Historical Knowledge*, pp. 85, 136; and Fischer, *Historians' Fallacies*, pp. 128–130.

33. See Jack S. Levy's chapter in this volume. For recent explorations of the interconnectedness of the international system and the unintended consequences that can arise, see Robert Jervis, "Complexity and the Analysis of Political and Social Life," *Political Science Quarterly*, Vol. 112, No. 4 (1997–98), pp. 569–578.

34. Brown, *Explanation in Social Science*, pp. 73, 109–132; and Stephen E. Pelz, *Race to Pearl Harbor: The Failure of the Second London Naval Conference and the Onset of World War II* (Cambridge, Mass.: Harvard University Press, 1974), pp. 149–151, 167–223.

numerous unique features of a limited series of events.[35] One of their functions is to provide a generalization about what is normal in a particular period, in order to explain what later changed and why. Another function is to provide a broad interpretation that explains a pattern of outcomes or a series of trends.[36] Alfred Thayer Mahan's theory of seapower, for example, holds true for the period of British dominance, before the rise of rail and truck transport, and the submarine and airplane. Paul Kennedy's account of changes in the financial and industrial resources of the great powers helps to explain the process of change in the balance of power since the industrial revolution, but perhaps not since the nuclear revolution. A limited set of generalizations may also deal with the incentives and disincentives of the peculiar Cold War international system, with its contradiction between nuclear deterrence as a force for stability on the one hand, and revolutionary pressures as a force for instability on the other.[37]

One major difference between political scientists and historians is that political scientists are primarily interested in the necessary conditions that explain a majority of similar cases, while historians are more interested in explaining the entire history of a single case in all its detail. Therefore historians frequently emphasize the sufficient conditions that produce the outcome. A historian will be satisfied to explain a nation's failure to ally against a potential hegemon by analyzing the decision-makers' personal and generational backgrounds, as many historians have done for the British appeasers of the 1930s. But a political scientist will emphasize the fact that repeated failures to balance in a timely fashion will lead to a series of unnecessarily long and costly wars, which may reduce the nation's power in the long run and allow other nations to rise.[38] Because what they are trying to explain is different, historians and political scientists emphasize different causal levels of analysis.

The generalizations, laws, and theories discussed thus far present a fairly deterministic picture of historical explanation, because standing conditions make outcomes probable. Thoroughgoing positivist historians would be environmental determinists, who would argue that their laws

---

35. Mandelbaum considers this type of generalization as most typical of what historians do; see *Anatomy of Historical Knowledge*, pp. 5–7, 121–124; see also Levy's chapter in this volume.

36. Gottschalk, *Generalization in the Writing of History*, pp. 113–114; and Fischer, *Historians' Fallacies*, pp. 103.

37. Pelz, "Changing International Systems," pp. 47–81.

38. I am grateful to Scott Sagan, Colin Elman, Miriam Fendius Elman, and Randall Schweller for these points.

and theories would combine with the learned behaviors of decision-makers to *compel* individuals to act with a great degree of predictability—the decision-makers would walk to their fates like people under hypnotic compulsion or like animals in the grip of instinctual or rote behavior.[39] Diplomatic historians usually do not write in this way, because humans are not pigeons or monkeys, programmed by instinctual drives or laboratory conditioning.

Intentionalist Explanations

International and domestic political, economic, and social systems, as well as the decision-makers' own backgrounds, usually allow the decision-makers some degree of freedom to reason, to choose purposes, and to choose policies that might achieve those purposes.[40] Decision-makers also can learn from experience and decide to change their behavior when they face the recurrence of a problem.[41] In many cases, then, decision-makers make free choices shaped by their individual desires and their reasoning processes, and these choices may ignore the structural conditions, systems, and norms that are operating. Motives and intentions are developed in the mind and do not arise directly from biological drives, learned behavior, or external stimuli.[42] Neville Chamberlain ignored the rule that he should help to oppose a potential hegemon, and he did so with terrible results, while Adolf Hitler eventually ignored the dangers of threatening to impose hegemony, with even more disastrous results. In short, many diplomatic historians assume that the decision-makers' choices and actions may bend, or even break, the probable course of history, at least over the short run.

One philosopher of history argues that diplomatic historians are primarily interested in these freely willed choices that national leaders make. According to the distinguished philosopher of history W. H. Dray, many diplomatic historians assume that the *intentions* of the decision-makers are the primary causes that explain historical outcomes. Decision-makers risk war by action or inaction, and they do so with their eyes open to the potential gains and dangers. Balance of power factors make war possible, and even somewhat probable, but it is the individual

---

39. Atkinson, *Knowledge and Explanation in History,* pp. 183–187.

40. Mandelbaum, *Anatomy of Historical Knowledge,* pp. 136–139; and Mink, "Philosophy and Theory of History," pp. 21–22.

41. Brown, *Explanation in Social Science,* p. 4.

42. Fischer, *Historians' Fallacies,* pp. 213–215.

leaders' decisions and actions that cause it.[43] While we may not wish to simplify our explanations in this way, many international historians will accept the assertion that some changing ideas and some individual decisions are important sufficient conditions of international events.

The historian makes such intentionalist explanations in a different way than he or she makes explanations that use changes in necessary conditions as determinants. To explain the actions of individuals who are choosing freely, the historian rehearses the decision-maker's thinking. The historian puts herself or himself in the decision-maker's position and tries to define its elements as the decision-maker did, reconstructing the decision-maker's knowledge, experience, and expectations. Thus the historian assumes that the diplomatic leaders' ideas are rooted in the information available to him or her about the real world and therefore are reconstructable, at least in part. He or she then evaluates the evidence of the decision-maker's values and goals and recreates the alternative paths which the decision-maker believed might lead to the decision-maker's objectives. The historian then tries to judge the apparent practicality of those alternatives by reasoning in the way that the decision-maker might. Thus the historian explains the choice of action on the basis of a recreation of the decision-making experience.[44]

International relations specialists have their own formal decision-making approach for this type of analysis, which diplomatic historians can use with profit. The most suitable approach to the study of decision-making comes from international relations theory and falls under the heading of foreign policy analysis, or comparative decision-making studies, that originated in the work of Richard Snyder, H.W. Bruck, and Burton Sapin, and was refined and developed by Michael Brecher, James Rosenau, Charles Kegley, Eugene Wittkopf, Pierre Renouvin, Jean-Baptiste Duroselle, and Alexander George.[45]

---

43. W.H. Dray, "Concepts Of Causation In A.J.P. Taylor's Account of the Origins of the Second World War," *History and Theory*, Vol. 17, No. 2 (1978), pp. 150–169. Louis Mink, in a comment on Arno Mayer's work, urged diplomatic historians to use a multileveled analysis to enrich their narrative—an analysis that included both balance of power considerations and class conflict; see Richard T. Vann, "Louis Mink's Linguistic Turn," *History and Theory*, Vol. 26, No. 1 (1987), pp. 8–9.

44. William H. Dray, *Philosophy of History* (Englewood Cliffs, N.J.: Prentice-Hall, 1964), pp. 10–12; for an explicit treatment of this method, see Ernest R. May, *The Making of the Monroe Doctrine* (Cambridge, Mass.: Belknap, 1975), pp. 259–260.

45. Richard C. Snyder, H.W. Bruck, and Burton Sapin, eds., *Foreign Policy Decisionmaking: An Approach to the Study of International Politics* (Glencoe, Ill.: Free Press of Glencoe, 1962); Michael Brecher, *The Foreign Policy System of Israel: Setting, Images, Process* (New Haven: Yale University Press, 1972), pp. 3–4; James N. Rosenau, "Pre-

This process of thought rehearsal is not primarily intuitive, but rather an empirical recreation of a thought process. What the historian is assuming is that rational actors with a certain set of information, experience, expectations, and goals will respond in the same way to very similar situations. Sometimes there is direct evidence of the decision-makers' goals and reasoning in the form of contemporary memorandums, but more often the historian has to reason in circular fashion from situation, goals, and actions back to intentions.[46] This reasoning assumes the form: Whenever decision-makers of such and such kind with such and such goals do A1 under conditions C1–Cn, then they intend to achieve E1.[47] By isolating the decision-maker's probable reasoning, we are pointing out another possible cause of his or her action. Many international leaders take pains to disguise their reasoning and purposes, and therefore much of the best work on such figures as Franklin D. Roosevelt consists of reconstructing their assumptions, goals, and images of the world from a variety of sources. For example, Robert Dallek has done so for Roosevelt at many critical decision points.[48]

Thus interpretations of the decision-maker's mental processes constitute another kind of explanation. Such explanations tend to be more singular than law-like or functional explanations, since they deal with the minds of different and sometimes complex individuals. And because these explanations sometimes enter the realm of hidden mental structures, they are suitable for the application of the techniques of the linguistic constructionists, cognitive psychologists, social psychologists, and

theories and Theories of Foreign Policy," in James N. Rosenau, ed., *The Scientific Study of Foreign Policy* (New York: Free Press, 1971), pp. 107–116; Charles W. Kegley, Jr., and Eugene R. Wittkopf, *American Foreign Policy: Pattern and Process*, 2nd ed. (New York: St. Martin's Press, 1982), pp. 11–31; Pierre Renouvin and Jean-Baptiste Duroselle, *Introduction to the History of International Relations*, trans. Mary Ilford (Oxford: Clarendon Press, 1967); and Alexander L. George, "Case Studies and Theory Development: The Method of Structured, Focused Comparison," in Paul Gordon Lauren, ed., *Diplomacy: New Approaches in History, Theory, and Policy* (New York: Free Press, 1979), pp. 43–68. See also the recent theoretical work on decision-making in this volume by Andrew Bennett and Alexander George.

46. Gottschalk, *Generalization in the Writing of History*, p. 125; and Fischer, *Historians' Fallacies*, pp. 213–215.

47. Brown, *Explanation in Social Science*, pp. 63, 67, 73–74.

48. Robert Dallek, *Franklin D. Roosevelt and American Foreign Policy, 1933–1945* (New York: Oxford University Press, 1979); and Ringer, "Causal Analysis in Historical Reasoning," pp. 162–167. Some decisions are less than rational, of course, due to faulty cognition, personality disorders, and a myriad of other causes; see Brown, *Explanation in Social Science*, pp. 86–98.

psychohistorians.[49] We may call such rational or irrational decisions the *proximate or sufficient causes* of the event that explain why the event occurred when it did and in the way that it did. This designation distinguishes sufficient causes from the *necessary conditions* that make the event possible and the *changes in necessary conditions* that make the event probable.

A historian must usually combine her study of decision-making with a sequential narrative that explores the effects of other causal levels of analysis as well as the decisions and actions of the other powers in the system. Thus, a single set of decisions as outlined above rarely explains a major event. Most historians move beyond the analysis of a single set of decisions to demonstrate for their reader a continuous series of conditions, events, decisions, and actions that makes the outcome very probable.[50] This chain of necessary conditions, causal mechanisms, and proximate causes reduces the decision-makers' options and finally leaves them little choice but to accept the outcome in question. Such a chain of standing conditions and proximate causes constitutes the sequential mode of explanation. Such an approach goes beyond simple decision-making analysis and is explored under the rubric "process tracing" by Andrew Bennett and Alexander George in Chapter 4.

In short, a particular chain of decisions and events demonstrates why the outcome occurred. A sequence of events may change both the incentives and the capacities for action and therefore shape the options from which a decision-maker will choose.[51] Thus there can be numerous factors that serve as a joint cause. Such sequences are not simple, especially given the impact of individual decision-making factors or complex international developments. The historian must break his or her narrative to explain the effects of such intervening and compounding variables on the options open to the decison-makers. Explanation by historical narrative (the sequential mode) moves beyond both law-like positivism and voluntaristic

---

49. Ringer, "Causal Analysis in Historical Reasoning," pp. 162-167; Ninkovich, "Interests and Discourse in Diplomatic History," pp. 159–160; and Chaiies A. Powell, James W. Dyson, Helen E. Purkitt, "Opening the 'Black Box': Cognitive Processing and Optimal Choice in Foreign Policy Decision Making," in Charles F. Hermann, Charles W. Kegley, Jr., and James N. Rosenau, eds., *New Directions in the Study of Foreign Policy* (Boston: Allen and Unwin, 1987), pp. 203–213.

50. William H. Dray, *Laws and Explanation in History* (Oxford: Clarendon Press, 1957), pp. 68–69.

51. Mandelbaum, *Anatomy of Historical Knowledge*, pp. 25–28, 69, 73, 110, 177–179, 186–187.

intentionalism, because it allows for unintended and unexpected consequences.[52]

In most cases, then, diplomatic historians are interested in explaining complex chains of events that do not lend themselves either to simple law-like statements about the effects of standing conditions, or straightforward portrayals of a decision-maker's thinking, or simple story-like narratives. For each event the analyst must include the standing conditions, C1-Cn, the decision-maker's reasoning, beliefs, and emotions, R1-Rn, and the intervening and compounding variables, IV1-IVn—all of which are necessary to produce the event E1. The event E1 then produces changed standing conditions, C4, C5, C6 . . . Cn and the new reactions of the decision-makers, R4, R5, R6 . . . Rn, etc., to produce E2. This stream of events up to En makes the outcome probable by reducing the options open to the decision-makers as they approach En. The decison-makers are usually free to choose among a number of options, especially early in the sequence. If we consider all of the relevant evidence and if we include everything in the causal chain that is necessary to produce the effect, then we can claim to have explained the event. Historians can emulate political scientists by being much more explicit about the necessary and sufficient conditions (and their relative weights) that lead to the events which they are trying to explain.

Historians who are willing to adopt such an approach will combine law-like statements about changes in necessary conditions with intuitive and retroactively reasoned explanations of sufficient conditions, and they will also be able to account for unanticipated historical accidents. If a sequence of events recurs fairly often, then the historian may need to use a functional explanation that will explain how international and domestic systems are combining to set the range for behavior, thereby establishing a likely pattern of events. The repeated U.S. interventions in Central America in 1900–30 and 1954–94 would be examples. Historians who are interested in broader changes over time will then show how the decision-makers' adoption of new goals and how changes in standing conditions toward positive feedback eroded the elements of stability in the system, leading to periods of breakdown, and eventually to the rise of a new system.[53] The contradictory goals and ideologies of the great powers and the arms races of the 1930s are a good example.

---

52. Atkinson, *Knowledge and Explanation in History*, pp. 34–35, 171. I am grateful to Colin Elman and Miriam Fendius Elman for highlighting this point; see also Richard Ned Lebow's chapter in this volume.

53. Fischer, *Historians' Fallacies*, pp. 162, 179; and Mandelbaum, *Anatomy of Historical Knowledge*, pp. 26–30.

Levels of Analysis and Theories of Causation

We can apply the concept of recurring necessary and sufficient conditions to the analysis of the fundamental factors that cause change in the international system over time. Louis Gottschalk has pointed out that many historical disputes do not revolve around what the data are, but rather what the basic forces are that operate in history and how they operate.[54] What are the typical standing conditions, proximate causes, and intervening variables that are associated with certain classes of events? When we ask such open-ended questions about the basic forces at work in international history, we should begin with clusters of questions and clusters of hypothetical answers, and these clusters should break the field of international history into its component parts.[55] To guide our search for the appropriate variables, international historians need a widely accepted, specific, organized set of concepts that will enable us to talk to each other about the same phenomena in the same terms—a taxonomy of the international, domestic, governmental, and personal variables that most diplomatic historians and international relations specialists consider important. Such a taxonomy will provide for the orderly arrangement and comparison of data at levels of analysis ranging from systemic standing conditions to intentionalist proximate causes.[56]

This sort of taxonomy seeks to solve the level of analysis problem that plagues our field by providing an extensive checklist of external environmental factors affecting the decision-makers' options; the perceived external environmental factors; the domestic environmental factors; the perceived domestic environment; the governmental sources of decision-makers' options; the perceived governmental sources; the individual sources of the decision-makers' options; the effect of decision-processes; the effects of implementation on the ultimate action; and the reaction of the target country.[57] The approach suggested by such a taxonomy will ensure that we use multivariate analysis to review all of the possible causes of an event. Multivariate analysis is necessary if we are

---

54. Gottschalk, *Generalization in the Writing of History*, p. 208.

55. Fischer, *Historians' Fallacies*, pp. 24, 38–39.

56. For a taxonomy for the subfield of U.S. diplomatic history, see Stephen Pelz, "A Taxonomy for American Diplomatic History," *Journal of Interdisciplinary History*, Vol. 19, No. 2 (Autumn 1988), pp. 259–276.

57. For a more general taxonomy for narrative history, see Dale H. Porter, *The Emergence of the Past: A Theory of Historical Explanation* (Chicago: University of Chicago Press, 1981), pp. 88–96. Porter's taxonomy includes items similar to those used in my taxonomy, such as individual, group, institutional, economic, and ecological forces.

to avoid either neglecting a level, or overemphasizing one level of causation, or comingling one level of analysis with another. This kind of taxonomy should also lead to a truly international history, because it forces the historian to seek causation in more than a single country.[58]

Because such a taxonomy makes explicit which levels of analysis historians are investigating, it can provide those who adopt it with consistent questions to ask from decision to decision, era to era, and country to country. Consequently, the adoption of such a taxonomy would make possible the systematic comparison of classes of events through time. Using such taxonomies we will be able to generate hypotheses for testing against several cases. The examination of a series of cases can help generate widely accepted hypotheses for testing, when there are a number of correlations between certain necessary and sufficient conditions and a certain outcome.

Correlation is not enough, however. David Dessler has shown that explanation requires an integrated causal theory to explain such correlations, and he uses the example of rainstorms to illustrate his point. Different necessary conditions can help to cause showers: the conjunction of cold and warm fronts; solar heating; and the presence of thermal updrafts around mountains. But the causal mechanism is the same in each case: as the air heats up, it rises, expands, cools, and eventually the humidity condenses into a torrent. One can observe the activities of rising and cooling columns of air to test the validity of the theory. The theory cannot predict exactly where and when the next shower will arrive, but it can explain why such storms are probable under certain conditions and in certain areas. If the causal mechanisms in question explain more aspects of the phenomenon more frequently in more important cases than competing theories, then it is validated, until something better comes along.[59]

The events that interest social scientists range from the simple to the complex, however, and causal mechanisms must have a similar range. Andrew Bennett and Alexander George have pointed out that causal models exist on at least three distinct levels: straightforward laws that explain a simple change and about whose operation there is intuitive understanding and agreement; midrange causal mechanisms that help to

---

58. For a brief description of ways to arrange levels of analysis, see J. David Singer, "The Level-of-Analysis Problem in International Relations," in Klaus Knorr and Sidney Verba, eds., *The International System: Theoretical Essays* (Princeton: Princeton University Press, 1961), pp. 77–92.

59. Dessler, "Beyond Correlation," pp. 345–353; for the last point, see Elman and Elman, "History vs. Neo-realism," p. 192.

explain a series of events, such as the operation of the spiral processes in arms races described above; and complex explanations in which multiple and often interdependent variables operate sequentially over a long period, such as the processes that caused the United States to delay its entry into World Wars I and II. In the latter case, the analyst does not know how to weight each variable, and the outcome might be caused by several of the variables, any one of which might have been enough. Historians have the most to learn from the midrange causal mechanisms tested in a series of comparable cases. Process tracing and narrative treatments may offer explanations of complex processes, but frankly I doubt whether we can overcome the problems of weighting the variables and interpreting the actions of individuals sufficiently to produce consensus on the operations of the causal mechanisms in complex cases. Complex cases can be compared analytically, but they are unlikely to yield law-like explanations.[60]

Certain generic problems recur that are amenable to process tracing analysis. Conventional and nuclear deterrence, coercive diplomacy, war termination, civil war mediation, insurgency and counterinsurgency, arms race spirals, power transitions, and paradigm shifts are all amenable to analysis over a series of cases. The generalizations produced in such studies will be conditional; they will be contingent on the nature of the international system existing at that time. Thus, the generalization will not take the form "arms races correlate with war," but rather, "arms races correlate with war under conditions of tight bipolarity among states with common borders during the prenuclear period."[61] Historians should learn from political scientists to test alternate causal theories against their data, instead of amassing evidence to support a single thesis.[62]

What theories should we be testing or using at which levels of the taxonomy? At the international system level, balance of power theory clearly operates at some times and under some conditions. At other times, power transition models may help explain what is going on.[63] Bargaining theories of non–zero sum games may explain the evolution of cooperative behavior in hostile bipolar environments.[64] At the state level, theories of

---

60. See Bennett and George's chapter in this volume.

61. See Alexander George, "Knowledge for Statecraft: The Challenge for Political Science and History," *International Security*, Vol. 22, No. 1 (Summer 1997), pp. 49–51.

62. Haber, Kennedy, and Krasner, "Brothers Under the Skin," pp. 35, 42–43.

63. Elman and Elman, "History vs. Neo-realism," pp. 183–188.

64. A number of these suggestions come from John Lewis Gaddis, "New Conceptual Approaches," pp. 418–422; and Robert Axelrod, *The Evolution of Cooperation* (New York: Basic Books, 1984).

interest group log-rolling, power elite corporatism, political culture, and bureaucratic politics can be tested as explanations; and at the individual level, rational choice theories, cognitive and social psychological models, and theories of threat perception can apply.[65] Jack Levy is correct in suggesting in Chapter 1 that diplomatic historians should have a toolbox of theories from which they can select the right implement to work at the proper level of analysis.

Testing Against Case Studies

To test midlevel generalizations, we can use the multiple case study method, comparing similar sets of events that occurred in the same type of international era to generate explanations that are limited as to time and place, but still more general than those of single narratives. These generalizations will cover far less than scientific laws do, but they will explain far more than idiosyncratic histories do. Eventually we may be able to construct limited inductive theories by grouping clusters of validated hypotheses on causation together. Success will come when we can present reproducible comparisons of patterns over a number of spatially and temporally defined cases.[66] Or, lacking comparable cases, the analyst may use counterfactual analysis to isolate which variables were critical to the outcome: If we exclude factor X or substitute factor Y in the taxonomy, for example, would the decision or outcome have been the same?[67]

One historian, Ernest R. May, has used the case study method to explain change in U.S. foreign policy. May has explained the brief rise and rapid fall of U.S. colonial expansionism in his book *American Imperialism*.[68] He tests the findings of political scientists that there must be a change in the outlook of the public opinion leaders and their attentive publics before there can be a reversal of policy. He then asks: Why did

---

65. Gaddis, "New Conceptual Approaches," pp. 418–422.

66. George, "Case Studies and Theory Development," in Lauren, *Diplomacy: New Approaches*, pp. 43–68; James Lee Ray, *Global Politics*, 3rd ed. (Boston: Houghton Mifflin, 1987) p. 77; and Colin Elman and Miriam Fendius Elman, "Diplomatic History and International Relations Theory: Respecting Difference and Crossing Boundaries," *International Security*, Vol. 22, No. 1 (Summer 1997), p. 13.

67. Raymond Grew, "The Case for Comparing Histories," *American Historical Review*, Vol. 85, No. 4 (October 1980), pp. 763–778.

68. Ernest R. May, *American Imperialism: A Speculative Essay* (New York: Atheneum, 1968). May has moved away from a belief in structured, focused comparisons as a method for drawing lessons for policymakers, however; see May, "History-Theory-Action," *Diplomatic History*, Vol. 18, No. 4 (Fall 1994), pp. 589–603.

the U.S. Congress refuse to accept President Ulysses S. Grant's proposal to annex Santo Domingo in 1871, but then go on an annexationist binge in 1898–99? In 1869–71 the opinion leaders were united in their opposition to colonialism, while in 1898 the opinion leaders were split, making dramatic change possible. May shows that the decisions existed in a large, multilevel context, but he does not use these various levels of analysis as a laundry list. Instead, he reviews which of them influenced the decisions of the policymakers at critical decision points.

What are the social science attributes that expand May's analytical toolbox? He uses a clear hypothesis that he then tests in carefully selected, clearly comparable case studies. He then searches through the levels of analysis and identifies, as other historians have, public opinion as the necessary condition which shaped McKinley's options. But he goes further than other analysts of public opinion have by using social science theory to identify the independent variables that might have caused the change in opinion in this period. He then uses a large number of varied and obscure newspapers, journals, and documents to build a picture of the division in elite opinion in 1898, as opposed to the consensus that existed in 1871. This depth of research lends authority to his argument that the split in the elite allowed expansion to happen during wartime. Thus he makes a sequential, narrative argument as well. May's work provides an example of the productive marriage of social science methods to traditional historical practice.

May's findings on the operation of public opinion fall into the category of limited generalization rather than covering law. His results might have been quite different if he had studied other eras in U.S. history with their different literacy rates, opinion leaders, and media. The processes of opinion formation and political intermediation change considerably over time, and the analyst has to adjust for these changing necessary conditions. In addition, May's findings probably would not translate well to some other countries and cultures. In the nineteenth century, his findings would not apply to Germany, Russia, or Japan. Thus social science methods can yield useful intermediate generalizations that are limited by the context of time and culture.

Learning from Each Other

The approach outlined above merely constitutes an intermediate step toward improved explanation in diplomatic history. The use of this approach can lead to more systematic and probabilistic explanations in international history, but it cannot produce many universally valid explanations. Certain factors may lead some decision-makers to act in the same way, while the identical factors might cause different decision-makers to respond in different ways.[69] Some of the constructionist historians' objections will still hold; the problems inherent to the selection of evidence will still remain as will the ideological differences between nationalist, realist, and new left historians. We may have to recognize that hypotheses that are supported by the evidence in one era or in one area of the world will probably not often apply in other eras or in other areas. Jack Levy makes the same point in Chapter 1.

In addition, some of our work will deal with unique combinations of causal factors. In some cases, history shows radical discontinuities, and unique factors comprise significant causes of the outcome. The proliferation of intercontinental ballistic missiles that can deliver hydrogen bombs is such a discontinuity, because it so forcefully deters warfare between the superpowers. Verification of arms control agreements by satellite photography is another example of a unique causal factor that would make comparisons of strategic arms control efforts across historical eras difficult.[70] We need also to recognize that the reconstruction of the decision-makers' motives and thought processes is such a difficult task that there will continue to be many honest disagreements that will remain unresolved, no matter how objective we try to be. By itself objectivity does not guarantee that we will produce correct accounts of the past, for objective historians are still as fallible as objective foreign policy decision-makers are, but we increase our chances of overcoming conflicting interpretations when we agree on our analytical categories and competing causal mechanisms.[71]

In sum, the prospects for positivism and behaviorism in international history and in the international relations field are somewhat limited by the idiosyncratic and complex nature of different historical events, even if they occur in the same era. Consequently we will probably find it impossible to move from observed regularities to validated theories and laws covering many similar phenomena in many different historical periods.[72] We must recognize that it may be impossible to move from such

---

69. Benjamin A. Most and Harvey Starr, "International Relations Theory, Foreign Policy Substitutability, and 'nice' Laws," *World Politics*, Vol. 36, No. 3 (April 1984), pp. 383–406.

70. See John Lewis Gaddis, *The Long Peace: Inquiries into the History of the Cold War* (New York: Oxford University Press, 1987), pp. 195–245.

71. Mandelbaum, *Anatomy of Historical Knowledge*, pp. 146–151.

72. See C. Behan McCullagh's review essay on William Todd, *History as Applied Science: A Philosophical Study* (Detroit: Wayne State University Press, 1972), in *History and Theory*, Vol. 12, No. 4 (1973), pp. 437–439, 451.

clusters of regularities to valid general theories of international behavior. James E. Dougherty and Robert L. Pfaltzgraff, Jr., have admitted that their fellow political scientists are still far from creating a science of international relations.[73]

On balance, however, serious diplomatic historians have far more to gain from adopting positivistic, behavioral methods than they have to lose. The use of systematic, multivariate analysis along the lines suggested above will link economic, technological, and social change to the actions of decision-makers. Thus it directs attention to the real-world, structural context, which diplomatic historians have tended to slight in their close analyses of the documentary records of negotiations and decisions. We may then maintain the balance in our narratives between the diplomatic decision-makers and their changing worlds. At the very least, if we agree on common modes of explanation, an overall taxonomy, and some general hypotheses, we will have better grounds for informed speculation on causation, because we will be comparing the same sets of causal mechanisms against the same data over time.

Those historians who are trying to deal with events over longer stretches of time need to be much more aware of changes in necessary conditions—the very structural and systemic changes that political scientists study. Historians can also learn, as Ernest May has, to do structured and focused comparisons of case studies, in order to generate useful midlevel generalizations in their field. As Jack Levy has suggested in Chapter 1, historians need to learn to differentiate between primary and secondary causes and specify the conditions under which the event they are studying was likely to occur. Adoption of such formal methods can sensitize us to structural causes, prevent exaggeration of intentionalist and accidental causes, and generally sharpen our analyses. Thus political scientists can help historians avoid a false voluntarism. Good comparative analytical histories can then become the basis for better narratives of single cases in all their peculiar detail. Analytical and narrative historians do not have to be enemies.

On the other hand, political scientists can profit from historians' accounts of decision-makers' reasoning. Decision-makers may reach the same kinds of decisions on different grounds, and intentionalist explanations may cast doubt on structural explanations of a case. Historians can

---

73. James E. Dougherty and Robert L. Pfaltzgraff, Jr., conclude that "the results of the theory-building efforts of the behavioral-quantitative phase [of development in the international relations field] have been slim indeed;" see their *Contending Theories of International Relations: A Comprehensive Survey*, 2nd ed. (New York: Harper & Row, 1981), p. 551.

remind political scientists of the role that free will and accident play in their cases and consequently temper their enthusiasm for generalizations that may be contingent on character, chance, era, or culture. In doing so, historians can help temper political scientists' tendency toward false determinism.[74]

Thus historians and political scientists can learn a great deal from each other. In addition, they have a common heritage. Both political scientists and historians are heirs to the rational tradition of the Enlightenment, and they have a duty to nurture and strengthen that tradition. As we leave a century of terrible slaughters that were conducted in the name of various mystical nationalisms and irrational utopianisms, we should dedicate ourselves to overcoming our differences and unite in our efforts to understand international relations.

---

74. Jack S. Levy, "Too Important to Leave to the Other: History and Political Science in the Study of International Relations," *International Security*, Vol. 22, No. 1 (Summer 1997), p. 31.

Chapter 3

Social Science and History: Ranchers versus Farmers?

Richard Ned Lebow

Ranchers and farmers were often enemies in the Old West. Ranchers wanted open land to graze their cattle herds and bring them to market. Farmers enclosed land to grow and protect their crops. As farms became more numerous, it became increasingly difficult for ranchers to drive their herds from the grass lands of Texas to the markets and slaughterhouses of the Middle West. Desperate ranchers sometimes resorted to violence in an ultimately futile attempt to preserve the open spaces of the West.

Like ranchers and farmers, historians and social scientists lay claim to the same terrain with very different purposes in mind. Historians study the past as a valuable exercise in its own right. They also use the past to illuminate the present by discovering the origins of values, ideas, and institutions and tracing their subsequent development. Social scientists regard the past as data that might help them develop and test theories of human behavior. Since the 1950s social scientists have had the upper hand, measured in salaries and access to jobs and research funds. Fortunately, the conflict between the two professions has never gone beyond rhetorical violence, but it has at times been acute and, in my opinion, counterproductive to both. This volume represents one of a growing number of opportunities to bring together interested representatives of the two intellectual communities to discuss matters of common interest.

I offer as my contribution a critical evaluation of the ongoing historical reevaluation of the Cold War. I identify some methodological pitfalls, and urge adoption of some conceptual tools not commonly employed by Cold War historians that could facilitate this enterprise. I use the Cold War as an accessible platform for my arguments, which are aimed at a wider audience of historians. Although I use some of the language and concepts of neopositivism, I am not urging historians to become social scientists. My paper is not intended—and I hope, is not read—as an exercise in disciplinary imperialism. Elsewhere, I have pleaded with international relations theorists to study the methods and findings of Cold War historians.[1] Learning in our scholarly neighborhood should be a two-way street.

Good research starts by identifying important questions or puzzles. I argue at the outset that Cold War history and international relations theory have been surprisingly unreflective about where their questions come from, and that this has led to some dead ends in both fields. The search for answers has been equally problematic. In Cold War history, answers most frequently take the form of single case narratives that attribute key decisions or events to multiple causes. I argue that failure to rank order these causes and explore the relationship between or among them can make such explanations difficult to refute and easy to confirm tautologically. Answers to questions require evidence, and I contend that Cold War history has been too narrowly based on the written record. Documentary evidence is obviously critical, but needs to be augmented—and often corrected—by oral history and interviews.

A common view holds that historians practice narrative-based explanation, and that this is something very different from theory-based explanation.[2] This is a false distinction. Narratives are compatible with and generally rooted in theory, although that theory may not be articulated. Historian Edward Ingram observes: "The historian's description is a form of analysis (it explains); likewise, narrative (which has nothing to do with chronology) is applied theory, an analytical test of a proposition; each presupposes the other and, without the other, neither can be carried out."[3] According to political scientist Jack Levy, the difference between political science and history "is not in the use or nonuse of theoretical concepts and models, but rather in how they use those concepts and in the importance they attach to being explicit about their analytic assump-

1. Richard Ned Lebow, "Rise and Fall of the Cold War in Comparative Perspective," *Review of International Studies*, Vol. 25 (December 1999), pp. 21–39.

2. See, for example, Edgar Kiser and Michael Hechter, "The Role of General Theory in Comparative-Historical Sociology," *American Journal of Sociology*, Vol. 97 (July 1991), p. 2; and John Lewis Gaddis, "Expanding the Data Base: Historians, Political Scientists and the Enrichment of Security Studies," *International Security*, Vol. 12, No. 1 (Summer 1987), pp. 3–21.

3. Edward Ingram, "The Wonderland of the Political Scientist," *International Security*, Vol. 22, No. 1 (Summer 1997), p. 53; see also Colin Elman and Miriam Fendius Elman, "Diplomatic History and International Relations Theory: Respecting Difference and Crossing Boundaries," *International Security*, Vol. 22, No. 1 (Summer 1997), pp. 5–21.

tions and models."[4] Historians attempt to explain the particular, but to do so they must resort to the general. If even some historical narrative is theory-driven, and implicitly employs theory to explain, then the historians who practice this form of narrative could benefit from a more self-conscious approach to the construction and evaluation of propositions.

Questions

Graduate education in the social sciences and history privileges explanation. Social science students are taught to build and test theories, and toward this end they study modeling, game theory, statistics, and other forms of data collection and analysis. History students are trained to make and evaluate interpretations. They learn languages and archival skills essential to using documents, on which most historical interpretations are based. Graduate education provides students in these disciplines with many of the conceptual and research tools they need to answer research questions, but little, if any, emphasis is placed on teaching students how to pose the questions that drive their research, or ascertain why they are interesting. The result is a haphazard research agenda where questions come and go in response to political agendas, intellectual fads, and the availability of data. Understandably, graduate students and assistant professors choose—and are often encouraged—to write about whatever is "hot" in their field to increase their chances of getting a job or tenure.

In a highly constrained market, it is understandable that many graduate students and assistant professors follow the path of least resistance. It is more difficult to sympathize with senior colleagues whose research agendas, which have the potential to shape entire fields, are driven by questions whose value rests on unarticulated and unexamined assumptions. My own field of international relations has paid a heavy price for this failing.

For international relations scholars in the 1980s, the preeminent question in the security subfield was the "long peace" between the superpowers. Specialists considered it remarkable that the superpowers had avoided war, unlike rival hegemons of the past. They were also impressed by the seeming durability of superpower spheres of influence. According to John Lewis Gaddis, "the very fact that the interim arrangements of

4. Jack S. Levy, "Too Important to Leave to the Other: History and Political Science in the Study of International Relations," *International Security*, Vol. 22, No. 1 (Summer 1997), p. 25.

1945 have remained largely intact for four decades would have astonished—and quite possibly appalled—the statesmen who cobbled them together in the hectic months that followed the surrender of Germany and Japan."[5] The burning question in international political economy was the survival of the postwar international economic order despite the seeming decline of the United States, the hegemon that had created this order. Some political economists were surprised that neither Germany nor Japan had attempted to restructure international economic relations to suit their respective interests.[6] Both questions assumed that the robustness of the political and economic status quo was an extraordinary anomaly that required an equally extraordinary explanation.[7]

Attempts to explain the unexpected stability of the postwar political and economic order, and the controversy these explanations provoked, pushed the problem of change out of the pages of the principal journals and into obscurity, where it remained until the Berlin Wall was breached.[8] No major theory of international relations made change its principal focus. Even theories that incorporated some concept of change made no attempt to specify the conditions under which it would occur.[9] In the absence of a theoretical interest in change, there was no debate about how or why the postwar order might evolve or be transformed. Scholars became insensitive to the prospect that such change could occur.

In a deeper sense, my field's blindness was attributable to the politi-

---

5. John Lewis Gaddis, *The Long Peace: Inquiries Into the History of the Cold War Era* (New York: Oxford University Press, 1987), p. 218.

6. See Charles Kindleberger, *The World in Depression, 1929–1939* (Berkeley: University of California Press, 1973); Robert Gilpin, *War and Change in World Politics* (Cambridge: Cambridge University Press, 1981). For critical discussions and alternate explanations, see Robert Keohane, *After Hegemony* (Princeton: Princeton University Press, 1984); Keohane, *International Institutions and State Power* (Boulder, Colo.: Westview, 1989); Duncan Snidal, "The Limits of Hegemonic Stability Theory," *International Organization,* Vol. 39 (Autumn 1985), pp. 579–614; and Volker Rittberger, ed., *The Study of Regimes in International Relations* (New York: Oxford University Press, forthcoming).

7. The focus of realism is great power relations. In describing the postwar political order as stable, realists are referring to the stability of Europe, and the de facto and later de jure acceptance of its division by East and West. The postwar political "order" in other regions of the world could hardly be called stable.

8. A literature search reveals that between 1970 and 1990, *International Organization, World Politics,* and *International Studies Quarterly* published no more than a half-dozen articles whose primary focus was major foreign policy or systemic change.

9. An exception is Gilpin, *War and Change in World Politics.* This point is also made by John Gerard Ruggie, "Continuity and Transformation in the World Polity: Toward a Neorealist Synthesis," Robert O. Keohane, "Theory of World Politics: Structural Realism and Beyond," and Robert W. Cox, "Social Forces, States and World Orders:

cal assumptions that shaped leading scholars' worldviews and research agendas. The absence of superpower war seemed extraordinary because of the widely shared belief that the Soviet Union was an aggressive and expansionist adversary; for some, it was the linear descendant of Hitler's Germany. If scholars had regarded Soviet leaders from Khrushchev as fundamentally satisfied with the status quo and concerned less with making gains than with avoiding losses—and there is much evidence to support this interpretation—the nonoccurrence of World War III would not have required any extraordinary explanation.

Cold War critics were equally myopic. Those who considered the nuclear arms race and its escalatory potential to be the major source of tension in East-West relations directed their scholarly attention to the domestic and international causes of the arms race and the ways it might be halted or stabilized through arms control and security regimes. Once again, there was little recognition or study of the possibility that the underlying conflict might undergo—or indeed, had already undergone—a profound transformation.

The same bias affected the study of political economy. The reigning orthodoxy, imported from classical economics, assumes that states are rational and seek to maximize gain. If scholars had started from the premise that German and Japanese bankers and industrialists, like their counterparts elsewhere in the world's capitalist establishment, were anxious above all else to preserve order and predictability—especially in a system from which they profited so handsomely—they would not have viewed the survival of the postwar international economic framework as anomalous. Japanese and Western European efforts to preserve the system would have been judged simple common sense.

Theory is supposed to free scholars from their political, generational, and cultural biases. In social science, it often does the reverse, and worse still, confers an aura of scientific legitimacy on subjective political beliefs and prejudices. Logical positivism and other "unity of science" approaches depict science as independent of the culture, life experiences, and personalities of scientists.[10] According to these epistemologies, sci-

---

Beyond International Relations Theory," all in Robert O. Keohane, ed., *Neorealism and Its Critics* (New York: Columbia University Press, 1986), pp. 148–149, 179–181, 197–198, 243–245. For a critique of cognitive psychology's failure to deal adequately with change, see Richard Ned Lebow and Janice Gross Stein, "Afghanistan, Carter and Foreign Policy Change: The Limits of Cognitive Models," in Dan Caldwell and Timothy J. McKeown, eds., *Diplomacy, Force, and Leadership: Essays in Honor of Alexander L. George* (Boulder, Colo.: Westview, 1993), pp. 95–128.

10. "Unity of science" approaches see no differences between the goals and proper practices of the social and physical sciences. Logical positivism has for many years

ence is supposed to respond to its own imperatives; previous discoveries unearth anomalies or open up promising lines of inquiry that are investigated by subsequent scientists. But the ideas that propel science to the next stage of inquiry rarely grow out of existing research. Thomas Kuhn and others have shown how revolutions in science are triggered by fundamental shifts in *gestalt* that identify new problems and new kinds of solutions to them.[11] To explain these gestalt shifts—in all scholarly enterprises—one must generally look beyond the lab and the archive.

Research agendas, especially in history and social science, reflect political, institutional, and personal agendas.[12] The historiography of World War I and the Cold War illustrate how ideology and current events drive scholarship. The Treaty of Versailles justified reparations by holding Germany responsible for war in 1914. The German government signed the Treaty, but categorically denied its responsibility for the war, and published a selective and carefully edited collection of documents to buttress its claim of innocence. Diplomatic history in the 1920s and 1930s was dominated by the *Kriegschuldfrage*. Predictably, works that upheld the Allied position provoked an equal and opposite reaction: revisionist scholarship shifted the mantle of blame onto the shoulders of Russia, France, and Britain, and attempted to undercut the justification for reparations. Decades later, the Berlin and Cuban missile crises revived interest in World War I. This time, concern that World War III might arise from miscalculation, accidents, loss of control, or runaway escalation led historians and political scientists to mine the crisis of 1914 for contemporary policy lessons. Around the same time, historians began to reexamine the deeper causes and meaning of World War I, its links to World War II, and

---

been associated with this position, but other approaches, among them positivism and empiricism, subscribe to it as well. There is a lot of confusion in political science; practitioners routinely use the term logical positivism to refer to all of these approaches. For appropriate definitions, see Friedrich Kratochwil, "Why Sisyphus is Happy: Reflections on the 'Third Debate' and on Theorizing as a Vocation," *Sejong Review*, Vol. 3 (November 1995), pp. 3–36.

11. Theodore S. Kuhn, *The Structure of Scientific Revolutions* (Chicago: University of Chicago Press, 1962).

12. Michael Oakeshott, *Experience and Its Modes* (New York: Cambridge University Press, 1990); Benedetto Croce quoted in E.H. Carr, *What is History?* (Harmondsworth: Penguin, 1964), pp. 20–21; Carr, *What is History?* pp. 16, 29–30; Levy, "Too Important to Leave to the Other," pp. 26–27; and Stephen H. Haber, David M. Kennedy, and Stephen D. Krasner, "Brothers Under the Skin: Diplomatic History and International Relations," *International Security*, Vol. 22, No. 1 (Summer 1997), pp. 34–43, especially pp. 37–38.

implications for developments elsewhere in the world.[13] This process has accelerated since the end of the Cold War.[14]

The historiography of the Cold War underwent a parallel evolution. In the 1950s and 1960s, scholarship focused on the question of Cold War "guilt." Conservatives and Cold War liberals blamed Stalin, communism, and the Soviet Union. Revisionist scholarship, which began in the 1950s but really flourished a decade later in response to the Vietnam War, held capitalism and the United States responsible for the Cold War. The collapse of the Soviet Union, and the access this permitted to hitherto unavailable documents, have led some anti-Stalinists in the West to claim victory, but by the 1970s the question of who started the Cold War had become largely passé. In response to détente, students of the Cold War shifted their attention to the questions of how a war-threatening conflict was gradually transformed into a more stable rivalry. Now that the Cold War is over, historians will presumably begin to examine the broader meaning of the Cold War, and do so with an eye on the issues of the moment. A case in point is a paper by Paul Schroeder that uses the concept of the *longue durée* to analyze World Wars I and II and the Cold War as a part of an iterative cycle of the creation, entrenchment, decline, collapse, and reconstitution of legitimate international orders.[15]

Research on World War I and the Cold War shifted in response to contemporary political developments. Scholars looked to the past for guidance about the present. The answers they found reflected their political views and starting assumptions. Neopositivism and the "new international history" are naive in their belief that anything else is possible. It is process, not motive, that distinguishes good from bad scholarship.

Process begins with the identification of an important question or puzzle. These arise when we encounter behavior at odds with our expectations. Expectations are always theory-driven; they are based on underlying beliefs about how the world works. Sometimes these beliefs are well specified, more often they are unspoken. When we observe a business buy dear and sell cheap, or a state attack a more powerful neighbor, we

---

13. See, for example, Hajo Holborn, *The Political Collapse of Europe* (New York: Alfred Knopf, 1963); and Arno J. Mayer, *Wilson versus Lenin: Political Origins of the New Diplomacy, 1917–1918* (New Haven: Yale University Press, 1959).

14. The historiography of World War I and the Cold War became intertwined in the Federal Republic of Germany in the 1960s. Anticapitalist and anti-American feeling ran high among intellectuals, and found expression in the Fischer thesis, which stressed the continuity of German history, from Bismarck through Adenauer.

15. Paul W. Schroeder, "The End of the Cold War in the Light of History," unpublished paper, January 1997.

consider the behavior anomalous because it appears to violate well-established principles of economics and international relations. If we dismiss the actors as ill-informed, incompetent, or crazy, the puzzle disappears, although it may give rise to the secondary one of how such people could have achieved positions of authority. To make "sense" of seemingly anomalous behavior, that is, to square it with accepted principles without relaxing the assumption of rationality, we look for other considerations specific to the situation that may have dictated choice and can ultimately be reconciled with the principles. A business may sell for a loss if there is a glut on the market or its managers expect prices to decline precipitously. A weak state may attack a strong one if its military has a strategy and tactics that it expects to negate the adversary's putative advantages.

Another way to make sense of anomalous behavior is to revise the beliefs or principles that make it appear anomalous. Do they rest on inappropriate assumptions? Ignore more important determinants of behavior? Leave unspecified, or improperly specified, the scope conditions under which they hold? The debate about the end of the Cold War is at its core a controversy about the validity of the assumptions that shaped Western understanding of the Soviet Union and its foreign policy. Conservatives, including some realists, insist that the end of the Cold War validated their assumptions that foreign policy is driven by power calculations; the Soviet Union's decline compelled Gorbachev to seek accommodation with the West on unfavorable terms. Other realists contend that their assumptions are valid, but that the outcome was anomalous because Mikhail Gorbachev made serious miscalculations. Critics of realism have used the end of the Cold War to argue that structure is indeterminate, and that policy choices are significantly shaped by ideas, domestic politics, and the preferences of leaders.[16]

Scholars must always remain open to the possibility that there is something wrong with their premises. Gerhard Weinberg maintains that historians, unlike social scientists, recognize the transience of their arguments and theories and are open to the possibility that new evidence may

---

16. See, for example, Kenneth N. Waltz, "The Emerging Structure of International Politics," *International Security*, Vol. 18, No. 2 (Fall 1993), pp. 5–43; William C. Wohlforth, "Realism and the End of the Cold War," *International Security*, Vol. 19, No. 3 (Winter 1994/95), pp. 91–129; Kenneth A. Oye, "Explaining the End of the Cold War: Morphological and Behavioral Adaptations to the Nuclear Peace?" in Richard Ned Lebow and Thomas Risse-Kappen, eds., *International Relations Theory and the End of the Cold War* (New York: Columbia University Press, 1995), pp. 57–84; Thomas Risse-Kappen, "Ideas Do Not Float Freely: Transnational Coalitions, Domestic Structures, and the End of the Cold War," in Lebow and Risse-Kappen, eds., *International Relations Theory and the End of the Cold War*, pp. 187–222; Richard Ned Lebow, "The Long Peace, the End of the Cold War, and the Failure of Realism," in Lebow and Risse-Kappen,

compel their revision or rejection.[17] The historiography of major controversies indicates to me that historians are just as committed to their
interpretations as social scientists are to their theories. They are more
likely to assimilate new "facts" to their theories than to use them as
catalysts for rethinking. Historians and social scientists alike need to
make explicit the underlying assumptions that guide their research, and
ask themselves what kinds of evidence could falsify their theories or
interpretations or lead them to approach the problem from a different set
of assumptions. Self-awareness and self-questioning is the most difficult
and most neglected part of good process, and, as the following section
argues, one of the most essential.

False Confirmation

Historical debates are most productive when they focus scholarly attention on underlying assumptions and principles. It often takes seemingly
anomalous behavior to spark such a debate. Gorbachev's withdrawal
from Afghanistan, liberation of jailed dissidents, push for free elections,
and willingness to let Eastern European people decide their own political
futures are cases in point. This is because of the cognitive tendency to
assimilate information, even disconfirming information, to existing beliefs, principles, or theories.[18] Motivated bias can reinforce this tendency.[19]

---

eds., *International Relations Theory and the End of the Cold War*, pp. 23–56; Robert G.
Herman, "Identity, Norms and National Security: The Soviet Foreign Policy Revolution and the End of the Cold War," in Peter J. Katzenstein, ed., *The Culture of National
Security: Norms and Identity in World Politics* (New York: Columbia University Press,
1996), pp. 271–316; and Jeffrey T. Checkel, *Ideas and International Political Change:
Soviet/Russian Behavior and the End of the Cold War* (New Haven: Yale University Press,
1977).

17. Comments at "History and International Relations Theory Conference," Tempe,
Ariz., January 15–18, 1998.

18. Human beings use knowledge structures, or "schemas," to cope with the enor-
mous amount of information they receive. Information is assimilated to these schemas.
On the limitations of human information-processing, see Richard Nisbett and Lee
Ross, *Human Inference: Strategies and Shortcomings of Social Judgment* (Englewood Cliffs,
N.J.: Prentice-Hall, 1980); and James Galambos, Robert Abelson, and John Black, eds.,
Knowledge Structures (Hillsdale, N.J: Lawrence Erlbaum, 1986). On biases and heuristics
in information-processing, see Daniel Kahneman, Paul Slovic, and Amos Tversky,
Judgment Under Uncertainty: Heuristics and Biases (New York: Cambridge University
Press, 1982). For a critique of this model, see Susan T. Fiske and Shelley E. Taylor, *Social
Cognition*, 2nd ed. (New York: McGraw-Hill, 1991), esp. pp. 554–558.

19. Irving L. Janis, *Victims of Groupthink: A Psychological Study of Foreign Policy Decisions and Fiascoes*, 2nd ed. (Boston: Houghton Mifflin, 1972); Irving L. Janis and Leon

Scholars who have built careers on particular interpretations are generally reluctant to recognize problems with those interpretations. When beliefs reflect strong emotional needs to maintain a particular construction of reality, they can be altogether impervious to discrepant information.

The deterrence debate—for many years, a nondebate—gives ample testimony to how cognitive and motivational biases can reinforce each other. Modern deterrence theory developed in response to the recognition that nuclear wars were too destructive to be a rational instrument of war, but that their very destructiveness might be exploited to prevent war. The classic formulation of this paradox is found in Bernard Brodie's 1946 study, *The Absolute Weapon*.[20] In the "golden age" of deterrence theory, the 1950s and 1960s, Bernard Brodie, William Kaufmann, and Thomas Schelling developed formal models of nuclear deterrence. They argued that it could be rational to threaten an irrational act, and explored ways in which deterrent and compellent threats of nuclear annihilation might be made credible.[21]

Deterrence theory gained widespread acceptance in academe and government for intellectual, political, and psychological reasons. Its elegance and simplicity appeared to offer scholars a powerful and widely applicable instrument to analyze and predict strategic behavior. For policymakers, it held out the prospect of exploiting an unusable weapon to achieve political goals. On a deeper level, deterrence was a psychological bulwark against nuclear war. If, as deterrence theory maintained, nuclear war could only come about because an adversary believed that its enemy could not retaliate in kind, war could be prevented by possession of a secure second-strike capability.[22]

Mann, *Decision Making: A Psychological Analysis of Conflict, Choice and Commitment* (New York: Free Press, 1977); and Richard Ned Lebow, *Between Peace and War: The Nature of International Crisis* (Baltimore: Johns Hopkins University Press, 1981).

20. Bernard Brodie, *The Absolute Weapon* (New York: Harcourt, Brace, 1946).

21. William K. Kaufmann, *The Requirements of Deterrence* (Princeton: Center of International Studies, 1954); Bernard Brodie, *Strategy in the Missile Age* (Princeton: Princeton University Press, 1959); Henry A. Kissinger, *The Necessity for Choice* (New York: Harper, 1960); Thomas Schelling, "Controlled Response and Strategic Warfare" (London: International Institute of Strategic Studies, June 1965); and Schelling, *Arms and Influence* (New Haven: Yale University Press, 1966).

22. For the psychological roots of deterrence, see Philip Green, *Deadly Logic: The Theory of Nuclear Deterrence* (Columbus: Ohio State University Press, 1966); Robert Jervis, *The Illogic of American Nuclear Strategy* (Ithaca: Cornell University Press, 1984), esp. pp. 22, 36, 37; and Steven Kull, *Minds at War: Nuclear Reality and the Inner Conflicts of Defense Policymakers* (New York: Basic Books, 1988).

Deterrence was confirmed tautologically. The United States buttressed its commitments in Berlin (1948–49, 1958–69, and 1961), the Taiwan Straits (1954 and 1958) and other parts of the world when they appeared threatened by the Soviet Union or China. When no military challenge occurred, politicians and analysts attributed communist restraint to U.S. deterrence. When deterrence failed—the most notable example is the Soviet attempt to deploy strategic missiles in Cuba in 1962—it was also explained in terms of deterrence theory. Kennedy administration officials and scholars assumed that Khrushchev challenged the United States because the president's youth and his lackluster performance in the Bay of Pigs crisis and at the Berlin and Vienna summits had given him good grounds to question U.S. resolve. They attributed Khrushchev's withdrawal of the missiles to Kennedy's credible display of military capability and resolve to use force, if necessary, to take the missiles out.[23] Deterrence was also given credit for the overall absence of nuclear war and the end of the Cold War. The conventional wisdom holds that Gorbachev sought an accommodation because the Soviet Union could no longer compete economically or militarily with the United States.

Recent evidence from Soviet and Chinese archives offers little support for any of these interpretations. In the Taiwan Straits crisis, the Chinese government's goal was to deter Taiwan and the United States from using force against the Chinese mainland.[24] Khrushchev sent missiles to Cuba not to force a trade-off in Berlin, as the Kennedy administration surmised, but to protect Castro from an expected U.S. invasion,

---

23. Elie Abel, *The Missile Crisis* (Philadelphia: Lippincott, 1962), pp. 35–36; James Reston, "What Was Killed Was Not Only the President But the Promise," *New York Times Magazine*, November 15, 1964, p. 126; Arthur M. Schlesinger, Jr., *A Thousand Days: John F. Kennedy in the White House* (Boston: Houghton Mifflin, 1965), pp. 391, 796; Theodore C. Sorensen, *Kennedy* (New York: Harper & Row, 1965), pp. 676, 724; Arnold Horelick and Myron Rush, *Strategic Power and Soviet Foreign Policy*, (Chicago: University of Chicago Press, 1966), pp. 142–143; Graham T. Allison, *Essence of Decision: Explaining the Cuban Missile Crisis* (Boston: Little, Brown, 1971), pp. 231–235; and Alexander L. George and Richard Smoke, *Deterrence in American Foreign Policy: Theory and Practice* (New York: Columbia University Press, 1974), p. 465. For a critique, and a different interpretation of Khrushchev's decision to send missile to Cuba, see Richard Ned Lebow, "The Cuban Missile Crisis: Reading the Lessons Correctly," *Political Science Quarterly*, Vol. 98 (Fall 1983), pp. 431–458; Raymond L. Garthoff, *Reflections on the Missile Crisis*, rev. ed. (Washington, D.C.: Brookings, 1989); and Richard Ned Lebow and Janice Gross Stein, *We All Lost the Cold War* (Princeton: Princeton University Press, 1994), especially chap. 4.

24. For an early version of this thesis, see Melvin Gurtov and Byong-Moo Hwang, *China Under Threat: The Politics of Strategy and Diplomacy* (Baltimore: Johns Hopkins University Press, 1980), pp. 63–98. See Shu Guang Zhang, *Deterrence and Strategic*

offset U.S. strategic superiority, and to get even with the president for deploying Jupiter missiles in Turkey. Kennedy had viewed these measures as prudent, defensive precautions against perceived Soviet threats. His actions had the unanticipated consequence of convincing Khrushchev of the need to protect the Soviet Union and Cuba from U.S. military and political challenges. Khrushchev withdrew the missiles to avoid war, but also because of Kennedy's public promise not to invade Cuba and his secret promise to withdraw the missiles in Turkey after a decent interval.[25]

The ultimate irony of nuclear deterrence may be that the strategy of deterrence undercut much of the political stability that the reality of deterrence should have created. The arms buildups, threatening military deployments, and confrontational rhetoric that characterized the strategy of deterrence obscured deep and mutual fears of war. Fear of nuclear war made leaders inwardly cautious, but their public posturing convinced their adversaries that they were aggressive, risk-prone, and even irrational. In Cuba, we now know, deterrence provoked the behavior it was meant to prevent.[26]

The intellectual history of deterrence highlights the disturbing ease with which beliefs can become entrenched. Even dramatically disconfirming events—this is how I read the Cuban missile deployment and Gorbachev's foreign policy revolution—can be explained away by true believers. Change, to the extent it occurs, is more likely to be generational; younger scholars, responding to novel political situations and intellectual currents, adopt new points of view. This is a slow and inefficient process. In the twentieth century it has also had disastrous political consequences. The hard-line deterrence strategy that characterized the U.S. approach to the Soviet Union throughout most of the Cold War was a response to the failure of appeasement in the 1930s. Appeasement in turn was a reaction to the more confrontational policies that were believed to have led to World War I. In each conflict, statesmen and generals prepared to prevent or fight the previous war.

Culture: Chinese-American Confrontations, 1949–1958 (Ithaca: Cornell University Press, 1992), for a more recent study making extensive use of Chinese documents and interviews.

25. Garthoff, *Reflections on the Missile Crisis;* Lebow and Stein, *We All Lost the Cold War;* and James G. Blight, Bruce J. Allyn, and David A. Welch, *Cuba on the Brink: Castro, The Missile Crisis and the Soviet Collapse* (New York: Pantheon, 1993).

26. Lebow and Stein, *We All Lost the Cold War;* and Ted Hopf, *Peripheral Visions: Deterrence Theory and American Foreign Policy in the Third World, 1965–1990* (Ann Arbor: University of Michigan Press, 1994).

Overdetermination

The late Sir Isaiah Berlin popularized the Greek poet Archilochus's distinction between hedgehogs and foxes.[27] Hedgehogs know one big thing, know it very well, and succeed by invoking it repeatedly. Foxes know many things, are inventive, and tailor their strategies to circumstances. Social scientists are more likely to be hedgehogs. They look for parsimonious explanations for seemingly complex events and assume that those explanations, and any strategies based on them, will be applicable in a wide range of situations. Historians are more likely to be foxes. They tend to treat every historical situation as unique, and are likely to propose varied and layered explanations on the assumption that complex events have complex causes. Reality, in the words of Melvyn Leffler, "is too complex to be captured by a single theory."[28] This approach has limitations of its own.

Multiple causation can take two forms. The first, known as overdetermination, occurs when several causes are present, any one of which could have produced the observed outcome. The second is when the combined effects of two or more causes are necessary to bring about the outcome. Historians, like their social scientist colleagues, need to specify which use of multiple causation they intend. Historical treatments of the Cold War sometimes fail to do this.

John Gaddis's writings illustrate this problem. In *The Long Peace,* he accepts Kenneth Waltz's contention that bipolarity was the principal structural cause of peace, and, Gaddis adds, of the unexpected stability of the postwar division of Europe.[29] It was an easy structure to maintain, encouraged stable alliances, and reduced the importance of individual defections from either alliance system. But Gaddis also contends that "what has really made the difference in inducing unaccustomed caution" was nuclear deterrence. He then offers a third cause of peace: the "rules" the superpowers evolved to regulate their competition. These rules in-

27.   Isaiah Berlin, *The Hedgehog and the Fox: An Essay on Tolstoy's View of History* (New York: Simon and Schuster, 1966).

28.   Melvyn P. Leffler, "New Approaches, Old Interpretations, and Prospective Reconfigurations," *Diplomatic History*, Vol. 19, No. 2 (Spring 1995), pp. 173–196, quote on p. 179; Edward Kiser, "Revival of the Narrative in Historical Sociology: What Rational Choice Theory Can Contribute," *Politics and Society*, Vol. 24 (September 1996), pp. 249–271, offers the view of theory as a "toolbox," an approach that should be appealing to historical "foxes."

29.   Kenneth N. Waltz, *Theory of International Politics* (Reading, Mass.: Addison-Wesley, 1979); and John Lewis Gaddis, *The Long Peace: Inquiring into the History of the Cold War* (New York: Oxford University Press, 1987).

cluded respect for each other's sphere of influence, and a commitment to avoid direct military confrontation and to use nuclear weapons only as an ultimate resort.

Waltz distinguished between "peace" (the absence of superpower war) and "stability" (the endurance of the bipolar system). Gaddis elides the two concepts, ruling out the possibility—which came to pass a few years after the publication of his book—that a bipolar system could be transformed without a war between its poles. Gaddis fails to tell us whether any or all of his structural and behavioral causes of peace are necessary and sufficient. Could peace have been preserved by any one of them? If not, which was (or were) the most important? And what about the relationship between these several causes? Surely, bipolarity and nuclear weapons were not unrelated; the latter helped to establish the former. Many realists would probably argue that the rules of the road Gaddis finds so important were a response to bipolarity or nuclear weapons.

His most recent book, *We Now Know: Rethinking Cold War History*, has the same problem.[30] He attributes the Cold War to Stalin's personality and ideology. Gaddis has no doubts about it; Stalin sought a Cold War the way "a fish seeks water."[31] Stalin also sought to extend Soviet territory and territorial control for security reasons. In Eastern Europe, where this control was ensured through military occupation and the imposition of Soviet-style puppet governments, Stalin's policy posed a direct challenge to Britain and the United States. But what *really* made the Cold War inevitable, Gaddis argues, was the coercive and crude way in which Stalin pursued his goals. Churchill, Atlee, Roosevelt, and Truman had to defend their policies to voters, and Stalin's failure to mask the extension of Soviet power behind the outward forms of democracy (plebiscites, elections, indirect rule through dependent but popularly elected governments) made it unacceptable to British and U.S. leaders.

Following Norman Naimark, Gaddis argues that Stalin's reliance on coercion and brutality was a reflection of the political-economic limitations of the Soviet system.[32] This was most evident in the occupation of Germany, where rape and pillage were unconstrained, and whole factories, rolling stock, equipment, and scientific personnel were forcibly removed to the Soviet Union. The United States was able to exercise

---

30. John Lewis Gaddis, *We Now Know: Rethinking Cold War History* (New York: Oxford University Press, 1997).

31. Ibid., p. 25.

32. Norman N. Naimark, *The Russians in Germany: A History of the Soviet Zone of Occupation, 1945–1949* (Cambridge: Harvard University Press, 1995).

influence in more subtle and effective ways, and worked collaboratively with elected governments. Washington also won the support of Western Europeans by providing extensive economic aid and credits for reconstruction. The asymmetry in political, administrative, and economic resources between the superpowers accounted "more than anything else, for the origins, escalation and ultimate outcome of the Cold War."[33]

Gaddis also maintains that Stalin's foreign policy was a direct extension of his domestic policy, and the overriding goal of both was to intimidate or, better yet, eliminate potential challengers. Cooperation, other than for purely tactical reasons, was alien to his nature. This leaves the door open to the possibility that another Soviet leader would have pursued a different policy in Eastern Europe and the Far East. But elsewhere Gaddis slams this door shut with his insistence that Stalin, and other officials, like Molotov, were prisoners of Marxist ideology. They believed that sooner or later—perhaps in as little as fifteen years—there would be another crisis of capitalism that would compel the leading capitalist powers to go to war to deflect domestic unrest. The United States would unleash a rearmed Germany against the Soviet Union. For protection, Soviet forces needed to control Germany and extend their defensive *glacis* as far west as possible.

There is an unresolved ambiguity in Gaddis's *We Now Know* about the Cold War and Stalin's relation to it. The regime, personality, and ideological explanations for the Cold War all point to an underlying defensive motivation: Stalin's personal, political, and *real politik*–driven need to expand Soviet influence. But Gaddis also advances a more offensive explanation. Stalin simply wanted to dominate Europe, and ultimately the world, but unlike Hitler, he was patient and "prepared to take as long as necessary to achieve his ambitions." But in Asia, Stalin threw caution to the wind, succumbed to "ideological euphoria," and allowed Kim Il-Sung to talk him into an invasion of South Korea. Some of these explanations are contradictory; others are related, but that relationship is left undefined; others may be epiphenomenal (i.e., due to other causes), and still others conflate cause and effect. Historians who offer multilayered explanations need to identify what kind of multiple causation they mean (Gaddis uses both interchangeably), distinguish *between* competing causes (offensive vs. defensive goals, and personality vs. ideology in this case), and rank order those that could be reinforcing (for Gaddis, regime capabilities, ideology, and personality). They also need to describe what-

---

33. Ibid., p. 17.

ever relationships exist between or among these causes. Failure to do this makes the overall argument impossible to sustain or falsify.

Counterfactual Arguments

Some prominent historians have dismissed counterfactual thought experiments as idle parlor games.[34] Counterfactual assumptions nevertheless lie at the core of all historical inference.[35] Implicit in every historical interpretation is the counterfactual that the outcome would *not* have occurred in the absence of the stated causes. If the Cold War was Stalin's fault, it follows that it would not have happened if a different leader had occupied the Kremlin—unless that leader had wanted that conflict for reasons of his own. Counterfactuals of this kind most often go unexamined. In the Soviet case, one counterfactual has received considerable attention: would communism have evolved differently if Lenin had lived longer, or if he had been succeeded by someone other than Stalin?[36] While this question is unanswerable, attempts to address it have usefully focused attention on the assumptions that guide and sustain different arguments about the role of Stalin and the nature of the Soviet system, and in doing so, have encouraged a more sophisticated historical debate.

Counterfactual thought experiments have an important role to play in Cold War scholarship. As noted above, they are a useful device for prodding historians and political scientists to make explicit the assumptions that guide their analysis and interpretations. They are also a useful tool to help formulate and specify these theories. John Gaddis alleges that Stalin was responsible for the Cold War. If Gaddis had asked himself if there still would have been a Cold War in the absence of Stalin, he would

---

34. According to A.J.P. Taylor, "a historian should never deal in speculation about what did not happen." *Struggle for the Mastery of Europe, 1848–1918* (London: Oxford University Press, 1954). M.M. Postan, writes: "The might-have beens of history are not a profitable subject of discussion," quoted in J.D. Gould, "Hypothetical History," *Economic History Review,* 2nd ser., Vol. 22 (August 1969), pp. 195–207. See also David Hackett Fischer, *Historian's Fallacies: Towards a Logic of Historical Thought* (New York: Harper Colophon Books, 1970), pp. 15–21; and Peter McClelland, *Causal Explanation and Model-Building in History, Economics, and the New Economic History* (Ithaca: Cornell University Press, 1975).

35. James D. Fearon, "Counterfactuals and Hypothesis Testing in Political Science," *World Politics,* Vol. 43 (January 1991), pp. 169–195.

36. George W. Breslauer, "Counterfactuals Reasoning in Western Studies of Soviet Politics and Foreign Relations," in Philip E. Tetlock and Aaron Belkin, eds., *Counterfactual Thought Experiments in World Politics: Logical, Methodological, and Psychological Perspectives* (Princeton: Princeton University Press, 1996), pp. 69–94, discusses this literature.

have been forced to decide if Stalin was a necessary and sufficient condition for that conflict. Removing Stalin from the scene would also have encouraged Gaddis to consider what else about the Soviet Union would have been different. Would foreign policy, for example, still have been subordinate to domestic policy, or subordinate in the same way? Counterfactual thought experiments of this kind could have helped Gaddis to rank order his explanations and the many links among them.

Counterfactual thought experiments are also useful in refuting others' explanations. Because every argument has its related counterfactual, critics have two strategies open to them: they can try to offer a different and more compelling account, or they can try to show that the outcome in question would still have occurred in the absence of the claimed causes. John Mueller's account of the Cold War is a nice example of the second strategy. In contrast to the conventional wisdom that attributed the "long peace" between the superpowers to nuclear deterrence, he argues that Moscow and Washington were restrained by their general satisfaction with the status quo, and secondarily by memories of World War II and the human, economic, and social costs of large-scale, conventional warfare. The unheralded destructiveness of nuclear weapons was redundant, and possibly counterproductive.[37]

Because historians typically study single cases, history confronts what social scientists call the "small-n problem." Single case studies can always be challenged as unrepresentative of the phenomenon in question. Validation is especially difficult when outcomes are attributed to multiple causes. Historians typically attempt to establish causation by process tracing. They try to document the links between a stated cause and an outcome. This works best at the individual level of analysis, but only when there is enough evidence to document the actors' calculations and motives. Even when such evidence is available, it may not permit historians to determine the relative weight of the several causes alleged to be at work, and which, if any, might have produced the outcome in the absence of the others.

Historians who focus on the behavior of actors generally want to understand it in a broader political, economic, or social context. They often posit underlying explanations for the actors' behavior or for the frames of reference they used to identify problems and appropriate re-

---

37. See John Mueller, *Retreat from Doomsday: The Obsolescence of Major War* (New York: Basic Books, 1989), and the debate on this subject between Mueller, "The Essential Irrelevance of Nuclear Weapons: Stability in the Postwar World," and Robert Jervis, "The Political Effects of Nuclear Weapons: A Comment," in *International Security*, Vol. 13, No. 3 (Fall 1988), pp. 55–90.

sponses to them. John Gaddis, as I have noted, believes bipolarity, nuclear deterrence, and the division of Europe were underlying causes of super-power restraint. The evidence for these or any other set of deeper causes is usually circumstantial; documents rarely show the extent to which they were responsible for the behavior in question. When the actor is a group, elite, bureaucracy, or mass movement, the influence of ideas, structures, and institutions are that much harder to track.

Case studies can generate and sometimes falsify propositions. To sustain causal inference it is generally necessary to engage in comparative analysis. Within the single-case format—the most common kind of his-torical scholarship—comparative analysis can take two forms: intra-case comparison and counterfactual analysis. Intra-case comparison breaks a case out into a series of similar interactions that are treated as separate and independent cases for purposes of analysis. Numerous studies of arms control and superpower crises have made use of this technique.[38] Like any form of comparative analysis, intra-case comparisons try to show as much variation as possible on dependent variables (what is to be explained) and independent variables. This is sometimes more difficult to do than in cross-case comparisons. It is also more difficult to establish the independence of cases, as the process and outcome of each case is more likely to influence policy in the next case than it would in cases involving different policymaking elites in different countries. But intra-case comparison confers a singular benefit: it examines variation within a relatively unchanging political and cultural context, controlling better than inter-case comparison for many factors that may be important but unrecognized. Thucydides' treatment of Athenian leadership at the out-break of war, during the sixth and seventh years of the war, and on the eve of the Sicilian expedition, provides a compelling example of how effectively this technique can be used by historians.[39]

Counterfactual analysis introduces variation through thought experi-ments that add or subtract contextual factors or possible causes, and ask how this would have influenced the outcome.[40] Thought experiments

---

38. See, for example, George and Smoke, *Deterrence in American Foreign Policy*; Alex-ander L. George and William E. Simmons, eds., *The Limits of Coercive Diplomacy* (Boulder, Colo.: Westview, 1994); Hopf, *Peripheral Visions*; Robert Jervis and Jack Sny-der, eds., *Dominoes and Bandwagons: Strategic Beliefs and Great Power Competition in the Eurasian Rimland* (New York: Oxford University Press, 1991); and Thomas Risse-Kappen, *Cooperation Among Democracies: The European Influence on U.S. Foreign Policy* (Princeton: Princeton University Press, 1995).

39. Thucydides, *A History of the Peloponnesian War*, in Robert B. Strassler, *The Landmark Thucydides: A Comprehensive Guide to the Peloponnesian War* (New York: Free Press, 1996).

40. Tetlock and Belkin, eds., *Counterfactual Thought Experiments in World Politics*.

allow researchers to build in the kinds of controls normally achieved only in a laboratory. They suffer from the obvious drawback: it is generally impossible to know the consequences of variation introduced by the experimenter. This uncertainty increases dramatically when the experimenter considers second- or third-level consequences of the counterfactual. Suppose we postulate that Archduke Franz Ferdinand was not assassinated in June 1914. This counterfactual involves a minimal rewrite of history; if the carriage carrying the archduke and his wife had not made a wrong turn, Prinzip "would not have had an opportunity to shoot the Royals at point-blank range." Deprived of the pretense provided by the assassination, it seems highly unlikely that Austria-Hungary would have presented Serbia with an ultimatum and would have gone to war when it was rejected. World War I would have been averted, at least temporarily. What would have happened next is very hard to say.

The speculative nature of counterfactual thought experiments makes many historians wary of them. But counterfactual analysis does not always have to be as speculative as the longer-term consequences of the survival of Archduke Franz Ferdinand. Deterrence offers a nice counterexample. One of the principal policy "lessons" of the 1930s is that appeasement whets the appetites of dictators whereas military capability and resolve is likely to restrain them. The failure of appeasement in the 1930s is readily apparent, but the putative efficacy of deterrence rests on the counterfactual that Hitler could have been restrained by France and Britain if they had credibly demonstrated their willingness to go to war in defense of the status quo. German documents make this possibility an eminently researchable question, and historians have used these documents to try to determine at what point Hitler was no longer deterrable.[41] Their findings have important implications for any assessment of French and British policy and the broader claims made for deterrence. The Cuban missile crisis is another evidence-rich environment in which to study counterfactuals. Key policy choices—Khrushchev's decision to send and remove missiles from Cuba, and Kennedy's decision to impose a blockade—and subsequent scholarly analyses were both contingent upon hypothetical antecedents. Kennedy believed, incorrectly, that Khrushchev sent missiles because Khrushchev doubted his resolve, and would not have sent them if he had taken a stronger stand at the Bay of Pigs and in Berlin. He reasoned that he had to prevent the installation of the missiles to convince Khrushchev of his resolve and deter a subsequent and more serious challenge to Berlin. Such counterfactuals are revealing

---

41. Yuen Foong Khong, "Confronting Hitler and Its Consequences," in Tetlock and Belkin, eds., *Counterfactual Thought Experiments in World Politics*, pp. 95–118.

in and of themselves; they indicate the underlying assumptions about international relations and adversarial goals that policymakers and scholars brought to the crisis. Recent written and oral evidence from Soviet and U.S. archives and former officials makes it possible to explore the validity of many of these counterfactuals.[42]

Even when counterfactuals are speculative, the difference between them and "normal" history is a matter of degree, not of kind. Documents are rarely "smoking guns" that allow researchers to establish motives or causes beyond a reasonable doubt. Historical argument is usually built on a chain of inference that uses documents or other empirical evidence as anchor points. Other historians evaluate these arguments on the quality and relevance of the evidence, the logic and propriety of the inferences based on it, and the extent to which that evidence permits or constrains alternative interpretations. Evaluation will also be influenced by the appeal of the underlying and generally unstated political and behavioral "principles" in which the inferences are rooted.

Counterfactual thought experiments are fundamentally similar to historical reconstruction. Suppose we attempt to evaluate the importance of Mikhail Gorbachev to the end of the Cold War by considering the likely consequences for Soviet foreign policy of Andropov's survival or Chernenko's replacement by someone other than Gorbachev.[43] To do this, we would study the career and policies of Andropov or an alternative successor to Chernenko (Grishin, Romanov, Ligachev?), and infer their policies on the basis of their past preferences and commitments, the political environment in 1986, and the general domestic and foreign situation of the Soviet Union. There is a lot of documentary evidence relevant to all three questions, evidence that sustains informed arguments about the kind of foreign policies any of these leaders might have pursued. Of course, random events, like Mathias Rust's May 1987 Cessna flight to Red Square, can have significant influence on policy, and these events, by definition, cannot be predicted. In the final analysis, counter-

---

42. Richard Ned Lebow and Janice Gross Stein, "Back to the Past: Counterfactuals and the Cuban Missile Crisis," in Tetlock and Belkin, eds., *Counterfactual Thought Experiments in World Politics*, pp. 119–148.

43. George Breslauer and Richard Ned Lebow, "Leadership and the End of the Cold War," unpublished paper, have conducted such an experiment. We identified other leaders who might have come to power in the Soviet Union, and other responses that the Reagan and Bush administrations might reasonably have had to them—or to Gorbachev—and played out the resulting interactions. We argue that different strategies or tactics by either superpower or their allies might have speeded up, slowed down, altered, or derailed the process of accommodation that let to the Soviet-American entente of 1990–91.

factual arguments, like any other historical argument, are only as compelling as the logic and "evidence" offered by the researcher to substantiate the link between the proposed alteration of history and its expected
consequence.[44]

Oral Evidence

Because many important Chinese and Soviet documents still remain
classified, Western students of Soviet foreign policy are often forced to
rely on the oral testimony of former officials to reconstruct critical decisions. Some scholars question the value of history constructed on the
basis of "hearsay," and contend that oral history is a poor substitute for
written sources and contemporary documents.[45] Oral history is rarely
intended as a substitute for documents, but rather as a supplement.
Discussion with former officials can help identify unknown documents
that may prove critical. It can put known documents in an appropriate
context. Historical accounts based solely on written documents can be as
incomplete and misleading as accounts derived entirely from interviews.

In the past decade, thousands of documents pertinent to the Cuban
missile crisis have been declassified. On the U.S. side, some of these
documents, especially the transcripts of the secret Ex Comm tapes, are of
enormous importance, but they do not reveal that behind the back of his
Ex Comm, President Kennedy engaged in negotiations with Khrushchev,

---

44. In this connection, counterfactual thought experiments should meet seven conditions. They should possess well-specified antecedents, connecting principles and consequences; pass the cotenability test (the hypothetical antecedent should not undercut
any of the principles or events linking it to the consequent); avoid the conjunction
fallacy (the intervening steps in the probabilistic sequence linking antecedent and
consequent should be as few as possible); pass the relevance test (preference should
be given to hypothesized antecedents that seem most likely to alter the fewest consequences in addition to the hypothesized one); pass the minimal rewrite test (preference
should be given to hypothesized antecedents that one can readily defend as feasible
without making major alterations in history); be consistent with the understandings
and principles of behavior that would be appropriate to normal historical analysis;
and consider the implications for the consequent of other changes in history the
hypothesized antecedent would introduce. See Philip E. Tetlock and Aaron Belkin,
"Counterfactual Thought Experiments in World Politics: Logical, Methodological, and
Psychological Perspectives," in Tetlock and Belkin, eds., Counterfactual Thought Experiments in World Politics, pp. 16–31.

45. Mark Kramer, "Remembering the Cuban Missile Crisis: Should We Swallow Oral
History?" International Security, Vol. 15, No. 1 (Summer 1990), pp. 212–216. In a personal communication to the author, November 2, 1999, Kramer insists that his objection was not to oral history per se, but to the uninformed sources used by early
scholars of the missile crisis.

made a secret concession on the Jupiter missiles in Turkey, and was willing to make a further concession if it was necessary to resolve the crisis. All of this information comes from revelations of former Kennedy administration officials. As they tell it, President Kennedy struggled to find the political room to reconcile the competing demands of foreign and domestic policy. He consequently kept some of his actions and decisions secret not only from the public but from many top government officials. He deliberately misled some of his most trusted officials and advisers like Secretary of State Dean Rusk to protect them and himself from subsequent congressional inquiries. A history of U.S. policy in the crisis based solely on documents would be very misleading.[46]

The same is true on the Soviet side. The most recent account of Soviet policy in the crisis, by Aleksandr Fursenko and Timothy Naftali, makes the most extensive use of declassified Soviet documents. Those documents say nothing directly about Khrushchev's motives for sending missiles to Cuba or his reasons for removing them. Nor do they shed new light on other key initiatives of Khrushchev during the crisis including the second, Saturday message that so baffled the President and his Ex Comm.[47] Khrushchev's motives, like Kennedy's, need to be inferred from the context, and from his off-the-record comments to close advisers and others.

Is the missile crisis unique? I think not. Extraordinary secrecy also surrounded the Bay of Pigs invasion. Within the Central Intelligence Agency, the Deputy Director of Intelligence and his directorate were not informed of the operation.[48] Secretary of State Dean Rusk remembers that he was not allowed by the White House to consult the Department's Bureau of Intelligence and Research, and that they almost certainly would have provided him with a critical evaluation. He was also prohibited from discussing the operation with senior officials at the State Department. This secrecy, Rusk insists, "made it very difficult for historians to reconstruct the Bay of Pigs operation, particularly its planning, because very little was put on paper. Dulles, Bissell, and others proposing the operation briefed us orally." The written records do not include the substance of these conversations.[49]

---

46. Garthoff, *Reflections on the Cuban Missile Crisis;* Lebow and Stein, *We All Lost the Cold War;* and Blight, Allyn, and Welch, *Cuba on the Brink.*

47. Aleksandr Fursenko and Timothy Naftali, *One Hell of a Gamble: Khrushchev, Castro, and Kennedy, 1958–1964* (New York: Norton, 1997).

48. Raymond L. Garthoff to Malcolm DeBevoise, May 22, 1991.

49. Dean Rusk as told to Richard Rusk in Daniel S. Papp, ed., *As I Saw It* (New York: Norton, 1990), p. 214.

U.S. policy during the 1973 Middle East war provides another example. None of the imperatives for secrecy at work in Cuba or the Bay of Pigs were present in this case. Even so, the documents, when released, will be misleading. Henry Kissinger frequently had different versions of documents prepared for different audiences and rarely put anything on record from his extensive back channel discussions. Future scholars, Kissinger noted, will have "no criteria for determining which documents were produced to provide an alibi and which genuinely guided decisions."[50] The documentary record is not only misleading but incomplete. As in the missile crisis, the most important decisions grew out of informal unrecorded conversations.

We must remain wary of interpretations of Cold War decisions and policies based largely, or entirely, on the written record. Archival research must be augmented by oral history. Interviews with former officials can help put documents in context, glean insights into the motives of actors, and ferret out secret understandings. In this connection, conferences that bring diverse policymakers together and encourage interaction among them are especially helpful. Experience indicates that these conferences are most likely to be productive when discussion is guided by relevant documents that are made available beforehand to all the participants. The documents can be used to refresh the memories of the participants and focus their attention on interpretative controversies or empirical lacunae surrounding critical decisions.

History and Social Science

My arguments have borrowed heavily from neopositivist epistemology. I have not spoken of prediction—the holy grail of neopositivism—because I think predictive theories are impossible in international relations and most other domains of social inquiry. I believed that explanation—identification of the causal mechanisms responsible for given outcomes—is a more realistic goal, and one to which many historians aspire. Studies of the Cold War that seek to explain its origins, dynamics, evolution, termination, or relationship to other conflicts indicate this commitment. Many of these studies reflect a "soft" positivist epistemology, and can accordingly be evaluated in terms of neopositivist protocols for hypothesis construction and testing.

Positivism, in both its "hard" and "soft" formulations, assumes that reality has an objective existence that is outside and independent of the

---

50. Cited by Walter Isaacson, *Kissinger: A Biography* (New York: Simon & Schuster, 1992), p. 827.

language and conceptual categories used to describe and analyze it. This assumption, and positivism more generally, has come under increasing attack in the social sciences. The principal alternative in international relations theory, "constructivism," is very much in the interpretivist tradition. Like other interpretivist approaches, it assumes that reason and irrationality are constitutive of actors and the societies in which they are embedded. Constructivists emphasize the intersubjective understandings actors have of themselves, other actors, and their relationships with these actors. Constructivist research suggests that categories of analysis used by international relations scholars often bear little relationship to the categories actors themselves use to frame problems, evaluate their interests, make policy, and draw lessons.[51]

For interpretivists, empathetic understanding from inside (*verstehen*), not explanation (*erklären*), is the goal of scholarly inquiry. The purpose of scholarship is to help us understand our lives, individually and collectively. History is a repository of human experience that each generation examines anew from the perspective of its own experience and concerns. There is not one correct way of framing or analyzing a problem, but multiple interpretations that generate different and often equally valuable insights. Interpretivist scholarship also aspires to high professional standards. It can be evaluated by the quality of its narrative. Does it provide a coherent explanation that makes sense of the empirical evidence in terms of the subjective understandings relevant actors have of this evidence, themselves, and the social context in which they operate? Other accounts may also "fit" the evidence, and competing accounts should be evaluated on the basis of their "generative" properties. Do they highlight and draw attention to hitherto unknown or neglected processes, turning points, and collective understandings that raise interesting research questions? An interpretivist research agenda may succeed in redefining in fundamental ways our conception of the Cold War.

Neopositivist and interpretivist epistemologies are both relevant to the study of the Cold War. On the whole, neopositivism is most appropriate to the "smaller" questions—those internal to the phenomenon under study. For the Cold War, these would include its origins, dynamics, and outcome. Historical analyses of such questions typically aim at "explanation," and mobilize evidence to document and justify their argu-

---

51. Robert Jervis, Richard Ned Lebow, and Janice Gross Stein, *Psychology and Deterrence* (Baltimore: Johns Hopkins University Press, 1985); "Beyond Deterrence," ed., George Levinger, also a special issue of the *Journal of Social Issues*, Vol. 43, no. 4 (1987);] Paul C. Stern, Robert Axelrod, Robert Jervis, and Roy Radner, eds., *Perspectives on Deterrence* (New York: Oxford University Press, 1989); and "The Rational Deterrence Debate: A Symposium," *World Politics*, Vol. 41 (January 1989), pp. 143–266.

ments. At least implicitly, their authors acknowledge that their arguments can be rejected if better and contradictory evidence emerges or if more persuasive interpretations are put forward. Theoretical work in international relations on these questions has been overwhelmingly neopositivist in orientation, although there is a growing corpus of interpretivist research that examines such questions as the emergence of norms of non-use of nuclear, biological, and chemical weapons, the roots of Gorbachev's foreign policy revolution, and the transformation of the conflictual Soviet-U.S. relationship into a more cooperative Russo-U.S. one.[52]

The interpretivist perspective is most appropriate to "bigger" questions that attempt to understand a phenomenon in a broader, external context. Such interpretations also rely on evidence, but do not rely on it to persuade. Evidence is more often used to illustrate the value of a particular frame of reference for providing insights and understanding. In history, interpretative research has always been common, and presumably, more interpretative studies of the Cold War will appear as that phenomenon has itself become history.

The ongoing epistemological debate in international relations theory has important implications for the relationship between international relations and history. For most of the Cold War, the international relations literature was realist and neopositivist, while Cold War history ran the gamut from interpretivist to neopositivist. These epistemological differences made dialogue difficult; the only real conversations were between realists in both disciplines, and between diplomatic historians and the small community of interpretivist political scientists who used primary historical sources to reconstruct events from the perspectives of the actors involved. Jack Levy argues that the prospect for dialogue is diminishing because of the "revival of narrative" and the "linguistic turn" in history, and the further spread of quantitative methods and game theory in international relations.[53] This is an unduly pessimistic view. If interpretivism makes more headway in political science, and if historians become self-conscious and sophisticated in their research strategies, we might move closer together and transcend our disciplinary cold war.

---

52.   See, for example, Martha Finnemore, *National Interests in International Society* (Ithaca: Cornell University Press, 1996); Richard Price, "A Genealogy of the Chemical Weapons Taboo" (Ph.D. dissertation, Cornell University, 1994); Herman, "Identity, Norms and National Security;" Addie Klutz, *Norms in International Relations: The Struggle Against Apartheid* (Ithaca: Cornell University Press, 1995); and Karin Fierke, *Changing Games, Changing Strategies: Critical Investigations in Security* (Manchester: University of Manchester Press, forthcoming).

53.   Levy, "Too Important to Leave to the Other," p. 23.

Chapter 4

Case Studies and Process Tracing in History and Political Science: Similar Strokes for Different Foci

Andrew Bennett and
Alexander L. George

$\mathbf{A}$ central theme in this volume is that the disciplines of political science and history must address schools of thought that question the value of theorizing upon historical events and studying individual cases. Postmodernists in both disciplines have critiqued positivist methods, arguing that language is so inherently open to multiple interpretations that cumulative theorizing on the basis of empirical evidence is unproductive. Meanwhile, some of the researchers using formal models and statistical methods have argued that satisfactory explanations need not empirically verify intervening causal mechanisms or processes in individual cases, or that studying single cases contributes little to theory development.

As a result of these challenges, case study researchers in history and political science have more in common with one another than they do with some schools of thought within their own disciplines. In particular, case study researchers share the conviction that the use of process tracing to study hypothesized causal mechanisms in individual cases is an important means of developing and testing historical and theoretical explanations. In this chapter we address the methodological challenges this shared commitment raises for case study researchers in history and political science, while also clarifying how researchers in the two fields differ in their use of case study methods in accordance with their different explanatory goals. We agree here with Jack Levy's assertion in this volume that the most salient distinction is that historians are more interested in explaining particular historical cases while political scientists place more emphasis on establishing generalizable causal patterns across cases or categories of cases.

We also address a related difference between political scientists and historians, specifically, political scientists' relatively higher concern for theoretical parsimony and historians' preference for descriptive richness. Tradeoffs between parsimonious models and explanatory richness involve both aesthetic decisions about what type of theory is most useful for given purposes and theoretical assumptions about which social phenomena exhibit causal relations that are simple, complex, or enigmatic. We argue that many social phenomena are characterized by complex causality, particularly equifinality (that is, the fact that the same outcome can arise through different causal paths in which there may be no single nontrivial necessary or sufficient condition). Building on our discussion of causal mechanisms, we suggest that complex causal relations like equifinality are best captured by what we call "typological theory." In contrast to the "covering law" conception of general theories, typological theories involve contingent generalizations that explicitly outline the differing background conditions under which the same value of an independent variable can have different effects (multifinality), or different mixes of variables can have the same effect (equifinality). Historians should find typological theory to be consistent with their own views of social relations as complex, path dependent, and contingent, even if typological theories are less rich than many historians would like.

This chapter first looks at the role of causal mechanisms in social science theorizing and historical explanation. It then discusses different uses of process tracing and points out its similarities to historical explanation, while noting the differences in how historians and political scientists use process tracing. Next, the chapter argues that in single case study research designs, process tracing can contribute to theory development even though political scientists usually prefer comparative case study designs. This is followed by a discussion of different types of causal relations, which we term "simple," "complex," and "enigmatic." The chapter then outlines the concept of typological theories, and it concludes with a brief illustration of how process tracing and typological theorizing might be applied to some of the issues of military innovation that John Lynn discusses in this volume. Many historians and political scientists are already aware that process tracing occupies a useful *methodological* middle ground between the two disciplines and among statistical studies, formal models, and postmodern narratives; we conclude that typological theories constitute a *theoretical* middle ground between parsimonious general theories and rich explanations based on specific sequences of causal mechanisms in individual cases.

Causal Mechanisms in Historical and Social Explanation

Efforts by postmodernists and some rational choice theorists to downplay the role of causal mechanisms have arisen, ironically, at the same time that a growing number of social scientists and philosophers of science have given causal mechanisms a central place in causal explanation.[1] Those who emphasize the explanatory role of causal mechanisms may be grouped loosely together as "scientific realists."

Despite growing agreement that causal mechanisms play an important role in causal explanation, agreement is lacking on an exact definition of a "causal mechanism." There is consensus that "causal mechanism" refers to an intervening connection between independent variables and dependent variables. There is also considerable agreement that an adequate explanation—and, by extension, an adequate theory—is not provided merely by correlational findings or laws, and that the identification, specification, or hypothesizing of a causal mechanism is also needed. For example, though readings on a barometer are correlated with the weather and even help predict it, the barometer does not explain the weather. Rather, air pressure, working through various causal mechanisms, helps explain changes in the weather and those in barometer readings as well as the correlation between the two. There is also substantial agreement that causal mechanisms operate within a given context or "causal field," and their effects depend on interactions with other variables. To capture these points of consensus without going beyond them, we define a causal mechanism as a component of a causal process that intervenes between agents with causal capacities and outcomes.[2] Causal mechanisms involve physical, social, or psychological processes that ultimately cannot be directly observed. We can only hypothesize about underlying causal mechanisms and make imperfect inferences about them on the basis of observed data. In the above example, air pressure has the causal capacity to affect both weather patterns and barometer readings, in combination

---

1. Philosophers of science and social science methodologists have given increasing emphasis in the past two decades to causal mechanisms. See David Dessler, "Beyond Correlations: Toward a Causal Theory of War," *International Studies Quarterly*, Vol. 35 (1991), pp. 337–355; Jon Elster, *Nuts and Bolts for the Social Sciences* (New York: Cambridge University Press, 1989); Daniel Little, *Microfoundations, Method, and Causation* (New Brunswick, N.J.: Transaction Publishers, 1998); Margaret Mooney Marini and Burton Singer, "Causality in the Social Sciences," in Clifford C. Clogg, ed., *Sociological Methodology* (Washington, D.C.: American Sociological Association, 1988); Wesley C. Salmon, *Four Decades of Scientific Explanation* (Minneapolis: University of Minnesota Press, 1990); Andrew Sayer, *Method in the Social Sciences: A Realist Approach* (London: Routledge, 1992); and Albert S. Yee, "The Causal Effect of Ideas on Policies," *International Organization*, Vol. 50, No. 1 (Winter 1996), pp. 69–108.

2. We rely on the counterfactual definition of causation here: a variable X is causally related to a variable Y in a given background context if a change in the value of X in that context would have changed the value of Y.

with air temperature, humidity, and other variables and through causal mechanisms involving thermodynamic processes.[3]

Several additional questions can be raised about causal mechanisms; here we attempt to clarify but not necessarily resolve them. Is a causal mechanism the smallest observable link between the value of one variable and that of another? In our view, while causal mechanisms do indeed reflect causal processes, the formulation of hypotheses about a particular causal mechanism is a theory-building choice made by the investigator, and this choice is influenced by the state of knowledge about the causal process that is operating as well as by the available instruments for observation and measurement. In our weather example, one generation of researchers might focus on Newtonian processes, while later researchers may push farther into relativistic processes at the atomic or even subatomic level.

A related question concerns whether macro-social causal mechanisms, such as macro-economic models, can be usefully posited. We maintain that they can, with the caveat that they must be based, at least in principle, on micro-causal mechanisms that explain individual behavior. Not all macro-causal mechanisms are of a character that makes it necessary in every study to explain or study them at the individual level, and the acceptable level of generality of causal mechanisms will vary depending on the particular research question and research objectives under investigation.[4] In contrast to those who argue that individuals need only behave *as if* the macro theory is true, however, we argue that the micro-level behavior or decision processes of individuals should also be studied and that if they are at odds with the mechanism posited by a macro-level theory, this anomaly requires explanation. For example, the finding that individuals behave according to psychological heuristics different from the profit-maximizing assumptions of some economic theories has led to modifications of these economic theories.

Causal mechanisms are more general than the specific causal processes evident in a particular case. At the same time, causal mechanisms can be usefully regarded as providing more detailed and in a sense more fundamental explanations than a general explanation for a particular phenomenon. Jon Elster's notes in this context that:

---

3. David Dessler, "Beyond Correlations," pp. 342–346.

4. Daniel Little is among those who argue that all macro-social causal mechanisms have to operate through the micro-social level of individual behavior. Little, *Microfoundations*, p. 198.

the scientific practice is to seek explanation at a lower level than the explanandum. If we want to understand the pathology of the liver, we look to cellular biology for explanation. To explain is to provide a causal mechanism, to open up the black box and show the nuts and bolts. . . . The role of mechanisms is two-fold. First, they enable us to go from the larger to the smaller: from molecules to atoms, from societies to individuals. Secondly, and more fundamentally, they reduce the time lag between the explanans and explanandum. A mechanism provides a continuous and contiguous chain of causal or intentional links. . . . The success of the reduction is constrained by the extent to which macro-variables are simultaneously replaced by micro-variables. . . . The search for micro-foundations is in reality a pervasive and omnipresent feature of science.[5]

Postmodernists, some rational choice theorists, and some statistical theorists have challenged the growing consensus on the role of causal mechanisms in causal explanation. Postmodernists question the validity of the entire positivist enterprise of using data to derive and test causal social theories. Rational choice theorists who downplay the role of causal mechanisms make the *as if* argument, critiqued above, that it is necessary only that individuals act *as if* they make decisions based on a rational choice calculation, not that they actually do so. Christopher Achen and Duncan Snidal, for example, argue that "rational deterrence [theory] is agnostic about the actual calculations that decision makers undertake. It holds that they will act as if they solved certain mathematical problems, whether or not they actually solve them."[6] Notably, some rational choice theorists have eschewed such "as if" assumptions.[7] In *Analytic Narratives*, prominent rational choice theorists Robert H. Bates, Barry R. Weingast,

---

5. Jon Elster, *Explaining Technical Change: A Case Study in the Philosophy of Science* (Cambridge: Cambridge University Press, 1983), pp. 23–24.

6. Christopher Achen and Duncan Snidal, "Rational Deterrence Theory and Comparative Case Studies," *World Politics*, Vol. 41, No. 2 (January 1989), p. 164. For a similar formulation, see John Ferejohn and Deborah Satz, "Unification, Universalism and Rational Choice Theory," *Critical Review*, Vol. 9, Nos. 1–2 (Winter–Spring 1995), pp. 74, 83 n. 3. For a critique of such "as if" assumptions that is similar to our own, see Colin Elman and Miriam Fendius Elman, "Diplomatic History and International Relations Theory: Respecting Difference and Crossing Boundaries," *International Security*, Vol. 22, No. 1 (Summer 1997), p. 18.

7. For example, Bruce Bueno de Mesquita argued at one point that "I do not suggest that decision-makers *consciously* make the calculations of the expected utility model. Rather, I argue that the leaders act *as if* they do" (cited in James Lee Ray, *Democracies and International Conflict: An Evaluation of the Democratic Peace Proposition* (Columbia: University of South Carolina Press, 1995), p. 134). Bueno de Mesquita rightly makes a considerable effort in his later work, however, to show that decision-makers actually

Avner Greif, Margaret Levi, and Jean-Laurent Rosenthal present an approach to integrating rational choice theories with case narratives using process tracing.[8] We concur with these authors that process tracing and case studies are compatible with rational choice approaches—the former constitute methods that can assess the theoretical claims of the latter. Similarly, case study methods can be and have been used to develop and test the theoretical hypotheses built from the deductive frameworks of game theory.

Gary King, Robert Keohane, and Sidney Verba have posed a different challenge to the role of causal mechanisms. In their work on scientific inference, these authors focus on the role of "causal effects" in causal explanation and they subtly downplay the role of causal mechanisms. To simplify a bit, these authors define causal effect as the change in the expected value of the outcome variable brought about by a specified change in the value of an independent variable. In other words, they argue, if we could run a perfect experiment in which the value of only one causal independent variable changes, the causal effect is the corresponding change in the dependent variable. These authors argue that the definition of causal effect is "logically prior to the identification of causal mechanisms . . . we can define a causal effect without understanding all of the causal mechanisms involved, but we cannot identify causal mechanisms without defining the concept of causal effect . . . we should not confuse a definition of causality with the nondefinitional, albeit often useful, operational procedure of identifying causal mechanisms."[9] The problem with this view is that it risks conflating the "definition of causality," and hence that of causal explanation, with the definition of "causal

go through rational types of calculations. See, for example, Bruce Bueno de Mesquita and David Lalman, *War and Reason: Domestic and International Imperatives* (New Haven: Yale University Press, 1992).

8. Robert H. Bates, Avner Greif, Margaret Levi, Jean-Laurent Rosenthal, and Barry R. Weingast, *Analytical Narratives* (Princeton: Princeton University Press, 1998), p. 13. As our emphasis on theory-building and testing in the present article suggests, we disagree with these authors' argument (pp. 13, 14, 16, 17) that our version of process tracing places less emphasis on theory development and testing than the approach in *Analytic Narratives*. For other examples that combine elements of rational choice theory with case studies and process tracing to develop explanations of complex events, see Jack S. Levy, "The Role of Crisis Management in the Outbreak of World War I," in Alexander L. George, ed., *Avoiding War: Problems of Crisis Management* (Boulder, Colo: Westview, 1991), pp. 62–102; and Brent Sterling, "Policy Choice During Limited War" (Ph.D. dissertation, Georgetown University, Washington, D.C., 1998).

9. Robert Keohane, Gary King, and Sidney Verba, *Designing Social Inquiry: Scientific Inference in Qualitative Research* (Princeton: Princeton University Press, 1994), p. 86. For their more technical definition of a causal effect, see pp. 81–82.

effect." This misses the key point that causal effects and causal mechanisms are equally necessary components of explanatory causal theories. True, we cannot posit a causal mechanism that has no effect, but neither can we theorize about a causal effect that has no underlying mechanism. Consequently, a growing number of social scientists and philosophers have placed equal weight on both causal mechanisms and causal effects as components of scientific explanation and sources of causal inferences. For example, Wesley Salmon, one of the pioneers in probabilistic notions of causality in the 1960s, surveyed three prominent theories of probabilistic causality in the late 1980s. He writes that "the primary moral I drew was that causal concepts cannot be fully explicated in terms of statistical relationships; in addition, I concluded, we need to appeal to causal processes and causal interactions."[10]

Moreover, the comparisons King, Keohane, and Verba make among ontological definitions and operational procedures are misleading. Statistical tests and controlled case study comparisons are operational procedures for estimating causal effects, which cannot be observed directly because we cannot run perfect experiments. Similarly, among its other uses process tracing is an operational procedure for attempting to identify causal mechanisms. It makes no sense to compare ontological entities like causal effects and causal mechanisms to the methodological procedures used for estimating them. Nor does it make sense to argue that causal effects are "definitionally prior" to causal mechanisms. Giving priority to causal effects, as King, Keohane, and Verba suggest, would unjustifiably privilege the statistical methods that are superior at estimating such effects. Conversely, giving priority to causal mechanisms would unjustifiably privilege the case study method of process tracing. Albert Yee has made this mistake, equal and opposite to that made by King, Keohane and Verba, by arguing that causal mechanisms are "ontologically prior" to causal effects because one cannot have a causal effect in the absence of an underlying causal mechanism.[11] Rather than arguing over the "definitional" or "ontological" priority of effects or mechanisms, it is essential to recognize that both are central to causal explanation. Hence, statistical methods, best suited to estimating effects, and case study methods, best adapted to exploring mechanisms, are essential and complementary sources of causal inference.[12]

---

10. Salmon, *Four Decades of Scientific Explanation*, p. 168.

11. Albert Yee, "The Causal Effects of Ideas," p. 84.

12. For an illustration of how case studies and statistical studies contribute complementary kinds of knowledge to a research program, see Andrew Bennett and Alexander L. George, "An Alliance of Statistical and Case Study Methods: Research on the

Process Tracing and Historical Explanation

Process tracing is the attempt to trace empirically the temporal and possibly causal sequences of events within a case that intervene between independent variables and observed outcomes. Several uses of process tracing can be distinguished.[13] Process tracing can help identify a specific causal process that may explain an instance of a particular phenomenon. It can also inductively identify general causal mechanisms that may be at work in other cases,[14] and it can test whether a given causal mechanism is at work in a particular case.

Process tracing is not a panacea for theory testing or theory development: its requirements are often difficult to meet and it has inherent limitations. However, it has many advantages for theory development and theory testing, some of them unique. It can identify paths to an outcome, point out variables that were left out in the initial comparison of cases, check for spuriousness, and permit causal inference on the basis of a few cases or even a single case. It can thus contribute in ways that statistical methods can do only with great difficulty, and it is often worthwhile even when sufficient cases exist for the concurrent use of statistical methods. Notably, Christopher Achen and Duncan Snidal, in an article criticizing how case studies have been used in practice, acknowledged that:

we emphatically believe they are essential to the development and testing of social science theory. . . . In international relations, only case studies provide the intensive empirical analysis that can find previously unnoticed causal factors and historical patterns. . . . The analyst is able to identify plausible causal variables, a task essential to theory construction and testing. . . . indeed, analytic theory cannot do without case studies. Because they are simultaneously sensitive to data and theory, case studies are more useful for these purposes than any other methodological tool.[15]

Interdemocratic Peace," *Newsletter of the APSA Organized Section in Comparative Politics*, Vol. 9, No. 1 (Winter 1998), pp. 6–9. A more detailed analysis of this issue will appear as a chapter in Alexander L. George and Andrew Bennett, *Case Studies and Theory Development* (Cambridge, Mass.: MIT Press, forthcoming).

13. Little, *Microfoundations*, p. 211.

14. This proposition is rejected by some rational choice theorists. Edgar Kiser and Michael Hechler, for example, argue that causal mechanisms cannot be derived inductively, but only from general theories. Kiser and Hechler, "The Role of General Theory in Comparative Historical Sociology," *American Journal of Sociology*, Vol. 97, No. 1 (July 1991), pp. 4, 6, 23, 24.

15. Achen and Snidal, "Rational Deterrence Theory," pp. 167–168.

While process tracing shares some of the basic features of historical explanation, historians and political scientists differ in the types and uses of process tracing that they emphasize because historians are most interested in explaining particular cases and political scientists seek to develop and test generalizable theories that explain categories of cases or phenomena.[16] Harry Eckstein and Arend Lijphart have offered typologies of case studies; their terminology differs but the types they identify are similar, although Lijphart adds a quite important type, the "deviant case":[17]

Lijphart	Eckstein
1) atheoretical case study	configurative-ideogrpahic case study
2) interpretative case study	disciplined-configurative case study
3) hypothesis-generating case study	heuristic case study
4) deviant case study	
5) theory-confirming or infirming case study	crucial, most-likely, least likely test cases

Historians' work usually falls into the first and second categories, mostly the latter, whereas most work by political scientists fits into the second, third, fourth, or fifth categories. Below, we discuss each of these kinds of case study, and the corresponding use of process tracing by historians and political scientists.

HISTORIANS' USE OF PROCESS TRACING IN HISTORICAL EXPLANATION

The simplest type of case study and process tracing, which Lijphart terms "atheoretical" and Eckstein labels configurative-ideographic, takes the form of a detailed narrative that purports to illuminate how an event came about. Such a narrative is highly specific and makes no explicit use of theory or theory-related variables. It may be supportable to some extent by explanatory theories, but these remain tacit.

---

16. We disagree here with Edward Ingram's argument that the distinction "between the political scientist's interest in generally applicable propositions and the historian's interest in particular instances" is "false," although this distinction is at times oversimplified and overstated. Edward Ingram, "The Wonderland of the Political Scientist," *International Security*, Vol. 22, No. 1 (Summer 1997), p. 53.

17. Harry Eckstein, "Case Study and Theory in Political Science," in F.I. Greenstein and N.W. Polsby, eds., *Handbook of Political Science* (Reading, Mass: Addison-Wesley, 1973), Vol. 7, pp. 79–138; and Arend Lijphart, "Comparative Politics and the Comparative Method," *American Political Science Review*, Vol. 65, No. 3 (September 1971), pp. 682–693. Eckstein also includes one type that Lijphart does not, the use of a "plausibility probe" case study that assesses the initial plausibility of a new theory before committing greater resources to its full study.

Most historical studies, however, do have an explanatory purpose and draw upon implicit theories to explain cases, even if they also maintain that the causal explanations underlying particular cases are unique. These studies generally fall into the category of "disciplined-configurative" or "interpretive" case studies, in which general propositions are used, often implicitly, to explain specific historical cases. Historians who implicitly or explicitly use theories on several levels of analysis—systemic, state, organizational, individual—to attempt comprehensive explanations of historical cases include John Lewis Gaddis, James Joll, Paul Kennedy, Paul Schroeder, Marc Trachtenberg, Barbara Tuchman, and many others.[18]

These historians' methods are insightfully articulated in Clayton Roberts's *The Logic of Historical Explanation*.[19] Roberts argues that each step or link in a causal process or historical explanation should be supported by an appropriate "law," defined by Carl Hempel as a statement of a regularity between a set of events. Roberts distinguishes, however, between universalistic and probabilistic laws. While the Hempelian "covering law" model is deductive in form, it is clear that no explanation using probabilistic laws can be strictly deductive. Since, as Ernest Nagel has observed, the covering law model cannot explain "collective events that are appreciably complex,"[20] Roberts argues that "historians rarely seek to explain the occurrence of a complex event by subsuming it solely under a covering law," a process he calls "macrocorrelation." In his view the few historians who have attempted macrocorrelation "have met with little success."[21] Instead, Roberts argues, historians explain their findings "by tracing the sequence of events that brought them about" and justifying each step as causal through reference to micro-level "laws."[22] Roberts terms this practice "microcorrelation," and argues that it involves "the

---

18. A few of these historians' many relevant works include John Lewis Gaddis, *We Now Know: Rethinking Cold War History* (New York: Oxford University Press, 1997); James Joll, *The Origins of the First World War* (New York: Longman, 1992); Paul Kennedy, *The Rise and Fall of the Great Powers: Economic Change and Military Conflict from 1500 to 2000* (New York: Vintage, 1989); Paul W. Schroeder, *The Transformation of European Politics, 1763–1848* (New York: Oxford University Press, 1994); Marc Trachtenberg, *A Constructed Peace: The Making of the European Settlement, 1945–1963* (Princeton: Princeton University Press, 1999); and Barbara Tuchman, *The Guns of August* (New York: Ballantine, 1994).

19. Clayton Roberts, *The Logic of Historical Explanation* (University Park: Pennsylvania State University Press, 1996).

20. Ernst Nagel, *The Structure of Science*, p. 574.

21. Roberts, *Logic of Historical Explanation*, pp. 9, 15.

22. Ibid., p. 16.

minute tracing of the explanatory narrative to the point where the events to be explained are microscopic and the covering laws correspondingly more certain."[23] At this microcausal level, "covering laws" begin to merge with "causal mechanisms" as we have defined them.

Accordingly, Roberts joins with the scientific realists in arguing that laws embody "regularities" and "correlations" but do not constitute adequate explanations. A mere statement of a correlation, such as that between smoking and cancer, may have some explanatory power but it is incomplete and unsatisfactory unless the causal relation or connection between the two terms is specified.[24] Since a correlation does not by itself constitute a causal explanation, Roberts asserts that efforts to explain complex events solely by invoking a covering law are insupportable as they forego the necessary process tracing.

Roberts rejects the widespread belief that historians do not make use of covering laws. He attributes this misconception to the fact that the laws historians employ are both "parochial" and implicit in their historical narratives. At the same time, Roberts recognizes that "the more microscopic the event to be explained, the more likely that the covering law will be a platitude . . . or a truism,"[25] and he consequently argues that to continually list them and assert their validity "would hopelessly clog the narrative."

POLITICAL SCIENTISTS' USE OF PROCESS TRACING IN DEVELOPING AND TESTING THEORIES

While political scientists also perform disciplined-configurative case studies, there is an important difference in emphasis. Roberts recognizes that historians have an obligation to make sure that the implicit covering laws they employ are true, but he does not address the question of how this is done, contenting himself with the observation that "reviewers and perceptive readers can readily tell the difference between histories based on sound covering laws and those that are naive and superficial." He adds that historians will occasionally make their supportive generalizations explicit, particularly when a controversy arises among historians

---

23. Ibid., p. 66. Roberts notes (p. 20) that a number of earlier writers have made the same point, referring to process tracing, variously, as "a genetic explanation" (Ernest Nagel), "a sequential explanation" (Louis Mink), "the model of the continuous series" (William Dray), "a chain of causal explanations" (Michael Scriven), "narrative explanations" (R.F. Atkinson), and "the structure of a narrative explanation" (Arthur Danto).

24. Ibid., p. 24.

25. Ibid., pp. 66–67.

over the truth of an explanation.[26] In theory-based process tracing, on the other hand, it is not desirable to rest explanations on implicit laws, which is why political science narratives are indeed "hopelessly clogged" with explicit theories.

Political scientists employ process tracing not only to explain specific cases but also to test and refine theories, to develop new theories, and to produce generic knowledge of a given phenomenon.[27] Such process tracing, which converts a historical narrative into an *analytical* causal explanation couched in explicit theoretical forms, is substantially different from historical explanation.

Sometimes political scientists do not construct a detailed tracing of a causal process in a case but instead seek a more general explanation. The investigator may resort to this either because the data or the theories necessary for a detailed explanation are lacking or because an explanation couched at a higher level of generality is the research objective. A decision to seek a more general explanation is consistent with the familiar practice in political science research of "moving up" the ladder of abstraction.[28]

Political scientists often use single or comparative case studies to help build new theories or test existing theories, purposes that historians pursue far less frequently. Many current theories in international relations, comparative politics, and U.S. politics do not specify in detail the causal process that leads from the independent variables to the variance in the outcomes.[29] Such underdeveloped theories cannot generate predictions or state expectations as to what should be observed regarding this

---

26. Ibid., pp. 87–88.

27. Roberts similarly notes that whereas history often limits itself to searching for the cause of a single event, "the purpose of science is to discover the laws governing the behavior of a phenomenon . . . to explain why a law exists, why a correlation occurs, one needs a theory," one which contains "a model that shows how the system works, the system that gives rise to the uniformities observed." Ibid., pp. 145–159.

28. See Giovanni Sartori, "Concept Misinformation in Comparative Politics," *American Political Science Review*, Vol. 64 (December 1970), pp. 1033–1053; and David Collier and Steven Levitsky, "Democracy With Adjectives: Concept Innovation in Comparative Research," *World Politics*, Vol. 49, No. 3 (April 1997), pp. 430–451.

29. Theories can be tested in two different ways. First, one can assess the ability of a theory to predict outcomes. This relates to the "congruence method" in case studies. See Alexander L. George, "The Role of the Congruence Method for Case Study Research," paper presented at the International Studies Association Convention in Toronto, March 18–22, 1997. This paper is available at http://www.georgetown. edu/bennett and a revised version will appear in George and Bennett, *Case Studies and Theory Development.* Second, one can assess the ability of a theory to predict the intervening causal process that leads to observed outcomes, which is the focus of the present chapter.

process in order to test the theory.[30] This is true, for example, of the first generation of studies on the democratic peace thesis, which rests on the results of correlational studies that seem to indicate that "democratic states" do not fight each other or seldom do so. While researchers offered several possible explanations for this phenomenon in the 1970s and 1980s, it was primarily in the 1990s that researchers began to specify the hypothesized causal processes in sufficient detail to permit them to be tested through process tracing of individual cases.[31]

The "heuristic" use of process tracing to develop and refine theories that are too general to generate testable predictions need not degenerate into an atheoretical enterprise. When a researcher uncovers a potential causal path not anticipated by any preexisting theory, there are several possible approaches for converting this finding into an analytical result couched in terms of theoretical variables. For example, the deductive logic or study of other cases may suggest a generalizable theory that includes the novel causal path. If so, it may be possible to specify and operationalize that new theory and test it against other cases, or even against new and conceptually independent process tracing evidence in the same case that gave rise to the theory.[32] Still another possibility is that upon further reflection the novel causal path will be identified as an exemplar of an existing theory which the investigator had overlooked or

---

30. For critiques of the frequent failure of theories of war to specify intervening causal mechanisms, see David Dessler, "Beyond Correlations," pp. 337–355; and Jack Levy, " The Causes of War: A Review of Theories and Evidence," in Philip E. Tetlock, Jo L. Husbands, Robert Jervis, Paul C. Stern, and Charles Tilly, eds., *Behavior, Society, and Nuclear War*, vol. 1 (New York: Oxford University Press, 1989) pp. 209–333.

31. For a recent review of this literature, see Miriam Fendius Elman, ed., *Paths to Peace: Is Democracy the Answer?* (Cambridge. Mass.: MIT Press, 1997), pp. 1–57 and 473–506. See also Bennett and George, "An Alliance of Statistical and Case Study Methods," pp. 6–9.

32. It is commonly asserted that a new theory cannot be tested against the same case that gave rise to it. If the evidence that suggested the theory is conceptually independent of other process tracing evidence in the case, however, this new process tracing evidence can test the theory. For example, when researchers looking at brain chemistry proposed a chemical mechanism that might help explain schizophrenia, they unexpectedly found that this same chemical mechanism was involved in the brain's reaction to the inhalation of cigarette smoke. The proposed mechanism thus also might explain the long-noticed but neglected fact that schizophrenics tend to be chain-smokers. As the researchers were not looking for or expecting an explanation of schizophrenics' chain-smoking, this finding is a relatively independent confirmation. See Denise Grady, "Brain-Tied Gene Defect May Explain Why Schizophrenics Hear Voices," *New York Times*, January 21, 1997, p. C-3. Although this study involved many schizophrenics, the logic of this kind of confirmation does not derive from sample size and it applies in single cases of the kind that historians often investigate.

thought irrelevant. The newly identified causal process may then contribute to the evaluation of the existing theory. Finally, of course, the novel causal path may remain ungeneralizable and unconnected to a useful theory pending additional research or deductive theorizing.

A particularly important type of case study for the development of new theories and testing of existing theories is the "deviant" case study. This is the study of cases whose outcomes are not predicted or explained adequately by existing theories. Deviant cases are frequently encountered in statistical studies and too often researchers in such studies make no effort to explain why they are "deviant," thus missing an opportunity to differentiate and enrich the general theory. Process tracing offers just such an opportunity. Witness, for example, the exemplary study of the International Typographical Union (ITU) by S.M. Lipset, Martin Trow, and James S. Coleman. They noted that the record of the ITU contradicted the "iron law of oligarchy" advanced by Robert Michels in his classic study, *Political Parties,* which argued that inherent in any large-scale social organization were motivations and means that led leaders of its bureaucratic structure to place the protection and exercise of their position ahead of a commitment to democratic internal procedures. Contradicting the generalization, the ITU governed itself through an elaborate and largely effective democratic system. The ITU, as Lipset later wrote, was an example of what Paul Lazerfeld referred to as a "deviant case." The authors' study of the ITU investigated whether there were new or specific factors present that explained the union's departure from the "iron law of oligarchy." A historical-structural study of the ITU employing survey research data and making some use of process tracing uncovered causal mechanisms and social-psychological processes that provided an explanation for the special character of the union.[33]

If a theory is sufficiently developed so that it generates predictions about causal processes that lead to outcomes, then—and only then—can process tracing test the predictions of the theory. The value of a case for

---

33. S.M. Lipset, Martin Trow, and James S. Coleman, *Union Democracy* (Glencoe, Ill.: The Free Press, 1956). Lipset provided a fascinating account of the origins and development of the study in "The Biography of a Research Project: Union Democracy," in Philip E. Hammond, ed., *Sociologists at Work* (New York: Doubleday Anchor Books, 1967), pp. 111–139. Stephen Van Evera emphasizes the importance of studying deviant cases, which he refers to as "outlier" cases, for theory development. Stephen Van Evera, *Guide to Methods for Students of Political Science* (Ithaca: Cornell University Press, 1997), pp. 22–23, 69.

The issue of deviant cases points to a difference in case selection criteria between historians and political scientists. Historians tend to focus on cases that are "important" in terms of their effects on subsequent history. In contrast, political scientists often focus on cases that are "important" in terms of their potential for developing

theory-testing depends on the strength and uniqueness of the process tracing predictions that alternative theories make regarding the case. If a theory makes a clear and strong prediction in a case, or the case is one in which the theory is "most likely" to hold true if the theory is true anywhere, and if the alternative theories make the same prediction, then the theory will be strongly impugned if the prediction does not prove true. The failure of the theory cannot be blamed on the influence of the variables highlighted by the alternative theories. Conversely, if a theory confronts a case in which it is "least likely" to hold true and the alternative theories make a different prediction, but the first theory's weak prediction proves true, this is the strongest possible evidence in favor of the theory. Usually, cases do not offer such decisive tests, but it is still worthwhile to note the strength of the findings of a case study.[34]

Although political scientists make more use than historians of process tracing for purposes of theory development and testing, historians at times also use process tracing for these goals. Historians with detailed knowledge of particular eras, events, or regions can provide valuable evidence on political science theories when these historians structure their narratives as tests of explicit theories or critiques of such tests. Paul Schroeder, for example, has drawn upon historical cases to test "whether neo-realist theory is adequate and useful as an explanatory framework."[35] Schroeder uses cases from 1648 to 1945 to carry out this test, arguing in

---

and testing theories on categories of cases, including deviant cases. For example, in the past few years political scientists have done numerous case studies of the 1898 Fashoda crisis between France and England because it might shed light on new theories on the relative absence of wars between democracies (Bennett and George, "An Alliance of Statistical and Case Study Methods," p. 8). This points to a wider constructive synergy in which political scientists frame theoretical questions in new ways that might rekindle research among historians on particular cases. Conversely, historians often unearth new historical evidence or case studies that force political scientists to rethink their theories.

34. For a similar view, see Van Evera, *Guide to Methods*, pp. 31–32. Two prior and often contentious issues in this theory-testing process concern whether a prediction is validly drawn from a theory and whether all predictions validly drawn from a theory are equally important as tests of that theory. For one view on these issues, see Imre Lakatos, "Falsification and the Methodology of Scientific Research Programmes," in Imre Lakatos and Alan Musgrave, eds., *Criticism and the Growth of Knowledge* (New York: Cambridge University Press, 1970), pp. 231–278. For an incisive critique of Lakatos, see Colin Elman and Miriam Fendius Elman, "Appraising Progress in International Relations Theory: How Not to be Lakatos Intolerant," presented at the annual meeting of the American Political Science Association, Atlanta, Georgia, September 2–5, 1999.

35. Paul W. Schroeder, "Historical Reality vs. Neo-realist Theory," *International Security*, Vol. 19, No. 1 (Summer 1994), p. 110. Although Schroeder asserts that his primary

effect that this is a "most-likely" test that applies neorealism "precisely to the historical era where it should fit best."[36] He finds, contrary to neorealist predictions, that states in fact differentiate their roles in the international system and that they often fail to balance against powerful states, sometimes instead "hiding" from threats, bandwagoning with them, or attempting to "transcend" them through new norms or institutions. Schroeder concludes that neorealist theory "gets the motives, the process, the patterns, and the broad outcomes of international history wrong."

Case Comparisons versus Single Case Studies

Political scientists use explicitly comparative case studies far more often than historians because of their greater interest in generalization.[37] Some political scientists even argue that causal explanation *requires* case comparisons, and that single case studies have limited uses in theory-building. James Lee Ray, for example, has argued that causal linkages cannot be identified within the context of one case.[38] Similarly, Robert Keohane, Gary King, and Sidney Verba have argued that "the single observation is not a useful technique for testing hypotheses or theories" unless it can be compared to other observations by other researchers. They add that single cases cannot exclude alternative theories, and that their findings are limited by the possibility of measurement error, probabilistic causal mechanisms, and omitted variables.[39]

We agree that the conclusions of single case studies are much stronger if they can be compared to other studies, but we suspect that most historians would join us in arguing that the limitations attributed to single case studies, while applicable, are not categorical. As Keohane, King, and Verba acknowledge, their view of the limits of single case studies is based in part on their definition of a case as having only one observation on the dependent variable, and they note that "since one case may actually contain many potential observations, pessimism is actually

---

aim is *not* to test neorealist theory with historical evidence (p. 111), his logic and evidence are generally consistent with those of theory-testing case studies.

36. Ibid., p. 147.

37. A well-known example of a comparative case study by a historian is Kennedy, *The Rise and Decline of the Great Powers.*

38. Ray, *Democracy and International Conflict*, p. 132.

39. Keohane, King, and Verba, *Designing Social Inquiry*, pp. 210–211.

unjustified."[40] Thus, while process tracing may not be able to exclude all but one of the alternative theories in a single case if some competing theories make similar process tracing predictions, many single case studies can exclude at least some explanations; some may be able to exclude all but one if an explanation makes a unique process tracing prediction that is validated.

As for measurement error, case study research is less prone to some kinds of measurement error because it can intensively assess a few variables along several qualitative dimensions, rather than having to quantify variables across many cases. Similarly, probabilistic causal mechanisms and the potential for omitted variables pose difficult challenges and limits to all research methods, but they do not necessarily invalidate the use of single case studies. The inductive side of process tracing may identify potential omitted variables through the intensive study of a few cases, and single case studies have changed entire research programs when they have impugned theories that failed to explain their most-likely cases.[41]

More broadly, process tracing offers an alternative way for making causal inferences when it is not possible to do so through controlled comparison. In fact, process tracing can serve to make up for the limitations of a particular controlled comparison. When it is not possible to find cases similar in every respect but one—the basic requirement of controlled comparisons—the possibility remains that one or another of several independent variables identified may have causal impact. Process tracing can test whether each of the potentially causal variables in the imperfectly matched cases can be ruled out as having causal significance. If all but one of the independent variables that differ between the two cases can be ruled out via process tracing, a stronger (though still not definitive) basis exists for attributing causal significance to the remaining variable.[42] In the same way, process tracing is capable of ameliorating the well-known limitations of Mill's methods of agreement and difference. For example, while Theda Skocpol's study of social revolutions has been critiqued for its reliance on Mill's methods, Skocpol in fact supplements her case comparisons with detailed process tracing as a means of further testing her theories.[43]

---

40. Ibid., p. 208.

41. Ronald Rogowski, "The Role of Theory and Anomaly in Social-Scientific Inference," *American Political Science Review*, Vol. 89, No. 2 (June 1995), p. 467.

42. For an example, see Ray, *Democracies and International Conflict*, pp. 158–200.

43. For a critique of Theda Skocpol's use of Mill's methods, see Elizabeth Nichols, "Skocpol on Revolution: Comparative Analysis vs. Historical Conjuncture," *Compara-*

Types of Causal Relations

Historians' and political scientists' differing emphases on generalizability rest in part on differing assumptions on what kind of causal relations are prevalent in social life. We distinguish between simple, complex, and enigmatic causal processes.[44] "Simple" causal relations include those in which there are limited or easily modeled interaction effects among independent variables. The simplest kind of causality is a linear relationship with limited interaction effects, so that an increment of change in one independent variable has the same effect on the outcome variable regardless of the context or the values of other independent variables. Some nonlinear relationships and interactions are also relatively simple and easy to model mathematically. The nearest examples of simple causal relations in political science might include the finding that across many different historical contexts democracies rarely if ever have fought wars with one another, even though democracies have often fought wars against nondemocracies. Another example of simple causal relations with strong empirical support is the finding that winner-take-all electoral systems in many different states have tended to produce two centrist parties while proportional representation electoral systems have produced more numerous and diverse political parties ("Duverger's Law").[45]

"Complex" causal relations involve interacting causal variables that are not independent of each other. Interaction effects may include "tipping points" at which the relations between variables change in magnitude or direction. Complex causal relations may also include equifinality, in which similar outcomes can arise through different combinations of variables or sequential paths in which no one variable is either necessary

---

tive Social Research, Vol. 9 (1986), pp. 163–186. For Skocpol's response, see her "Analyzing Causal Configurations in History: A Rejoinder to Nichols," Comparative Social Research, Vol. 9 (1986), pp. 187–194. On Skocpol's use of process tracing to supplement Mill's methods, see Daniel Little, Microfoundations, Methods, and Causation, pp. 233–235.

44. For a similar discussion of different types of causal relations, see Robert Jervis, System Effects: Complexity in Political and Social Life, (Princeton: Princeton University Press, 1997) pp. 34–60. We use the term "enigmatic" causality to distinguish our concept from chaos theory, which is similar but which also deals with systems that may be ordered despite seeming disorder. Because of strategic interaction and the endogeneity of social structures and human agents, it is possible that some social relations are even less orderly than the complex biological and physical relationships most often used as examples in chaos theory.

45. Interestingly, Duverger's "law" has become more contingent as it has undergone further study. See Robert G. Moser, "Electoral Systems and the Number of Parties in Postcommunist States," World Politics, Vol. 51, No. 3 (April 1999) pp. 359–384.

or sufficient. Case study methods provide opportunities for inductively identifying complex interaction effects. For example, process tracing can be especially useful in determining whether the phenomenon being investigated is characterized by equifinality. This is particularly important in supplementing statistical analyses that have not addressed the possibility of equifinality. In addition, typological theories, discussed below, can capture and represent interaction effects and equifinality if a relatively small number of variables is involved. Statistical methods can also capture interaction effects and perhaps even equifinality, but they are usually limited to interactions that reflect simple and well-known mathematical forms; when interaction terms are added to statistical models, the sample size necessary to get significant empirical results increases.

A still more complex form of causal relations might be termed "enigmatic," representing causal relations that pose strong challenges for attempts at theory building and testing. These relations include tight endogeneity in which variables cannot be spatially or temporally disentangled, probabilistic causal mechanisms operating at low levels of probability, and large numbers of variables interacting in nonlinear ways. When these kinds of causal relations are present, each case will be unique in important respects, generalization will be severely limited, and even highly contingent predictions will not be possible. Still, if endogeneity can be set aside, explanation may be possible through historical narratives that draw on numerous causal mechanisms.

Most social scientists would probably agree that each kind of causal relation—simple, complex, and enigmatic—may be present in at least some social relations on some levels of analysis. An important difference among and between political scientists and historians, however, involves the different initial working assumptions researchers make about which kind of causal relation usually holds in the puzzles that interest them. Some political scientists, including rational choice theorists and neorealist international relations theorists, tend to assume that simple causal relations hold, and that "covering law" type generalizations can be derived about behaviors across a wide variety of contexts. Many historians' emphasis on the uniqueness of historical cases suggests an assumption that enigmatic causal relations, particularly probabilistic causal mechanisms or large numbers of interacting variables, are prevalent. Postmodernists also tend to assume that enigmatic causality is pervasive, though they place more emphasis on the problem of endogeneity in relations among agents and structures, arguing that linguistic representations of social life both constitute and are constituted by human agents and cannot be objectively studied.

Our own view is that while simple causality holds in some spheres and enigmatic causality applies in others, many of the phenomena of interest in international relations and comparative politics involve important elements of complex causality. Patterns, conjunctions of interacting variables, and path dependent causal sequences recur with sufficient similarity that they can be usefully modeled even though elements of cases remain unique and theoretical concepts are socially constructed. The most appropriate form for modeling such complexity, we argue, is often that of typological theories, to which we now turn.

Typological Theory

Corresponding roughly to the three types of causality—simple, complex, and enigmatic—are three different conceptions of "theory."[46] Social scientists who believe that important phenomena are characterized by simple causal relations tend to embrace Hempel's "covering law" conception of theories as highly general and abstract propositions that hold true in a wide variety of contexts.[47] Historians are generally skeptical of this conception of theory, and many would agree with Clayton Roberts's assertion that the corpus of historical writing contains few nontrivial covering law theories that have stood the test of time.

As Roberts observes, the failure generally of the social sciences to find meaningful laws (with economics perhaps a partial exception), has led Jon Elster to conclude that "the basic concept in the social sciences should be that of a mechanism rather than of a theory."[48] Roberts finds this conception of theory to be consistent with his own view of historical explanation, and social scientists who believe enigmatic causality to be pervasive are likely to find it acceptable as well (except for postmodernists, who emphasize the endogeneity problem). Yet Elster himself is not entirely satisfied with the causal mechanism conception of theory because causal mechanisms can have different effects depending on the context. That is, Elster raises the challenge of identifying the different conditions under which a causal mechanism applies: "Moving from a plurality of mechanisms to a unified theory would mean that we should be able to identify in advance the conditions in which one or the other mechanism would be triggered. . . . My own view is that the social

---

46. Our treatment of these issues has benefited greatly from discussions with David Dessler, who is in no way responsible for whatever loose thinking remains.

47. The classic 1948 statement of the covering law model is C.G. Hempel and Paul Oppenheim, "Studies in the Logic of Explanation," in C.G. Hempel, ed., *Aspects of Scientific Explanation* (New York: Free Press, 1965).

48. Roberts, *Logic of Historical Explanation*, p. 155.

sciences are currently unable to identify such conditions and are likely to remain so forever."[49] Elster's conclusion is too pessimistic. His remarks point to the need for a third conception of theory, one that can address complex causal relations such as interaction effects and equifinality. This conception of theory, which we term "typological theory," identifies recurring conjunctions of causal mechanisms and provides theories on the pathways through which these conjunctions produce effects.[50] It constitutes a conceptual middle ground: typological theories do not attempt to state broad "covering law" generalizations about phenomena, but differentiate these phenomena into more specialized types about which contingent generalizations can be formulated. Typological theories draw upon discrete causal mechanisms, but focus on the effects of specified configurations of these mechanisms.

A typological theory is not the same as a historical explanation of a particular event. A historical explanation traces a series of specific connections in an extant historical case. In contrast, typological theory identifies generalized pathways, whether the path in question has occurred only once, or a thousand times, or is merely hypothesized as a potential path that has not yet occurred at all.[51] A pathway is characterized in terms of variables rather than by the values of these variables associated with a historical explanation. It might focus, for example, not on the "Russian revolution" per se, but on this revolution as one example of the type of revolutions that: follow an international war, replace weak state institutions, and take place amidst an economic crisis. Even if there is only one revolution fitting this type, a typological theory on this type of revolution states how the underlying causal mechanisms interact and allows us to generalize, albeit in a limited way, to possible future revolutions that fit the same type. Such generalized pathways are what is distinctive about

---

49. Jon Elster, *Political Psychology* (New York: Cambridge University Press, 1993), p. 5. Similarly, Andrew Sayer recognizes that "the operation of the same mechanism can produce quite different results and, alternatively, different mechanisms may produce the same empirical results." He thus notes the need to identify how the effects of causal mechanisms vary by contexts, though does not express the same pessimism as Elster on whether this can be done. See *Method in Social Science: A Realist Approach*, 2nd ed., (London: Routledge, 1992), pp. 107, 111, 121.

50. On theorizing about contingent causality and interaction effects, see Charles Ragin, *The Comparative Method* (Berkeley: University of California Press, 1987); and Little, *Microfoundations*.

51. A fully specified typological theory provides hypotheses on all of the mathematically possible combinations of independent and dependent variables under inquiry, but typological theories are almost never fully specified because researchers are usually interested only in the types that are relatively common or that have the greatest implications for theory-building or policymaking.

typological theory. They are abstract and theoretical even though they are "closer" to concrete historical explanations than are claims about causal mechanisms or covering laws. Specific pathways, in turn, can be explained by known causal mechanisms. Prospect theory, for example, provides a causal mechanism—the tendency of individuals to take greater risks to prevent a perceived loss than to attain a perceived gain of the same magnitude—that under certain conditions supports explanations of recurring patterns of behavior.

Some of the distinctions among the three types of theory are simply differences in degree. For example, the distinction between a few interacting variables in complex causality and many interacting variables in enigmatic causality is a fuzzy one. Also, "covering laws" could be phrased in a contingent way that makes them indistinguishable from typological theories, or in a narrow way that equates them with causal mechanisms. Causal mechanisms can be recast at different levels of generality, and what one social scientist considers a mechanism another might consider a conjunction of mechanisms.[52] Also, a mechanism that is probabilistic at one level of analysis may become almost deterministic at a higher level of generality. For example, if there is a probability of .50001 that any individual voter will choose candidate A in a winner-take-all two-party election, we cannot predict very well how individuals will vote but as the number of voters grows we become almost 100 percent confident that A will win.

But there are also distinctions in kind among the three categories of causal relations. The move from simple causality, where interaction effects are for practical purposes zero, to complex and enigmatic causality, where interactions are important, is a distinction in kind. Similarly, complex causality is distinguished from enigmatic causality by the presence in the latter of probabilistic causal relations at low levels of probability.

In view of the subtlety of these distinctions, investigators need not be overly concerned with classifying whether a particular hypothesis involves simple, complex, or enigmatic causality. Rather, researchers should focus on specific hypothesized causal relations for the phenomenon under study and model it through whatever mathematical formulae or typological theories best represent the hypotheses of interest. It may even be possible to use a mathematical formula to model equifinality and to test this model statistically. What is most important is that researchers

---

52. Interestingly, in response to various critiques from other philosophers of science, Hempel attempted to devise a probabilistic conception of covering laws, but this effort and subsequent similar projects by other philosophers encountered fundamental difficulties. On these developments, see Salmon, *Four Decades of Scientific Explanation*.

can choose from a well-developed repertoire of both causal mechanisms (such as evolutionary selection, socialization, emulation, collective action problems, principal-agent problems, problems of credible commitments, two-level games, and learning) and functional forms (such as linearity, path dependency, tipping points, geometric progressions, equifinality, multifinality, and asymptotic limits) in formulating their hypotheses.[53] Still, the terms "covering laws," "causal mechanisms," and "typological theories" are useful for the present general discussion, even though the demarcation among these terms and the correspondence to types of causal relations are inexact.[54]

Case studies can be used inductively to develop and refine typological theories through a "building block" approach that maps out the alternative causal paths to the outcome of interest. This approach explicitly addresses the phenomenon of equifinality. The building block approach is particularly important in new or emerging research programs, but it can also involve the explanation of "deviant" cases that are not sufficiently explained by existing theories. The aim is to proceed incrementally toward the goal of developing a typological theory. In opting for this more flexible strategy, the investigator seeks to gradually build a typology and a typological theory via empirical analysis of cases within a theoretical framework. While this strategy relies on induction, it is analytical, theory-driven induction. The use of analytical induction does not exclude making use of deductive theoretical ideas, particularly theories on discrete causal mechanisms that may form the building blocks for more ambitious or integrative theories, to help guide the empirical approach.

For example, an empirical approach relying on historical explanations for different cases of deterrence failure enables the investigator to discover more general types of deterrence failures, some of which may encompass several cases, and to identify generic explanations for each type of failure. The different causal patterns of deterrence failure become part of a typological theory of deterrence. Such a differentiated theory of failures is significantly different from, and often more useful than, a

---

53. These illustrative causal mechanisms and functional forms are drawn largely from Bates et al., *Analytic Narratives* pp. 234–236; and Jervis, *System Effects*.

54. A related distinction is that between "variable-centered" approaches and "case-oriented" approaches, or those that treat cases as "configurations" of variables. See Ragin, *The Comparative Method*; and Ira Katznelson, "Structure and Configuration in Comparative Politics," in Mark Irving Lichbach and Alan S. Zuckerman, eds., *Comparative Politics: Rationality, Culture, and Structure* (London: Cambridge University Press, 1997), pp. 81–112.

theory that attempts to provide a single explanation for all deterrence failures.[55] Differentiated explanations of the outcomes of the cases that are all instances of the class of events being investigated become a part of a cumulative typological theory, or a "repertoire of causal mechanisms" of that phenomenon.[56]

One may object that such a procedure will lead to an infinite number of types if each case is idiosyncratic enough to warrant the creation of a new type to encompass it. This danger need not arise; the number of variables in the theoretical framework will limit the variance in explanation. In addition, the investigator should exercise judgment about the usefulness of constructing more and more refined, narrowly circumscribed subtypes. Typological theories become exponentially more complex as variables are added. They are difficult to present, interpret, and remember after about five to six independent dichotomous variables, or thirty-two to sixty-four possible types. Research usually focuses on only a fraction of the mathematically possible types, however, and variables can be recast at different levels of generality or the range of types under consideration can be reduced.[57] Researchers might choose to focus on one or a few well-specified subtypes and a few variables that are hypothesized to have the greatest causal weight.[58] For example, in a study by Alexander George and Richard Smoke on deterrence, three major types of deterrence failure emerged from the cases studied; the possibility of introducing subtypes of the three types was recognized but not pursued since the objectives of the investigation did not require it.[59]

---

55. Alexander L. George and Richard Smoke, *Deterrence in American Foreign Policy: Theory and Practice* (New York: Columbia University Press, 1974).

56. Dessler, "Beyond Correlations," p. 343, citing Richard W. Miller, *Fact and Method: Explanation, Confirmation and Reality in the Natural and the Social Sciences* (Princeton: Princeton University Press, 1987) p. 139.

57. See Alexander L. George and Andrew Bennett, "Developing and Using Typological Theories in Case Study Research," paper presented at a MacArthur Foundation workshop on case study methods at Harvard University, October 17–19, 1997, and available at http://www.georgetown.edu/bennett

58. Alternatively, it is often possible to reduce substantially the number of relevant types that can be logically derived in a complex typological space. See Bennett and George, "Developing and Using Typological Theories."

59. George and Smoke, *Deterrence*, p. 535.

Military Innovation and Change: A Potential Venue for Typological Theory

The study of military innovation provides a useful example of the potential of typological theory. John Lynn argues in Chapter 14 that there is no definable body of literature dealing with the *general* phenomena of military change to compare with the theoretical literature on international relations. While he is correct, there have been important efforts, particularly by Barry Posen and Stephen Rosen, to theorize about the sources of military innovation.[60] Unfortunately, however, the theoretical literature on military innovation has not been cumulative. As Lynn notes, this literature has largely produced a set of "lists and lessons" without identifying the contingent conditions under which particular lessons apply, as a typological theory would. The works by Posen and Rosen illustrate this problem, and they also point toward the potential development of typological theories of military innovation.

Posen and Rosen address military innovation in the same period, the years leading up to World War II, and they even address one of the same cases, the British Royal Air Force's (RAF's) development of its air defense forces. They provide radically different theoretical arguments, however, and they disagree in their interpretations of the RAF case. Posen argues that innovation from within military organizations is rare and that civilian intervention in military affairs, defeat in battle, the presence of "maverick" innovators in or from the military, or some combination of these, are often the sources of military innovation.[61] In contrast, Rosen argues that civilians and maverick innovators who leave the military or are marginalized within it have little influence, and he maintains that the key requirement for innovation is the presence of top military leaders who enjoy legitimacy within their service branches, recognize the need for innovation but pursue it with political skill and patience, and create career paths for junior officers to rise to the top from the new or reorganized military service that is the subject of the innovation.[62]

These views appear to be diametrically opposed, but they are easily reconciled within a single broad typological theory if we assume that military innovation is characterized by equifinality. In other words, Posen

---

60. Barry Posen, *The Sources of Military Doctrine: France, Britain, and Germany between the World Wars* (Ithaca: Cornell University Press, 1984); and Stephen Peter Rosen, "New Ways of War: Understanding Military Innovation," *International Security*, Vol. 13, No. 1 (Summer 1988) pp. 134–168.

61. Posen, *Sources of Military Doctrine*, pp. 54–57.

62. Rosen, "New Ways of War," pp. 134–143.

and Rosen may be talking about different paths to military innovation, and it may be that no single variable is necessary or sufficient for such innovation and that the interactions among the variables distinguish different paths or types. A typological theory of military innovation could be constructed based on six variables discussed by Posen, Rosen, and Lynn: change in technology originating from military laboratories or the domestic economy; maverick innovators; reformist military leaders; civilian intervention in military affairs; the international context; and the structure of military organizations.[63] Each of these variables could be defined with various degrees of generality. The international context, in particular, might itself be a typology defined by wartime versus peacetime and the presence or absence of expansionist states, military innovation by other states, and ongoing power transitions.[64] For simplicity, let us consider all the variables to be dichotomous, with the first four measured as present or absent, the international context measured as wartime or peacetime, and military organizations measured as centralized (a strong general staff system) or decentralized, with pronounced interservice rivalries.

Even this "simple" typology has sixty-four possible combinations of independent variables, or 128 possible types if we include a dichotomous outcome variable of innovation/no innovation. This seems an impossibly large typological space, but if we code the cases studied by Posen and Rosen and place them within these possible types, several conclusions quickly emerge. First, as a consequence of Rosen's research design and case selection, the cases he studied essentially fall into a single type. They all took place in peacetime and in the presence of great technological change, maverick innovators were present to some degree in each case (although Rosen's process tracing discounts their influence), reformist military leaders and civilian intervention were present, the military organizations involved were not centralized under a strong general staff system, and the outcome in each case was that innovation took place. The fact that all the cases fit one type does not mean that Rosen cannot draw any significant conclusions. He is able, for example, to dismiss suggestions that either wartime or failure in war are necessary conditions for

---

63. This list is preliminary and illustrative, and other variables could be added. While it captures most of the factors discussed by Posen, Rosen, and Lynn, for example, it leaves out Lynn's reference to wider societal and cultural changes as sources of innovation.

64. Posen gives a sophisticated analysis of the systemic constraints faced by France, Germany, and Britain in his case studies, and his analysis cannot be easily reduced to a few parsimonious types of international contexts.

innovation.[65] But Rosen's focus on one type of case means that his conclusions are necessarily contingent, as he recognizes by acknowledging that other cases may fit other patterns or types. Specifically, Rosen notes that U.S. nuclear doctrine may have been largely created by civilians inside and outside of the Defense Department.[66]

Second, the disagreements between Posen and Rosen are not as fundamental as they appear at first glance. For the most part, they are talking about different types or paths. Neither says that a maverick, civilian intervention, or the presence of reformist military leaders is a necessary condition for innovation, though Rosen comes close to this claim for reformist leaders and Posen does so for civilian intervention. Thus their cases largely talk past one another, addressing different types without claiming to identify any single necessary condition. Posen's case study of French military doctrine before World War II demonstrates that France lacked innovative military leaders, civilians did not intervene on behalf of innovation, and mavericks such as Charles de Gaulle who favored strengthening offensive capabilities lacked support from top military or civilian leaders. It is thus consistent with both Rosen's and Posen's views that French doctrine was not innovative, as neither the factor that Rosen emphasizes (reformist military leaders) nor that which Posen highlights (civilian intervention) was present. Posen's case study of Germany presents more of a challenge for Rosen's views, as it shows civilian intervention under Hitler combining with the efforts of the maverick General Heinz Guderian to impose a blitzkrieg strategy on reluctant top military officers. Because Rosen has not argued that reformist military leaders are a necessary condition for innovation, however, this case does not invalidate Rosen's findings on the type of cases he has chosen or his argument that military reformers are key to one path to innovation. A more serious challenge for both authors' theories would be a case in which civilian intervention and reformist military leaders were both present but innovation did not take place, or where they were both absent but innovation did take place.

Third, interaction effects are important. Both authors note this, but on the issue of civil-military relations they understate interaction effects in their debate on the case of the RAF. Posen presents RAF Air Chief Marshall Sir Hugh Dowding as a maverick proponent of air defense who was opposed by the dominant bomber-oriented culture of the top RAF

---

65. Failure in the previous war could be treated as another independent variable, but in the current presentation its effects are captured in the other variables since mavericks, reformist leaders, and civilian intervention are all more likely after failure in war.

66. Rosen, "New Ways of War," p. 166.

officers but who was able to rapidly increase Britain's air defenses because of civilian support. Although he notes the interaction effect this involves between political actors and military mavericks, in Rosen's view he gives too much emphasis to the civilians' role and overstates the reluctance of top RAF officers to spend on air defense.[67] Conversely, Rosen underemphasizes the possibility that Dowding might have been marginalized within the RAF if he had not received civilian support. This important debate arises from the conflicting process tracing evidence presented by the two authors, but it pushes into the background the authors' evident agreement that the joint presence of civilian support for innovation and military reformers or mavericks is a much more powerful source of innovation than any of these factors acting alone. Mavericks or reformers in the military can help stimulate civilian intervention, and civilian intervention can encourage mavericks and reformers to risk a struggle against top officers opposed to innovation. If few or no cases can be found of strictly civilian-imposed or solely military-motivated innovations, this is an important theoretical finding.

Placing Posen's and Rosen's arguments in the framework of a wider typological theory not only puts their actual and apparent disagreements in context, it also points to the directions in which the research program on military innovation might develop. As suggested above, one direction is to try to find cases that fit other types in the framework. Are there any cases of innovation where only one of the three variables—civilian intervention, mavericks, military reformers—is present? Are there cases where two or three of these are strongly present but no innovation takes place? Are there cases of major technological change but no innovation, or of innovation in the absence of technological change? How does wartime innovation differ from that in peacetime?

A second direction for developing the research program is to develop subtypes by further differentiating the independent and dependent variables. How does emulation of other states' military innovations differ from innovative efforts to counter or offset innovations by others? How do such internationally motivated innovations differ from home-grown innovations? How does innovation by military laboratories differ from that of dual-use innovations by the domestic economy? How do the politics of "technology push" and "mission pull" innovation differ? Under what conditions do different subtypes of civilian intervention (by executives, parliaments, or defense industries) using different instruments (budgets, investigations, personnel changes, or material rewards)

---

67. Posen, *Sources of Military Doctrine*, pp. 120, 165–176; and Rosen, "New Ways of War," pp. 143–150.

result in innovation? If we reverse our explanatory goal and cast military innovations as independent variables, what kind of typological theories might we construct on the dependent variables of societal change, state formation, or civil-military relations? Systematically casting the variables, types, and subtypes relating to military innovation in terms of typological theory can allow for greater cumulation of knowledge on these kinds of questions. It can also provide a clearer framework for historians to critique the work of political scientists who have omitted important variables or interaction effects.

Conclusions

Underlying the debates among formal modelers, postmodernists, and case study researchers in history and political science are differing theoretical assumptions about what kinds of causal relations are common in social life and differing aesthetic decisions on the tradeoffs among parsimony, rigor, and explanatory richness. We have not attempted to move any formal modelers or postmodernists out of their views on these issues. Rather, we have attempted to highlight the common middle ground for historians interested in historical explanation and political scientists sensitive to the complexities of historical events. The epistemological middle ground consists of the assertion that causal mechanisms and causal effects are both essential to causal explanation. The methodological middle ground is the use of process tracing to identify and test hypothesized causal mechanisms in historical cases. The theoretical middle ground centers on typological theories. These theories allow for equifinality, path dependency, interaction effects, and nonlinear relations. They also sacrifice a substantial degree of parsimony to achieve greater explanatory richness. They are thus more amenable to historians who are drawn to causal complexity, and more useful to historians who attempt to situate their cases with respect to political science theories and case studies, than the covering law or causal mechanism notions of theory.

Still, many historians will find even the richer confines of typological theory too constraining. They will argue for the unique aspects of historical cases, and for the need to include far more variables and interactions than even typological theories can easily accommodate. But we do not aspire to convert historians into political scientists. It is essential for our work that historians remain experts on particular historical eras, events, or regions. Then, when political scientists take a sudden interest in, for example, the British-French Fashoda crisis of 1898, which many researchers view as an important case for testing theories on the absence of wars between democracies, there will be historical case studies to draw upon and historical experts to critique our work. Our hope is that historians will continue to check in on our theorizing, draw upon our typological theories in deciding what evidence to look for and what implicit or explicit theories to employ in explaining their cases, and critique our case studies when they omit important variables or fail to use the historical record adequately. As long as historians contribute in these ways to the development of typological theories, and political scientists develop theories that are sensitive to the complexities of historical cases, we can fruitfully continue to go our separate ways together.

Part II
Cases

Chapter 5

World War II: A Different War

Gerhard L. Weinberg

This paper will focus on the differentiation which I believe must be made, but all too often is not made, between World War I and World War II. Because the numbers are used, there appears often to be a mistaken sense of continuity, a continuity analogous to that between the First and Second Burmese Wars and other such numerically named conflicts. It was this mistaken view which, alongside some additional ones, led me to try to write a global history of World War II in the first place. My own prior work on the role of Germany in the origins of World War II had led me to see how different the new conflict was certain to be when compared with the prior war that was so vivid in the memories of its survivors. It is, therefore, the differentiation between World War II and its predecessor, as well as the extent to which that predecessor in fact belonged into a category with numerous prior wars, that became the focus of my thinking about World War II and is the burden of this paper. Every effort, like that of Randall Schweller, which reduces World War II to one of a somewhat similar series subject to general theories that can either be applied to or derived from them, is guaranteed to mislead and confuse rather than enlighten because it requires that entirely different conflicts be shoehorned into a mold that does not fit, with key characteristics necessary for any understanding of events eliminated because they would invalidate the thesis or break the mold.

There is a critical clue to this in the date of the beginning of World War II, September 1, 1939. The Germans initiated the war by their invasion of Poland on that day. In preceding years, some individuals inside Germany had argued for the initiation of a program for the killing of

A different version of this paper has appeared in the *New Zealand Army Journal,* No. 20 (December 1998), pp. 1–9.

"useless lives": the aged, the crippled, the mentally sick, babies with serious birth handicaps. Adolf Hitler had answered that such a program could be carried out only during a war, and since he intended to go to war, this was not an evasion but a deferral. In October 1939 he signed a secret order that was to provide a cover for the large-scale killing of the handicapped—but he backdated it to September 1, 1939. Does anyone believe that his calendar was wrong?

In the winter of 1938–39, when he was deciding that in 1939 he would not again allow himself to be deprived of a war as he felt had happened in 1938, he also looked forward to new measures against the Jews; in a conversation with the foreign minister of Czechoslovakia he referred to the coming extermination of the Jews and in public in a speech on January 30, 1939, he predicted that the Jews of Europe would be exterminated if there were another war, a war he already intended to initiate later that year. In subsequent years, Hitler repeatedly referred back to this public prophecy, but whenever he did so, he always claimed that this had been in his speech of September 1, 1939. Why this misdating that anyone could check in the National Socialist Party's official publication of Hitler's speeches? The answer seems to me to be obvious: in his thinking, the war was not fought because Germany had military forces and did not know what else to do with them; it was fought for racial aims that were integral and essential parts of the war and in fact were central to its purpose.

When scholars examine wars, they should be very careful to distinguish between aims and means. The two certainly can and do have major effects on one another, but changes in one can take place essentially independently of changes in the other. The expeditions sent by the rulers of ancient Egypt up the Nile and into the Sinai utilized different weapons in the Old, Middle, and New Kingdoms. The substitution of bronze for copper in the first transition and the addition of chariots in the second certainly altered the details of fighting. The aims, however, did not change substantially, and the different campaigns can best be understood by historians as essentially similar, even if centuries apart. That similarity rests in their aims: the control of certain mineral resources, the extraction of tribute, the security of trade routes, the acquisition of slaves.

A very large proportion of the wars of the ancient Mediterranean world may be grouped in a similar fashion. Territorial expansion, imperial status, and control of adjacent tribal areas could be added to the list of aims, but there were few exceptions to these goals. The converse, revolt against the victor in an earlier war, ought to be added as another major category, but it would generally take place only after a prior conquest by an expanding power considered alien, oppressive, or both.

One could make a case for the Third Punic War being in a way an exception, and one I shall return to subsequently. There is a way in which the determination of the Romans to end the existence of Carthage as an entity—the leveling of the city and the removal as slaves of its surviving population, all as a means of slaying their fears of the long-deceased Hannibal—does belong in a separate category. It should be noted, however, that the Phoenician settlements and towns in the vicinity of Carthage were *not* molested. In fact, some of them were rewarded for their neutrality or aid to Rome in the war; the province of Africa, into which the newly acquired land was organized, was thereafter ruled in a manner essentially similar to that of other provinces under the control of the Roman Republic and Empire.

This short lesson in ancient history is inserted here in order to help set the stage for a discussion of the two great conflicts of this century. There has been a tendency to lump them together as a European civil war in two stages, as another Thirty Years War interrupted by a brief armistice, as two German bids for hegemony in the way Ludwig Dehio placed them in his thought-provoking book, *The Precarious Balance*.[1] Professor Schweller and others similarly look upon World War II as similar in its origins to others without regard to the war's distinguishing aims. It seems to me that these constructs obscure rather than enlighten; they make understanding more rather than less difficult. The major reason for the confusion generated by such views is that they ignore the absolutely fundamental difference in aims between the two wars.

What contemporaries came to call "The Great War," and what is now more frequently referred to as World War I, was fought for aims that were essentially similar to those of prior wars. Expansion of territory and perhaps colonial possessions, influence and status, control of raw materials and strategic points, defense of what one already had against real or perceived threats—all these were as much a factor in such earlier conflicts like the Seven Years War as in the war begun in 1914. That similarity in aim is also apparent in the agreements and disagreements among the allies on both sides, at least in the early stages of the war. Austria-Hungary's expectation about Serbia and Germany's about Belgium, Bulgaria's hopes of regaining territory previously held, Romania's aspirations for Hungarian territory, Italy's promissory notes in the Treaty of London, the division of Germany's Pacific empire between the British and Japan, Russian interest in control of the Straits—the list could be extended, but the point should be obvious. It might be argued that the

---

1. Ludwig Dehio, *The Precarious Balance: Four Centuries of European Power Struggle*, trans. Charles Fullman (New York: Vintage, 1962).

aims of the United States, at least when it entered the war, were not that different from those of the others, even if phrased rather differently.

The field in which the war of 1914–18 could be said to differ from its predecessors is surely that of means. It turned out that the social mechanics at the disposal of the modern state were capable of drawing resources out of the participants on a scale that was extraordinarily high and that, combined with the physical mechanics of the weaponry provided by the level of industrialization of the time, made the new conflict infinitely more destructive of life, property, and institutions in all sorts of ways than almost anyone had anticipated. The strains this imposed on many of the participants in turn changed them in both their aims and their internal structures in ways that were equally unanticipated. But there are two aspects of this which must be noted.

First, the inability of the participants to extricate themselves from the descent into mutual self-destruction was to a very great extent the result of a fortuitous development in German strategy: the change from the war plans of the elder Helmuth von Moltke, Prussia's army chief of staff in the 1880s, to the lunacies of Alfred von Schlieffen, the chief of staff at the turn of the century. Instead of fighting a basically defensive war to retain the positions of Germany and Austria-Hungary in Europe, Schlieffen had come up with the really crazy idea that the way to defend Austria against Russia—the original purpose of Germany's making an alliance with Austria-Hungary—was to invade Belgium with units that Germany did not have and the creation of which he opposed since he did not want the officer corps' aristocratic character diluted by the great increase in officers such units would require. Modified but not abandoned by the younger Helmuth von Moltke, chief of staff at the beginning of World War I, this project led to a stalemate with German forces deep inside Belgian and French territory rather than somewhere near the pre-war borders, thus giving one side the illusion of hope for victory and the other an enormous incentive to keep going. Unlike the Korean War, in which the fighting by 1953 had returned practically to the original dividing line between North and South Korea, after swinging back and forth in both directions, there could be no relatively easy disengagement in World War I as there was in Korea from a conflict whose continuation was unlikely to do either side much good.

Second, the overwhelming majority of the physical damage of the war, both in terms of casualties and destruction of property, was caused by relatively minor changes in weaponry that had been available and had been used for some time: artillery and rapid-firing infantry weapons. New weapons—airplanes, tanks, and gas—certainly contributed their share; and the war at sea was fought with ships dramatically different from the naval fighting of the Napoleonic Wars, but even in this field the smaller wars of the nineteenth century had seen plenty of precursors.

The fundamental change in this century would come with World War II. Here was a war in which the major initiating power had aims that were entirely different from those of prior conflicts. The fact that Germany's allies, on the other hand, had aims that were basically like those of the previous wars—Italy for more colonies and a larger role in the Balkans; Romania, Finland, Hungary, and Bulgaria to regain losses of prior wars and settlements; Japan for a continuation of its previous expansion in Asia—would make their relationship to Germany impossibly difficult in ways that make the frictions in the Anglo-U.S.-Soviet alliance look like harmony itself. And the German-led alliance eventuated in its members' actually shooting at each other in several instances: the Germans fighting the Italians, Romanians, Finns, and Bulgarians before it was all over—and at the end breaking their no-separate-peace agreement with the Japanese.

In fact, Germany's most important military allies in World War II, Italy, Japan, and Romania, had all fought on the other side in the preceding conflict. This switch from being Germany's enemies to becoming its allies took place because they imagined that they could more easily attain their traditional objectives on the side of Germany rather than on the side of Germany's enemies, as in the preceding conflict, not understanding until too late that Germany's objectives were in the long run incompatible with their own.

It is the aims of Germany that have to be examined, and it is the neglect of those aims in much of the relevant literature that has obscured the nature of the history of World War II from so many. All during the 1920s Adolf Hitler assured his audiences that he was unlike all the others who also thought of themselves as the self-anointed saviors of the country after its defeat in the last war. He referred to them disdainfully as *Grenzpolitiker*, border politicians, who merely wanted to undo the peace treaty of 1919 and regain for Germany what had then been lost. An obvious sign of their utter stupidity, such a policy would only lead Germany into big and costly wars at the end of which it would be where it had been in 1914: unable to feed its population on its own land. He described himself by contrast as a *Raumpolitiker*, a politician of space, who would lead Germany to the conquest not of the snippets of land lost by the peace treaty of Versailles but of hundreds of thousands of square kilometers. These lands would be Germanized with settlers who would raise large families to replace the casualties lost in the wars of conquest and provide soldiers for the wars that would follow. That process would end only when the Germans had inherited the earth.

This is not the time and place to analyze the way Hitler attained power in Germany but rather to point out how the racial revolution pointing to a demographic reordering of the whole globe began in 1933, not 1939, with war a significant and essentially integral portion of the whole process. At the same time a one-party dictatorship was established in Germany and a vast rearmament program initiated, the racial policies were inaugurated as well. In the negative sense, the persecution of Jews and Sinti and Roma, the Gypsies, began in 1933. The procedures for sterilizing those Germans thought likely to transmit hereditary defects were instituted on July 14, 1933, a date picked quite deliberately. In the positive sense, measures designed to increase the birthrate of those Germans deemed of appropriate racial background also started in the same year. In 1938 and the early months of 1939, the regime moved forward *simultaneously* on both the internal and the external front.

On the internal front, there were the drastic new measures against the Jews, symbolized for the world by the pogrom of November 1938, and followed by internal discussion of far more violent measures, first publicly heralded in the previously mentioned Hitler speech of January 30, 1939, asserting that in any new war the Jews of Europe would be killed. In those same months, preparations went forward for the establishment of a vast program of so-called euthanasia, the killing of those non-Jewish Germans whose physical or mental handicaps were believed to make them "unworthy of life." It is not a coincidence that both the January 30 speech and the order Hitler signed in late October 1939 for the "euthanasia" program were intentionally and knowingly misdated at the time and in official Nazi publications to September 1, 1939. Why of all the days of the year was that one picked? The day Germany initiated World War II was deliberately picked both for official publications and for a secret internal decree because in the eyes of those in charge the demographic revolution inside and outside Germany was perceived as a single entity.

Hitler had intended to begin the first of his wars in 1938. Czechoslovakia was to be conquered to improve Germany's strategic position for war against Britain and France and to increase the population base of its army. He backed down at the last moment and regretted it to the end of his life, determined never to repeat what he considered the worst error of his career. When the attempt to subordinate his Eastern neighbors to Germany while he attacked in the West did not succeed with Poland in the winter of 1938–39, he decided to attack that country either separately or simultaneously with the Western powers if they came in on Poland's side. Why war with the Western powers at all? Why had Germany's military buildup been focused on that war from 1933 on? Not because he wanted to see the Eiffel Tower but because war in the West was the prerequisite in his eyes for the seizure of enormous land in the East from a Soviet Union believed to be hopelessly feeble. That would provide the land for the first great numbers of Germanic settlers, and also the mineral resources, especially the oil, needed for the next war, that against the United States, a war for which he had ordered weapons systems begun in 1937.

It was this war for space that Germany launched in 1939 and would fight thereafter with unbelievable ferocity until utter defeat. And the strategy followed both in the fighting outside and policies inside Germany and German-controlled territory can be understood only if the racial preconceptions and aims of German policymakers are taken into consideration. I will cite only a few examples from both the realms of strategy and the internal processes, but it should be understood that the convenience of analysis has nothing to do with the simultaneity of the events and their interaction with one another.

Just as soon as it looked to the Germans as if victory in the West had been attained in the early summer of 1940, the plans for the next wars, those against the United States and the Soviet Union, were set in motion. On July 11 the resumption of preparations for war against the United States was ordered; by the end of that month Hitler had been persuaded to wait for the attack on the Soviet Union—originally scheduled for that fall—until the spring of 1941. By that time, one of the most radical steps in racial policy was moving forward: the systematic slaughter of the handicapped. By the summer of 1941, over a hundred thousand Germans had fallen victim to this program; it was in that process that the bureaucratic, mechanical, and recruitment procedures for systematic murder had been developed. This plan was slightly altered in the summer of 1941 when the growing difficulties in the campaign in the East made it inadvisable to impress on German soldiers the thought that if they were seriously wounded, their own government would kill them; however, the killing went on in a decentralized fashion, taking over another hundred thousand lives by 1945 and in addition being extended into German-occupied territory. And those carrying out this awful activity were so enthusiastic about it that they did what they could to continue it even after the German surrender of May 1945.[2]

By the summer of 1941, the next segment of the demographic revolution was also in full swing. On the one hand, hundreds of thousands of Germans were being resettled in places from which the local peoples

2. Henry Friedlander, *The Origins of Nazi Genocide: From Euthanasia to the Final Solution* (Chapel Hill: University of North Carolina Press, 1995), pp. 49–50, 162–163.

had been expelled or killed. On the other hand, the systematic killing of Jews had been initiated, and Hitler in late July 1941 personally explained to the visiting Croatian Minister of Defense that the countries of Europe would be emptied one by one, with Hungary likely to be the last country to give up its Jews. But that was not all; not only would the Sinti and Roma be included in the killing, but it was to be extended outside Europe. Again Hitler was quite explicit. In November 1941, as the Germans hoped to take over the Middle East and Northwest Africa, he explained in considerable detail that all Jews living among *aussereuropäische Völker*, those living among non-European peoples, would also be destroyed.

The German general Erwin Rommel had initially been sent to Libya to rescue the last portion of Mussolini's African empire still held at least in part by Italian forces and thereby simultaneously salvage the Fascist Party's control of Italy, but thereafter Rommel was not urged on to Cairo so that the Germans could dismantle the pyramids and move them to Berlin. The aim was to make it possible to arrange the *Vernichtung*, the destruction, of the Jewish communities of Palestine, Syria, Iraq, Egypt, and other African nations. The Suez Canal could be and repeatedly was closed by German planes laying mines—a point generally disregarded in accounts of the war—but the systematic killing of portions of the population of the Near East required actual control of the territory.

Needing a large surface fleet to fight the United States but not having had time to complete one of his own, Hitler urged the Japanese forward with the promise to join them and did so the moment he heard of the attack on Pearl Harbor—he did not want to wait the few days until the formal celebration of war with the United States could get underway in Berlin. Once the large Japanese navy was involved on Germany's side, any delay in actually starting hostilities against the United States was unnecessary. And German racial preconceptions about the United States were about as solid—and as silly—as those concerning the peoples of the Soviet Union.

The other aspects of the racial and demographic revolution were certainly not lost sight of. The killing of the handicapped and of Jews and Gypsies went forward. High family allowances were provided for German soldiers, and propaganda proceeded for the soldiers to have lots of children, inside marriage and out. And "Germanic looking" children were kidnapped in very large numbers in the eastern occupied territories in the belief that this would both weaken the local population and increase the Germanic base. Inside the German government there was considerable discussion of multiple marriages for surviving soldiers and other drastic ways of increasing the birthrate after the war of those considered to be of the favored racial stock.

The pervasiveness of belief in such simultaneous measures to increase the birthrate of some and accept the killing of others as an integral part of the war is dramatically illustrated by two collections of letters. At the top, the letters of Hitler's main administrative aide, Martin Bormann, reflect Hitler's view; after he wrote his wife who had borne him ten children that he was now busy impregnating a mistress, she replied that "it would be a good thing if a law were to be made at the end of this war . . . which would entitle healthy, valuable men to have two wives." A sentence that Bormann annotated with the comment that "the Fuehrer is thinking on similar lines!"[3] At the bottom, a collection of letters of an ordinary German soldier published in the former German Democratic Republic show him in full accord with the message of racial policy in both directions, raising the birthrate of the racially superior and eliminating those deemed inferior. In December 1941, he wrote to his wife that "we must replace" the children not born to soldiers killed in the fighting; that there "is no excuse anymore today" for those who hesitate to bring children into the world; and that "we must clear away the terrible prejudice against unmarried mothers"; in April, 1944, he explained to her how wonderful it was that an uncle fully understood the regime's concept of sterilizing those likely to have "hereditarily defective descendents."[4]

One further question belongs in this context. There were the terrible medical experiments in some of the camps in which means were to be found for the mass sterilization of large groups *without* individual surgical procedures. The latter were reserved for Germans; by the end of the Third Reich there had been more than four hundred thousand (one of many reasons why physicians were for the most part such enthusiastic Nazis). But then who were to be the victims of mass sterilization techniques if these had ever been developed? In a world without Jews, without Gypsies, without the handicapped, and with all those considered of superior background but suspected of possibly passing on genetic defects already surgically sterilized, who was left? The answer seems clear: any peoples, like the Slavic population of Eastern Europe, whose labor was needed until they could be replaced by Germanic settlers. These people and their labor could then be exploited, but they would

---

3. Hugh R. Trevor-Roper, ed., *The Bormann Letters*, trans. R.H. Stevens (London: Weidenfeld and Nicolson, 1954), p. 45; compare to Oron J. Hale, ed., "Adolf Hitler and the Post-War German Birthrate: An Unpublished Memorandum," *Journal of Central European Affairs*, Vol. 17, No. 2 (July 1957), pp. 166–175.

4. Kurt Pätzold, ed., *Briefe des Soldaten Helmut N. 1939–1945* (Berlin [East]: Aufbau-Verlag, 1988), pp. 133–134, 220.

have no progeny. The whole globe was eventually to be not only inherited but also populated by the self-worshipping Germans.

The aims of the Germans, who launched the war and primarily determined its initial course, were entirely novel. In prior wars there had certainly been mass slaughter and enslavement, the razing of cities, and the transplanting by deliberate policy of large groups of people. The example of Carthage cited earlier is an extreme one, but here too one should not overlook a fundamental difference. The tens of thousands carted off to Rome as slaves became a portion of the large slave society of the Republic; nothing suggests that many of them or their descendants were not freed at a later date and entered Roman society, and with the real possibility of themselves or their descendants entering the equestrian and even the senatorial order. There is no evidence that those from Carthage were treated any differently from manumitted slaves who had been seized elsewhere.[5] In this general field the Germans of World War II were indeed innovators of the most grisly variety.

In the area of weapons, on the other hand, we see development, not innovation. Clearly there were bigger and faster planes, larger bombs, new kinds of fuses and larger armored fighting vehicles, somewhat differently configured warships, and scientific breakthroughs in radar, rockets, and medicine. The first appearance of ballistic missiles, proto-computers, and atomic bombs certainly point to a different military technology in the future, but all three of these developments appear to be as much a matter of coincidence in the timing of scientific advance as an integral part of the war. That does not make them unimportant, but the war hastened rather than precipitated these innovations. Initiatives on all three antedate the war. The combination of the two most dramatic technological breakthroughs, the German ballistic missile and the U.S. atomic bomb, would create the super-weapon of the postwar era, the intercontinental ballistic missile, and open up the possibility of ending human life on earth, but that is another story.

Here we should perhaps conclude by bringing the history of war to those most directly affected by it: individual human beings. I want to talk about three: Heather Whitestone, Albert Sabin, and Jonas Salk. If the Germans had won World War II, these three would have been killed; the Miss America of 1994 because of her handicap, the other two as Jews. The ravages of polio could have continued, and those surviving it crippled

---

5. Although the case of Carthage is included as an example of genocide in the volume edited by Frank Chalk and Kurt Jonassohn, *The History and Sociology of Genocide: Analyses and Case Studies* (New Haven: Yale University Press, 1990), the differentiation discussed in this paper is alluded to (p. 92).

would also have been killed in the so-called euthanasia program. Does anyone seriously believe that if the Germans had won World War I that would have happened? The next time the origin of World War II is described as the product of traditional diplomacy and the fighting as a sort of dangerous chess game, and an account is offered that abstracts the purpose from the conflict, it is the question just mentioned that should be raised.

Chapter 6

The Twenty Years' Crisis, 1919–39: Why a Concert Didn't Arise

Randall L. Schweller

E.H. Carr attributes the twenty years' crisis to the English-speaking countries' "almost total neglect of the factor of power."[1] The victors' repudiation of "normal" balance of power politics might not have proven as fatal as Carr suggests had a concert system arisen in its place. The "crisis" of 1919–1939 was one of creating a legitimate international order in the absence of *any* functioning security system. This structural problem largely explains how another world war came only twenty years and two months after Versailles. To be sure, Hitler and his powerful contemporaries also played a significant role in shaping the course of history between the two wars. The difficult task "of balancing the relative importance of 'personality' and impersonal 'structures' and forces,"[2] which is general to interpretations of all historical periods, has proven a singularly acute and divisive one with regard to the interwar years. Perhaps this is because the story of the origins of World War II has been told so many times. Like all important historical events, it will be endlessly researched, revisited, rethought, reviewed, and revised.[3] But while it shall remain an unending story in an interpretive sense, World War II is not a mystery.

The purpose of this chapter is therefore not to uncover some new fact or set of facts that calls for a radical reinterpretation of the origins of the war; nor is it to offer *the* definitive explanation of events leading up to the outbreak of war in 1939—only a pretentious fool would consider such an absurdity. Instead, consistent with Jack Levy's claim that political scientists are driven by theoretical puzzles and "base their explanations

---

1. Edward Hallett Carr, *The Twenty Years' Crisis, 1919–1939: An Introduction to the Study of International Relations* (New York: Harper and Row, 1964), p. vii.

2. Ian Kershaw, *Hitler* (London: Longman, 1991), p. 4.

3. John Lukacs, *The Hitler of History* (New York: Knopf, 1997), pp. 1–2.

on theoretical models," my primary interest in studying the interwar period and World War II is to "generalize about the relationships between variables and construct law-like statements" about state and international systemic behavior.[4]

The value of the World War II story for my purposes is that it contradicts many of the key behavioral predictions of realist balance of power theory and suggests a modification of the research program's auxiliary hypotheses in ways that accord with realism's "hard core" propositions.[5] Recognizing that many states did not balance against threatening increases in power during the 1919–1939 period, I do not simply discard realist theoretical insights because the historical record does not conform to the conventional view of how the balance of power is expected to work. This alone is not evidence that realism is a degenerative research program. Instead, following standard Lakatosian metatheory and international relations disciplinary practice, I retain realism's core propositions but make changes in the more secondary hypotheses, yielding new predictions that can be tested against the case.

In summary, World War II is an important case for international relations theory because it suggests ways to revise, reformulate, and amend realist balance of power theory "for the purposes of (1) better explanations and more determinate predictions, (2) refinement and clarification of the research program's theoretical concepts, and (3) extension of the research program to cover new issue areas."[6]

The paper opens with a short discussion of the epistemological and methodological ground rules that inform my work. Next, I point out the merits of systems theory as a research tool for understanding the origins and prosecution of World War II. This is followed by a discussion of the causal role of Hitler. Finally, I outline the nature of the twenty years' crisis (that a concert among the victors of WWI did not emerge), and explain why there was so little security cooperation among the victors of the Great War.

---

4. Jack S. Levy, "Too Important to Leave to the Other: History and Political Science in the Study of International Relations," *International Security*, Vol. 22, No. 1 (Summer 1997), pp. 22, 25.

5. For an insightful discussion of Lakatosian metatheory and a useful description of the neorealist hard core, see Colin Elman and Miriam Fendius Elman, "Lakatos and Neorealism: A Reply to Vasquez," *American Political Science Review*, Vol. 91, No. 4 (December 1997), pp. 923–926.

6. Randall L. Schweller, "New Realist Research on Alliances: Refining, Not Refuting, Waltz's Balancing Proposition," *American Political Science Review*, Vol. 91, No. 4 (December 1997), p. 927.

Neoclassical Realism

My work embraces the epistemological and methodological premises of neoclassical (or neotraditional) realism.[7] In Gideon Rose's view, this new "school explicity incorporates both internal and external variables, updating and systematizing certain insights drawn from classical realist thought."[8] Neoclassical realists, like their predecessors, identify the relative power and interests of states as the key causal variables in explaining world politics and foreign policy behavior. What most clearly distinguishes them from other realists (e.g., structural, defensive, aggressive, contingent, etc.) is their assumption that, while an objective distribution of capabilities does exist and the intentions of other states can be known, the impact of these causal factors on countries' external behavior is indirect, complex, and problematic; it must first "be translated through intervening variables at the unit level" such as leaders' perceptions and domestic state structure.[9]

Members of this new school are generically "realist" because they believe that international politics is best understood as a perpetual struggle for security, prestige, and power and influence, that is, control over territory, scarce resources and the distribution of those resources, the behavior of other groups (primarily states in the modern system), and the world economy; and they embrace a political philosophy or worldview that is profoundly pessimistic about the human condition, moral progress, and the capacity of human reason to create a world of peace and harmony. Both of these propositions (or assumptions) about international relations spring from realism's emphasis on international anarchy and its consequences—consequences that can be mitigated (e.g., by be-

---

7. According to Gideon Rose, the other members of the neoclassical realist school are Aaron Friedberg, Fareed R. Zakaria, Thomas J. Christensen, Melvyn P. Leffler, and William C. Wohlforth. See Gideon Rose, "Neoclassical Realism and Theories of Foreign Policy," *World Politics*, Vol. 51, No. 1 (October 1998), pp. 144–172. John A. Vasquez similarly calls me, Jack Snyder, Thomas Christensen, Stephen Walt, Colin Elman, and Miriam Fendius Elman neotraditional realists. See John A. Vasquez, "The Realist Paradigm and Degenerative versus Progressive Research Programs: An Appraisal of Neotraditional Research on Waltz's Balancing Proposition," *American Political Science Review*, Vol. 91, No. 4 (December 1997), pp. 899–912. Finally, I have been called a "motivational realist" because of my focus on the intentions of states. See Andrew Kydd, "Sheep in Sheep's Clothing: Why Security Seekers Do Not Fight Each Other," *Security Studies*, Vol. 7, No. 1 (Autumn 1997), pp. 114–154; also see Randall L. Schweller, "Neorealism's Status-Quo Bias: What Security Dilemma?" *Security Studies*, Vol. 5, No. 3 (Spring 1996), pp. 90–121.

8. Rose, "Neoclassical Realism and Theories of Foreign Policy," p. 146.

9. Ibid.

nign international structures, skillful diplomacy, military technology, etc.) but not transcended altogether. As long as states exist in a self-help realm under conditions of material and social scarcity, they will continue to compete with each other. The enduring context of anarchy makes conflict and war inevitable and international cooperation difficult to achieve and harder to maintain.

What is "new" about neoclassical realism is its attempt to systematize traditional realist propositions and to test them using sound methodological techniques—ones that stress precise measurement and include variables (such as system polarity and state power) not found in earlier realist works. And because "neoclassical realism stresses the role played by both independent and intervening variables," as Rose observes, "it carries with it a distinct methodological preference—for theoretically informed narratives, ideally supplemented by explicit counterfactual analysis, that trace the ways different factors combine to yield particular foreign policies."[10]

More broadly, neoclassical realists emphasize problem-focused research that (1) seeks to clarify and extend the logic of basic realist (classical and structural) propositions, (2) employs the case study method to test general theories, explain cases, and generate hypotheses, (3) incorporates psychological, domestic-political, and international-systemic variables, (4) addresses important questions about foreign policy and national behavior, and (5) has produced a body of cumulative knowledge. A partial list of theoretical questions explored by neoclassical realism includes: Under what conditions do nations expand their political interests abroad?[11] What is the relationship between a nation's external behavior and its domestic mobilization?[12] How do political elites perceive and think about power in world politics?[13] How do states assess and adapt to changes in their relative power?[14] How do states respond to threats and opportunities in their external environment, and do different kinds

---

10. Ibid., p. 153.

11. Fareed Zakaria, *From Wealth to Power: The Unusual Origins of America's World Role* (Princeton: Princeton University Press, 1998).

12. Thomas J. Christensen, *Useful Adversaries: Grand Strategy, Domestic Mobilization, and Sino-American Conflict, 1947–1958* (Princeton: Princeton University Press, 1996).

13. William C. Wohlforth, *The Elusive Balance: Power and Perceptions During the Cold War* (Ithaca: Cornell University Press, 1993).

14. Aaron L. Friedberg, *The Weary Titan: Britain and the Experience of Relative Decline, 1895–1905* (Princeton: Princeton University Press, 1988); and Zakaria, *From Wealth to Power.* Friedberg investigates this question from the perspective of a declining power, while Zakaria's study is of a rising power.

of states respond in different ways?[15] What explains variation in state alliance strategies, whether they choose to balance, buck-pass, band-wagon, chain-gang, or avoid alliances altogether?[16]

In their examinations of these questions, which lie outside the scope of neorealist theory, neoclassical realists have not rejected systemic theory but instead incorporated its insights, since, as Fareed Zakaria suggests, "a good account of a nation's foreign policy should include systemic, domestic, and other influences, specifying what aspects of policy can be explained by what factors."[17] Likewise, Jack Snyder writes: "theoretically, Realism must be recaptured from those who look only at politics between societies, ignoring what goes on within societies. Realists are right in stressing power, interests, and coalition making as the central elements in a theory of politics, but recent exponents of Realism in international relations have been wrong in looking exclusively to states as the irreducible atoms whose power and interests are to be assessed."[18]

While my research focuses on a variety of international problems and issues, all of it is informed by one central theme: international politics and foreign policy are largely a function of the interaction between state (or unit) attributes and international structure. To uncover these often complex structural and unit interactions, I employ a holistic approach known as systems theory, which should not be confused with purely structural theory.[19] Generally speaking, a system refers to a set of elements interacting to form a whole, such that "reciprocal impact [is]

---

15. Randall L. Schweller, *Deadly Imbalances: Tripolarity and Hitler's Strategy of World Conquest* (New York: Columbia University Press, 1998), chap. 3.

16. Thomas J. Christensen and Jack Snyder, "Chain Gangs and Passed Bucks: Predicting Alliance Patterns In Multipolarity," *International Organization*, Vol. 44, No. 2 (Spring 1990), pp. 137–168; Thomas J. Christensen, "Perceptions and Alliances in Europe, 1865–1940," *International Organization*, Vol. 51, No. 1 (Winter 1997), pp. 65–98; and Randall L. Schweller, "Bandwagoning For Profit: Bringing the Revisionist State Back In," *International Security*, Vol. 19, No. 1 (Summer 1994), pp. 72–107.

17. Fareed Zakaria, "Realism and Domestic Politics: A Review Essay," *International Security*, Vol. 17, No. 1 (Summer 1992), p. 198. For further elaboration, see Jennifer Sterling-Folker, "Realist Environment, Liberal Process, and Domestic-Level Variables," *International Studies Quarterly*, Vol. 41, No. 1 (March 1997), pp. 1–25.

18. Jack Snyder, *Myths of Empire: Domestic Politics and International Ambition* (Ithaca: Cornell University Press, 1991), p. 19.

19. This is consistent with Kenneth Waltz's definition of a system as "composed of a structure and of interacting units. The structure is the system-wide component that makes it possible to think of the system as a whole." Kenneth N. Waltz, *Theory of International Politics* (Reading, Mass.: Addison-Wesley, 1979), p. 79. For a discussion of how traditional and structural realists differ in their understanding and usage of the term "system," see Randall L. Schweller and David Priess, "A Tale of Two Realisms:

feasible, if not unavoidable" and the whole cannot be known by simply summing or otherwise studying just its parts.[20] Specifically, systems consist of both a structure and interacting units, and changes at either level may alter systemic outcomes.[21]

Systems Theory and World War II

On four fundamental issues regarding the origins of World War II, Gerhard Weinberg and I are in complete agreement. First and most significant, we agree on the importance of taking a systemic, or holistic, approach to the origins and prosecution of World War II. Weinberg writes: "In the first place, I am convinced that the war must be seen as a whole, and that the presentation of it in discrete segments covering the European and Pacific portions separately distorts reality and obscures important aspects of the war on both sides of the world."[22] Second, we agree that World War II was not merely a continuation of World War I (the reasons for which I will outline later); they were two distinct wars with very different origins and motivations, and the twenty years' crisis and World War II cannot be properly understood otherwise. Third, we view World War II as a truly hegemonic struggle. Weinberg observes: "A total reordering of the globe was at stake from the very beginning, and the leadership on both sides recognized this."[23] This view conforms to Robert Gilpin's tripartite definition of the theory of hegemonic war:

[First,] a hegemonic war is distinct from other categories of war; it is caused by broad changes in political, strategic, and economic affairs. [Second,] the

---

Expanding the Institutions Debate," *Mershon International Studies Review*, Vol. 41, Suppl. 2 (April 1997), pp. 7–8. For the most comprehensive and sophisticated treatment of systems theory in international relations, see Robert Jervis, *System Effects: Complexity in Political and Social Life* (Princeton: Princeton University Press, 1997). For the application of a systems theory to a specific historical case, see Schweller, *Deadly Imbalances*.

20. Inis Claude, *Power and International Relations* (New York: Random House, 1962), p. 42. In Jervis's view: "Interconnections and emergent properties define systems, whether or not humans are part of them." Jervis, *System Effects*, p. 28.

21. Kenneth N. Waltz, "Reflections on *Theory of International Politics:* A Response to My Critics," in Robert O. Keohane, ed., *Neorealism and Its Critics* (New York: Columbia University Press, 1986), p. 327.

22. Gerhard L. Weinberg, *World in the Balance: Behind the Scenes of World War II* (Hanover, N.H.: University of New England Press, 1981), p. xi.

23. Gerhard L. Weinberg, *A World At Arms: A Global History of World War II* (Cambridge: Cambridge University Press, 1994), p. 2.

relations among individual states can be conceived as a system; the behavior of states is determined in large part by their strategic interaction. [Third,] a hegemonic war threatens and transforms the structure of the international system; whether or not the participants in the conflict are initially aware of it, at stake is the hierarchy of power and relations among states in the system.[24]

Fourth, we agree that the outcome of World War II was not a foregone conclusion. Hitler was not simply a psychopath determined to destroy Germany in a suicidal, unwinnable war. As the historian Justus D. Doenecke points out, during the years 1939–41, "Western Europe was subjected to a German occupation that gave every indication of becoming permanent, the Soviet Union stood in mortal danger, and Japan appeared to be poised for lasting domination of Asia."[25] Similarly, Weinberg argues that as late as 1942, the Axis had enjoyed a string of victories that might well have continued had they only coordinated their military strategies.[26]

24. Robert Gilpin, "The Theory of Hegemonic War," in Robert I. Rotberg and Theodore K. Rabb, eds., *The Origin and Prevention of Major Wars* (Cambridge: Cambridge University Press, 1989), p. 16.

25. Justus D. Doenecke, "U.S. Policy and the European War, 1939–1941," *Diplomatic History*, Vol. 19, No. 4 (Fall 1995), p. 669.

26. The argument goes as follows. U.S. entry into the war threatened a large-scale Allied intervention in the Western Mediterranean and on the Atlantic coast of French West Africa, and with it a greater likelihood of Vichy defection and Spanish reluctance to side with the Axis. Hitler responded by shifting his attention from the Eastern Front to the Mediterranean theater, advising his Italian and Japanese allies that the key aim of Axis policy in the spring and summer of 1942 would be a meeting in the Indian Ocean. If successful, this rendezvous operation would disrupt the entire Anglo-U.S. supply system, gain Axis control of the Middle East oil resources, cut the southern supply route to the Soviets, and permit the flow of critical materials between Germany and Japan. It was a high-stakes role of the dice that, one way or the other, promised to tilt irrevocably the balance of the entire war. The Italians, of course, did not need to be convinced of the supreme importance of the Mediterranean theater and the need to defeat Britain.

The strategy, which might well have succeeded, was never attempted. Japan, for all intents and purposes, simply abandoned its European partners. Instead of following up their offensive in the Indian Ocean, wnich they had initiated with great success in April, the Japanese foolishly disregarded Hitler's advice and turned in the opposite direction to meet the U.S. forces that had landed on Tulagi and Guadalcanal on August 7. In five months of bitter fighting in the Solomons, Japan suffered heavy losses in warships, ground combat assault troops, and naval air units that precluded the anticipated return to the offensive in the Indian Ocean. With Japan diverting its resources to the South Pacific, the British took Madagascar and the United States opened a supply route across Iran that sustained the Red Army in its battle against the new German offensive. For the Indian Ocean strategy, see Gerhard L. Weinberg, *Germany, Hitler, and World War II* (Cambridge: Cambridge University Press, 1996), chap. 16.

WHY SO FEW SYSTEMIC INTERPRETATIONS OF THE WAR?

If an understanding of World War II requires a holistic approach, as Weinberg and I believe, why has the overwhelming mass of published material on this war, in contrast with World War I, ignored the systemic view? There are many reasons for this, but I suspect that the bulk of the explanation centers on two aspects of World War II that clearly distinguish it from World War I: the enormous charisma of the interwar leaders, especially compared with their rather faceless counterparts in World War I (with the exception of Kaiser Wilhelm II); and the standard characterizations of World War I as a tragic accident and of World War II as a Manichean struggle between the forces of light and darkness.

Both historians and political scientists tend to pay more attention to the particular world war that better "fits" their discipline's explanatory focus. It is not surprising that political scientists, who seek to develop parsimonious and powerful theories that also yield policy-relevant generalizations, have studied World War I far more thoroughly than World War II. This is because the origins of World War I appear as an exemplar of how structural influences and unintended consequences can cause an outcome (in this case, world war) that none of the actors desired and none preferred over any of the other possible outcomes. This "unintended" nature of World War I (that leaders intended only to risk and not to fight a major war) also made the case especially attractive for generating policy-relevant knowledge during the height of the Cold War; it allowed scholars to study the dynamics of crisis escalation and thereby explain how a nuclear war might occur even if neither superpower had any rational reason to initiate one.[27]

Conversely, World War II is an ideal case for the idiographic orientation of the historian, with an eye for the particular, the unique, the individual. World War II's unique cast of "larger than life" characters— Hitler, Mussolini, Roosevelt, Chamberlain, Stalin, Daladier, and Churchill—explains why international relations theorists have tended to ignore the case and historians seemed obsessed by it, especially those persuaded by "great leader" approaches to history.[28]

---

27. The use of World War I as an analogous case for the outbreak of nuclear war seems to contradict the view put forth by the Elmans that international relations theorists are guilty of "(un)intended presentism." See Colin Elman and Miriam Fendius Elman, "Diplomatic History and International Relations Theory: Respecting Differences and Crossing Boundaries," *International Security*, Vol. 22, No. 1 (Summer 1997), pp. 8–9, 13–14.

28. I am indebted to the editors, Colin Elman and Miriam Fendius Elman, for pointing this out.

In light of the gigantic scale of these leaders' personalities, it is all the more astonishing how completely Adolf Hitler's life and career overshadows those of his contemporaries. This is particularly true today. Starting in the 1960s, the revival of the public's fascination with Adolf Hitler has grown each year. Recognizing the public's prurient curiosity about any incarnation of evil, the so-called Jack the Ripper syndrome,[29] it is nonetheless undeniable that "Adolf Hitler was," as John Lukacs claims, "the most extraordinary figure in the history of the twentieth century."[30] In the insightful eyes of Joachim Fest:

History records no phenomenon like him. Ought we to call him "great"? No one evoked so much rejoicing, hysteria, and expectation of salvation as he; no one so much hate. No one else produced, in a solitary course lasting only a few years, such incredible accelerations in the pace of history. No one else so changed the state of the world and left behind such a wake of ruins as he did. It took a coalition of almost all the world powers to wipe him from the face of the earth in a war lasting nearly six years, to kill him—to quote an army officer of the German resistance—"like a mad dog."[31]

So it is not surprising that the temptation to posit Hitler as a sufficient cause of the war has proven almost irresistible for both historians and political scientists. Lukacs asserts: "That [the] war would not have come in 1939 except for Hitler, and that the course of that entire war would have been *entirely different* but for Churchill, Stalin, and Roosevelt, needs no further explanation."[32] Similarly, Emerson Niou and Peter Ordeshook "sympathize . . . with the analyses that interpret Hitler's personality . . . as critical to the outbreak of World War II rather than some breakdown in traditional balance of power forces."[33] John Mueller argues that Hitler alone caused World War II, since "it almost seems that after World War I the only person left in Europe who was willing to risk another total war was Adolf Hitler."[34]

Yet, declares E.H. Carr, "to say that the second World War occurred

---

29. See Lukacs, *The Hitler of History*, pp. 2–5, 43.

30. Ibid., p. xi.

31. Joachim C. Fest, *Hitler*, trans. Richard and Clara Winston (San Diego: Harcourt Brace Jovanovich, 1974), p. 3.

32. Lukacs, *The Hitler of History*, p. 41 (emphasis added).

33. Emerson M.S. Niou and Peter C. Ordeshook, "Stability in Anarchic International Systems," *American Political Science Review*, Vol. 84, No. 4 (December 1990), p. 1231.

34. John Mueller, "The Essential Irrelevance of Nuclear Weapons: Stability in the Postwar World," *International Security*, Vol. 13, No. 2 (Fall 1988), p. 75.

because Hitler wanted war is true enough but explains nothing."[35] At best, it is a flimsy explanation that borders on tautology and ignores situational factors that were crucial antecedent causes of the war. At worst, the force of Hitler's personality and his unmatched ability to make history has blinded too many scholars to the importance of the structural environment in which the actors made the fateful decisions that led to war. Far too few analysts have asked the questions: What was the structure of the international system from 1933 to 1939? What opportunities and constraints did international structure provide the actors? As I have argued elsewhere and will again here, the structure of the international system prior to World War II was tripolar—not multipolar, as commonly believed—and this needs to be taken into account in explaining the alliance patterns and foreign policy strategies of the major powers prior to and during the war.[36]

To restrict the analysis to structural elements alone, however, would be just as wrongheaded as focusing entirely on individual personalities or other unit-level factors. Structural conditions are merely permissive or "profound" causes of specific actions: they allow certain things to happen by providing opportunities for and constraints on actors' behavior.[37] As Arnold Wolfers explained years ago, where less than national survival is at stake, conditions of danger or opportunity emanating from the external environment do not approach what could be called inexorable (or irresistible) compulsion—compulsion capable of producing uniform reaction, of leaving policymakers with no other choice but to act the way they did.[38] The many historical instances of political leaders' shaping events and changing the course of history, though often in unforeseen and unintended directions, suggest that systemic-structural factors rarely dictate behavioral conformity among actors.

Complex historical events, like World War II, are the product of many causes, both general and specific. Any interpretation of the origins of the

---

35. Edward Hallett Carr, *What is History?* (London: Macmillan, 1961), p. 81.

36. See Schweller, *Deadly Imbalances*; and Randall L. Schweller, "Tripolarity and the Second World War," *International Studies Quarterly*, Vol. 37, No. 1 (March 1993), pp. 73–103. For multipolar accounts of World War II, see Waltz, *Theory of International Politics*; Barry Posen, *The Sources of Military Doctrine: France, Britain, and Germany Between the World Wars* (Ithaca: Cornell University Press, 1984); and Christensen and Snyder, "Chain Gangs and Passed Bucks."

37. See William Dray, *Perspectives on History* (London: Routledge and Kegan Paul, 1980), chap. 4; and Kenneth N. Waltz, *Man, the State, and War: A Theoretical Analysis* (New York: Columbia University Press, 1959), pp. 232, 234, 238.

38. Arnold Wolfers, *Discord and Collaboration: Essays on International Politics* (Baltimore: Johns Hopkins Press, 1962), chap. 1.

war must therefore include the particular interests and goals of the major actors as specific causes that supplement the more general causes, providing greater determinateness to the explanation.[39] Most historians agree that both objective situations (e.g., standing conditions that make the event possible and changes in standing conditions that make the event probable) and human characteristics (e.g., intelligence, heroism, wickedness, and blunders) make history; the two causal levels complement each other. Disputes over historical interpretations, when they are not the result of conflicting appeals to evidence or of basic interpretations of the facts, often turn on the relative weight assigned to the two levels of causation. Establishing a hierarchy of causes and specifying their relations to one another is not the exclusive task of the social scientist, it is the essence of historical interpretation. Different causal judgments tend to reflect, therefore, competing assessments of the interplay among unit- and structural-level factors—proximate causes and standing conditions—and the relative weight assigned to each level.[40]

The Causal Role of Hitler?

Let us return to the question of Hitler's role and significance as a cause of World War II and engage in an "idiographic" counterfactual thought experiment.[41] Historians have conventionally viewed the emergence of Hitler as a necessary and sufficient condition for the war. His revisionist

---

39. For an insightful discussion of proximate causes and standing conditions and the interplay among independent, intervening, compounding, decision-making, and dependent variables, see Stephen Pelz's chapter in this volume.

40. On this point, I am somewhat at odds with Richard Ned Lebow, whose comments on overdetermination and multiple causation suggest that historians, unlike social scientists, often fail to rank order causal variables and specify causal linkages in their multilayered explanations. It is my experience that "good" history, like "good" social science, explains how causes fit together and assigns causal weights to variables, putting some in the foreground and keeping others in the background. The problem of underspecification of causal linkages equally plagues both political science and diplomatic history; that is, both disciplines could do a far better job of explicitly stating everything in the causal chain—the sequences of standing conditions and proximate causes—that is necessary to produce the posited effect. See Richard Ned Lebow's chapter in this volume.

41. For five ideal-type patterns of counterfactual reasoning, including the idiographic case study, see Philip E. Tetlock and Aaron Belkin, "Counterfactual Thought Experiments in World Politics: Logical, Methodological, and Psychological Perspectives," in Philip E. Tetlock and Aaron Belkin, eds., *Counterfactual Thought Experiments in World Politics: Logical, Methodological, and Psychological Perspectives* (Princeton: Princeton University Press, 1996), pp. 6–15. Also see Geoffrey Hawthorn, *Plausible Worlds: Possibility*

aims, they contend, were far more ambitious than those of his predeces-sors.[42] While Hitler's predecessors, Gustav Stresemann and Heinrich Brüning, would have gladly accepted the frontiers of 1914, for instance, Hitler not only rejected these borders but made it clear that he would not be satisfied with a restoration of the huge gains Germany made by the Treaty of Brest-Litovsk (1917). Furthermore, Weimar leaders showed little enthusiasm for Hitler's ideas on race and space and would not have even contemplated, much less carried out, Hitler's barbaric policies of exter-minating and enslaving Jews and the inhabitants of those territories mapped out for future German "living space."[43]

Revisionists counter that Hitler did not invent the doctrines of race and space and that he was not the only German of his day who believed in them. Indeed, Hitler's beliefs were fairly popular among Germans and other Europeans and they were rooted in old ideas and theories. For example, Hitler's call for German "living space" was inspired by nine-teenth-century German geopolitics; his vulgarized, racist version of Social Darwinism had, by 1900, gained wide acceptance in German academic circles and among the masses; and his claim that Germany had not been defeated in World War I but instead stabbed in the back by Jews or those inspired by Jews was also commonly believed in Germany after the war.

Yet, even if we concede that Hitler's ideas on race and space and the expansiveness of his territorial aims distinguished him from prior Ger-man leaders, the key question remains: Was Hitler's ideology or one similar to it necessary for the outbreak of World War II? Throughout history, the diversity of interests and ideological concerns that have mo-tivated states to wage large-scale war for the purpose of overthrowing the established order suggests that Naziism was not a necessary cause of the war. "Napoleonic France and Hitlerite Germany," notes Gilpin, "gave very different governances to the Europe each united."[44] What defines all revolutionary states is not a specific set of interests or radical ideology

and *Understanding in History and the Social Sciences* (Cambridge: Cambridge University Press, 1991), chaps. 1 and 5; Richard Ned Lebow's chapter in this volume; and Schweller, *Deadly Imbalances*, pp. 180–181. For criticism of "parlour-games with might-have-beens," see Carr, *What Is History?* p. 91.

42. See, for instance, Hugh Trevor Roper, "A.J.P. Taylor, Hitler and the War," in William Roger Louis, ed., *The Origins of the Second World War: A.J.P. Taylor and His Critics* (New York: John Wiley, 1972), pp. 44–63.

43. For Hitler's ideology of race and space, see Gerhard L. Weinberg, *The Foreign Policy of Hitler's Germany: Diplomatic Revolution in Europe, 1933–1936* (Chicago: Univer-sity of Chicago Press, 1970), chap. 1.

44. Robert Gilpin, *War and Change in World Politics* (Cambridge: Cambridge Univer-sity Press, 1981), p. 37.

but a strong conviction that the status-quo order is illegitimate and must be overturned, if necessary, by force of arms.[45] By this definition, post-1919 Germany could not have been anything other than a revolutionary state. All German parties and statesmen were calling for drastic revision of the peace settlement and the German people were willing to fight to achieve this goal. The revisionist foreign policy goals espoused by Nazi ideology were not unique—they were the ordinary expressions, albeit in an especially vicious anti-Semitic tone, of the average German's hostility toward what was perceived as an unduly harsh and unjust treaty.

Of course, Weinberg is certainly correct in saying that Hitler's aims—his demographic and racial revolutions—were anything but traditional; that Hitler despised "*Grenzpolitiker*, border politicians, who merely wanted to undo the peace treaty of 1919 and regain for Germany what had then been lost;" and that Hitler promised to "lead Germany to the conquests not of snippets of land lost by the peace treaty of Versailles but of hundreds of thousands of square kilometers."[46] But Weinberg is incorrect, in my judgment, in implying that traditional war aims, which he lists as "expansion of territory and perhaps colonial possessions, influence and status, control of raw materials and strategic points, defense of what one already had against real or perceived threats,"[47] would not have sufficed to bring about World War II.

Indeed, to the onlooking great powers at the time, the objectives of Germany's invasion of Poland, which triggered the war, looked essentially similar to those of prior wars. That Hitler's long-run goals of world conquest and racial purity proved to be fundamentally different from the traditional objectives of prior German leaders matters little in predicting the outbreak of World War II; because the novelty of Hitler's aims—his racial policies and long-range plan to establish a German world empire—were either unknown, uncertainly believed, or given little credence by the leaders of Nazi Germany's actual or potential enemies in 1939, it is extremely unlikely that this "fact," which only became a certainty in hindsight, significantly altered the probability that war would break out when it did. Here, Weinberg commits the common mistake of "creeping determinism," whereby "outcome knowledge" or the certainty of hindsight contaminates our understanding of the past.[48] By focusing on the

---

45. For the aims of "revolutionary states," see Henry A. Kissinger, *A World Restored: Castlereagh, Metternich, and the Problem of Peace, 1812–1822* (Boston: Houghton Mifflin, 1957).

46. Gerhard L. Weinberg's chapter in this volume.

47. Ibid.

48. Tetlock and Belkin, "Counterfactual Thought Experiments," p. 15.

novelty of Hitler's aims, he implies that this explains World War II, that such aims were a necessary or sufficient antecendent condition for World War II, and that the pursuit of more traditional German aims would have produced a different outcome.

Structuralists point out that the legacy of Versailles was a dangerous imbalance of power that placed Germany in an unnatural position of "artificial inferiority." Denied its "natural weight" by the terms of the treaty, Germany was nevertheless left intact at the insistence of the Anglo-Saxon powers and remained potentially the strongest power in Europe. Since "powers will be powers," A.J.P. Taylor argues, it "was perfectly obvious that Germany would seek to become a Great Power again."[49] In his view, Germany was a "normal" state, acting as any other state would have behaved under similar objective conditions. Further, Taylor's Hitler was a "normal" statesmen, who, in principle and doctrine, was "no more wicked and unscrupulous than many other contemporary statesmen."[50] Unlike his pusillanimous counterparts, however, Taylor's Hitler was a daring improviser, who capitalized on the opportunities his feckless opponents dropped in his lap. If anyone is to be blamed for the war, therefore, it is not Hitler, who quite naturally sought to undo Germany's defeat and, like most statesmen, "had an appetite for success."[51] Rather, it is the leaders of Britain and France: "They were the victors of the first World war. They had the decision in their hands. It was perfectly obvious that Germany would seek to become a Great Power again. . . . Why did the victors not resist her?"[52]

Taylor's charitable characterization of Hitler as a responder and not an initiator of the crucial events leading up to the war has been ridiculed and rejected by most historians, and rightly so. Yet, this does not invalidate the essential thrust of his argument that "acute structural imbalance" was a sufficient cause of World War II. That is, we may concede that Hitler was not a "normal" statesman, that he intended World War II, sought world conquest, and planned for it long in advance, and still conclude that these factors were not sufficient causes of the war or even necessary ones but rather irrelevant or epiphenomenal to the outcome; at best, they made a highly probable event more likely to occur.

According to this interpretation, an underlying "geopolitical reality"

---

49. Taylor, *The Origins of the Second World War*, p. xiii.

50. Taylor, *The Origins of the Second World War*, p. 71. For a discussion of the "normal statesman" assumption, see Dray, *Perspectives on History*, chap. 4.

51. Taylor, *The Origins of the Second World War*, p. 106.

52. Ibid., p. xiii.

operates in accordance with objective laws such that the outcome could not have been any different from what it was, regardless of the policies and decisions of human agents. Adherents of "geopolitical determinism" claim that Germany's power and prestige would have risen without Hitler, and that the resulting structural imbalances made violent change inevitable. As Taylor writes: "All Germans, including Hitler, assumed that Germany would become the dominant Power in Europe once she had undone her defeat."[53] German liberation from the "slave" treaty of Versailles meant German domination of Europe. So what did it matter that Hitler rather than someone else came to power in Germany in 1933? A united Germany at the center of Europe was simply "too big and dynamic for any stable European state system."[54] All one needs to assume is that Germany acts like any other great power, and it becomes akin to a destructive force of nature. And like nature, it is blameless for the damage it unleashes; for nature does not have a strategy, it does not make choices, it simply sets the state of the world.

In this spirit, unless post-Versailles Germany proved to be an extremely "abnormal" state in an altruistic, self-abnegating sense, it was destined to become a rising, dissatisfied power; and when such states have gained sufficient strength to wage hegemonic wars against the established order, more often than not, they have done so. At a minimum, they have threatened or risked war in an attempt to get others to redress their grievances. Thus, World War II was an accident waiting to happen. It was only a matter of time before the tension between Germany and its neighbors boiled over; the established powers could do little or nothing to keep the lid on the kettle.

In contrast with this deterministic notion of structure, the neoclassical realist approach sees structure as a permissive cause of action, providing the conditions that "let" rather than "make" things happen. Thus, while most of Hitler's ideas were not original and were shared and accepted by the majority of the German people, the rise of Hitler was not epiphenomenal to the war; he was, in my judgment, one of several jointly sufficient but not necessary antecedent conditions for the outbreak and severity of World War II. That is, while the war may have still occurred in the absence of Hitler, once he or someone very much like him came to power in Germany it became highly improbable that World War II could be avoided or kept limited. This view is similar to Lord Alan Bullock's argument that neither Hitler nor Stalin "created the circumstances which

---

53. Ibid., p. xviii.

54. David Calleo, *The German Problem Reconsidered: Germany and the World Order, 1870 to the Present* (Cambridge: Cambridge University Press, 1978), p. 1.

gave them their opportunity. But I do not believe that circumstances by themselves in some mysterious way produce the man; I am not convinced that if Hitler or Stalin had failed to seize the opportunity, someone else would and the result would have been much the same."[55] The historian, Ian Kershaw, puts it more precisely:

In historical explanation *both* the intentions of the leading actors *and* the external conditions which promote or negate those intentions are centrally important. The motives, aims and intentions of powerful political leaders are indeed of vital significance. But they are not 'free floating'. They have to operate for the most part in circumstances which extend beyond the control and manipulation of any single historical personage, however great the political power possessed by that individual.[56]

The goals and policy decisions of statesmen, sometimes even those of extraordinarily unremarkable ones, can (and often do) exert a profound effect on the course of history, and so human agency must be taken into account. But structure matters too. If Hitler had been the leader of Equador rather than Germany, he could not have started World War II. If the United States had not disengaged from Europe and demobilized its armed forces, Hitler would have been denied his "window of opportunity" to grab the Continent. In short, Hitler was not an altogether sufficient cause of the war; he alone could not and did not cause the war or determine its course.[57]

Systemic Causes of the Twenty Years' Crisis and World War II

In this section, I advance a systemic argument for the twenty years' crisis that builds on an influential theoretical work by Robert Jervis, "From Balance to Concert: A Study of International Security Cooperation."[58] Jervis asks: Why does security cooperation among states in the form of a concert system arise, disrupting the continuity of balance of power systems? He begins by listing four conditions necessary for the operation of

---

55. Alan Bullock, "Have the Roles of Hitler and Stalin Been Exaggerated?" The Government and Opposition/Leonard Schapiro Lecture, 1996, *Government and Opposition*, Vol. 32, No. 1 (Winter 1997), p. 82. I disagree with Bullock to the extent that he posits Hitler and Stalin as necessary, not just sufficient, antecedent causes of World War II.

56. Kershaw, *Hitler*, p. 8.

57. For a similar view, see William R. Thompson's chapter in this volume.

58. In Kenneth A. Oye, ed., *Cooperation Under Anarchy* (Princeton: Princeton University Press, 1986), pp. 58–79.

a balance of power system: there must be several actors (the minimum number is two) of relatively equal power; all states must wish to survive; states cannot be so constrained by ideologies, personal rivalries, national hatred that they are unable to align with each other on the basis of short-run interests—that is, there must not be many strong "alliance handicaps;" and war must be a legitimate tool of statecraft.[59]

"The most obvious clue," Jervis notes, "is provided by the timing of the concerts. They occur after, and only after, a major war fought to contain a potential hegemon."[60] This is because the aftermath of such wars weakens the last two conditions of a balance of power: "no alliance handicaps" and "war is a legitimate tool of statecraft." Hegemonic wars create two types of alliance handicaps: unusually strong bonds among the members of the victorious coalition, and hatred and distrust for the defeated near-hegemon, which is seen as an abnormal state unfit to be a potential ally. Concert members cooperate with each other by scheduling frequent and regular meetings to discuss major issues, jointly negotiating with third parties, and exchanging high-level security information to enhance the transparency of their military postures and strategies.

The horrible costs of hegemonic wars also make war unthinkable as an instrument of foreign policy. In Jervis's words: "After such an experience, the winners will be highly sensitive to the costs of war and will therefore be hesitant to resort to armed force unless their most vital interests are at stake. That is particularly true because in most cases the war against the hegemon will have been accompanied by, or will have led to, large-scale social unrest."[61]

The twenty years' crisis suggests that the weakening (or absence) of these two balance of power requirements may be necessary but insufficient to produce a concert system; that is, Jervis identifies jointly necessary causes but not jointly sufficient ones for the emergence of a concert system. World War I qualifies as a large-scale war that exhausted the combatants, created alliance handicaps, and made war an unacceptable tool of statecraft for the victors; why, then, did its aftermath not yield a concert system? The answer, I believe, lies in *how* World War I undermined these two balance of power conditions and one other crucial condition for a properly functioning balance of power system: it must not be composed of three equally strong actors.

---

59. Ibid., p. 60.

60. Ibid., p. 60.

61. Ibid., p. 61.

ALLIANCE HANDICAPS

Strong alliance handicaps among the great powers appeared after World
War I. These impediments to alignments for short-run interests formed
in entirely different ways and for very different reasons than those engendered by the Napoleonic wars, after which a concert emerged. In
contrast with the strong bonds that developed among the victors after
the defeat of Napoleonic France, interwar alliance handicaps centered on
ideological differences that *divided* the former allies and prevented their
further cooperation against the defeated aggressor. As a result of the
Russian Revolution and reaction against it, the conflict of nation-states
that began with the French Revolution yielded to the conflict of ideologies
among communism, fascism-Nazism, and liberal democracy. The most
important effect was that France (under great pressure from Britain)
could no longer ally with Russia, its traditional ally against Germany.
Similarly, ideological affinities, rather than short-run strategic interests,
brought the Axis partners together. The extent to which ideology rather
than *raison d'état* governed relations within the Axis often surprised Hitler
himself, who many believe was more a political realist than an ideologue.
Consider Hitler's reaction to Mussolini's acquiescence to Germany's occupation of Austria in March 1938. Of the great powers, Italy stood to
lose the most by the *Anschluss* and the presence of a Greater Germany at
the crest of the Alps. Thus, when Hesse reported from Rome that Il Duce
"had accepted the whole thing in a very friendly manner," Hitler "was
thrown into transports of joy and said, repeating himself hysterically
many times: 'I will never forget him for this.'"[62]

The interwar system was also divided into three "interest-based"
camps: those that aimed to defend the status-quo order, those that sought

---

62. *Documents on German Foreign Policy* [hereafter DGFP], Series D, Vol. 1 (Washington, D.C.: U.S. Government Printing Office [GPO], 1956), pp. 573–576; Edmonde M.
Robertson, *Hitler's Pre-War Policy and Military Plans, 1933–1939* (London: Longmans,
1963), pp. 115–116; and Albert Speer, *Inside the Third Reich,* trans. Richard and Clara
Winston (New York: Macmillan, 1970), pp. 109–110. Years after the Rome-Berlin Axis
and with reliable evidence that Mussolini had written off Austria, Hitler was nevertheless relieved by Mussolini's decision. As John Lukacs observes, Hitler "had feared
that, after all—or in the end, or at the crucial moment—Mussolini's *Staatsräson, raison
d'état*, would kick in, more important than their ideological comradeship." Lukacs, *The
Hitler of History*, p. 119. Weinberg disagrees with this interpretation. He claims that
Hitler had told Mussolini that Germany would annex Austria and that it would be
done in stages; and that Hitler could count on Mussolini's not intervening militarily
in Austria because of the large number of Italian troops commited to the Spanish Civil
War. Hitler, he writes, "originally envisaged a lengthy process of annexation of Austria
which would last several months and would allow Rome time to accustom itself to
the new conditions rather than being confronted by a fait accompli overnight." Weinberg, *Germany, Hitler and World War II,* p. 103. In the end, however, Mussolini was

to overthrow it, and those that wanted simply to be left alone. For two reasons, this ideational global rift thwarted any hope of the balance of power operating effectively. First, it created a dangerous imbalance of power by the mid-1930s, which could only have been restored by an actively engaged U.S. presence in Europe. With the United States unwilling to assume the role of offshore balancer, the revitalization of German power tilted the scales heavily against the status-quo states in favor of the revisionist camp, which included Italy, Japan, Soviet Russia, and various other smaller states such as Hungary. In essence, this meant that the Versailles order would eventually be overturned; the only questions that remained were when, how, and to whose advantage.

Second, the presence of several powerful revisionist states created alliance handicaps that severely disrupted the operation of the balance of power. The most basic requirement of a balance of power system is that states side with the weaker state or coalition; they must balance against, and not bandwagon with, the stronger side. Yet, revisionist states, unlike defenders of the status quo, have little incentive to balance a strong revisionist challenger; they seek to unravel, not preserve, the established order.[63] Accordingly, dissatisfied states are attracted to rising revisionist powers calling for a New Order. For instance, in 1936, Mussolini believed that Italy would be more appreciated and politically autonomous as Hitler's satellite than as a member of the weaker Anglo-French coalition. Unlike Britain and France, Nazi Germany supported Italy's goal of turning the Mediterranean into an "Italian Lake."[64]

The tendency of revisionist states to flock together also worked against an alliance between France and Russia and drew the Soviets (as well as Italy, Japan, and Hungary) into Hitler's embraces. As status-quo powers, France and Britain could offer the Soviets only the prospect of survival in a long war against Germany—a war in which the Red Army would probably find itself at the outset fighting German forces alone. They could not offer Stalin either short-term security or territorial gains at the expense of the status quo. In contrast, a rapprochement with Germany offered Stalin both short-term security and significant territorial

---

presented with a fait accompli. Moreover, though Hitler may have expected Mussolini to accept the *Anschluss*, as Weinberg claims, we will never know what Hitler truly believed prior to the annexation; and Hitler himself could never be entirely certain how Mussolini would actually react once the *Anschluss* began in earnest.

63. See Schweller, "Bandwagoning For Profit."

64. "Any future modifications of the Mediterranean balance of power," Hitler told Ciano in 1936, "must be in Italy's favour." Count Galeazzo Ciano, *Ciano's Diplomatic Papers,* ed. Malcolm Muggeridge (London: Odhams Press, 1948), p. 57.

gains. Indeed, Soviet expansion was possible only in collusion with Hitler. In the end, the two countries' shared interest in revisionism bridged their ideological divide.

THE ILLEGITIMACY OF WAR AS A TOOL OF STATECRAFT

After fighting an exhausting war to contain a potential hegemon, the victors are, as Jervis asserts, extremely sensitive and averse to the costs of war. In the eyes of the victors, therefore, war is no longer viewed as an acceptable policy option. Indeed, after World War I, the United States retreated into isolation; Britain sought to avoid war through appeasement of Germany's grievances; and France, having been showered by international opprobrium in response to Poincaré's adversarial posture toward Germany in 1923, grudgingly adopted a conciliatory and purely defensive grand strategy. What all the victors feared most was another long and bloody war against Germany. This shared goal did not, however, result in a concert or any significant security cooperation among them. Even when the German threat became undeniable in 1936, France and Britain failed to coordinate their military strategies.

One reason for British ambivalence toward France was that, to the British interwar mind, tight alliances and the lining up of states into opposing blocs caused the outbreak of World War I; the proposition that alliances provoke war rather than deter it was, for the British, an important lesson of the last war. Thus, in 1938, the British Chiefs of Staff opposed staff talks with the French on the grounds that "the military advantages of closer collaboration with the French regarding concerted measures against Germany . . . would be outweighed by the grave risk of precipitating the very situation we wish to avoid, namely the irreconcilable suspicion and hostility of Germany."[65] The British saw conferences and collective actions of any sort among only some of the European powers as impediments to the prospects of European peace.

A further and perhaps more important reason that a Concert did not emerge was that the Versailles settlement represented a compromise between the divergent views held by Britain and France regarding how best to preserve the new and fragile peace. Initially, the French staunchly supported the status quo, believing that only a clear preponderance of power on the side of the status-quo defenders and a firm, demonstrated resolve to use that power strictly to enforce the terms of the Treaty in its entirety would prevent a revolt by the dissatisfied powers. Most impor-

---

65. Quoted in R.A.C. Parker, "The Failure of Collective Security in British Appeasement," in Wolfgang J. Mommsen and Lothar Kettenacker, eds., *The Fascist Challenge and the Policy of Appeasement* (London: Allen and Unwin, 1983), p. 26.

tant, the French strategy called for containment and deterrence of Germany by ensuring that France maintained superior power over its potentially stronger and inherently aggressive neighbor.

Convinced that they had already "lost the peace" at Versailles, France, unlike Britain, violently opposed German expansion in the east for several reasons.[66] First, they feared that any change in the territorial status quo in Europe would set a dangerous precedent that might unleash a general assault on the Versailles order. "*Une fois le premier détail de l'architecture tombé,*" Herriot warned, "*tout l'édifice tomberait lui-même.*"[67] Second, French security now relied on the assistance of precisely those countries in Eastern Europe, particularly Poland and Czechoslovakia, which it considered substitutes for its traditional ally, czarist Russia. Lastly, the French feared that Germany, if it expanded in the east, would become so powerful that it could turn around and defeat France. German expansion of any kind contradicted the main goal of French policy, which was to prevent Germany from actualizing its potential power; to keep it in a permanent state of "artificial weakness." The French could hardly be expected to sanction an increase in Germany's relative power through the absorption of its allies. As it was, the "German menace" already possessed natural advantages over France and posed, in the minds of the French, a very real and most dangerous threat to their country's survival.

Similarly motivated by fear of another war with Germany, British policymakers attempted to eliminate the danger of another European explosion not by containment and deterrence of Germany but rather by removing the causes of revolt. "This meant," as Arnold Wolfers describes, "taking the new order merely as a starting point in a process of continuous adjustment, intended eventually to produce a new and more generally satisfactory settlement."[68] Paul Kennedy describes British appeasement as a policy of settling international quarrels "by admitting and satisfying grievances through rational negotiation and compromise, thereby avoiding the resort to an armed conflict which would be expensive, bloody, and possibly very dangerous."[69] In adopting this type of benevolent "engagement" strategy toward the revisionist powers, Britain

---

66. This discussion is drawn from Arnold Wolfers, *Britain and France Between Two Wars: Conflicting Strategies Since Versailles* (New York: Harcourt Brace, 1940), chap. 1.

67. "Once the first detail of the architecture falls away, the entire edifice will crumble." As quoted in ibid., p. 19.

68. Ibid., p. 5.

69. Paul Kennedy, "The Tradition of Appeasement in British Foreign Policy, 1865–1939," in Paul Kennedy, ed., *Strategy and Diplomacy, 1870–1945* (London: Allen and Unwin, 1983), p. 16 (emphasis omitted).

hoped not only to prevent war but also to moderate the course of change and render it less provocative. Support for peaceful and limited revision as opposed to a policy of deterrence and forceful defense of the status quo, the British believed, would ultimately reconcile the dissatisfied states with the essential framework of the established order and convert them into status-quo powers.

The driving motive behind British appeasement was not international justice, however, but rather fear of war, which was to be avoided at all costs. Capturing the British mood, William R. Rock writes:

Of all the factors in British appeasement, none was more potent than the abhorrence of war as a means of settling international difficulties in the twentieth century. Surely the historical lesson of the First World War was clearly writ: the total nature of that great struggle had rendered war in its traditional role as senseless beyond contemplation. It was not that the whole nation had converted to philosophical pacifism, for only a wing of the Labour party had taken that route. Nor was it a matter of cowardice, irresponsibility, or fear. It was simply a poignant realization of the terrible destruction wrought by modern war; a keen appreciation that its costs vastly exceeded any benefits which might accrue to a prospective victor, in name only; a plain recognition that Europe had reached a stage of moral development where war must be considered a barbarity incompatible with civilized life; and a deeper commitment to rationality as the foundation stone of human behaviour. War, in short, had emerged in the British mind as the ultimate evil. Nothing would justify another one.[70]

Though often mischaracterized as having wholeheartedly embraced Wilsonian liberalism, the British were actually quite wary of cooperative security regimes and multilaterism in general. The League of Nations and collective security were seen by the British as essentially antirevisionist instruments, and as such they tended to work against the goals of peaceful revision and the avoidance of war. Specifically, the British thought that "the multilateral negotiation implied by League procedures facilitated obstructiveness and made mutual bargaining more difficult."[71] Further, as Sir Eric Phipps observed, the League (or, for that matter, any form of collective security) would not be fully acceptable to British governments until it was converted "from a purely passive into a really active instrument, not for the preservation of obsolete treaties but for their revision"; similarly, Churchill opined that "those who are devoted and sincere supporters of the Covenant of the League of Nations do not confine their

---

70. William R. Rock, *British Appeasement in the 1930s* (New York: Norton, 1977), p. 41.

71. Parker, "The Failure of Collective Security," p. 23.

position to an armed and combined defence of the *status quo*. We contemplate machinery for the redress of legitimate grievances between nations, and we must contemplate that if a grievance is shown to be justified it shall be corrected even against the wishes of nations who would be unwilling to make the sacrifice."[72]

For Britain, the legacy of Versailles was a sense of guilt—a guilt that not only prompted the British to give Germany every benefit of the doubt but that also made war with Germany over revision of the Treaty even more senseless.[73] Many Englishmen shared John Maynard Keynes's fear that the Treaty's harsh terms "might impoverish Germany now or obstruct her development in the future."[74] "Ashamed at what they had done," Martin Gilbert and Richard Gott suggest, the British "looked for scapegoats, and for amendment. The scapegoat was France; the amendment was appeasement. . . . France was blamed for having encouraged Britain in an excess of punishment. Justice could only be done by helping Germany to take her rightful place in Europe as a Great Power."[75]

In the eyes of British appeasers,[76] a stable and constructive peace required that "a large part of 'Eastern Europe' proper should be reconstructed under German leadership"; the states of Eastern Europe "ought to be as efficiently connected with Germany along the whole course of the Danube as are the American States along that other 'ole man river,' the Mississippi."[77] They welcomed German revision in the east because it would satisfy Germany's legitimate prestige demands and appetite for expansion; divert German attention away from the west; prevent the danger that Germany and the Soviet Union might draw together; and replace the chaos and weakness of Central Europe with a strong and coherent German bloc—one that would effectively buffer the West from the poison of Russian communism. Thus, in 1936, when sanctions against Italy were ended, "the British Cabinet came near to deciding on a public repudiation of British obligations under the Covenant in Eastern Europe

---

72. Phipps and Churchill quotes cited in ibid., pp. 22, 25.

73. See Rock, *British Appeasement in the 1930s*, p. 43.

74. John Maynard Keynes, *The Economic Consequences of the Peace* (London: Macmillan, 1919), p. 102.

75. Martin Gilbert and Richard Gott, *The Appeasers* (London: Weidenfeld and Nicolson, 1963), p. 21.

76. The list of British appeasers includes, among others, Lloyd George, Marquess of Londonderry, Lord Lothian, T. Philip Conwell-Evans, Lord and Lady Astor, Neville Chamberlain, Stanley Baldwin, Arnold Wilson, Thomas Moore, and Sir Horace Wilson.

77. J.L. Garvin, editor of *The Observer*, as quoted in ibid., p. 49.

and it was in effect agreed that those obligations would not be carried out in practice."[78] This logic proved expedient, if short-sighted, in 1938, when the British realized that war could only be avoided not by stabilizing the status quo in Central Europe but rather by actively promoting its change, at Czechoslovakia's expense, in the hope of satisfying the revisionist powers.

For its part, the United States was able but unwilling to assume the role of a strong offshore balancer. Rather than working to stabilize Europe, the United States turned its back on the Continent, refusing to ratify the Versailles Treaty and trying to insulate itself from future war through neutrality legislation. Most Americans came to believe that U.S. entry into World War I had been a terrible mistake; the four years of senseless carnage in Europe clearly showed that war was no longer a legitimate tool of statecraft. Reflecting this view, Congress objected to Articles 10 and 16 of the League of Nations' Covenant, which were regarded as requiring the United States to guarantee by sanctions and military force the territorial integrity of all League members against any act of "aggression." With regard to the status quo in Europe, the United States was indifferent and determined not to expend any blood or treasure in support of it.

The Neutrality Acts of August 31, 1935, and February 29, 1936, showed that, prior to 1937, the United States had no immediate concern either with the maintenance of the status quo or with its revision in any specific direction. Hitler's remilitarization of the Rhineland only reinforced the prevailing U.S. mood of isolation; U.S. Secretary of State Cordell Hull called it a purely European development that did not affect the United States.

Prior to May 1940, the Roosevelt administration sought a return to the pre-war status quo without any U.S. commitment. To accomplish this goal, Roosevelt consistently tried to appease Hitler with offers of arms limitations, tariff reduction, and access to raw materials and markets.[79] It was not until the passage of the Lend-Lease Act in March of 1941, which

---

78. Parker, "The Failure of Collective Security," p. 24.

79. See Arnold A. Offner, *American Appeasement: United States Foreign Policy and Germany, 1933–1938* (Cambridge, Mass.: Harvard University Press, 1969); and Arnold A. Offner, "Appeasement Revisited: The United States, Great Britain, and Germany, 1933–1940," *Journal of American History*, Vol. 64 (September 1977), pp. 373–393. For the most outspoken view of Roosevelt as an appeaser before 1940, see Frederick W. Marks III, *Wind Over Sand: The Diplomacy of Franklin Roosevelt* (Athens, Georgia: University of Georgia Press, 1988).

discriminated against Germany, that the United States chose sides in the European war.[80] Yet, as late as the spring of 1941, Roosevelt refused to provide naval escorts for convoys bound for Britain. Indeed, prior to Pearl Harbor, it is doubtful that Roosevelt ever sought to enter the conflict.[81] Instead, the goals of Roosevelt's foreign policy centered on "the containment of Hitler, the survival of Britain, and the elimination of any need for large-scale American intervention."[82] Roosevelt envisioned the U.S. fighting a proxy war, one in which the United States supplied arms to the Russian and British armies, which would do the fighting; at most, the U.S. would contribute naval and air power but not ground troops.

In sum, the victors of World War I all shared the view that war was no longer a legitimate tool of statecraft, but disagreed about how best to avoid another large-scale war: Britain championed appeasement and peaceful revision; France supported deterrence and containment of Germany; and the United States chose isolation from the Continent. These discrepant views, primarily over the value of preserving the international order created by the Versailles peace settlement, led, in turn, to divergent grand strategies that prevented the emergence of a Concert or any other form of security cooperation among them. While one can cite various contributory causal factors for this failure (e.g., domestic politics in each state), the linchpin, in my view, was U.S. nonengagement. If, as Jervis argues, "the U.S. had been willing to guarantee Britain's security, Britain would have been willing to guarantee France's, which would have generated a very different pattern of international politics." Because systems are composed of interconnected parts, the seemingly "indirect" effect of U.S. isolationism set in motion a destabilizing "positive feedback" dynamic.[83] This process, by amplifying the initial indirect effect, produced significant consequences for the stability of the European subsystem and eventually the global one.

---

80. In 1937, the United States adopted a policy of permitting belligerent trade on a cash-and-carry basis; when the war commenced in 1939, it repealed the arms embargo. Both policies benefited sea powers and so were more favorable to Britain than Germany—but they were a far cry from any type of active U.S. engagement in the war.

81. See Weinberg, *A World at Arms*, pp. 86–87, 238–263; and Weinberg, *World in the Balance*, pp. 75–95.

82. Warren F. Kimball, *The Juggler: Franklin Roosevelt as Wartime Statesman* (Princeton: Princeton University Press, 1991), p. 12.

83. Jervis, *System Effects*, p. 20.

THE TRIPOLAR STRUCTURE OF THE INTERWAR SYSTEM

As mentioned, Jervis claims that the smooth operation of balance of power systems requires "several actors of relatively equal power."[84] I disagree. Sometimes inequalities among several actors enhance the stability of a balance of power system, whereas equality of strength among the actors can be destabilizing. Consider, for instance, a tripolar system composed of three actors of relatively equal power. Here, any two-against-one coalition will be twice as strong as the isolated third. Moreover, because any combination of actors yields the same strength, assuming that the purpose of allying is power aggregation, no coalition is more likely to form than another. Compare this type of triad to a tripolar system in which the actors are of unequal strengths. Now any coalition will comprise a stronger and a weaker partner. The unbalanced nature of the coalition works against the destruction of any member of the triad because, if this occurred, the weaker member of the victorious coalition would be at the mercy of its stronger partner. Now consider a triad in which the strengths of the members are: $A = 2$, $B = 2$, $C = 4$. Here a natural coalition exists between A and B against C. The triad behaves as if it were a stable bipolar system.

The unique properties of tripolar systems explain why the balance of power system did not function properly during the interwar period; and this, in turn, partly explains the outbreak of the war.[85] The structure of the international system changed during the 1930s, moving from multipolarity to tripolarity. According to data generated by the Correlates of War (COW) project, by 1938 the combined capabilities of the United States, the Soviet Union, and Germany accounted for over 70 percent of the total power capabilities held by the great powers, and this 70 percent share was evenly distributed among the three powers.[86]

---

84. Jervis, "From Balance to Concert," p. 60.

85. This argument is fully developed in Schweller, *Deadly Imbalances*.

86. The Correlates of War Project, "The Capability Data-Set Printout," made available through the Inter-University Consortium for Political and Social Research at the University of Michigan, December 1987. COW capability scores reflect three distinct measures of national power: military (forces in being), industrial (war potential), and demographic (staying power and war-augmenting capability). Each component is divided into two subcomponents. The military dimension consists of the number of military personnel and military expenditures; the industrial component is measured by production of pig iron (pre-1900) or ingot steel (post-1900) and fuel consumption; and the demographic component is divided into urban and total population. The composite power index is the sum of each state's mean score for the six measures as a percentage of all scores within the Great Power subset. William B. Moul has refined

Prior to 1935, the international system was bipolar, with the United States and the Soviet Union as the two poles.[87] The remaining major powers—Britain, France, Germany, Italy, and Japan—were lesser great powers because they each possessed less than half the capabilities of the most powerful state in the system (the United States). Germany, however, was on the verge of attaining polar status.

By 1935, the bipolar system evolved into a tripolar system, as Germany attained weak third pole status. During this early stage of rearmament, Germany would require allies to counterbalance either of the other two poles. By 1938, German strength had substantially increased, creating a virtual equilateral tripolar system; that is, all three poles possessed roughly equal shares of between 20–25 percent of total great power capabilities and were far stronger than any of the other major powers.

As I have argued at length elsewhere, Hitler recognized the tripolar structure of the international system, and his grand strategy reflects this understanding.[88] Hitler's original program consisted of four stages.[89] First, Germany would rearm and secure alliances with two key lesser great powers—Britain and Italy. Next, Germany would unleash several lightning wars against its neighbors in order to bolster its military and economic resources and to pacify its western flank in preparation for the eastern campaign. Under the shelter of British neutrality or, better still, with its help, the Reich would then strike quickly to eliminate the nearest pole, the Soviet Union, before the more distant pole, the United States, could intervene. The defeat of Soviet Russia would transform the tripolar system into a bipolar one, pitting the stronger German-led European continent against the weaker North American continent (Hitler believed that the United States would annex Canada). Germany would now be "entirely self-reliant and capable of withstanding any economic blockade which might have been staged by the major maritime powers."[90]

With Europe as the nucleus of the German empire, Hitler would then set in motion the next step of his program: the defeat of the United States

---

the COW index by substituting iron production for the demographic components of the COW index. See William B. Moul, "Measuring the 'Balances of Power': A Look at Some Numbers," *Review of International Studies*, Vol. 15, No. 2 (April 1989), pp. 101–121.

87. For the data that supports this, see Schweller, *Deadly Imbalances*, chap. 1.

88. Ibid., esp. chaps. 2 and 6.

89. See Weinberg, *World in the Balance*, pp. 53–74.

90. Milan Hauner, "Did Hitler Want a World Dominion?" *Journal of Contemporary History*, Vol. 13, No. 1 (January 1978), p. 24.

and the creation of a global German empire. In preparation for this final war, the Reich would expand overseas from its continental base and retool its armed forces—with the Luftwaffe and navy receiving priority over the army. After establishing power bases in Europe, Africa, and the Atlantic, Germany would attack and crush the United States, converting the international system from bipolarity to unipolarity.

In his discussions of the balance of power, Hitler spoke of the international system in tripolar terms. France and Britain, he believed, were decaying powers that had long ago fallen to second-class status.[91] Of the remaining great powers, only Stalinist Russia and the United States were capable of thwarting Germany's drive for hegemony. During the 1930s, however, Russia and the United States were both preoccupied with internal problems, and so showed little interest in the fate of Europe. Likewise, Europe seemed scarcely to notice the affairs of the two great powers on its flanks. This state of affairs—the unactualized potential power of Germany's most dangerous rivals and the mutual disinterest among Russia, the United States, and Europe—offered Germany a window of opportunity to defeat Russia and grab the Continent.

Because the United States was disengaged from Europe at the outset of the war, from 1936 until the fall of France in June of 1940, Nazi Germany, the Soviet Union, and an Anglo-French combination were the three poles; and from June 1940 till the end of the war, the United States replaced the Anglo-French coalition as the third pole. The story becomes one of shifting tripolarity in terms of the membership and identity of the third pole; but, in both cases, the system was composed of three poles of roughly equal strength.[92] According to my discussion of the properties of tripolar systems, this equilateral configuration is particularly volatile and less stable than a tripolar system composed of unequal actors. The Nazi-Soviet pact demonstrates this logic quite nicely.

---

91. For Hitler's view on the balance of power and the demise of Britain and France, see Conversation, Hitler-Teleki, April 29, 1939, *DGFP,* Series D, Vol. 6 (Washington, D.C.: U.S. GPO, 1956), pp. 377–378. Similarly, Joachim von Ribbentrop declared in a conversation with M. Cincar-Markovic, the Yugoslav Foreign Minister, "Let there be no doubt about it, Germany could face calmly any combination of enemies." "Conversation, Ribbentrop-Cincar-Markovik," April 25, 1939, *DGFP,* Series D, Vol. 6, p. 326. See also "Conversation, Ribbentrop-Teleki and Csaky," April 30, 1939, *DGFP,* Series D, Vol. 6, p. 372, wherein Ribbentrop says, "If . . . Britain and France wanted such a trial of strength, they could have it any day."

92. In fact, it is incorrect to treat France and Britain as a single pole because this confuses polarity (a structural element that tells us how many poles exist) with polarization (a behavioral attribute of the system that tells us how many blocs or alliances exist). Nevertheless, some of the contemporary actors (most important, Stalin) conceptualized the system as tripolar with an Anglo-French pole.

STALIN'S FAILED TERTIUS-GAUDENS STRATEGY. Like Hitler, Stalin conceived of the pre–World War II international system in tripolar terms. But unlike Hitler, who saw the European system as bipolar with the United States out of the picture, Stalin's tripolar vision was based on his belief that Britain and France together constituted a third European pole—one that could effectively balance Germany. In his speech at the plenary session of the Central Committee in January 1925, Stalin revealed the *tertius-gaudens* strategy that would guide Soviet foreign policy in the next world war:

The preconditions for war are getting ripe. War may become inevitable, of course not tomorrow or the next day, but in a few years. . . . But, if war begins, we shall hardly have to sit with folded arms. We shall have to come out, but we ought to be the last to come out. And we should come out in order to throw the decisive weight on the scales, the weight that should tilt the scales.[93]

For the Soviet Union to become the enjoying third, Stalin had first to ensure not only that war broke out in the west but that it would be a protracted one—and for that both sides must be formidably strong. Consistent with his desire to instigate a "second imperialist" war from which the Soviet Union could safely abstain, Stalin supported the victory of fascism in Germany but not the further spread of fascism throughout Europe. A triumph of fascism in Western Europe would not only prevent its division into rival camps but would seriously threaten the Soviet Union.

Stalin's strategy required that the Anglo-French combination be militarily strong enough to keep from being overrun and speedily conquered by German and Italian forces. In the short term, therefore, Stalin supported the strengthening of a collective security coalition led by France and directed against Germany. He also encouraged the democracies to rearm, and instructed the French Communists to call off their campaign against the government's plan to extend the period of French military service from one to two years. Robert Tucker comments:

By his collective-security diplomacy, in combination with his popular-front tactics in the Comintern, Stalin was assisting events to take their course toward a European war. An accord with Germany remained a basic aim because it would offer an opportunity to effect a westward advance of Soviet rule while turning Germany against the democracies in what Stalin envisaged

---

93. Stalin quoted in Isaac Deutscher, *Stalin: A Political Biography*, 2nd ed. (New York: Oxford University Press, 1949), p. 411.

as a replay of World War I, a protracted inconclusive struggle that would weaken both sides while neutral Russia increased her power and awaited an advantageous time for decisive intervention. But to make sure that the European war *would* be protracted, he wanted Britain and France to be militarily strong enough to withstand the onslaught that Germany under Hitler was becoming strong enough to launch against them. That explains his moves to encourage ruling elements in both these major states to rearm with dispatch, and his order to the French Communists to support the French military buildup.[94]

Viewing the European system as a tripolar structure of roughly equal poles, it is easy to see why Stalin made a deal with Hitler. A nonaggression pact with Germany would destroy the status quo, afford easy spoils in Eastern Europe and Finland, and instigate a war of attrition among the capitalist powers. Better still, the Soviet Union enjoyed the role of kingmaker, as both Germany and the democratic powers needed it to form a winning coalition. Thus, Germany would be made to pay heavily for Soviet assistance in a war from which Russia could safely abstain. Stalin used his bargaining power to prolong the Anglo-Franco-Soviet negotiations just long enough to extract additional concessions from Hitler, in exchange for which the Soviet leader put his signature to the pact with Germany that he desperately wanted anyway. It appeared that Stalin had succeeded in the role of abettor: Germany was deflected to the west, while the Soviets comfortably looked on from the sidelines, gaining at the others' expense.[95] Speaking of the pact, Stalin commented: "Of course it's all a game to see who can fool whom. I know what Hitler's up to. He thinks he's outsmarted me, but actually it's I who have tricked him."[96]

In the end, Stalin's calculation "that the oncoming war between them would be a protracted one that would result in their mutual weakening or exhaustion while Soviet Russia was at peace and rebuilding its own strength"[97] proved incorrect. His "major blunder," as Isaac Deutscher points out, was that "he expected Britain and France to hold their ground

---

94. Robert C. Tucker, *Stalin in Power: The Revolution From Above, 1928–1941* (New York: Norton, 1990), p. 345.

95. Supporting this view of Soviet foreign policy, Sir Nevile Henderson wrote: ". . . I always believed that Moscow's chief aim was to embroil Germany and the Western Powers in a common ruin and to emerge as the *tertius gaudens* of the conflict between them. This was, up to August, similarly the professed view of all Germans from Hitler downward who commented on our Russian negotiations." Nevile Henderson, *Failure of a Mission: Berlin, 1937–1939* (New York: G. P. Putnam's Sons, 1940), p. 259.

96. Stalin is quoted in Tucker, *Stalin in Power*, pp. 597–598.

97. Ibid., pp. 587, 592.

against Germany for a long time . . . he overrated France's military strength; and he underrated Germany's striking power."[98]

Stalin's *tertius-gaudens* strategy hinged on his perception that the Anglo-French pole and the German one were roughly equal in strength. Had he known that France and Britain would not behave as a single pole (that is, that their military forces and doctrines would not be fully integrated) and that, even if they had, their combined strength would be less than Germany's, Stalin would have likely aligned with France and Britain at the outset of the war. In short, a tripolar European system composed of clearly unequal actors would have been more stable than one of equally strong poles.

Conclusion

John Lewis Gaddis has pointed out that one of the great ironies of history is that after World War I the statesmen attempted to construct security arrangements to keep the peace only to find themselves at war twenty years later, while after World War II there was no such attempt, and yet there followed "the long peace" that still endures today.[99] Commenting on Gaddis's observation, Jervis says, "it is not strange that the [international system] that lasted was not designed and the one that was designed worked in a very different way than anyone expected. Interconnections and interactions create sufficient complexity so that it would be surprising if the results conformed to statesmen's anticipations."[100] In this chapter, I have presented a different view. It was not the unintended consequences of statesmen's designs that led them to an undesired destination. Rather, it was their firm intention to discontinue—to thwart—balance of power politics, coupled with their failure to agree (also intended) on any security design to replace it, that caused a prolonged crisis and eventually the collapse of international peace.[101]

Three crucial requirements of balance of power were absent after 1919, two of which must be absent for a concert system to arise. That neither type of system emerged produced the twenty years' crisis and

---

98. Deutscher, *Stalin*, p. 441. For Stalin's overestimation of Anglo-French strength, see Adam B. Ulam, *Expansion and Coexistence: Soviet Foreign Policy, 1917–73*, 2nd ed. (New York: Holt, Rinehart and Winston, 1974), pp. 227, 229, 264.

99. John Lewis Gaddis, *The Long Peace* (New York: Oxford University Press, 1987), pp. 215–216.

100. Jervis, *System Effects*, p. 65.

101. In contrast, after World War II the statesmen deliberately did nothing to thwart the normal functioning of balance of power dynamics.

World War II. First, significant alliance handicaps impeded the fluidity in alliance patterns required for a balance of power system to work. With little flexibility to choose appropriate alliance partners, the defenders of the status quo could not, initially, muster enough strength to deter or defeat the potential hegemon. Ironically, it took Hitler's attack against Soviet Russia and declaration of war against the United States to create finally an effective—indeed, overwhelmingly powerful—countervailing coalition.

Second, because the goal of balance of power is not the preservation of peace but rather the survival of the essential actors, war must be a legitimate tool of statecraft. If states act as if they are more interested in peace than their own survival as independent states, then the balance of power will not operate effectively or as the theory predicts. None of the principal victors of World War I viewed war as a normal instrument of statecraft. Yet, a concert among them did not arise to replace balance of power politics. Instead, each went its own way, pursuing counterproductive policies that enabled aggressors to make piecemeal gains at the expense of the Versailles order.

Finally, the interwar system became tripolar with three roughly equal poles. For several reasons, this structure is least conducive to the operation of a balance of power system. First, there is a tendency to gang up on one of the three poles because the spoils can be divided equally among the two victors and because none of the poles wants to be the one ganged up on. Second, because there are no power disparities among the three poles, no coalition is more likely to form than any other; this uncertainty produces anxiety that can lead to, among other things, preventive war. Third, external balancing cannot stabilize the system because any coalition (*AB*, *BC*, or *AC*) will be twice as strong as the isolated third pole. And fourth, as Soviet behavior shows, because all three poles are roughly equal in strength, one of them can attempt a *tertius-gaudens* (or advantaged third) strategy, whereby it attempts to make relative gains by instigating, aiding, and abetting conflict between the other two poles. This strategy will misfire badly if the perception of relative equality among the poles is incorrect. Accordingly, imbalances of power in tripolar systems can and will be stabilizing *only* when they are recognized; which is to say that perceptions of power often matter as much as actual power.

Chapter 7

Postscript: September 1939

Carole K. Fink

I sit in one of the dives
On Fifty-Second Street
Uncertain and unafraid
As the clever hopes expire
Of a low dishonest decade

W. H. Auden, "September 1, 1939"

Randall L. Schweller and Gerhard L. Weinberg present two almost dia-metrically opposite interpretations of the origins of World War II, one taking a systemic and structural approach, the other an actor-centered explanation.[1] One draws on theoretical literature based on a few centuries of state behavior under the balance of power system; the other frames his argument of the uniqueness of Hitler's aggression in both a short and very long historical perspective going back as far as ancient Rome. Implicitly, they both address the old Churchillian question, whether World War II was avoidable or inevitable.[2]

Let us note the issues on which Schweller and Weinberg agree. Both reject the venerable, palliative formulas that World War II was caused by vengeance for Versailles, or that it was the climax of a thirty-year Euro-pean civil war after a brief, twenty-year truce.[3] Both regard World War II

1. I thank Richard Ned Lebow for recommending the enlightening discussion by Alexander E. Wendt, "The Agent-Structure Problem in International Relations Theory," *International Organization*, Vol. 41, No. 3 (Summer 1987), pp. 335–370.

2. Winston S. Churchill, *The Second World War*, vol. I: *The Gathering Storm* (London: Cassell, 1948). For a useful review of the historiography, see Andrew J. Crozier, *The Causes of the Second World War* (Oxford: Blackwell, 1997), pp. 226–259.

3. Despite the numerous and impressive rebuttals in the scholarly literature, the "Versailles" thesis not only retains an astonishing durability in textbooks and popular lore; it is now also applied as a warning against Russia's demotion in world affairs

as distinct from World War I—as a global, total, hegemonic struggle whose outcome was unforeseeable as late as 1942.[4]

These shared "holistic" approaches to World War II lead, however, in two fundamentally opposite directions, which Schweller ascribes to the "enormous charisma of interwar leaders," particularly the Nazi führer. Quoting E.H. Carr, Schweller maintains that "to say that World War II occurred because Hitler wanted war is true enough but explains nothing"[5] without an understanding of the "structural environment" in which the actors made the fateful decisions that led to war." Weinberg, on the other hand, basing his presentation on Hitler's pronouncements and the Nazis' deeds after 1933, characterizes World War II as the climax of a purposeful and methodical "racial and demographic revolution." In December 1936, Thomas Mann had already predicted:

The meaning and purpose of the National Socialist State is this alone and can be only this: to put the German people in readiness for the "coming war" by ruthless repression, elimination, extirpation of every stirring of opposition, to make them an instrument of war, infinitely compliant, without a single critical thought, driven by a blind and fanatical ignorance.[6]

Both writers have largely omitted these four issues from their essays: the global dimension of the outbreak of World War II; the economic determinants of structural volatility and national policy (neither discuss the impact of reparations, war debts, the Great Depression, and Stalin's and Hitler's various development and armament plans); the role of small, secondary actors, such as Piłsudski and Beck, Beneš and Schuschnigg as positive, passive, or negative factors in Hitler's and Stalin's designs; and the importance of social, cultural, and intellectual factors in failing to

---

(for example, in the remarks of former Ambassador Oleg Grinevsky to the Mershon Center of the Ohio State University on October 16, 1998.) The "thirty-year-war" thesis is best represented in Ludwig Dehio, *Deutschland und die Weltpolitik im 20. Jahrhundert* (Munich: Oldenbourg, 1955); and David Calleo, *The German Problem Reconsidered: Germany and the World Order, 1870 to the Present* (Cambridge: Cambridge University Press, 1978).

4. See Gerhard L. Weinberg, *A World at Arms: A Global History of World War II* (Cambridge: Cambridge University Press, 1994); also Peter Calvorcoressi and Guy Wint, *Total War: Causes and Courses of the Second World War* (London: Allen Lane and Penguin Press, 1972).

5. E.H. Carr, *What is History?* (London: Macmillan, 1961), p. 81.

6. Thomas Mann, Letter to the Dean of the Faculty of Philosophy of the University of Bonn, December 19, 1936, published in *Achtung Europa! Aufsätze zur Zeit* (Stockholm: Bermann-Fischer Verlag, 1938), pp. 106–107.

prevent, or precipitating, World War II, such as the melancholy history of interwar pacifism and internationalism.

Where do we go from here? Our purpose is to examine the divergent approaches of historians and international relations theorists to significant issues of the past in order to gain greater analytic sophistication and wisdom—if not greater predictive capabilities. Should we simply split the difference between the two theses, combining a vile, purposeful Hitler with a malfunctioning system caused by Stalin's cunning, British and French weakness, and U.S. isolation? Restated, would a dead Hitler in World War I *and* a better Versailles have prevented World War II? Would such syncretism provide greater understanding to students, colleagues, and the general public of a now-distant war that caused 40 million casualties, untold destruction, and revolutionary consequences throughout the world? Let me make a modest attempt to raise some critical points about both essays and then suggest some tentative conclusions.

The Faulty Edifice

Schweller, seeking to avoid a purely structural determinism or a Hitler-centered explanation, presents a dynamic picture of the twenty years' crisis. His argument is that the scale and ferocity of World War I, followed by a bitterly contested peace, left the victors unwilling or unable to establish a balance of power to preserve the status quo. Without a solid concert system bolstered by firm alliances and collective security, the more volatile tripolar system emerged, which Hitler and Stalin could easily manipulate.

Many historians would dispute Schweller's model concert, the post-Napoleonic period, as the measure of the failures of the interwar period. After all, the Metternich system was an ephemeral phenomenon. The motley coalition of Austria, Great Britain, Prussia, and Russia collapsed in peacetime; it not only failed to exclude France but was incapable of maintaining collective control in Europe and overseas. After the last concert played at Verona in 1823, each state went its own way.[7]

Moreover, the victors in World War I were even more quarrelsome and leaderless than one hundred years earlier, and the ex-enemy was far more formidable. Napoleonic France had been decisively trounced and

---

7. Paul W. Schroeder, *Metternich's Diplomacy at Its Zenith, 1820–1823* (Austin: University of Texas Press, 1962); also Enno Kraehe, ed., *The Metternich Controversy* (New York: Holt Rinehart & Winston, 1971), and Norman Rich, *Great Power Diplomacy, 1814–1914* (New York: McGraw Hill, 1992).

occupied; but Imperial Germany, which had won its war in the East and was not invaded by the Allies, emerged from the peace settlement—according to Weinberg's decisive refutation of Keynes—potentially the strongest economic and military power in Europe.[8]

What blocked the creation of an effective interwar alliance system that could have prevented World War II? Schweller's interpretation, framed in classic Cold War terms, has a bickering Britain and France ostracizing and failing to appease Soviet Russia, an isolationist United States "unwilling to assume the role of offshore balancer," and a Stalin joined by other avaricious statesmen abetting Hitler's drive to destroy Europe and the world.[9]

Schweller tends to underrate historical and practical factors. By stressing ideology, he underplays Great Britain's *long* aversion to peacetime commitments in Europe based on its domestic and imperial considerations; he ignores the fact that Mussolini's adherence to the Axis reflected weakness more than fascist solidarity; and he minimizes the fact that the two autocratic states that banded together in August 1939 to start World War II—Nazi Germany and Soviet Russia (with the tacit support of Japan, but with Italy now on the sidelines)—shared a greater zest for revisionism than a common ideology.[10]

Schweller explains the victors' failure to band together to protect the status quo as based on their fear of "another long and bloody war against Germany" and their disagreement over how to avoid it. To be sure, once the treaties were signed, each took a separate path to escape their treaty responsibilities. From Lloyd George's defection from his partners at Fontainebleau in April 1919 to Chamberlain's ardent revisionism at Munich in September 1938, Great Britain's leaders were critical of Versailles, opposed to France's efforts at enforcement, lukewarm toward the League and collective security, and determined to appease Germany in order to

---

8. Gerhard L. Weinberg, "The Defeat of Germany in 1918 and the European Balance of Power," *Central European History*, Vol. 2 (1969), pp. 248–260.

9. See Jonathan Haslam, "Soviet-German Relations and the Origins of the Second World War: The Jury is Still Out," *Journal of Modern History*, Vol. 69, No. 4 (Dec. 1997), pp. 785–797.

10. On Great Britain, see, for example, P. Catterall and C.J. Morris, eds., *Britain and the Threat to Stability in Europe, 1918–1945* (Leicester: Leicester University Press, 1993), as well as P. Haggie, *Britannia at Bay: The Defence of the British Empire against Japan, 1931–1941* (Oxford: Oxford University Press, 1981). On Italy, see D.C. Watt, "The Rome-Berlin Axis, 1936–1940: Myth and Reality," *Review of Politics*, Vol. 22, No. 4 (1960); Dennis Mack Smith, *Mussolini's Roman Empire* (London: Longman, 1976). And on the Soviet-German relationship, see B. Wegner, ed., *From Peace to War: Germany, Soviet Russia, and the World, 1939–1941* (Oxford: Berghahn Books, 1997).

prevent another Somme, which had caused a half million casualties. France, with its crucial demographic disadvantage, the loss of its strong eastern ally, and dread of another bloodbath, postured against the "German menace" but also built the Maginot line, was slow to modernize its army and economy, and silently betrayed its East European allies. The United States, although one of the main architects of the peace treaties, resolutely refused political and military engagements with its former allies while establishing firm economic ties with both Weimar and Nazi Germany.[11]

But Schweller overstates his case by accusing the victors of failing to develop Concert habits: "regular meetings to discuss major issues, jointly negotiating with third parties, and exchanging high-level security information to enhance the transparency of their military postures and strategies." In the 1920s, there was no lack of Allied consultations in the Supreme Council, the Conference of Ambassadors, and the Reparations Commission as well as in the periodic meetings of the Council of the League of Nations. There was no dearth of bilateral and also multilateral diplomacy, from the annual meetings of the League Assembly, to the international conferences of the 1920s in Brussels, Genoa, Locarno, and Geneva. And a significant number of private national and international organizations worked to create international harmony and eliminate the causes of war.[12]

To discover why Britain, France, and the United States failed to build an edifice strong enough to sustain their victory goes beyond their appalling losses between 1914–18, their subsequent disenchantment with the peace settlement, and their aversion to binding commitments. As soon as World War I ended, the three democracies, with their global interests, were engaged in cutthroat competition over resources and markets as well as over power and influence in their respective colonial and neocolonial realms. Well before Hitler seized power, the Allies had been challenged by bold, revisionist states, Soviet Russia and Hungary, Turkey and Italy, Poland and Lithuania, Weimar Germany and Japan. Far from charismatic figures, the figures responsible for building and maintaining collective security—Ramsay MacDonald and Austen Chamberlain, Raymond Poincaré, Edouard Herriot, and Aristide Briand, Calvin Coolidge and Herbert Hoover—were fairly run-of-the-mill statesmen who, in Anthony Adamthwaite's memorable characterization "lacked a victory cul-

11. Sally Marks, *The Illusion of Peace: International Relations in Europe, 1918–1933* (New York: St. Martin's, 1976).

12. See, for example, Leila Rupp, *Worlds of Women: The Making of an International Women's Movement* (Princeton: Princeton University Press, 1997).

ture."[13] All had personal limitations, all failed to master the civilian and military structures of their governments, all were too deferential to the leaders of finance and business, all lacked the political courage needed to maintain European peace.

The failure of Allied statesmen was not inevitable. Beneath the surface, Britain and France had fundamental economic, military, and demographic weaknesses that made them cower before any direct threat to the peace treaties. That is why they appeased Kemal's Turkey at Lausanne, waffled over Mussolini's aggression in Corfu, removed military control over Weimar Germany despite massive treaty violations, created the anodyne Kellogg-Briand peace pact, twice scaled down reparations, evacuated the Rhineland early, and relentlessly pursued the will-o'-the-wisp of disarmament. At the same time, the so-called victors of World War I established a dismal record of squandered opportunities to arrange for coherent, peaceful treaty revision under the aegis of the League of Nations. By the 1930s, their successors were even less equipped to maintain their commitments to collective security and to resist the greater threats posed by Hitler.[14]

Schweller claims that the tripolar structure, the result of the Allies' weakness and Hitler's determination to establish the Third Reich's hegemony, made World War II inevitable. Nazi Germany's rearmament in the mid-1930s gave it a virtually equal standing with its two mightiest potential enemies, the United States and the Soviet Union, leaving Britain and France far behind. According to Schweller, Hitler's great achievement was to dominate this tripolar world by luring the Soviet Union into his camp. Stalin, who had reckoned on an Anglo-French counterweight to Germany, gambled on a short-term gain in 1939 in order to achieve his ultimate goal of dominating all of Eastern Europe.

Using the concept of tripolarism, featuring Hitler as the new coachman and Stalin as the cunning if maladroit exploiter, helps to explain the heightened tensions of the 1930s from the perspective of perceptions and misperceptions of national power. The problem with this theory is that it is steeped more with hindsight than explanatory power. Tripolarism does not, for example, explain why Europe went to war in 1939 rather than 1938, over Danzig instead of the Sudetenland. It minimizes the importance of Asia and of secondary European states. It ignores the process by

---

13. *Grandeur and Misery: France's Bid for Power in Europe, 1914–1940* (London: Arnold, 1995).

14. Marc Bloch, *Strange Defeat: A Statement of Evidence Written in 1940,* trans. Gerard Hopkins (New York: Norton, 1968), chap. 3, contains an eloquent analysis of France and its allies' shortcomings.

which a significant segment of Western public opinion became mobilized against Nazi expansion. Above all, it leaves us baffled as to why the leaders of the "decaying powers," Britain and France, decided unexpectedly in September 1939 to deny Hitler a free hand in Eastern Europe after two decades of appeasement, and after the virtual balancers had refused to halt the Third Reich; why the Poles fought valiantly; and why Italy stayed out.

Schweller, seeking to integrate agent with structure, has cited conscious actors for having betrayed the rules of balance of power after World War I; but he has not sufficiently recognized, or explained, those who defied the constraints of tripolarism to precipitate the outbreak, and to some extent affect the outcome, of World War II.

Hitler's War

Gerhard Weinberg's essay focuses exclusively on Hitler's racism as the cause of World War II. He argues that Hitler surpassed his Wilhelmine and Weimar predecessors, to whom he referred disparagingly as *Grenzpolitiker*, and was a self-proclaimed *Raumpolitiker* seeking to acquire huge amounts of space for German domination and colonization. According to Weinberg, the Nazi seizure of power on January 30, 1933, was accompanied not only by a vast rearmament program but also by a deliberate and organized racial policy that included the persecution of Jews, Sinti, and Roma, the sterilization of people with physical and mental handicaps, and, we might add, the persecution of homosexuals. Henry Friedländer's prize-winning monograph has shown how the widespread, well-organized euthanasia program was the precedent for the later mass killings during World War II.[15]

Nazi Germany's drive for territorial and racial domination has long been acknowledged. Hitler's threats against the Jews began in the early 1920s, and the order of events after the seizure of power is quite clear. Yet, do brash words always indicate intention, and does chronology explain everything? Some of Hitler's plans were fulfilled, but others were not. The fact that sterilization began in 1933, euthanasia in 1939, and mass killing in 1941 might, but does not necessarily, link these barbarities with the outbreak of World War II. After all, sterilization did not begin or end with the Nazis. The onset of euthanasia nine months after Hitler's threatening speech against the Jews and one month after the attack on Poland may or may not be connected with Hitler's overall war aims. Even the

---

15. Henry Friedländer, *The Origins of Nazi Genocide: From Euthanasia to the Final Solution* (Chapel Hill: University of North Carolina Press, 1995).

exact dating of the origins of the final solution—still a matter of controversy among historians—cannot be precisely linked to the outbreak of war in the East.[16]

Weinberg has given us an argument difficult to refute but also difficult to generalize, or to learn from. On a specific, historical level, how can we explain the links between Hitler's wild musings, the nature of the Nazi bureaucratic-ideological state, and the outbreak of World War II? Weinberg's Hitler has an ironclad consistency impervious to internal or external factors; the German people speak with one voice aimed solely at global domination; and the issues of September 1939, detached from almost every context except racial war, have been conflated with the events of the following two years.

On a more general level, these questions remain: Could Nazi Germany have been challenged effectively by more resolute foes? Would a revived Germany without Hitler have pursued the same war for racial as well as territorial domination? Are Hitler's genocidal policies truly unrelated to, and incomparable with, those of other countries?

Some Tentative Conclusions

Hitler's sole responsibility for the outbreak of World War II, once almost universally acknowledged, is now open to fresh investigation. Throughout the long Cold War, the monolithic Nuremberg verdict was contested by conservative and revisionist scholars as well as by political leaders engaged in a global ideological struggle. With the official end of "Hitler's war"—and the Cold War—in 1990, the link between our world and September 1939 is no longer self-evident.[17] Over the past half-century there has been a great swell of testimonies, documentation, and memorials to Hitler's millions of victims; but serious questions have also been raised over the exercise of historical memory, objections voiced over the reification of the Holocaust, and doubts expressed over our ability ever to achieve scholarly objectivity in reading the evidence of Hitler's war.

Sixty years ago, one of Britain's sagest historians, E.H. Carr, framed the structure of international relations during the interwar period in terms of the venerable Western tradition of dualities: utopia versus reality; power versus morality; the sanctity of treaties versus the impulse for

---

16. Christopher Browning, *The Path to Genocide: Essays on the Launching of the Final Solution* (Cambridge: Cambridge University Press, 1992).

17. Compare Bradley F. Smith, *The War's Long Shadow* (New York: Simon & Schuster, 1986) with John Lukacs, *The End of the Twentieth Century and the End of the Modern Age* (New York: Ticknor & Fields, 1993).

change.[18] Carr also taught us that because utopians and realists need the other's company—the utopians to establish their virtuousness, the realists to borrow a road to somewhere—international history derived much of its moral and intellectual texture from the interplay between these two symbiotic forces.

From Schweller and Weinberg, we have two opposite, mutually reinforcing theories that can launch us on a new way of conceiving the interwar crisis and the origins of World War II. Schweller's structural formulation will require a broader understanding of historical actors and a more nuanced comprehension of historical models. Why, for example, were the Allies able to contain, largely by peaceful means, czarist and Bolshevik Russia but *not* Hitler's Reich? Weinberg's compelling, exceptionalist formulation, sustained by the data and chronology, will ultimately require infusions of structural analysis and comparison to attain a more balanced assessment of this increasingly distant era. May our younger colleagues and students who study the interwar period, equipped with new questions, insights, and methodology, profit from the Schweller-Weinberg debate.

---

18. Edward Hallett Carr, *The Twenty Years' Crisis, 1919–1939* (New York: Harper and Row reprint [1940], 1964).

Chapter 8

Hegemony, Global Reach, and World Power: Great Britain's Long Cycle

Edward Ingram

Great Britain as a world power found new life after World War II in a "special relationship" with the United States that looks different seen from the United States or Britain and by historians or political scientists. British historians and American politicians treat the relationship as imaginary; imagined by British politicians to buttress their self-importance and justify postponing difficult and supposedly unpopular decisions. British politicians, on the other hand, who still pretend that the relationship exists, even if they no longer believe it, are abetted by American political scientists. Both imagine an alternative special relationship between the late-twentieth-century United States and an imaginary nineteenth-century Great Britain.

American political scientists often encourage British politicians to daydream by ignoring today's pygmy and focusing on yesterday's world power seen as the ancestor to the present and future United States. Britain's experience tells political scientists, who examine classes, not incidents, about the U.S. experience as a world power; joining Louis XIV's France and the sixteenth-century Habsburg Monarchy in a class of (purported) hegemons.[1] Thus, British politicians and American political scientists are tied together like Siamese twins joined back to back and facing in opposite directions. Although one looks to the past and the other to the future, both see the future of the United States in the mirror of Britain's past. Paul Kennedy's appearance in March 1988 before the Senate Armed Forces and Budget Committees to explain that, unless the

---

The author thanks George Modelski for helpful criticism.

---

1. Christopher Layne, "From Preponderance of Offshore Balancing: America's Future Grand Strategy," *International Security*, Vol. 22, No. 1 (Summer 1997), pp. 86–124.

United States took care, his theory of imperial overstretch might apply to it in the twenty-first century, momentarily turned the history of Britain as a world power into an issue in U.S. domestic politics. Although Kennedy claims to explain the rise and fall of all of the modern great powers, the others are only Britain in disguise, which accounts for his popularity among American political scientists who see Britain as the United States in disguise.[2]

Unfortunately for political scientists, Britain as a world power was not the sort of state they have in mind. Discussion of the possible versions of Britain as a world power and the problems they cause political scientists is followed here by a critique of long cycle theory. Progressive as well as cyclical, the theory postulates five cycles of leadership in the modern international system that begin with fourteenth-century Portugal and reach their apotheosis in the postwar United States, and claims to explain the structural characteristics that determine successful and failed bids for leadership. As the theory stipulates that sea power, on account of its global reach, always outbids land power, boxed into a particular region, it offers Britain a star part. World leader in two of the cycles, Britain plays the role of tadpole between Portuguese frogspawn and United States frog.

Empires and Nation-States

In an era in which neorealism still provides one of the leading paradigms in the United States for the study of international relations, empires are out of fashion. They have been replaced by nation-states: separate, autonomous, equal, and struggling to preserve themselves in an anarchic system by means of balancing, formerly against power and, more recently, against threat.[3] Paul W. Schroeder shows that states often do not struggle and rarely balance, a statement true of Britain, given its fondness for appeasement during its era of world power.[4] The political scientists' international system often baffles historians, therefore, by taking for granted a model of a great power that never existed, though one under-

---

2. Paul Kennedy, *The Rise and Fall of the Great Powers* (New York: Random House, 1987).

3. Kenneth N. Waltz, *Theory of International Politics* (Reading, Mass.: Addison-Wesley, 1979); and Randall L. Schweller, "Bandwagoning for Profit: Bringing the Revisionist State Back In," *International Security*, Vol. 19, No. 1 (Summer 1994), pp. 72–107.

4. Paul W. Schroeder, "Historical Reality vs. Neo-realist Theory," *International Security*, Vol. 19, No. 1 (Summer 1994), pp. 108–48; and Paul W. Schroeder, "Munich and the British Tradition," *Historical Journal*, Vol. 19, No. 1 (March 1976), pp. 223–243.

stands the appeal to American nationalism and exceptionalism of pretending that it did. Before fitting Britain's actions to any of the political scientist's models, the historian has to ask three simple questions beneath the political scientist's notice but difficult to answer. What political form did Britain take? Where should one look for it on the map? And when did it exist?

As historians differ from political scientists in asking questions rather than stating theoretical assumptions, their work goes off in a different direction. Political scientists, despite their name, resemble postmodernists. For them both, theory is all. Even if "good theory must be validated over a wide range of conditions," as Jack S. Levy claims, the theory cannot be invalidated by contrary examples.[5] To validate it, political scientists make a list of events and conditions (like hegemony) borrowed from, but not found in, the past, because political science exists outside time, both historical and clock. They disguise time and place with a large white sheet, in which they cut holes to allow the items to be placed on the list, labeled, and analyzed to poke through. Historians, who do not own a sheet and find list-making and labeling difficult, are often puzzled by the labels political scientists pin to items and by the lists they make: great power wars, the coding of diplomatic events, and the test of naval capability for global power. The lists appear quaint because slightly changing the labels (the tests of eligibility) dramatically changes the items listed.

Unlike political scientists, historians distinguish between two sorts of reality: the past as it existed and the past as it can be recovered (constructed by imagining). The evidence recovered does not speak for itself: historians must decide what it signifies. Historians wonder, for example, whether sophisticated statistical analysis can be applied to haphazard scattered materials, when one does not even know whether one knows how many have been lost. Thus, historians have to do *some* archival work, not because archive-based works command the highest respect—for they do not; the prize goes to generally applied theories like Kennedy's of imperial overstretch and Schroeder's of equilibrium—but for Deborah Welch Larson's reasons: to learn how to construct and to assess how others are handling their materials. In no other way can historians ensure that a theory meets Robert Jervis's test of validity by providing more satisfactory explanations of past events.[6]

---

5. Jack S. Levy's chapter in this volume.

6. Deborah Welch Larson's chapter in this volume; and Robert Jervis, commenting on the work of Morton Kaplan, in *International History Review*, Vol. 20, No. 2 (June 1998), p. 502.

Whereas political scientists cannot decide whether to kill off the author, in history the author is dead. Historical narratives are collages (or paintings), a group of related items with foreground, background, high-lights, and shadows, waiting for readers whose readings will differ according to their knowledge, tastes, and viewpoint. Readings of our own works change along with our readings of the past. Political scientists, however, claim to support authors against readers. As their arguments derive from theory and are to be laid out in ways that prohibit varieties of meaning, author and reader, in refining the same theory, are expected to agree about what is meant. Deferential to one another, political scientists nonetheless kill off the historians whose works they ransack for "empirical" evidence. They use histories as if nobody wrote them—their intention irrelevant, their purpose to supply on command colorful flotsam from grandmother's attic to test (or fit) a theory. As political scientists allow themselves lives as authors, historians wonder why they are refused the same favor.

To find out why answers are needed to the historian's simple questions about Britain, one need look no further than the back cover of one of the many editions of Kennedy's study of the domestic constraints on British foreign-policymaking in the late nineteenth and twentieth centuries, *The Realities behind Diplomacy*.[7] There one finds both a definition of the state and an account of its decline. The blurb, presumably written by the publishers, not by Kennedy himself, states: "In 1865, when Palmerston died, the small group of islands that is Britain constituted the leading nation in world affairs. A century later, Britain had been devastatingly cut down to size: economically, militarily, territorially, it is today less than a second-rate power."

This statement contains two sorts of sleight of hand. The first disguises the nature of the state. Whereas the Scots would not describe Britain as a nation, but might use the term nation-state, the Irish, who would not use that term for a state their ancestors wished to leave, would use United Kingdom not Britain. Even the United Kingdom was a multinational empire. The second sleight of hand disguises the fact that the shrunken territories are a different state; the devastating territorial losses must refer to the British and Indian Empires, not merely to carving the Republic of Ireland out of the United Kingdom. But if colonial and Indian territories were peripheral to power in the nineteenth century, why should the loss of them have contributed to decline in the twentieth? Why

---

7. Paul Kennedy, *The Realities behind Diplomacy: Background Influences on British External Policy, 1865–1980* (London: Fontana, 1985 ed.).

not cast them off as the burden and distraction nineteenth-century critics of empire had called them? Had they suddenly become more important?

Whatever else Britain may have been, it was not a nation-state but an empire: its power (meaning its influence in world affairs during peacetime, not its ability to win coalition wars: American political science is obsessed with war) came from being one of Robert C. Binkley's "federative polities" long after he had, with regret, deprived them in 1870 of a future.[8] The world power of the nineteenth and twentieth centuries known as Britain was not formed of the United Kingdom. It was formed either of the British Empire, still reformulating the constitutional relationship among its parts as late as the Statute of Westminster of 1931, or of a dual monarchy composed of the United Kingdom and the Indian Empire and ruled after 1876 by a Queen-Empress. The Indian Empire was a separate state from the United Kingdom, though not independent of it, and after World War I was set on the road to Dominion status in the footsteps of Canada. The government of India (copying Hungary in Austria-Hungary in its dealings with Austria) was able to constrain the British government by acting, in Arthur Balfour's words, as an unfriendly ally.[9]

Even if one allowed historians to quibble with the definition, one would not allow political scientists to quibble, because they define great powers by their capability in war. In the Crimean War, the Boer War, and two world wars, the British Empire fought as one. One may ask whether a particular colony strengthened or weakened the state, but not whether it had a separate identity: nobody would ask that of Bavaria or Wyoming. Thus, Stephen M. Walt may not attribute Australia's decision to fight alongside Britain in two world wars to ideological compatibility.[10] In 1914, Australia had no choice: it was not independent. And if it became independent by 1939, Hitler did not notice: he offered the British Empire, not the United Kingdom, a bargain. Whether His Britannic Majesty may declare one of his realms, but not the others, to be at war with Germany is a nice point of international law. Australia thought not.

Political scientists should be more willing than historians, preoccupied with social structure and culture, to recognize the importance of constitutional relationships. They should be able to see through Little Englanders like Kennedy and his mentor A.J.P. Taylor, who write the

---

8. Robert C. Binkley, *Realism and Nationalism* (New York: Harper, 1935).

9. Balfour to Kitchener, Dec. 3, 1903, Balfour MSS, British Library, Additional MSS 49726.

10. Stephen M. Walt, *The Origins of Alliances* (Ithaca: Cornell University Press, 1987), p. 35.

history of Britain as the history of the United Kingdom's ships, manufactures, and foreign investments. The figures for population, raw materials, and industrial production—what political scientists call the war-capability index—that Taylor gave at the beginning of *The Struggle for Mastery in Europe* and promptly forgot, have been given a new lease on life by Josef Joffe.[11] They underpin the figures Kennedy used to prove Britain's inability in the twentieth century to win a coalition war and they resemble the figures compiled by the Correlates of War (COW) project on which political scientists, most recently Randall L. Schweller, are too willing to rely.[12] But the figures cited by Kennedy and Schweller and compiled by COW are the figures for the United Kingdom, not Britain. Count Indian heads, and Britain contains more people than the United States. Count Indian and Canadian raw materials, and Britain is better supplied than Germany.

Historians accuse political scientists of being illusionists rather than scientists because they rig the course before they roll the ball. Let's take the figures for Gross National Product (GNP) in 1897, the year Britain is supposed to have begun to try to counteract the effects of its notorious relative decline.[13] Angus Maddison gives the United States a figure of 100 in recognition of its status as the world's largest economy. It is followed, in descending order, by China (98), Britain (60), Russia (58), India (57), France (37), and Germany (35).[14] If Britain was a dual monarchy, at 117 its GNP was nearly twenty percent larger than the United States' and three and a half times as large as Germany's. Where is the German challenge? Although GNP may explain little, George Modelski and William R. Thompson, who emphasize the economy's "leading sectors" like Taylor and Kennedy, concede that they predict the future, not rate power at the time.[15] The figures for GNP predict a different future for Britain from theirs, however, in which an Asian state, unable to militarize its economy, declined in the twentieth century along with all other Asian

---

11. Josef Joffe, "'Bismarck' or 'Britain'? Toward an American Grand Strategy after Bipolarity," *International Security*, Vol. 19, No. 4 (Spring 1995), p. 100.

12. Randall L. Schweller, *Deadly Imbalances: Tripolarity and Hitler's Strategy of World Conquest* (New York: Columbia University Press, 1998), pp. 26–31.

13. See Charles A. Kupchan, *The Vulnerability of Empire* (Ithaca: Cornell University Press, 1994), pp. 106–130; and Keith Neilson, "'Greatly Exaggerated': The Myth of the Decline of Great Britain," *International History Review*, Vol. 13, No. 4 (November 1991), pp. 695–725.

14. "The Century the Earth Stood Still," *Economist*, December 20, 1997, p. 67.

15. George Modelski and William R. Thompson, *Leading Sectors and World Powers* (Columbia: University of South Carolina Press, 1996), pp. 70–103.

states except Japan. Its geography and political structure prevented it from harnessing its population and strategic raw materials.

Defining Britain not only requires the reexamination of its relative decline (the other mode, along with hegemony, in which political scientists debate the United States's future in terms of Britain's past), but also the function of alliances and the idea of the democratic peace. Few historians would accept Walt's definition of the origins of alliances—"In short, how do states choose their friends"—or treat alliance and alignment as interchangeable labels.[16] Walt's example of Israel's close alignment with the United States without being its ally points up the problem rather than solves it. Israel, aligned so closely with a European state, would be labeled its colony, part of its informal empire (in the 1950s Israel did urge Britain to admit it to the Commonwealth), and would be used to illustrate the relationship between imperial patron and colonial client.

Britain's alignment with the United States was just as peculiar: so extreme a version of an alliance as a tool of management that it became a strangling alliance in which one party uses the alliance to destroy the other. The relationship between the United Kingdom and Britain is shown in the U.S. offer during World War II to defend the United Kingdom but not the British Empire. As the destruction of Britain as a world power was the price to be paid for the safety of the United Kingdom, Englishmen and Scots were asked to buy safety for themselves by throwing Britons and Indians to the wolves.[17] Owing to the onset of the Cold War, which the British had every reason to promote, the Americans later redefined Britain by enlarging their umbrella to cover some of the remaining British colonies, most obviously the Malay States and Hong Kong. Thus, for Britain, colonization by the United States proceeded simultaneously with decolonization, a form of Dominion status for the United Kingdom on the road away from world power.[18]

To define Britain as the British Empire or as a dual monarchy composed of the United Kingdom and the Indian Empire is to pose a series of questions about the nature of the actors in a multipolar system rather

---

16. Walt, *The Origins of Alliances*, p. 1.

17. William Roger Louis, *Imperialism at Bay: The United States and the Decolonization of the British Empire, 1941–1945* (New York: Oxford University Press, 1978). For the democratic peace, see Miriam Fendius Elman, ed., *Paths to Peace: Is Democracy the Answer?* (Cambridge, Mass.: MIT Press, 1997).

18. William Roger Louis and Ronald Robinson, "The Imperialism of Decolonization," *Journal of Imperial and Commonwealth History*, Vol. 22, No. 3 (September 1994), pp. 462–511; and Andrew J. Rotter, "The Triangular Route to Vietnam: The United States, Great Britain, and Southeast Asia, 1945–1950," *International History Review*, Vol. 6, No. 3 (August 1984), pp. 404–423.

than to suggest answers. Even if one relies solely on constitutional relationships and confines attention to the formal empire when defining Britain, where does an empire end? Is the end of it marked by a frontier? Or by a buffer zone? In the Indian Empire, the administrative, military, and political frontiers, always found in three different places, spent the nineteenth century moving northwestwards behind one another. For example, although in 1837 the administrative frontier of the Indian Empire ran along the river Sutlej, southeast of Punjab, the military frontier, at which the state would defend itself from attack, ran northeast of Punjab along the river Indus, and the political frontier ran further northeast, beyond the Hindu Kush, in order to prevent another powerful state from being organized within striking distance.[19] Later, the Indian Empire spread from British-ruled areas to areas their subsidiary allies ruled, to areas with whose rulers they had treaties of friendship and non-interference, to buffer zones, to island bases, to gunboats protecting trade at sea and missionaries converting the heathen on land. To tell when one had left the Indian Empire and how far its arm might reach was difficult both for its inhabitants seeking protection and foreigners fearing its wrath.

States are not separate and sovereign (as if sovereignty were identifiable and indivisible): in empires, sovereignty is divisible and territory shared, because in a multipolar system in which states are pinned into a hierarchy, they often overlap. Historians, who project forward from before the treaty of Westphalia, rather than backward from the Cold War, treat international relations as the extension of dynastic and imperial relationships and assume that the sovereign territorial state is, and always has been, a model, not a commonplace. As most great powers retain the characteristics of the dynastic agglomerates from which they descend, the suzerain-state system cannot be separated—in history if not in theory—from the sovereign-state system.[20] Thus, the late eighteenth-century Indian states system, in which states defined themselves by their share in the revenue instead of the territory from which it was collected, was not as different from the European states system as political scientists suppose. The European Union is taking up traditional habits.

Nor can the open frontier be dismissed as a problem occurring only beyond Europe, an aspect of global relations in the periphery rather than regional relations in the core. After the treaty of Kutchuk-Kainardji of 1775 awarded Russia undefined rights in the Ottoman provinces of

---

19. Edward Ingram, *Empire-building and Empire-builders* (London: Cass, 1995), pp. 160–192.

20. Martin Wight, *Systems of States*, ed. Hedley Bull (Leicester: Leicester University Press, 1977), p. 17.

Moldavia and Wallachia, Britain put forward claims to similarly un-defined rights, for similar geopolitical reasons, in the province of Bagh-dad. After 1882 Egypt belonged to both the Ottoman Empire and Britain. The status of Bosnia and Herzegovina, which belonged between 1878 and 1908 to both Austria-Hungary and the Ottoman Empire, was not uncom-mon.

Where a state will be found partly depends on its type. Both Ronald Robinson and John Gallagher and their successors and rivals, P.J. Cain and A.G. Hopkins, treat informal empire as more important than formal empire in defining the British empire and perhaps Britain as a world power.[21] Nonetheless, they are looking at different sorts of interests and relationships in different parts of the world. Robinson and Gallagher's emphasis on the geopolitical tie between the United Kingdom and the Indian Empire draws them to the Middle East and Africa. For them, the partition of Africa was driven by Britain's need to prevent another great power from controlling the routes to the East by way of the Suez Canal and the Cape of Good Hope. Cain and Hopkins not only turn the empire into a pattern of investments, they also move it westward: Egypt, the hub of Robinson and Gallagher's empire, barely rates a mention in Cain and Hopkins's. Except that Cain and Hopkins ignore the United States, this westward shift ought to remove one of the most noticeable milestones on the road to Britain's relative decline: the turn-of-the-century withdrawal from the western hemisphere. Of course Britain did not object when the United States took control of the Panama Canal. How could it, when it controlled the Suez Canal? Nor did Britain withdraw. Its investments in the United States *were* its most important interest in the western hemi-sphere. Canada, Brazil, and Argentina paled by comparison.

The definition and location of a state determines the chronology of its rise and fall. Britain, the victor in World War I, which reached its widest extent in 1922, needs to be seen as a more powerful state in the early twentieth century, but as less powerful seventy years earlier; a warning against following John Brewer and Stephen D. Krasner in as-suming that power accompanies wealth.[22] Wealth only matters if states

---

21. Ronald Robinson, John Gallagher, and Alice Denny, *Africa and the Victorians: The Official Mind of Imperialism* (London: Macmillan, 1962); P.J. Cain and A.G. Hopkins, *British Imperialism: Innovation and Expansion, 1688–1914* (London: Longman, 1993); and P.J. Cain and A.G. Hopkins, *British Imperialism: Crisis and Deconstruction, 1914–1990* (London: Longman, 1993).

22. John Brewer, *The Sinews of Power: War, Money, and the English State, 1688–1783* (New York: Knopf, 1989); and Stephen D. Krasner, "State Power and the Structure of International Trade," *World Politics*, Vol. 28, No. 3 (April 1976), pp. 317–347.

are willing to spend it and, in a crisis, can persuade or compel their inhabitants to die for it. Britain in the nineteenth century could not; nor did U.S. wealth and "leading sectors" win the Vietnam War. The Pax Britannica was an illusion. The 1850s and 1860s were not the apogee of Britain's power, the era of Christopher Layne's hegemony or Michael W. Doyle's "unipolar world peripheral system" in which Britain was unchallenged in the wider world.[23] Nor were they an age of mid-Victorian equipoise in which social harmony followed from a sustained rise in the standard of living. Both the Crimean War and the Indian Mutiny of 1857 that preceded the unipolar period and the U.S. Civil War that followed it, not only acted as missed moments when Britain failed to anticipate the future, but also caused a structural upheaval in Britain equivalent to the upheaval in the Continental European states that followed the revolutions of 1848. That Britain could not have been met with an overwhelming European coalition in 1860 did not make it the "arbiter" of Europe, as Layne claims. Nor did it withdraw from European affairs owing to its "so pronounced" dominance.[24] It did not withdraw (it scored a great victory at the congress of Berlin in 1878) and it failed in the 1860s to intervene effectively. Between 1915 and 1922, on the other hand, Britain turned itself into the world's foremost military power. Land power, not sea power, was crucial to Britain's victory in World War I. The event was not exceptional. Britain had relied on military power more than sea power since its victories in Bengal and later the Deccan allowed it to create a substitute in Asia for the American state it had lost.

World Power and Global Power

One way to define Britain and its role in the international system is by examining George Modelski, Karen A. Rasler, and William R. Thompson's theory of geopolitical long cycles in the modern international system—operating independently of, but not unconnected with, economic cycles—which leads them to misperceive the nature and degree of Britain's power in the nineteenth century and the circumstances of its relative decline. Being political scientists, they ask the dead to show us the way to our future. And being Americans, they assume that Britain handed the torch of progress to the United States in the face of a challenge from Germany that led to World War I. If one assumes instead that Britain bandwagoned

---

23. Michael W. Doyle, *Empires* (Ithaca: Cornell University Press, 1986), p. 236.

24. Christopher Layne, "The Unipolar Illusion: Why New Great Powers Will Rise," *International Security*, Vol. 17, No. 4 (Spring 1993), pp. 5–51.

in 1914 with France and Russia rather than balanced against Germany, Britain's role in the international system will change.

In order to change Britain's role, one has to play it down as well as up. Political scientists are fascinated with the world wars because they offer an important test of a myriad of theories. The fact and type of war is treated as given, however, because political scientists study the role of the wars in the system, not their history. Thus World War I, caused by the Anglo-German naval rivalry, of all the unlikely things, is fought between Germany and Britain (which becomes the United States in disguise) and World War II between Germany and Britain as agent for the United States and, after the United States joins in, as its (suffocating) sidekick. In fact both wars were fought between Germany and Russia; closed down in the west until Russia lost the first and won the second. Without looking at wars from the right angle, one misses the relationship between the core and the periphery of the international system crucial to long cycle theory.

The theory posits a modern world system since the late fifteenth century composed of five progressive cycles of world leadership ("capability concentration") that move westward, though not without backtracking, toward their apotheosis, or "maturity," in the post–World War II United States.[25] Indeed, the United States provides the model of a mature world leader, one deconstructed backward through time by way of Britain "Two" (as long cycle theory calls nineteenth- and twentieth-century Britain), Britain "One" in the eighteenth century, and the United Provinces in the seventeenth century to reach its embryonic form in sixteenth century Portugal. Ming China, recently tacked on as a "prototype" first cycle, is ignored here because the poor fit with the other cycles reminds one of a soprano voice with bad breaks between registers.[26]

Each cycle is divided into four phases—global war, world power, delegitimation, and deconcentration (the last two meaning emergence of potential rivals, and failure to anticipate the challenge from a regional rival at the core)—and these four phases govern the rise and fall during each cycle of the world leader, which is "selected" by the system during the first phase of the cycle, the global war. The two world wars are combined to become the equivalent of the wars of the Grand Alliance and the Spanish Succession and the French Revolutionary and Napole-

---

25. George Modelski, ed., *Exploring Long Cycles* (Boulder, Colo.: Lynne Rienner, 1987); and George Modelski, *Long Cycles in World Politics* (Seattle: University of Washington Press, 1987).

26. Modelski and Thompson, *Leading Sectors*, pp. 153, 170.

onic Wars: a global war lasting thirty years and dividing cycle four, Britain Two, from cycle five, United States.

The cycles are viewed from two different standpoints. The global war becomes the first phase when the leader's decline is explained. When its rise is explained, however, global war becomes the third phase and world power the fourth and last phase. The first two phases, which precede the global war and occur during the delegitimation and deconcentration of the previous world leader, are marked by agenda setting and coalition building. The relationship between decline and rise is difficult to follow, therefore, when one state, Britain in cycles three and four, has both to decline and rise at the same time. A state in relative decline, whose power is in deconcentration owing to the alliance building and capability of its competitors, will emerge as the dynamic and exuberant victor from the forthcoming global war.

As Modelski correctly remarks, the theory as summarized here is "descriptive" and, in his view, has since progressed to "explanation" by applying evolutionary theory.[27] Perhaps it has. Nonetheless, the later work begins by summarizing the earlier (using previously published diagrams and tables), and if the system described leaves one puzzled, the explanation built on it may not persuade. Nor do historians, unlike political scientists, separate description from explanation: one presupposes the other, like the two faces of a coin. If what is explained did not happen, how is one to believe the explanation?

What happened is always a more difficult problem for historians than why it happened. The chronology of the fourth cycle of the system is as follows. Britain Two emerged during the French Revolutionary and Napoleonic Wars (global war) after two generations of agenda setting and coalition building during its own delegitimation and deconcentration as Britain One; flourished until 1850 (world power); was presented with new rivals until 1873 (delegitimation); and failed before 1914 to meet the challenge (deconcentration), thus surrendering its world leadership to the United States, which made in 1914 a successful macro-bid for the succession. The chronology is flawed, because the definition of Britain, the nature of its power, and the location of the challenge to it are all misconceived.

One may doubt whether Britain fit in the nineteenth century the specifications of a world leader. Second, one may doubt whether Britain played the role of one. And third, one may doubt whether the challenge to Britain came from Germany (a regional power) in Europe (at the core)

---

27. George Modelski, letter to author, February 8, 1998.

rather than Russia (a world power) in the wider world (in the periphery). The Anglo-Russian rivalry that lasted throughout the fourth cycle—from the Ochakov Crisis of 1791 until the Suez Crisis of 1956—may have determined the cycle's chronology, by providing both a lever by which to obtain or block indirect global reach and a buttress to the political structure of an imperial state.

WORLD LEADER OR WORLD POWER

Long cycle theory demands a sleight of hand as one elides the word "global" into the word "world." The subject of study, which remains constant—whereas it changes in the spreading oil-slick of Immanuel Wallerstein's system—is the globe. The system, however, is a world system in which global relations form an inter-regional level of operation and analysis separate from regional and national relations, the other two levels. The leader of the system is called a world leader and its moment of greatest influence, phase two of the four, is called world power. Not that *the* world power is allowed to become *a* world power, one of the many "oceanic world powers" foreshadowed by Ming China. It is strictly enjoined not to fall into "the quagmire of world power."[28]

One of the requirements for world leadership is global reach and the leader's task is to manage global relations, although they, if worldwide, do not extend throughout the world. Similarly, the leader is required by means of its global operations to manage the world's economy.[29] For global relations, therefore, one should read oceanic relations—for everything that takes place on land is regarded as regional—and for global reach, one should read sea power. The world leader is required to possess 50 percent of the world's naval capability at the end of the global war.

But how does a world leader lead a world system, if anything outside the range of sea power exceeds its capability? And if the leader does not bring order on land as well as at sea—for where do people live?—and in Asia as well as in Europe and the Americas, why is it not considered merely a global leader, confined to acting at the global level of the system, rather than a world power? Even then, how can it protect inter-regional trade? Not that the change of title and role would alter the nature of the Anglo-Russian rivalry, which limited nineteenth-century Britain's ability to act as either world leader or world power by threatening to curtail its global reach.

The decisive phase of each cycle is the global war, in which the new

28. Karen A. Rasler and William R. Thompson, *The Great Powers and the Global Struggle, 1490–1990* (Lexington: University Press of Kentucky, 1994), pp. 146–147.

29. Ibid., p. 16.

world leader is selected following two generations in which it has proved its fitness, partly by economic dynamism, and partly by taking a macro-decision to bid for selection by showing its capability to perform. But it is not allowed to show capability for world leadership by successful empire-building. This disqualifies it: nobody shall say that the United States is a mature form of colonizer. Nor is the global war a world war. It is not necessarily fought worldwide, nor between all the existing great powers. If it is fought merely between states with global reach, about global relationships, and at the global level of the system, however, it can have little to do with the "great regional wars," as Modelski calls wars such as the Thirty Years War, which are waged in Europe at the regional level of the system and in fact select the new world leader.[30] Levy argues that global relationships derive from, rather than determine, relationships in the system's core region—Europe throughout long cycle theory's five cycles.[31]

But how much power must the world leader deploy? Enough to contribute to the outcome of a crisis, or enough to decide the outcome? The choice one makes partly determines whether or not one regards Britain as a world power. Although Britain undoubtedly decided the outcome of World War I by turning itself into the foremost military power in the world, and is claimed by patriotic historians without much justification to have decided the outcome of the war of the Spanish Succession, they are hard pressed to make such claims for the Napoleonic Wars. Save, of course, for devotees of the Duke of Wellington, who mistake countermarching in Spain and Portugal for the invasion of Russia and the battle of Leipzig.

SPECIFICATIONS OF THE WORLD LEADER

The six specifications for world leadership in long cycle theory are as follows: to be an island or peninsula safe from attack by land (which gives away the Americans' view of Canada and Mexico); to be a nation-state (though all great powers are empires); to show economic dynamism; to be the strongest seapower (measured by Thompson in numbers and tonnage of ships) and thus to possess global reach; not to be driven by ideology (which gives away the Americans' view of the United States as the repository of truth); and to be selected in the global war that follows

---

30. Modelski, *Long Cycles*, p. 45.

31. Jack S. Levy, *War in the Modern Great Power System* (Lexington: University Press of Kentucky, 1983).

the macro-decision to bid for world leadership. One does not need much in the way of an army.[32]

SELECTION IN A GLOBAL WAR. To begin with selection in a global war, one cannot tell whether the new leader has to win the war or only profit from the work of others. Although Thompson allows the leader merely to run off with the spoils, as Britain may have done in 1815, Modelski, more exacting, demands victory. To cite Modelski's example of William Pitt the Younger's controlling the First Coalition in the French Revolutionary Wars as the victory over the challenge from France that turned Britain One into Britain Two, however, merely calls patriotic English history to the service of patriotic American political science. The Revolutionary and Napoleonic Wars were regional wars fought between France, on the one hand, and Austria and Prussia, managed by Russia, on the other. Although Britain went to war, often it did not fight; and it neither defeated Napoleonic France nor starved it into submission. Victory at Trafalgar could not anticipate the nightmare that followed defeat at Austerlitz: Napoleon and Alexander I's plan in 1807 by the treaty of Tilsit to divide Europe and the Middle East between them. Russia and Britain were jointly winners over Napoleonic France.[33] They became dual (though not joint) monitors of the Concert of Europe and during the system's fourth cycle, sometimes as rivals, sometimes in cooperation, they managed global relations between them. Britain used the rivalry to ensure that it would never again have to fight France and Russia at the same time. This rule, which governed the conduct of British foreign policy throughout the nineteenth century, was applied on the outbreak of general European (regional, not world or global) war in 1914.

SHAPE AND STRUCTURE. As Britain was neither an island or peninsula, nor a nation-state, but a dual monarchy made up of the United Kingdom and the Indian Empire—two islands and a peninsula half the world away from one another—its geographical peculiarity explains the other purpose of its rivalry with Russia: the attempt to stabilize the area between its two halves by preventing another powerful state from seizing control. Britain first tried to prevent the opening of new routes across the Middle East—the Suez Canal was the most famous, disliked, and threatening—and second, tried to create a precursor to the Northern Tier of the 1960s.

---

32. For the role of sea power, see William R. Thompson, *On Global War: Historical-Structural Approaches to World Politics* (Columbia: University of South Carolina Press, 1988), chap. 7.

33. Paul W. Schroeder, *The Transformation of European Politics, 1763–1848* (Oxford: Clarendon Press, 1994).

This Middle Eastern echo of the Burgundian Circle, stretching from the Ottoman Empire by way of Persia to Afghanistan, was designed to enable the Indian Empire to turn its back on the Heartland to face the wider world, thus separating global affairs from Eurasian regional affairs.[34]

Nor was Britain, though an island and a peninsula, insular politically: it was denied the privilege of the offshore balancer of being able to choose when, and how far, to involve itself in continental affairs. Britain seemed to have the choice in Europe, although the Crimean War makes one wonder, but lacked it in Asia, where unruly subjects, unfriendly neighbors, and poor frontiers compelled it to forestall events, not wait to respond to them. In this it resembled the Habsburg Monarchy more than any other state: it had to make similar attempts to preempt by effective geopolitics and diplomacy the need to use military power. When Joffe offers the United States the choice of following "Britain" or "Bismarck," the principle he enunciates for Britain of "anti-hegemonism without entanglement" is false.[35] In Asia, Britain demanded hegemony for itself, either alone or in partnership with Russia.

Britain was precisely what world leaders are forbidden to be in long cycle theory: a "structural heterogeneity . . . built piece by piece" with "malintegrated subunits"; an empire preoccupied with territorial expansion and defense, having leaped into the forbidden "territorial trap" which supposedly was "the final nemesis of global power."[36] The empire was created between 1784 and 1818 (in response to the loss of most of British America), precisely when Britain Two took the macro-decision to bid for world leadership, is supposed to have shown economic dynamism during the early phases of industrialization, and was selected in a global war. For Britain, victory in the global war partly took the form of state-building in India: victory over Mysore in 1799 and over the Marathas in 1804 and 1818 turned Britain into the paramount power and completed the swing to the east that Geoffrey Parker regards as Britain's principal

34. Edward Ingram, *The Beginning of the Great Game in Asia, 1828–1834* (Oxford: Clarendon Press, 1979).

35. Joffe, "'Bismarck' or 'Britain?'" p. 103.

36. Karen A. Rasler and William R. Thompson, *War and State Making: The Shaping of the Global Powers* (Boston: Unwin Hyman, 1989), pp. 71–72; William R. Thompson and Gary Zuk, "World Power and the Strategic Trap of Territorial Commitments," *International Studies Quarterly*, Vol. 30, No. 3 (September 1986), pp. 249–267; and George Modelski, "The Long Cycle of Global Politics and the Nation State," *Comparative Studies in Society and History*, Vol. 20, No. 2 (April 1978), p. 229.

contribution to the rise of the West.[37] Thompson and Gary Zuk, by sleight of hand, transpose Britain's victories over Mysore and the Marathas into a response to a global challenge from France.[38] Although that is how the British authorities in India portrayed them, everybody—including, Napoleon, the Emperor, and the tsar—knew that they were inventing victories over imaginary French enemies to pass off state-building in the periphery as support for allies in the core.[39]

The creation of the Indian Empire can hardly have been one of the "signs of deterioration and decay" Modelski would have it be, when it occurred at the beginning of cycle four, phase two, world power.[40] The disagreement over chronology is crucial. Modelski will only allow Britain to take over India in 1858, the date at which Rasler and Thompson begin to count Indian Army troops as a component of Britain's military capability. But a minister responsible for the government of India's foreign, military, and political affairs (as opposed to the commercial activities of the East India Company) sat (usually) in the cabinet from 1784; large numbers of British troops were stationed in India paid for by local taxes; and the British government intervened decisively in 1857 to put down the rebellion, only the most serious of many, *before* it abolished the East India Company.[41] Nor should one exaggerate the degree of direct British control following the takeover. The Indian budget remained separate from the United Kingdom budget, and the secretary of state for India did not have to obtain approval of it from the House of Commons. Control of finance, the hallmark of parliamentary sovereignty, was lacking in Britain.

ECONOMIC DYNAMISM AND POLITICAL HEGEMONY. Although Britain did show economic leadership and possess global reach, neither was of the sort prescribed by long cycle theory. Even if the so-called Industrial Revolution began in the United Kingdom, which one may doubt, it was not finished. The emphasis placed by the theory on manufacturing and

---

37. Geoffrey Parker, *The Military Revolution: Military Innovation and the Rise of the West, 1500–1800* (Cambridge: Cambridge University Press, 1988), pp. 135–136.

38. Thompson and Zuk, "World Power," p. 152.

39. Edward Ingram, *Commitment to Empire: Prophecies of the Great Game in Asia, 1797–1800* (Oxford: Clarendon Press, 1981), chaps. 4–5.

40. George Modelski, "Long Cycles of World Leadership,' in William R. Thompson, ed., *Contending Approaches to World System Analysis* (Beverly Hills, Calif.: Sage, 1983), p. 122.

41. Francis G. Hutchins, *The Illusion of Permanence: British Imperialism in India* (Princeton: Princeton University Press, 1967), chap. 4.

free trade is mistaken: 1822 was the last year in which Britain showed a favorable balance on its visible trade. Britain, during its phase of world power down to the 1850s—the era of the Pax Britannica when the Royal Navy supposedly ruled the waves—was a preindustrial state. Little different from other European states, it was run by noblemen, civil servants, army and navy officers, and bankers, not by industrialists, manufacturers, and merchants. The new elites resembled the groups in France who won a victory during the first phase of the Revolution, which the British welcomed. Their victory stands for the triumph of aristocracy over absolutism; for liberty as privilege and property rights at the expense of equality. Russia became the British bogeyman partly because it stood for the persistence of absolutism; for limits to property rights and a larger role for the state in society.

The new old-style Britain was manifested in the nineteenth century in two new old-style empires. The first, created between 1784 and 1842, was authoritarian and militarist. It was created by force; metropolitan control over it was tightened, whenever possible, not relaxed into responsible government by choice; and in India, the state preserved an agrarian society in which the tax structure was designed to pay for a larger army.[42] Its unofficial successor, created after 1870, was found outside as often as inside the territories left over from its predecessor and was shaped by investments and the financial weapons, like credit ratings, used to protect them. Neither of the alternatives offers a suitably progressive bridge between eighteenth-century Britain in cycle three and the late twentieth-century United States in cycle five.

Financial clout, not heavy industry and cotton goods, was the foundation of Britain's wealth and power. W.D. Rubinstein and Cain and Hopkins differ here from Martin Weiner and Correlli Barnett, who blame lack of interest in industry and science for Britain's decline.[43] And they differ from Kennedy, who blames lack of raw materials and heavy industry able to make the weapons needed to win a coalition war.[44] Whereas

---

42. Christopher A. Bayly, *Imperial Meridian: The British Empire and the World, 1780–1830* (London: Longman, 1989); and Douglas M. Peers, *Between Mars and Mammon: Colonial Armies and the Garrison State in Nineteenth Century India* (London: British Academic Press, 1995).

43. W.D. Rubinstein, *Capitalism, Culture and Decline in Britain, 1750–1990* (London: Routledge, 1993); Martin J. Weiner, *English Culture and the Decline of the Industrial Spirit, 1850–1980* (New York: Cambridge University Press, 1981); and Correlli Barnett, *The Collapse of British Power* (New York: Morrow, 1992).

44. Paul M. Kennedy, *The Rise and Fall of British Naval Mastery* (New York: Scribner, 1976).

long cycle theory claims that economic dynamism *precedes* world power, the new Britain's greatest wealth and economic dynamism *followed* it, during the years after 1870 when the alternative hegemonic version of Britain dominated by manufacturers began to fear the challenge from Germany.

Nor did Britain's economic dynamism *derive* from world power. Whereas the limits to sea power were shown whenever Britain tried to drive Russia out of Europe and prevent the expansion of Prussia across Germany, the 1850s and 1860s were far from being an age of equipoise at home after the structural upheavals accompanying the Industrial Revolution had ended: a generation of prosperity and social harmony bridging the two forms of empire. A two-way, not one-way, street runs between Britain's two halves. In the 1850s, the Indian half came charging into Victorian daily life. The Great Rebellion of 1857, the name properly given to the Indian Mutiny—not in recognition of its nationalist goals, but of its significance as an example of the possibility of destroying a world leader from inside in peacetime rather than outside during a global war—was a more important event in the United Kingdom than in India. The British response to the Mutiny buttressed authoritarian political and social structures and the differences between the sexes, and confirmed that Britain was not a liberal constitutional monarchy, but a militarist despotism, however supposedly enlightened.

SEA POWER AND GLOBAL REACH. Britain's global reach was no better suited than its economic system and social structure to the requirements of long cycle theory. It was owed to the Indian Army, not the Royal Navy. In the wider world, unlike Europe, Britain was less a naval than a military power: its stability depended upon its capability to turn global power into world power by projecting power inland. Unless Britain could contain Russia in the Middle East, the rebellion expected the moment the outposts—or proxies—of the Russian empire reached the frontier of Afghanistan would confine the army in India to the role of garrison and prevent it from performing the role of imperial expeditionary force the state required. The Indian Army served in Egypt in 1801 and in Italy in 1945. Between times, it served in China, New Zealand, Burma, Malaya, Turkistan, the Ottoman Empire, Abyssinia, Malta, South Africa, and on the Western Front. It met all Britain Two's needs as a global power, even world power. When it could not meet Britain's needs as a regional power in Europe, the British created a field army in 1916 in the Continental style, belatedly declared and later won a regional (not a global) war, and perhaps were selected as Britain Three for the role of world leader in the Locarno System. The 1920s, when Britain proved more suited to the role of world power than it had eighty years earlier, were a decade of British unipolar-peripheral hegemony embodied in the Prince of Wales smiling down at the world from the deck of H.M.S. *Hood*.[45]

The task of fighting a regional war, accepted unwillingly, was treated as a momentary, if unavoidable, aberration. World leaders and global powers must be confident that other states will be ready, and willing, to fight regional wars on their behalf. The British in 1940, who expected to fight the Nazis to the last Frenchman, were miffed when the French, asked by Winston Churchill to hold up the Germans as long as possible, refused to burn down Paris. Any offshore balancer looks for a stooge. Britain, turned down by France, foolishly switched roles by offering itself to the United States.

DELEGITIMATION AND DECONCENTRATION

If Britain met none of the prerequisites of a world leader, nor did it play the role of one in the prescribed manner, in the prescribed sequence. Instead of providing order for the international system, its concept of balance of power in Europe promoted, perhaps demanded, disorder and it lacked sufficient power to provide order in phase two—the early and middle decades of the century—when it acted as world power, partly owing to the need to contain challengers bidding, albeit indirectly, to obtain global reach. It failed during the Crimean War in a bid to foreshadow the treaty of Brest-Litovsk by driving Russia out of Poland and Ukraine, and to deny the United States its future by supporting the South in the U.S. Civil War. Conversely, however, in phase four, when it should have succumbed after 1900, it outlasted its challengers. The "new imperialism" of the 1880s and 1890s, culminating in "Splendid Isolation," successfully demonstrated Britain's global reach and solved the problem of the security of India. It is a far cry from "delegitimation."

The challengers to Britain as world leader were France and Russia, not Germany. If the world leader's task is to manage global relations, challengers with the longest global reach are to be feared more than states limited to a regional role in the system. Thus France (directly) in phases one, two, and three and Russia (indirectly) in phases two, three, and four acted as the challengers; Austria in phases one, two, and three and Germany in phases three and four acted in the core region—in Taylor's words—as Britain's necessary ally: a stronger state more interested and

---

45. Anthony Clayton, *The British Empire as a Superpower, 1919–1939* (London: Macmillan, 1986); and John Ferris, "'The Greatest Power on Earth': Great Britain in the 1920s," *International History Review*, Vol. 13, No. 4 (November 1991), pp. 726–750.

on the same side in a European question, which will head off a crisis and prevent the need for a stooge in dealing with it.

That Britain declared war in 1914 against its necessary ally (Germany) alongside its challengers (France and Russia), though at a time when it did not plan to fight, illustrates the curious relationship between the regional and global levels of the international system. Even if one looks at commercial-financial cycles, rather than geopolitical cycles—which would make Britain better suited to be world leader in Cain and Hopkins's system than in long cycle theory—Germany need not be portrayed as the challenger and the United States, which used British finance and merchant shipping, was anything but one.[46] And if geopolitical cycles operate independently of commercial-financial cycles, and global relations operate independently of regional relations, one expects to find a different challenger challenging a different sort of state as world leader, even if the world leader bears the same name.

In studies of Britain's role in the outbreak of World War I, the wrong question is asked: what happens if France and Russia lose? The right question is: what happens if they win? Britain's decision to declare war in 1914 alongside its challengers—it did not plan to *fight* alongside them—is explained by the sort of war expected. By bandwagoning (with the potentially most deadly rival rather than the potentially strongest state) instead of balancing, and working in the fashion of an appeaser with France and Russia in an attempt to control them, the British were trying in 1914 to anticipate the worst-case scenario: a Franco-Russian victory, which would have more dangerous worldwide repercussions for Britain than a German victory in the short, limited war everyone pretended to expect and was ready to fight. Britain went to war preoccupied with its global relationships: not necessarily expecting a Franco-Russian victory, but hoping to act as offshore balancer in a stalemate. The likelihood by the autumn of 1915 of a Franco-Russian defeat, however, left Britain wondering whether victory in the wider world might cost the loss of too much influence in the core region. Thus the decision to gear up for a regional war, at first merely to encourage the French to fight harder; a decision long cycle theory should call a macro-decision to bid for the renewal of world leadership.

At issue here is the relationship between discussion and decision and why some paradigms, the Anglo-German rivalry for one, do not change. Although the foreign office archives for 1906 to 1914 are full of discus-

---

46. Suzanne Y. Frederick, "Germany and Britain," in William R. Thompson, ed., *The Evolution of Great Power Rivalries* (Columbia: University of South Carolina Press, 1998), pp. 306–336.

sions about the challenge to Britain from Germany, no notice need be taken. If G.P. Gooch and Harold Temperley had edited the *British Documents on the Origins of the War* properly, they would have paid more attention to Britain's second foreign office, housed at the India office, and shifted the balance of threat away from Germany toward Russia.[47] Cain and Hopkins ignore the sheaves of documents Robinson and Gallagher cite to show that worry about the Indian Empire drove Britain to occupy Egypt in 1882 and lead the partition of Africa that followed. Kennedy ignores the bigger sheaves explaining why Britain in the 1930s could not stand up to Hitler and even, what a joke, Mussolini. Either appeasement is said to be overdetermined, or all the documents are read as talk, allowing the correspondents to discuss other issues, in secret, as if in a foreign language or code. Listening to the Marquess Wellesley describe the defeat of Mysore in 1799 as a victory over Napoleon leads one to think one has joined Alice in Wonderland—a world, like political science, in which space, time, and distance follow incomprehensible rules: far is near, unlikely is urgent, forwards is backwards, and one must run as fast as one can in order to stand still.

If Britain was dominated by the landed, financial, and service elites who represented the City's interests, and if British imperialism reached its zenith in the late nineteenth century, the use of British capital and financial services during the industrialization of Germany was a godsend, not a challenge—as Lloyd's explained when warning the Committee of Imperial Defense that, in the event of war, it would have to honor its insurance contracts and pay out on German ships sunk by the Royal Navy.[48] The "made in Germany" scares scared nobody who mattered. Britain's decline in the twentieth century paralleled its rise in the nineteenth the moment foreigners placed their capital elsewhere and looked elsewhere for financial services—developments over which Britain had little control.[49]

Despite Fritz Fischer and Gerhard L. Weinberg's undoubtedly correct analysis of Germany's long-term hegemonic goals, Britain and Germany

---

47. Keith Wilson, "The Imbalance in *British Documents on the Origins of the War, 1898–1914*: Gooch, Temperley, and the India Office," in Keith Wilson, ed., *Forging the Collective Memory: Government and International Historians through Two World Wars* (Providence, R.I.: Berghahn Books, 1996), pp. 230–264.

48. Paul M. Kennedy, "Strategy versus Finance in Twentieth Century Great Britain," *International History Review,* Vol. 3, No. 1 (January 1981), pp. 50–51.

49. B.R. Tomlinson, "The Contraction of England: National Decline and Loss of Empire," *Journal of Imperial and Commonwealth History,* Vol. 11, No. 1 (October 1982), pp. 58–72.

found themselves in 1914 and 1939 fighting wars that neither of them expected or desired. Hitler and even Wilhelm II may have desired another war at a different moment, but not that war at that moment. Anglo-German relations were tense after 1900 because both states took their shared interests and shared rivalry with Russia for granted. They merely disagreed about which of them benefited more from the relationship, needed it more, and should pay the higher price for it. At any moment, disagreement about the future might take precedence over agreement about the present and understanding of the past.

If global reach is all long cycle theory's world leader needs to enable it to provide order, the system need not select the strongest sea power. Modelski's claim that "the only effective and cost-efficient method of global interaction involved the sea" overstates the case.[50] A state does not need global reach to control global politics; it may control them indirectly by the use of levers. Britain's worst-case scenario, which explains its decision to go to war in 1914, was a repeat of the treaty of Tilsit, which laid out an alternative global, if not world, system to the Vienna Settlement: Franco-Russian cooperation predicated on divided hegemony over the Eurasian region, followed by a joint or parallel thrust for global reach.

Britain, which had learned how a regional power can control the global politics of a global power during the war of the Second Coalition, never forgot. The French army occupying Egypt after 1798 did nothing. By doing nothing in Egypt, however, and despite Britain's so-called decisive naval victory at the battle of the Nile, it disrupted Britain throughout the world by acting as a magnet powerful enough to control the Royal Navy's movements from the Channel reaches to the South China Sea. It drew one British expeditionary force eastward up the Mediterranean toward Alexandria, another westward into the Red Sea toward Suez. As the result, Manila was saved for Spain, Mauritius for France, and Batavia for Holland; privateers played havoc with British trade in the bay of Bengal; Austria was left to defeat at the battle of Hohenlinden; and Britain, fearful of letting Russia into the Middle East as the price of driving out France, occupied Malta at the risk of provoking the quarrel with Russia it wished to avoid, and found itself in 1801 at war with France and Russia, the two strongest military powers, at the same time. It was compelled to make peace at Amiens on unfavorable terms.[51]

Memories of Tilsit and the French expedition to Egypt determined

---

50. George Modelski, "Long Cycles," in Modelski, ed., *Exploring Long Cycles*, p. 130.

51. Edward Ingram, "The Geopolitics of the First British Expedition to Egypt: I–IV," *Middle Eastern Studies*, Vol. 30, Nos. 3–4 (July–October 1994), pp. 435–460, 699–723; Vol. 31, Nos. 1–2 (January–April 1995), pp. 146–169, 339–367.

how Britain played the role of world leader throughout the nineteenth and early twentieth centuries. They provided the template into which the British fitted intelligence about world affairs. As the challenge Britain feared most was a Franco-Russian alliance, it worked to the rule of not risking a quarrel with both at the same time, and of working *with* one, not *against* the other, but to keep the two apart. To head off the challengers, however, and enable Britain to play the role of world leader, two requirements had to be met: France should not control Egypt, and Russia should be contained along a line drawn from Constantinople to Kabul, the line of the Northern Tier. Although the fate of Cairo always mattered more to Britain than the fate of Constantinople, because France was Britain's most immediate challenger, Russia became the most dangerous challenger despite its apparent lack of global reach, owing to its potential in Central Asia to reach around the British fleet. Germany became Britain's necessary ally, asked to supply a counter-lever to meet the expected challenge.

Thus the July Crisis pointed to disaster for Britain. Who cared what happened to Archduke Franz-Ferdinand or the Serbs? Or the Czechoslovaks, as Neville Chamberlain might have said? Or if the Russians joined in? Another bloody nose for them suited Britain. But once France joined Russia, the policy of keeping the two rivals apart with German help had failed disastrously. As the U.S. Civil War and the Franco-Prussian War had proved the risk from neutrality, Britain had no choice but to join in, in order to restrain—the classic form of appeasement first tried by George Canning during the Greek Revolt—and in the hope of mediating. No wonder Chamberlain was reading Harold Temperley's study of Canning's foreign policy on the flight to Munich.

Limits to Sea Power

Rasler and Thompson measure a state's global reach and its eligibility for global power and world leadership by its naval capability. Ten percent of the world total is required for global power; fifty percent by the world leader, so that however scattered its units around the globe, it can concentrate sufficient force to meet any single challenger or coalition. States other than Japan are ineligible if their forces operate in only one region or if, like the Ottoman Empire, they operate in two oceans but with the wrong technology.[52] One suspects a Mahanian tendency: the percentage is of warships able to fight in the line of battle, not of merchantmen

---

52. Rasler and Thompson, *Great Powers*, p. 17, and *War and State Making*, p. 21.

converted in wartime to frigates and winning a *guerre de course* by following the rules of the *jeune école*.

One of the oddities of Britain as a world power was its inability to turn sea power into global power. It could use sea power against France indirectly, therefore overtly, for example during the Second Syrian Crisis of 1838, or directly, therefore disguised (as mobilization), for example during the Fashoda Crisis. If war *had* broken out in 1898, however, France's strategy of *guerre de course* might have disrupted trade, injuring Britain's economy more effectively than the attack on the French colonies recommended by Mahan would have injured France; this may explain why Britain soon afterwards reexamined the role of the battleship.[53] But Britain had greater difficulty in using sea power against Russia. In the revolving door stretching from Turkistan to Transcaucasia that shaped the Anglo-Russian rivalry and often led to a rivalry of mutual restraint or joint self-denial, the Russian army had the advantage over the British fleet, and not only later in the century when it could travel toward India along the Transcaspian railway.[54] Sea power, despite Britain's best efforts, could not hold a ring around Russia and prevent it breaking out of the Eurasian regional system into the wider world.

Let us take a quick tour from west to east through five unsuccessful British attempts to hold the ring. First, the Gulf of Bothnia freezes over in winter; access to it depends on control of the Sound; and its shallows prevent battleships firing cannon ball from moving close enough inshore to do damage. Britain was neither able in 1801 to exploit a victory over Denmark against Russia, nor in 1854 to move the Crimean War from the Black Sea. Second, Britain could not force the Dardanelles under sail, and any attempt to force them under steam would drag it into regional politics by requiring control of the sultan or cooperation with Austria-Hungary to earn the goodwill of Germany. The difficulty of forcing the Dardanelles was increased after the occupation of Egypt in 1882 by the ill will of France and, after 1894, by the Franco-Russian alliance. Third, although Britain in the 1830s chose the Tigris-Euphrates river system for a symbolic demonstration of its capability to project sea power inland by drawing a line Russia must not cross in an area in which probably it would not try, the expedition to Basra in 1914, leading to defeat by the Ottomans at Kut, proved the difficulty of turning symbol into substance. Fourth, the plan to use the Persian Gulf as a springboard for troops

---

53. Charles H. Fairbanks, "The Origins of the Dreadnought Revolution: A Historiographical Essay," *International History Review,* Vol. 13, No. 2 (May 1991), pp. 246–272.

54. Edward Ingram, "Britain and Russia," in Thompson, ed., *Great Power Rivalries,* pp. 269–305.

launched northward to cause havoc in Persia—what Britain called keeping the peace—foundered for lack of a base, or "police station" to borrow the postwar euphemism. Fifth, this left the Japanese alliance in the Far East, again a symbol of intent rather than the demonstration of capability it turned out to be. Britain expected Japan to lose a war with Russia.

Thus, sea power and global reach could not contain Russia within the Eurasian region, nor prevent it from thrusting for global reach and challenging Britain at the global level: expanding into the Middle and Far East or threatening to use the lever of a feint against India. As neorealists do not take account of intentions, only of potentialities and capabilities, the question whether Russia ever intended to invade India is irrelevant. The debate during phase three of cycle four between the Bombay (or Forward) School of Indian defence and the Punjab (or Backward) School showed that Britain knew that Russia's challenge could only be met by an offensive in Turkistan mounted from India, that is by fighting a regional war in Asia to preserve global reach—the price of the Bombay School's offensive strategy—or by the threat of an alliance with Germany in the core region—the price of the Punjab School's defensive strategy of "masterly inactivity" along the Indus. To make the point in Turkistan, Britain twice sent troops to occupy Afghanistan, twice suffered tactical defeats, and twice won geopolitical victories.

The failure of Britain's sea power to ensure global reach can be shown even in areas out of Russia's reach: during the crises of 1826–29 arising from Russia's attacks on Persia and the Ottoman Empire and 1832–33 arising from Mehemet Ali's attack on Mahmud II; in 1840–42 in Argentina and China; and during the Crimean War, the first two falling within long cycle theory's phase of world power.

Britain could not force agreement in 1826–29 on the role of Persia and the Ottoman Empire in the international system, because it dared not try to restrain Russia by sending the Mediterranean fleet into the Black Sea. In 1832–33, it lacked two fleets to manage simultaneous crises in Portugal and Syria, although both were vulnerable to sea power. Russia intervened in the Syrian crisis instead and, by the treaty of Unkiar Skelessi, turned the Ottoman Empire into a Russian protectorate and promised Russian troops in Syria to replace the French troops formerly in Egypt; in itself an effective bid to extend Russia's global reach, both directly and indirectly, by the use of leverage against Britain outside the Eurasian region. In the Crimean War, Britain failed in its counterattacking bid to foreshadow the treaty of Brest-Litovsk by driving Russia away from the Black Sea and out of Poland, and depended for the limited victory which left Russia vulnerable by demilitarizing the Black Sea on the Austrian army's mobilization in Galicia.

The incidents of 1840–42 in China and Argentina, in which Britain worked with France in a restraining alliance, at the same time working against France in the Middle East in a restraining alliance with Russia, illustrate the limits to sea power most clearly. Robinson and Gallagher cite the incidents as the classic example of the use of sea power to open up world markets to industrial goods. Christopher Platt counters that in both cases success depended upon conditions at the regional level—the state being coerced must be strong enough not to collapse into anarchy but weak enough not to resist effectively—and anyway was illusory.[55] China, preoccupied with rebellion, agreed to trade, but refused to buy; Argentina countered with the threat of retreat, asking how long and to what effect a European force could hover off Buenos Aires. Whether or not the incidents represent the inability of the world power to provide order, or to cause effective havoc, at the global level of the world system, they do represent the lack of the capability of sea power to turn global power into world power.

Conclusion: King of the Castle

Three criticisms of long cycle theory's conception of Britain as world leader may be summarized as follows. First, the Anglo-Russian rivalry defines the role of Britain as world leader in the nineteenth and twentieth centuries. The Anglo-German wars, which the British did not intend to fight, even after they declared war, were temporary, unexpected disruptions to a sustained predictable pattern.[56] Second, the Anglo-Russian rivalry points to the need to reexamine the challenger's identity in each of the cycles, owing to the potential of great powers for indirect global reach. Third, the rivalry separates the global and regional levels of the system. When Rasler and Thompson leave Russia (and the Ottoman Empire) off their list of European regional powers and confine it to the wider world as a global (and Asian regional) power, they move the system's core region to Central Asia and the Middle East during the

55. John Gallagher and Ronald Robinson, "The Imperialism of Free Trade," *Economic History Review*, 2nd series, Vol. 6, No. 1 (February 1953), pp. 1–25; D.C.M. Platt, "The Imperialism of Free Trade: Some Reservations," *Economic History Review*, 2nd series, Vol 21, No. 3 (August 1968), pp. 296–306; and D.C.M. Platt, "Further Objections to an Imperialism of Free Trade," *Economic History Review*, 2nd series, Vol. 26, No. 1 (February 1973), pp. 77–91.

56. John A. White, *Transition to Global Rivalry: Alliance Diplomacy and the Quadruple Entente, 1895–1907* (New York: Cambridge University Press, 1995); and Keith Neilson, *Britain and the Last Tsar: British Policy and Russia, 1894–1917* (Oxford: Clarendon Press, 1995).

fourth and fifth cycles.[57] If during these two cycles the rivalry shapes a tripolar system in which the United States first replaces Britain then emerges preeminent, system change is confined to world powers acting at the global level: it does not depend on intrusions from the (European) regional level in an unsuccessful regional bid for world leadership. Unfortunately, it allows for a global challenge from China to the United Staes and upsets Modelski, who now wishes to reverse the westward motion of his cycle of world leadership.

Long cycle theory illustrates two differences in the way historians and political scientists approach international relations. American political scientists are mesmerized by the Cold War: whether it was a bipolar system, the United States, unknowing, was a hegemon all along, and how the United States can prolong its unipolar moment—in other words with who is, how one gets to be, and the best way to stay top dog. Historians assume a multipolar system in which empires, not nation-states, of equivalent (but not equal or similar) power are tied (by agreement as well as constraint) into a customary system designed to ensure (if possible) that no top dog emerges. The system resembles a ratking, in which a group of rats, closely confined, become tied together by their tales. Some are big, some small and, just as important, some are tied closer to the knot than others. The small with greater manoeuverability are able to evade, and sometimes even to restrain, the big with less.

The argument among political scientists between balancers and bandwagoners arises from their search for the King of the Castle and knowing he is the United States. The (pretended) refinement of balance of power theory into balance of threat attracts American scholars who assume that once the refinement becomes standard, the United States will prolong its role as world leader. Other states, aware of U.S. preeminent power, do not (well, should not) perceive it as a threat because its actions obviously benefit all actors within the system other than rogue states (living beyond Kipling's Pale).[58] Tell that to Britain's Labour government watching the Ford administration lever the World Bank in 1973 into ratchetting up the terms of its loan.[59] In "special relationships," punishment is the reward for good behavior.

Political scientists therefore misunderstand the relations between

---

57. Rasler and Thompson, *Great Powers*, p. 29.

58. Samuel P. Huntington, "Why International Primacy Matters," *International Security*, Vol. 17, No. 4 (Spring 1993), pp. 82–83; and Walt, *The Origins of Alliances*, pp. 282–285.

59. Mark D. Harmon, *The British Labour Government and the 1976 IMF Crisis* (London: Macmillan, 1998), originally entitled *Ties that Bind.*

states, especially alliances. Britain, the tattered Phoenix rising from the ashes of World War I, was placed in an unenviable geopolitical position. Despite acting as world leader by providing order, or stable disorder, owing to the destruction of both the challengers with the potential for global reach (France and Russia) and the necessary allies in the core region (Imperial Germany and Austria-Hungary), it was placed in the most dangerous of all situations: left alone with its friends (Japan and the United States). A state aware of its relative decline, more threatened by its allies than its enemies, tries harder to prevent its allies from winning decisive victories than to ensure its enemies' decisive defeat.

Lastly, long cycle theory points to historians' and political scientists' different ideas about the relationship between theory and evidence. Theory helps historians to tease more out of the evidence, to find some where none existed, and to shape it. Imagine a whale-bone corset lying on a table. Although it has no shape itself and cannot stand alone, it transforms the ungainly flesh of the Prince Regent. Used by political scientists, however, the corset becomes a suit of armor. It stands upright, takes its own shape, and gives not an inch to accomodate the size and figure of the wearer. Long cycle theory's account of Great Britain as world leader prefers the comforting, constraining certainties of political science to the liberating uncertainties of history.

Chapter 9

Martian and Venusian Perspectives on International Relations: Britain as System Leader in the Nineteenth and Twentieth Centuries

William R. Thompson

There must be something distinctive about international relations that generates such grossly varying interpretations of what is believed to be going on at any given point in time. Some of the reasons are obvious. Even though most people do not possess much information about the subject, everyone has an opinion. Yet international relations can encompass extremely complex processes and, for that reason alone, analysts will tend to disagree about how best to capture and package the complexity. Then, too, and hardly unrelated to the first two reasons, almost every academic department that teaches international relations is likely to do it differently. In political science, it is usually not necessary to ask with what theories an analyst is working. All one really needs to ask is where the analyst was trained. If the answer is University X or any other letter in the alphabet, one is likely to be able to guess not only the topic that is being studied but also how it is being studied. A similar technique can be used for scholars outside the United States although sometimes one only needs to know the country in which someone was trained to be able to guess the probable epistemological stance.

But there is more to wildly dissimilar interpretations than simply complexity of world politics, the deficit in information, the surplus number of opinions about it, and disparate academic training. There is also the question of attitudinal predisposition toward various analytical choices. In this chapter, I develop a modest thesis about different predispositions, with particular emphasis on the question of structure, and then generate an extensive illustration of one facet of the consequences by looking at arguments about how we should interpret Britain's status in the world system between 1816 and 1945. I extract seventeen antistructuralist criticisms of structuralist interpretations from the literature and examine them critically from an avowedly structuralist position.

The discussion of the assertions, and the responses to them, should serve double duty. The critical assertions are all made by historians about misinterpretations of nineteenth- and twentieth-century international relations put forward mainly, but not exclusively, by political scientists. In juxtaposing assertion and counterassertion, one can see the collision of two very different ways of thinking about the same phenomena. Demonstrating the differences will serve one purpose by illustrating some ways in which historians and social scientists diverge in their analytical approaches. However, a second purpose of the exercise is to rebut the criticisms. It is not sufficient to note that some historians and some social scientists approach related phenomena differently and to leave it at that. Social science assertions about historical phenomena can be shown to be wrong. So, too, can historians' evaluations of social science assertions.

The subject matter is too important to simply be left to a "different strokes for different folks" shrug of the shoulders. It would be naive to expect to convert historians into political scientists, or vice versa. We would be even more remiss, however, if we ignore each other's assumptions, arguments, and findings. Both sides might even learn something about their own perspectives when forced to deal with the other side's slant on things. Even if nothing is resolved, it is important that we continue to pay attention to other camps' perspectives. Otherwise, we are apt to become too comfortable with our own assumptions and explanations.

Martian and Venusian Predispositions

One school of thought in world politics contends that international relations is fairly structured. There is a hierarchy of elite actors based in large part on their respective shares of technological innovation, economic resources in general, and military capability. However, the hierarchy is neither constant nor stable in the long term. The structure changes when elites ascend or decline the hierarchy as they either improve their relative economic standing or experience positional deterioration. International conflict—who fights, who wins, and who loses—is to some considerable extent influenced by these structural changes. When the structure is reasonably stable and one state predominates over the rest, a condition that is most likely immediately after an intensive struggle over succession to the apex of the hierarchy, conflict is less probable. When the systemic leader's position is challenged by newly ascending or reemerging competitors, conflict becomes more probable.

Calling this structural interpretation a school of thought glides over the many disagreements among the analysts who subscribe to the general outlines. For instance, structuralists disagree about which actors are elites and why some actors should be given special weight in analyses. They disagree about which international conflicts are important and why they are important. They disagree about the role of political economy and the sources of power and influence in the world system. Disagreements about actors, conflicts, and central processes lead to varying historical scripts and calendars so that there may be major conflicts of interpretation between any two structural interpretations.

Taking an ecumenical or generic structural position in this chapter might be desirable in the abstract but extremely awkward to execute as different structural interpretations would respond differently to antistructural criticisms. Therefore, I should state at the outset that my comments will be couched primarily in the terms of one structural framework—the leadership long cycle perspective.[1] This perspective distinguishes between global and regional structures. Global politics are about the management of long distance, interregional commerce, and other interactions. Global powers are those actors with sufficient global reach to engage in long-distance commerce and applications of military force. Historically, this has translated primarily into sea power. Regional powers are more locally oriented and are more likely to specialize in military power that emphasizes land applications useful for the extension of territorial control. In contrast, trading states, armed with sea power, are limited in their interest in, and capability to, control extensive territory around the world.

The most critical actor in this framework is the world power. This actor is the leading global power. Its foundation for global leadership is established by its initial control of major economic innovations in commerce and industry. These innovations are crucial for long-term economic growth and tend to be generated in clusters that are highly spatially and temporally concentrated. One example is the late eighteenth century's Industrial Revolution emphasis on ways of producing cotton and iron

---

1. The principal long cycle works are George Modelski, *Long Cycles in World Politics* (London: Macmillan, 1987); George Modelski, "Evolutionary Paradigm for Global Politics," *International Studies Quarterly*, Vol. 40, No. 3 (1996), pp. 321–342; George Modelski and Sylvia Modelski, eds., *Documenting Global Leadership* (London: Macmillan, 1988); George Modelski and William R. Thompson, *Seapower in Global Politics, 1494–1993* (London: Macmillan, 1988); George Modelski and William R. Thompson, *Leading Sectors and World Politics: The Coevolution of Global Politics and Economics* (Columbia: University of South Carolina Press, 1996); William R. Thompson, *On Global War* (Columbia: University of South Carolina Press, 1988); William R. Thompson, *The Emergence of the Global Political Economy* (London: University College London Press-Routledge, 2000); Karen Rasler and William R. Thompson, *War and State Making: The Shaping of the Global Powers* (Boston: Unwin and Hyman, 1989); and Karen Rasler and William R. Thompson, *The Great Powers and Global Struggle, 1490–1990* (Lexington: University Press of Kentucky, 1994).

products, which gave way to an emphasis on steam and railroads in the mid-nineteenth century. Britain led in these two technological waves only to be displaced in subsequent waves focusing on electricity, chemicals, and automobiles in which Germany and the United States took the lead in the late nineteenth century.[2]

In the leadership long cycle framework, a new world power emerges at the end of a period of global war fought at least in part over which state's decision-makers will have the opportunity to make policy for the global system. It has demonstrated its authority during the global war by putting together and leading a coalition of states to defeat the opposing coalition. The world power also emerges from the global war as the world's leading sea power—a military capability that was useful in winning the global war and that will be useful in enforcing the consequent global order.

Yet none of this hierarchy last forever. The world power loses its monopoly on economic innovations and its leading seapower position. Its position is challenged by other global powers that seek to ascend to the lead position. Ultimately, in conjunction with other factors—such as growing concentration of power in the world system's primary region—another bout of global war is fought to determine who will become the next world power. The last two rounds of global war were fought in 1792–1815 and 1914–45.[3] Between these periods of global combat, Britain ascended to, and declined, as the system leader or world power.

A directly opposed school of thought exists. It denies that world politics is structured. Or, if it is, that it is impossible to measure relative positions among the elite actors. Position and influence hinge on too many intangible factors that have no fixed interpretation. The resources states deploy in one instance may have no or little impact in another instance, region, or in time. For instance, strategic bombers may have one kind of impact in a highly urbanized setting and quite another in jungle terrain. The only thing that really matters is whether decision-makers are successful in achieving their goals in specific applications of power. And success in this context is as much a function of such attributes as clever-

---

2. Prior to the post-1815 British systemic leadership, the long cycle framework has a sequence extending back to the tenth century that includes the Northern and Southern Sung, Genoa, and Venice as prototypical leaders and Portugal, the United Provinces of the Netherlands, and eighteenth-century Britain. After 1945, the United States assumed the role.

3. Global wars are an institution that emerged only after 1494 and the development of a close interdependence between global affairs and regional western European developments. Global wars occurred in the following periods: 1494–1516, 1580–1608, 1688–1713, 1792–1815, and 1914–45.

ness, will, reputation, bluff, and idiosyncratic behavior by other actors as it is a function of material resources.

Even more to the point, the contrary position is that Britain did not possess the appropriate attributes for systemic leadership, that its sea power was of limited utility, and that its economic resources that were most applicable to world politics had little to do with industrial innovations. Britain's success was instead predicated on its empire—in marked contrast to arguments that maritime powers are supposed to eschew territorial entanglements—and finance. But successful as it might have been, Britain never had the sort of global predominance depicted in structural perspectives. Moreover, it is argued that the structuralists have it backwards. Structuralists argue that Britain was strongest in the early nineteenth century and in decline in the latter half of that century. Antistructuralists contend that Britain was strongest immediately after World War I—both relative to the preceding century and in comparison with its rivals.

These schools of thought produce seemingly night and day or, to be more *au courant*, Venusian and Martian interpretations of international relations. What an analyst from one school calls black, another analyst labels white. Nowhere is this more obvious than in the interpretation of the British role in world politics in the period between 1816 and 1945. The structural school portrays Britain as the leader of the successful coalition against Napoleon, the leading economic producer of the first half of the nineteenth century, and that century's preeminent sea power. Toward the end of the nineteenth century, other states, most prominently Germany and the United States, began to catch up with and to surpass the British economic lead. Britain, in relative decline, was forced to retrench in order to deal with the new competition. World Wars I and II were fought in large part to decide who would succeed to the systemic leadership role once occupied by a Britain no longer capable of defending its former leading position.

The antistructural school of thought contends that this interpretation of British leadership and decline is nonsensical. Britain was never that powerful in the first two-thirds of the nineteenth century and only became influential in European politics toward the end of that century—at the same time that the structural school perceives Britain in a free-fall economic decline. Britain, according to this antistructural view, was successful because European circumstances had changed in such a way as to create an opportunity for British balancing that had not prevailed before the 1890s and because British decision-makers exploited the opportunity in defense of their widespread empire. Not only did Britain emerge the winner in World War I, its postwar position was superior to any position attained by Britain in the previous century and a half. That is to say, Britain did not experience any meaningful decline before 1939. Consequently, one cannot explain British behavior in terms of something that never happened. Things fell apart only in the 1930s because the Soviet Union and France would not or could not play their traditional roles and because British decision-makers made the wrong choices—not so much due to relative resource weaknesses but more as a function of missed opportunities and a lack of will. It was World War II and its aftermath, the destruction wrought by the Axis powers, and the postwar behavior of colonial subjects and Cold War allies, especially the United States, that "did in" the British Empire.

While these interpretations come across as opposite or Martian and Venusian reconstructions of what transpired between 1816 and 1945, they are not necessarily as far apart as they seem. At least, it can be argued that the structural interpretation is not quite as incompatible with the antistructural point of view as the antistructuralists would have us believe. The incompatibility that is apparent reflects a perennial blind spot in the structural perspective and a fundamental misunderstanding or blind spot (or perhaps more than one) on the part of the antistructuralists. To the extent that the disputed interpretation revolves around whether capability absolutely determines power and influence, it is not clear that anyone is in disagreement.[4] The question then becomes more one of why antistructuralists believe that structuralists think that structure dictates outcomes in both the short and long term.

Nevertheless, these disagreements are not inherently a function of different disciplinary ways of doing things. The same disagreements are found within history and political science as well as between representatives of the two disciplines. The real distinction separates what might be termed humanities approaches versus social scientific ones. While historian antistructuralists are likely to be more comfortable with the humanities (and perhaps it is fair to say that historian structuralists are not as uncomfortable with social science as historian antistructuralists), it does not follow that political science antistructuralists are also likely to feel discomfort operating in a social scientific form of discourse. On the contrary, antistructuralists predominate in social science research focused on international relations.

---

4. Karen Rasler and William R. Thompson find that the empirical influence of relative capability (military and economic) on war outcomes, in general, has declined over time in "Predatory Initiators and the Changing Landscape for War," *Journal of Conflict Resolution*, Vol. 43, No. 4 (August 1999), pp. 411–433.

I first attempt to clarify these generalizations about the distinctions between historians and political scientists and then proceed to an extended example focused on the seventeen antistructural assertions about the roles and status of 1816–1945 Britain.

Making Distinctions About Historians and Political Scientists

The *International Security* symposium exchange among Elman and Elman, Levy, Haber, Kennedy, and Krasner, George, Ingram, Schroeder, and Gaddis is quite useful in establishing differences of approach, attitude, and instinct between diplomatic historians and political scientists who study international politics.[5] Historians focus on specific problems such as why did France retreat at Fashoda or why did Britain not intervene in the U.S. Civil War. The stories they tell are based to a considerable degree on a description of what took place in 1898 or in 1861–65. Generalizations about what people do are uncommon—in part due to a heightened sensitivity to fluctuations in context. Things are never quite the same from episode to episode. That rule of thumb, in its own turn, is due in part to the perception that individual personalities loom large in these event stories. It is not Germany that acts in the late nineteenth century but Bismarck and Kaiser Wilhelm and a cast of other very specific characters who formulate and execute German foreign policy. To be able to come to grips with the complexities surrounding distinctive events and personalities, one needs access to various sorts of material, but for diplomatic history, governmental archives of memorandums and reports are thought to be indispensable. If for no other reason than that governmental archives are slow to be opened, historians are focused on events that have happened in the past. But, of course, historians need no special excuse to appreciate the past for its own sake.

Historians try to avoid arguments about whether complete analytical objectivity is conceivable and proceed with their analyses as honestly as

5. See Colin Elman and Miriam Fendius Elman, "Diplomatic History and International Relations Theory: Respecting Difference and Crossing Boundaries," pp. 5–21; Jack S. Levy, "Too Important to Leave to the Other: History and Political Science in the Study of International Relations," pp. 22–33; Stephen H. Haber, David M. Kennedy, and Stephen D. Krasner, "Brothers Under the Skin: Diplomatic History and International Relations," pp. 34–43; Alexander L. George, "Knowledge for Statecraft: The Challenge for Political Science and History," pp. 44–52; Edward Ingram, "The Wonderland of the Political Scientist," pp. 53–63; Paul W. Schroeder, "History and International Relations Theory: Not Use or Abuse, but Fit or Misfit," pp. 64–74; and John Lewis Gaddis, "History, Theory and Common Ground," pp. 75–85, all in *International Security*, Vol. 22, No. 1 (1997).

they can. Given the perceived complexity of events and personalities, the very notion of causality is often suspect. In particular, simple causal arguments must be wrong if only because they are too simple. Evidence is obviously important but it cannot be disentangled from its specific context and, in any event, it tends to be evidence about why X did or thought Y at time Z. Theories may or may not be useful in illuminating some dimensions of a specific story. Alternatively, specific stories may be useful in discrediting certain theories. But there is no question that theory is and should be subordinated in the search for greater historical understanding.[6]

In marked contrast, political scientists are oriented toward more general problems. They seek to explain arms races or wars as a categorical phenomenon—not the outcomes of the Anglo-French naval arms race or World War I. If asked to explain a specific case, the first instinct should be to identify what the particular case represents in general because theories only offer explanations about general phenomena, not specific events. In their own research (as opposed to answering pesky questions about current events), political scientists are supposed to begin with theories and then move toward cases that can help assess the relative utility of the theories that exist. Explanation is accomplished if general theoretical propositions (or hypotheses derived therefrom) receive empirical support. Prediction is important in this context because that is how political scientists test the degree of conformance between what is expected theoretically and what is observed empirically. This meaning of prediction is not the same thing as forecasting future probabilities based on extrapolations from current trends, a fairly rare practice that nevertheless seems particularly vexsome to historians.

Political scientists, in general, prefer generalizations that apply universally. Spatial and temporal modifiers and exceptions are thought to be undesirable because they represent factors that simply have no specific meaning or have yet to be theorized about successfully. Conceivably, one could take this generic approach to any particular period in history, but more recent problems and cases are usually preferred to more distant ones. Empirical data tends to be more readily available for more recent cases, and the knowledge that is gained by explaining relatively current phenomena seems more relevant and the work is therefore more likely to be both funded and appreciated. Moreover, there is always the suspicion that the farther back in time one goes the more key parameters must have changed. Since we do not know much about those key parameters

---

6. See Jack S. Levy's chapter in this volume for more discussion on the distinctions between historians and political scientists on the roles of theory and generalization.

or, alternatively, because the existing key parameters have more policy relevance, it is more prudent to work with relatively recent phenomena.

Objectivity is thought to be both possible and highly desirable, or at least conceivable, for political scientists as long as one's values are made explicit and somehow kept out of the analysis as much as possible. Causation is taken for granted and parsimonious causation is better than complex causation.[7] The focus is on the interaction of variables—not on personalities operating in specific contexts with proper place names. The existence of the past cannot be denied; path dependencies are acknowledged at least in the abstract. But, in general, history should be subordinated to the quest for better theory.

Having repeated these distinctions found in the literature, I must note that the descriptions of historians who study international relations sound more accurate than the descriptions of political scientists who study international relations. The reason for that is that historians are a much more homogeneous population than are political scientists. Jack Levy is correct to point out that we need to stick to describing central tendencies.[8] The only problem is that it seems easier to discern central tendencies characterizing historians than it is to make generalizations about political scientists. After all, we have a good number of area specialists, philosophers, institutional historians, ideologues, journalists, and wannabe policymakers within our political science community. Quite often, their approach may seem to more closely approximate the historian's way of doing things than that of the mythical political scientist's. One solution to this problem is to contrast historians with social, as opposed to political, scientists. It does not solve all of the problems of over- or inaccurate generalization, but it helps to reduce some of the error. It may also eliminate a sizable proportion of the political science population from the comparison.

Even so, the attributes discussed above should be viewed as opposing polarities on continuums along which individuals may be located. For instance, there is some variance among historians on the extent to which their analyses are narrative-based. Some historical treatments are sheer narrative. Other historians would be aghast if someone accused them (rightly or wrongly) of narrative-based explanation. Similarly, social scientists vary by how much theory and what sort of theory (e.g., single hypothesis, middle range, grand) is introduced into their inquiry. So, we

---

7. See Richard Ned Lebow's chapter in this volume for similar observations on the historian's preference for complex causation.

8. Levy, "Too Important to Leave to the Other," p. 23.

can imagine a scale on which individuals place themselves according to how they approach their subject matter. At one end is pure description and the other pure theory. Undoubtedly, very few analysts always work at the polar ends of the continuum. Nor need we assume that analysts are always consistent in operating at the same scalar point as they move from topic to topic. But some rough level of consistency can probably be anticipated.

While each of these various attributes that I am linking to historians and political scientists suggests a different scale, it is unlikely that analysts place themselves on each possible scale differentially. It is more likely that they, not unlike attitudinal attributes, cluster. We can, for example, easily visualize a historian who is strongly narrative bound, highly impressed by contingent relationships among major personalities and extremely uneasy about how causation works. There are also historians who are more comfortable with generalization, causation, and theory. There are social scientists who abhor the thought of non-universal principles, cannot or prefer not to think in terms other than simple causality, and believe that predictive success is the only criteria, besides parsimony, by which to judge theoretical arguments. Then, there are social scientists who have a healthy respect for context, can tolerate some level of contingency, and do not expect to find universal principles or laws.

STRUCTURE AND ANALYTICAL TYPES

What does all this speculation have to do with the disputed role of structure in world politics? At the risk of some overgeneralization, I will advance the thesis that the two "types" of historians and social scientists used as examples in the paragraph above tend to view the role of structure differently. The type A historian (narrative bound, emphasizing contingency and personalities, and uneasy about causation) and the type A social scientist (seeks universal principles, simple causality, parsimony, and predictive success as the primary evaluation criterion) are least likely to embrace structural ideas. For these types of analysts, structural arguments simply do not fit their versions of reality. They generate cognitive dissonance and, therefore, are likely to be ignored or dismissed out of hand. The more closely an analyst approximates the ideal A type, the more dismissive he or she is likely to be.

In contrast, some Type B historians (relatively comfortable with generalization, causality, and theory) and at least some type B social scientists (relatively sensitive to context, contingency, and non-universal generalizations) are more apt to appreciate structural arguments because structural ideas generate less cognitive dissonance for these types of analysts.

Instead, it is the analytical products of type A analysts which give them generic discomfort.[9]

To be sure, there are exceptions to these generalizations. Most important, there are few pure type A and B analysts. Most historians and social scientists are found scattered on points somewhere in between the A and B continuum poles within their respective "disciplinary" domains. Fortunately or unfortunately, depending on one's point of view, one would also have to admit that both analytical populations are skewed toward the A points. Type B analysts are clearly in the minority everywhere. There is also the irony that type A historians have absolutely no lines of communication to type A social scientists and vice versa since they represent polar opposites on still another scale but type B analysts at least have some obvious potential for profitable, mutual interaction.

Nonetheless, I submit, the differential clustering of scholarly attitudinal predispositions is one prime reason for Martian and Venusian versions of international relations. Type A and B analysts are inclined psychologically to see different things going on in the real world. As a consequence, their interpretations give the appearance of emerging from completely different planets.

This is why the debate over the utility of structural interpretations of international relations goes on within history, within political science, and between historians and political scientists. It is not derived from inherent differences between disciplines. It is derived from inherent differences among historians and political scientists about how best to approach their preferred subject matters.

Yet if type A and B products create genuine cognitive dissonance for the other type of analyst, on what basis can we communicate across types? It is not clear that successful interaction across types of analysis and analysts is feasible. Still, we need to make the effort because there is something to be gained. Structuralists and antistructuralists can each learn from the other. There is also some strong probability that the two

---

9. Some readers may find these distinctions regarding type A and type B political scientists counterintuitive. What I am leaving out of the argument is a variable appreciation for history. Type A political scientists, with a commitment to parsimony and universal generalizations, prefer for the most part to ignore history as an inconvenient obstacle to theorizing. Structural approaches usually (but not always) entail some assumption that history matters and, therefore, are accompanied by some form of historical script or interpretation that is important to their theoretical framework. Pure type A political scientists thus will dismiss historical-structural analysis as too historicist and atheoretical for their tastes. On the other hand, some type B political scientists will also dismiss historical-structural analysis as too theoretical or not sufficiently open to countless contingencies.

points of view are simply talking past one another. They give the appearance superficially of totally rejecting the other side's basic assumptions and conclusions. But, abstractly speaking, there are ways to accommodate seemingly diametrically opposed views and profit from the exchange. Whether all or any concerned will in fact perceive profit is another question entirely.

In the next section of this paper, I turn to a point-by-point examination of selected assertions made by antistructuralist historians primarily about the work of structural historians on interpreting Britain's status in world politics in the nineteenth and twentieth centuries. This structure—historians criticizing historians—helps to illustrate the argument that the debate over structure is not due to disciplinary distinctions alone.

While the critical assertions are aimed at the work of specific historians, I do not see it as my task to defend the specific works under attack. Rather, I am more interested in responding generically to the claims as a structurally oriented social scientist, for the same criticisms could just as easily be leveled against the type of work in which I and others like myself are engaged.

Specific Assertions by the Antistructuralist School

Table 9.1 lists the seventeen assertions in one set. They were not selected randomly. Rather, the rationale was to develop a set of statements that summarized as fairly as possible the antistructuralist positions on questions of particular interest to structural interpretations of Britain's nineteenth- and twentieth-century roles. In addition, the assertions were organized to move from more general to more specific statements and, as much as possible, to move chronologically over the 1816–1945 era.

There is a limit to how exhaustive one can be in assembling these assertions. Antistructuralist analysts have advanced other assertions. The list in Table 9.1 should thus be viewed as a both a representative and a purposive sample.[10] While it is difficult to respond to the set of assertions as a group in a meaningful way, it should make more sense to take them one at a time.

---

10. My present focus on antistructuralist arguments is restricted primarily to John R. Ferris, "The Greatest Power on Earth: Great Britain in the 1920s," *International History Review*, Vol. 13, No. 4 (1991), pp. 726–750; Ingram, "The Wonderland of the Political Scientist"; Edward Ingram's chapter in this volume; Gordon Martel, "The Meaning of Power: Rethinking the Decline and Fall of Great Britain," *International History Review*, Vol. 13, No. 4 (1991), pp. 662–694; B.J.C. McKercher, " 'Our Most Dangerous Enemy': Great Britain Pre-eminent in the 1930s," *International History Review* Vol. 13, No. 4

1. *Structural approaches to world politics and the 1816–1945 role of Britain are exercises in economic determinism.*[11]

The antistructuralist school repeatedly describes structural approaches as economic-deterministic in nature. Yet it is interesting to note that antistructural analysts do not describe themselves as power-, influence, prestige, will-deterministic. As a consequence, one senses that the "economic determinism" charge is some sort of coded denigration, as, indeed, the determinism accusation is usually meant to be derogatory and dismissive rather than a neutral description of a school of thought. Whatever the case, most structural approaches are far less deterministic than their critics claim. Structural approaches do, however, tend to privilege economic variables in their theoretical hierarchies. By "privilege" I mean to say that it is usually assumed that economic variables have more influence on political variables than the other way around. That assumption neither rules out reciprocal influences (political variables influencing economic variables), nor does it attribute all the variance in political variables to economic causation. The bottom line is not determinism; it is that actors are more likely to have greater influence when their relative economic position is greater than when it is lesser. That leaves a great deal of theoretical room for the operation of other processes and relationships.

A case in point is Paul Kennedy's argument.[12] Since many of the antistructuralists to whom this chapter responds have focused on Kennedy as a main target of their scorn, it is appropriate to look at just what this particular structural version actually argues.[13] Essentially, Kennedy

---

(1991), pp. 751–783; and Keith Neilson, "'Greatly Exaggerated': The Myth of the Decline of Great Britain before 1914," *International History Review*, Vol. 13, No. 4 (1991), pp. 695–725.

11. Neilson, "'Greatly Exaggerated,'" p. 696; and McKercher, "Our Most Dangerous Enemy,'" p. 756.

12. Paul Kennedy, *The Rise and Fall of the Great Powers* (New York: Random House, 1987).

13. One explicitly stated reason for targeting Kennedy was that he had the temerity to advance the rise and fall of Britain as a paradigm for international history. While Kennedy's *The Rise and Fall of the Great Powers* is certainly compatible with Kennedy's *The Rise and Fall of British Naval Mastery* (New York: Scribners' Sons, 1976) and his *Strategy and Diplomacy, 1870–1945* (London: Allen and Unwin, 1983), one would be hard pressed to attribute paternity for structural arguments on rise and decline politics to Kennedy. Some alternative structural interpretations would include A.F.K. Organski, *World Politics* (New York: Knopf, 1968); Andre Gunder Frank, *World Accumulation, 1492–1789* (New York: Monthly Review Press, 1978); Robert Gilpin, *U.S. Power and the Multinational Corporation* (New York: Basic Books, 1975); Robert Gilpin, *War and Change*

Table 9.1. Seventeen Antistructuralist Assertions About Britain's Role as System Leader.

1. Structural approaches to world politics and the 1816–1945 role of Britain are exercises in economic determinism.

2. Structural arguments that portray Britain as a relatively special case and one that exemplifies categorical systemic leadership are exercises in anglocentrism that rival U.S. exceptionalism. Long cycle structuralism goes even further by developing a model of progressive cycles predicated on the United States as the mature end point and then projecting backwards to reinterpret the Portuguese-Dutch-British leadership sequence as an evolutionary maturation process, not unlike the transition from tadpole to frog.

3. Since many of the components of power and influence that matter most are too intangible to measure systematically, it is impossible to create rank orders of states in the international system.

4. Since no weapon is inherently superior to other types of weapons, even the most simple types of capability counting are meaningless and therefore demonstrate the impossibility of comparing the relative strengths of states.

5. In the 1792–1815 global warfare, Britain was no match for France on the continent. The advantages of sea power in this type of confrontation are exaggerated, for sea powers are inherently limited as to the damage they can inflict on continental opponents. What was most important to the outcome was the coalition of European states that formed to defeat Napoleon. If the ostensible new system leader could not decide the Napoleonic outcome with its own resources and instead only profited from the work accomplished by land powers, in what sense can it be regarded as a system leader? Moreover, the subsequent limitations on British influence in Europe were more due to the strategic limitations of sea power than to decline. For instance, British sea power could not be expected to impose order within Europe or to fully contain Russia within Eurasia. Contrary to the emphasis placed on sea power by the long cycle approach, Britain's global reach was based more on the Indian Army than on the Royal Navy.

6. Britain "flourished in peculiar historical circumstances." Britannia could rule the waves in the nineteenth century because no other state cared to challenge it.

7. If Britain was so powerful in the mid-nineteenth century, why were its interests threatened by Russia? Why could Britain not deter the outbreak of the Crimean War?

8. Britain at its peak never equalled Rome.

9. No great power, certainly including Britain, is or ever was omnipotent.

10. At the turn of the nineteenth and twentieth centuries, Britain retreated from the Americas and made new arrangements with Japan, France, and Russia to share its security burden. These developments cannot be attributed to British relative decline. Rather, they demonstrated British strength in international politics.

11. It was German policy and not German power that led Britain to identify Germany as a threatening adversary prior to World War I.

Table 9.1. continued

12. The emphasis on British relative decline in manufacturing and trade ignores the critical role played by Britain's leadership in providing investment capital and international finance, especially after 1870. In any event, wealth in Britain continued to be based on land ownership. For much of the nineteenth century Britain remained a preindustrial state, run by aristocrats, bureaucrats, and bankers, and not industrialists and merchants.

13. "Britain had the money, the technology, the industrial capacity and the will to maintain the underpinnings of deterrence [in 1914]."

14. Britain and Germany twice found themselves fighting wars which neither of them expected or desired. Throughout the nineteenth and early twentieth centuries, Britain's challengers were France and Russia. At different times, Austria and Germany acted as Britain's continental allies to contain the threat of French and Russian expansion. Britain's decision to go to war in 1914 was thus not predicated on balancing against German expansion. Rather, it was based on a fear that a Franco-Russian victory would lead to their shared domination of Eurasia and a subsequent, joint bid for global supremacy. Britain had no choice but to bandwagon with the side that was likely to win, in hopes of restraining their future appetites.

15. Global relations do not determine relations in the system's core region (Europe between 1494 and 1945). Global relations are derived from relations in the system's core region. If global wars were fought only between states with global reach and about global relationships, they would have had little impact on the world's great power clashes.

16. World War I can only be seen as a triumph for Britain. In the twenty years following the war, Britain was as strong, if not stronger, than it had been in the preceding 150–200 years.

17. Britain was great because of its empire, not despite it. One interpretation is that the real British problem was its failure to create a tightly integrated empire in 1919 that could generate the resources necessary to compete effectively in international politics. If one counted the population and resources of the Empire as opposed to those of the United Kingdom, one would construct a different impression of the relative position for "Britain," as well as little evidence of relative decline. This failure of imperial integration was compounded by the losses experienced in World War II. But the real sources of the demise of the British Empire were colonial agitation for independence after World War II and the pernicious policies aiming at decolonization and the destruction of the Empire by Britain's ally, the United States.

contends that economic and technological growth is *a* central dynamic in international relations—not the only dynamic conceivable. Moreover, the way this central dynamic operates gives a temporary advantage to one state for a period of time. The rise and fall dynamic also ultimately affects military power and is closely related to the probability of great power warfare. The propositions outlined in Table 9.2 hardly read as if they were a manifesto of economic determinism. What determinism is there is a long-run determinism. In the long run, states and decision-makers cannot evade their structural constraints. Nothing in the argument suggests that states and decision-makers cannot be creative in ignoring or sidestepping their structural constraints in the short run.

As it happens, the antecedence of some economic variables deemed important to the creation of structure and hierarchy over some important military-political variables has been established empirically. Rasler and Thompson and Reuveny and Thompson have repeatedly found that indicators for economic innovation (growth rates in leading sector production) and concentration (shares in leading sector production) antecede naval concentration (shares in sea power capability) and warfare (percent of gross national product devoted to military spending or percent of military personnel as a proportion of total population).[14] These relation-

---

in World Politics (Cambridge: Cambridge University Press, 1981); Robert Gilpin, *The Political Economy of International Relations* (Princeton: Princeton University Press, 1987); Kenneth N. Waltz, *Theory of International Politics* (Reading, Mass.: Addison-Wesley, 1979); A.F.K. Organski and Jacek Kugler, *The War Ledger* (Chicago: University of Chicago Press, 1980); Fernand Braudel, *The Perspective of the World*, trans. by Sian Reynolds (New York: Harper and Row, 1984); Immanuel Wallerstein, *The Politics of the World-Economy* (Cambridge: Cambridge University Press, 1984); Modelski, *Long Cycles in World Politics*; Modelski, "Evolutionary Paradigm for Global Politics"; Joshua Goldstein, *Long Cycles: Prosperity and War in the Modern Age* (New Haven: Yale University Press, 1988); Manus Midlarsky, *The Onset of World War* (Boston: Unwin Hyman, 1988); Modelski and Thompson, *Seapower and Global Politics*; Modelski and Thompson, *Leading Sectors and World Politics*; Thompson, *On Global War*; Christopher Chase-Dunn, *Global Formation: Structures of the World-Economy* (New York: Basil Blackwell, 1989); Rasler and Thompson, *War and State Making*; Rasler and Thompson, *The Great Powers and Global Struggle*; Charles F. Doran, *Systems in Crisis* (Cambridge: Cambridge University Press, 1991); and Mark R. Brawley, *Liberal Leadership: Great Powers and Their Challengers in Peace and War* (Ithaca: Cornell University Press, 1993). It might be interesting to try and trace who influenced whom and how in the development of these often different arguments.

14. This is a Granger causality test. One dimension of causal arguments is that if variable X is a cause of variable Y, a change in X's values must antecede an impact on Y's values. Granger causality tests are fairly conservative statistical tests to establish whether X and Y are systematically related in a statistically significant fashion and whether variable X's influence really does antecede variable Y's movement over time.

Table 9.2. Paul Kennedy's Theory of Structural Change.

---

1. The central dynamic of change in international politics is driven primarily by developments in economic growth and technology. These developments, in turn, bring about changes in social structures, political systems, military power, and the hierarchical position of actors.
2. The pace of change is non-uniform due to irregularities in the unevenness of growth, technological innovation, entrepreneurial invention, and other intervening factors such as climate, geography, and war.
3. Different regions and states have experienced faster or slower rates of growth due to shifts in technology, production, and trade as well as to their variable receptivities to adopting new modes of increasing wealth.
4. Military power ultimately depends upon economic wealth derived from an infrastructure integrating production, technology, and finance. Uneven economic growth, therefore, significantly impacts the relative military power and strategic position of states.
5. Great power warfare has been closely related to the rise and fall of major actors. The new territorial order established at the end of each great power coalition war, in which victory always goes to the side with the greatest material resources, confirms longer-term shifts in economic capabilities and the redistribution of international power.
6. A peculiar set of historical and technological circumstances facilitates the emergence of states that are enabled to acquire, temporarily, a disproportional share of wealth and power.
7. While the relative erosion of disproportional wealth and power is inevitable, the pace of erosion can be accelerated by attempts to maintain commitments that exceed the diminishing means to sustain them.

Source: Karen Rasler and William R. Thompson, *The Great Powers and Global Struggle, 1490–1990* (Lexington: University Press of Kentucky, 1994), pp. 143–144.

---

ships characterize both the British era of leadership prior to 1914 and the U.S. era after 1945. Naval concentration and warfare do feed back into the economic realm in significant ways, but these reciprocal influences do not diminish the causal priority and primacy of economic innovation and concentration.

Nevertheless, the principal Achilles' heel of structural approaches is that the lion's share of attention is devoted to the rise and fall of the

---

At this point in time, these types of examinations appear to be about as close to an approximation of causality as we can come.

See Karen Rasler and William R. Thompson, "Technological Innovation, Capability Positional Shifts and Systemic War," *Journal of Conflict Resolution*, Vol. 35, No. 3 (1991), pp. 273–294; Rasler and Thompson, *The Great Powers and Global Struggle;* and Raphael Reuveny and William R. Thompson, "War, Systemic Leadership and Economic Growth: The United States Case," *Journal of Conflict Resolution*, Vol. 43, No. 5 (1999), pp. 570–595.

economic foundation and not enough attention has been directed at what might be called the capability-influence gap that the antistructuralists emphasize. In other words, in the long run it can be argued that capability (the resources an actor possesses or can access) roughly approximates influence (whether actors obtain the outcomes they desire). But that does not imply that capability equals influence in the short run from a structural point of view. The primary value of the antistructural school of thought is to point out that a rapidly deteriorating relative economic position need not spell immediate political disaster. Eventually, relative decline "catches up" with decision-makers and they will find their options so circumscribed that retrenchment becomes nearly inevitable. In the British case, though, relative economic decline set in some time in the second half of the nineteenth century and it might be said that British policy did not fully adjust to its deteriorating economic position for another century. Hence there is clearly a lag between declining position and fully delimited options that is both material and perceptual in nature. In the interim, there is much room for nimble strategy and adroit maneuvering. And it very well may be true that decision-makers are not necessarily the first to realize or to admit that their nation's capability foundation is eroding. The perceived rate of decline is always a matter of debate. Therefore, it should not be surprising if, on occasion, decision-makers speak and act as if they are unaware that their former preeminence has slipped away from them. Some would even say that is part of their job description.

2. *Structural arguments that portray Britain as a relatively special case and one that exemplifies categorical systemic leadership are exercises in anglocentrism that rival American exceptionalism.*[15]

Long cycle structuralism goes even further by developing a model of progressive cycles predicated on the United States as the mature end point and then projecting backwards to reinterpret the Portuguese-Dutch-British leadership sequence as an evolutionary maturation process, not unlike the transition from tadpole to frog.[16]

There are elements of anglocentrism (and other types of exceptionalism) in structural models of international relations but, if so, they are probably due primarily to the prominence of the British example in relatively recent history. On the other hand, Ingram contends that the long cycle approach is U.S.-centric because the authors in question knew

---

15. Martel, "The Meaning of Power," p. 674.

16. See Ingram's chapter in this volume.

what the U.S. system leader looked like and whiggishly traced its pre-sumed antecedents back in time through the British and the Dutch to the Portuguese.[17] The core criticism is that the authors in question presumed a development process at work. If one knows what the mature product looks like, it is then necessary to find the less developed precedents. Since Ingram does not believe there is a development process at work in the first place, arguments to the contrary are viewed as figments of over-wrought social science imagination. As it happens, the leadership long cycle perspective that Ingram is criticizing now traces the origins of contemporary (or most recent) U.S. leadership to origins in Sung China five centuries before the Portuguese breakthrough into the Indian Ocean.[18] The argument is that the long wave type of modern economic growth first manifested in Sung China a millennium ago (see, for in-stance, the partially parallel argument of the historian William McNeill) can be tracked forward in time continuously via the successive growth experiences of the Northern Sung, Southern Sung, Genoese, Venetians, Portuguese, Dutch, British, and the United States.[19] While isolated epi-sodes of long-term growth can be discerned before the Sung period (i.e., before the tenth century C.E.), the continuous succession of growth lead-ers cannot be traced before the tenth century. Therefore, it is presumed that something changed in the parameters of the world economy around the tenth century. Does that mean leadership long cycle analysis has become Sungcentric?

Are these cycles progressive? Is there a maturation process involved? These are highly debatable issues. What is less debatable is that while an evolutionary process is thought to be at work, the evolutionary assump-tion is that change is open-ended. There need not be a next leader—nor is any specific leader necessarily an improvement on its predecessors in all spheres. As we make the transition between any two leaders, the naval technology may or may not have improved, the underlying leadership resource base may or may not have expanded, the global wars may or may not have become more extensive and deadlier, the scope of leader-ship operation may or may not have been enlarged, and the level of global order established may or may not have been extended. Over the past thousand years, in contrast, all of these criteria have changed for better or worse. For example, leadership in the global political economy

17. See Ingram, "The Wonderland of the Political Scientist," and his chapter in this volume.

18. Modelski and Thompson, *Leading Sectors and World Politics.*

19. William H. McNeill, *The Pursuit of Power: Technology, Armed Force and Society Since AD 1000* (Oxford: Oxford University Press, 1982).

no longer depends on slavery as it once did. That is certainly a progressive feature. However, the potential lethality of another global war seems markedly less progressive.

There are no tadpoles in the Sung-U.S. leadership sequence; they are all frogs of varying size and capability performing somewhat similar roles in the global political economy.[20] The United States has never been the ideal role model on which the long cycle theoretical apparatus rests. On the contrary, what is amazing is that after a thousand years of change, the global political economy stumbles along with much the same form of political leadership with which its "modern" era started.

More interesting is Gunder Frank's charge that almost all of the current theorizing about structural change is highly Eurocentric.[21] His argument is that the center of the world economy was located in eastern Asia until about 1800, and shifted only briefly (for about two centuries) to Western Europe and North America. It is now shifting back to eastern Asia, according to Frank's Sinocentric perspective. But, putting aside the question of the accuracy of Frank's location of the world economy's center in the 1500–1800 period, the world's center of economic innovation was once clearly located in the Near East some five thousand years ago. If one made this argument must we then call it a Sumerocentric point of view?

The answer is probably yes and the general point is that we create models based in part on our interpretation of international "realities." Where else are our models to originate? To accuse a perspective of harboring some type of centricity, then, does not have much meaning unless it is implied that the interpretation fits only that patch of geographical territory at some point in time and no other or, alternatively, exaggerates the appearance of some territory's attributes or behavior into a general model. The antistructural critique comes closer to the latter than the former but since it is denying that the structural perspective fits the British experience in the first place, the implications of "anglocentricity" are left vague.

There is also the perhaps amusing question of who is more genuinely anglocentric—one group that sees British ascent and decline as a phase that other states have experienced in history, or another group that argues that Britain is difficult to compare with similar political units and, in any event, never declined until it was stabbed in the back by its U.S. ally? Or

---

20. The different types of frogs, as opposed to the tadpole-frog sequence, was suggested by George Modelski.

21. Andre Gunder Frank, *ReOrient* (Berkeley: University of California Press, 1998).

is the root question one of whether emphasis should be placed on Britain as opposed to the British Empire? This question of state centricity versus imperial centricity emerges again below.

From a structural point of view, one highly appropriate question is whether the center of the action is identified correctly. From an antistructural point of view, there presumably is no center to identify correctly or incorrectly. The question then revolves around whether an empirical case can be made for or against some group's alleged centrality.

3. *Since many of the components of power and influence that matter most are too intangible to measure systematically, it is impossible to create rank orders of states in the international system.*[22]

If the components of power and influence are mainly intangible, a rank order of states in the international system would be difficult to construct. However, the adherents to the antistructural perspective seem a bit confused on this issue. While they stress the intangible, they also insist on the continued preeminence of Britain up to 1914 and even, amazingly, to 1939. The antistructural position is that Britain was the only global or world power prior to the two world wars.[23] All other possible contenders were either isolated, confined to regional theaters, or both.[24] Hence, one gathers that it is possible to at least rank order the geographical scope of influence. Antistructural analysts also claim that Britain was the world's leading sea power and financial power at a time when structural analysts are describing Britain as a declining power.[25] Does that imply that it is possible to rank order sea and financial power but not other types of capability?

---

22. Martel, "The Meaning of Power," p. 677.

23. Neilson, "'Greatly Exaggerated,'" pp. 696, 725; and McKercher, "'Our Most Dangerous Enemy,'" pp. 751, 783.

24. Antistructuralists appear to use the "global" and "world" modifiers for the "power" term to signify the geographical scale of foreign policy interests. A global or world power, therefore, is one that has worldwide foreign policy interests. Some structuralists, in constrast, tend to reserve these terms for states with the capability to operate on a global or world scale. For instance, in leadership long cycle vernacular, a global power is a state with the minimum global reach capability to operate beyond its local region. A world power must possess half or more of the global power capability pool at the outset of its incumbency.

25. Neilson, "'Greatly Exaggerated'"; and McKercher, "'Our Most Dangerous Enemy.'"

4. *Since no weapon is inherently superior to other types of weapons, even the most simple types of capability counting are meaningless and therefore demonstrate the impossibility of comparing the relative strengths of states.*[26]

This statement, taken on its face value, is clearly untrue.[27] History is replete with examples of people with iron swords defeating other people armed only with bronze swords, of people with rifles that fire more quickly defeating other people with rifles that fire more slowly, and of people with the capability to hurl projectiles farther defeating people with less hurling capability. Without any doubt, some weaponry is inherently superior over other types of weaponry. Other things being equal, an eighteenth-century ship captain engaged in a sea battle would rather have a fifty gun ship-of-the-line than a frigate with twenty-five guns. That is exactly how the concept of ships-of-the-line emerged as the number of guns escalated and lesser-gunned ships could no longer engage competitively in the front line of the fleet. Over time, this escalation in artillery numbers expanded to encompass armor thickness and how far the artillery could fire its shells. Wooden ships gave way to iron and steel ships just as galleys had given way to sailing ships in earlier blue water clashes. Dreadnoughts made earlier battleships obsolete because Dreadnought artillery could engage and destroy the older style battleships before they could bring their guns to bear on the opposition. Aircraft carriers took this idea one step further by launching aircraft to attack ships that were not yet in sight. Once that principle became dominant, battleships were forced to yield their front-line status.

It is quite conceivable to quantify weaponry capability as long as one is reasonably careful.[28] Historically, decision-makers have spent some time counting their opponent's ships-of-the-line, battleships, carriers, attack submarines, and so on—and not without reason. The outcome of an encounter between any two ships equally armed and armored may be

---

26. Martel, "The Meaning of Power," p. 678.

27. In all fairness, Martel is attempting to suggest that capabilities that may work in one region will not necessarily work the same way or as effectively in another region. The point is well taken but it leads the author to overstate his case considerably. See his "The Meaning of Power."

28. Naval historians tend to prefer the greater detail found in Glete's naval data set over Modelski and Thompson's data, which was designed to examine hypotheses about naval concentration over a 500-year period. While there are problems in using Glete's data for serial purposes, the same general decay patterns can be observed in both data sets, although Glete's data stops short of addressing the question of British relative decline before 1939. Compare Jan Glete, *Navies and Nations: Warships, Navies and State Building in Europe and America, 1500–1860* (Stockholm: Almquist, 1993); and Modelski and Thompson, *Seapower and Global Politics.*

difficult to call without reference to crew training, skill, and luck. But a fleet with twice as many first-line ships as an opponent's is, other things being equal, more likely to win a battle between the two fleets. Similarly, a state with more front-line ships than all of its opponents combined is a better bet to become the world's leading sea power than is a state with only 10 percent of the naval capability pool. However, presumably no one argues that sea power is guaranteed to be of much use in combat waged in interior deserts, mountains, or jungles.[29] Nor is anyone arguing that a battleship equals an infantry battalion. And it cannot be assumed that the possession of weapons means that those weapons will be utilized wisely or at all. There are indeed limitations to weaponry quantification and the uses to which it may be applied. Yet these limitations do not prevent us from separating major from minor powers or system leaders from followers.

5. *In the 1792–1815 global warfare, Britain was no match for France on the continent. The advantages of sea power in this type of confrontation are exaggerated, for sea powers are inherently limited as to the damage they can inflict on continental opponents. What was most important to the outcome was the coalition of European states that formed to defeat Napoleon. If the ostensible new system leader could not decide the Napoleonic outcome with its own resources and instead only profited from the work accomplished by land powers, in what sense can it be regarded as a system leader? Moreover, the subsequent limitations on British influence in Europe were due more to the strategic limitations of sea power than to decline. For instance, British sea power could not be expected to impose order within Europe or to fully contain Russia within Eurasia. Contrary to the emphasis placed on sea power by the long cycle approach, Britain's global reach was based more on the Indian Army than on the Royal Navy.*[30]

There should be no question that the statements concerning the limitations of sea power in confrontations with continental opponents and the need for coalitions of sea and land powers to suppress an attempt at regional hegemony are correct. However, none of these arguments is alien to structural perspectives, which are ordinarily highly sensitive to the distinctions between sea and land power. It is helpful to emphasize, as does leadership long cycle theory, that there are really two different

---

29.   See C. Harvey Gardiner, *Naval Power in the Conquest of Mexico* (Austin: University of Texas Press, 1956) for an example of how sea power sometimes turns up where least expected.

30.   Martel, "The Meaning of Power," p. 680; Ferris, "'The Greatest Power on Earth,'" p. 732; and Ingram's chapter in this volume.

games at play. One group of states has specialized in long-distance trade, sea power, and the avoidance as much as possible of continental (in this case, read European) entanglements. Another group of states has specialized in territorial expansion within Europe and developing its instruments of land power. While not all major powers (since 1500 anyway) clearly belong exclusively to one species or the other, the most lethal wars have been fought when the leader of the sea power group has organized a coalition of states to suppress the regional hegemony of a European land power (e.g., Spain, France, and Germany).[31]

The system leader's role as a coalition organizer is particularly important. To the extent that the system leader has specialized in sea power, there are very real limitations on what it could do militarily against an entrenched land foe. This is the classical whale versus elephant dilemma.[32] They cannot get at each other very well or conclusively. Either the whale must enlist its own elephants or the elephant must enlist its own whales. In modern history, the whale coalition leader has always triumphed over European elephants, in part due to a two-front strategy combining sea and land power against a would-be hegemon relying largely on land power.[33] Once the coalition has been victorious, the coalition leader has not emerged as a world hegemon. Rather, an aspiring regional hegemon has been defeated, thereby suppressing a potential threat to the global system of long-distance trade and advanced technological production. It is this global system over which the system leader is preeminent due to both its coalition leadership and its near-monopoly position in controlling long-distance trade and advanced technological production. However, preeminence in the global system does not necessarily translate into influence in and over regional affairs. Moreover, that global preeminence is likely to be maintained longer if the system leader is able to avoid entanglement in regional politics. Even so, no global system leader has managed to isolate itself from regional problems for very long. Its own position is likely to erode. Equally likely is the emergence of new competitors and challengers.

---

31. See William R. Thompson, "Long Cycles and the Geohistorical Context of Structural Transitions," *World Politics*, Vol. 43, No. 1 (1992), pp. 127–152; and Rasler and Thompson, *The Great Powers and Global Struggle* for the development and application of Ludwig Dehio's arguments to European regional politics since 1494.

32. William R. Thompson, "Principal Rivalries," *Journal of Conflict Resolution*, Vol. 39, No. 1 (1995), pp. 195–223.

33. See Modelski and Thompson, *Seapower and Global Politics;* and Colin S. Gray, *The Leverage of Sea Power: The Strategic Advantage of Navies in War* (New York: Free Press, 1992).

Britain did not win the Napoleonic Wars singlehandedly any more than the United States won World War II on its own. It has instead been the task of system leaders to cajole, subsidize, and, if necessary, intimidate fellow global war coalition members. At the same time, sea power has been critical to the process of a wartime coalition leadership's moving its own troops and supplies. It also must deny the same maritime benefits to the other side. These are tasks that Britain became quite proficient at in its heyday.

Sea power is also critical in acquiring and maintaining the system leader's global network of bases around which imperial territorial control tends to cluster and expand. System leaders do not initially plan to control extensive territory, but ever since Venice it has proven difficult to avoid this byproduct of success. The Indian Army did prove critical in maintaining and expanding the territorial frontiers of the British Empire in a relatively inexpensive way. However, the utilization of the Indian Army was greater in the second half of the nineteenth century than in the first half. From a leadership long cycle perspective, Britain had already peaked in the first half of the nineteenth century. The deployment of the Indian Army along the turbulent African and Asian frontiers thus was more a matter of hanging on to positions already achieved than a matter of constructing new sources of wealth and global power. But if one views the Empire as the source of wealth and power, it is the second half of the nineteenth century and the continuing imperial expansion that seems more critical. This disagreement seems to be a matter of assumptions and interpretations—and not one of disputes over the facts of the nineteenth century.

6. Britain "flourished in peculiar historical circumstances." Britannia could rule the waves in the nineteenth century because no other state cared to challenge it.[34]

From a structural perspective, there was little that was peculiar about Britain's flourishing in the nineteenth century. The general situation that Britain exploited to its advantage has been iterative. One state has developed an overwhelming lead in sea power and commercial or industrial innovation. At the end of a period of intensive global war, its main competitors are weakened or exhausted. It is not that competitors do not choose to challenge the system leader's postwar maritime authority, they either cannot or dare not do so. But this type of situation only lasts so long. Competitors eventually begin developing their capability to chal-

---

34. Ferris, "'The Greatest Power on Earth,'" p. 733.

lenge at sea and in the marketplace. Hence, the Pax Britannica was no more "artificial" or illusory than the Pax Americana that some skeptics attribute to the temporary effects of the aerial bombardment of German and Japanese factories. The generalization is that system leaders improve their edge over their competitors even more by exhausting them in an intensive global war. At a minimum, time is required to recover. In that interim, the system leader is less likely to be challenged in the management of the global system's preoccupation with long-distance trade and advanced technological production. This interim situation does not mean that the international system will be completely peaceful or that the system leader's governance will be effective, widespread, or even visibly manifested in regional affairs. It does mean that a conclusive global war is likely to be followed by a period characterized by a significant absence of serious challenges to the political-economic status quo.

7. If Britain was so powerful in the mid-nineteenth century, why were its interests threatened by Russia? Why could Britain not deter the outbreak of the Crimean War?[35]

There are two easy responses to this assertion. One is that Britain was most powerful at sea in the mid-nineteenth century. The Balkans and the Crimea are not easily accessed by sea power. Therefore, Russia could contemplate predominantly land attacks on the Ottoman Empire. A second answer is that the Crimean War took place in the mid-nineteenth century: it did not take place for some thirty-five years after the end of the Napoleonic Wars, despite earlier opportunities for Russian-British antagonism in the Near East.[36] In structural perspectives, the system leader's position erodes and challenges become more probable. In the case of the Crimean War, the challenge turned out to be less than formidable. So, too, was the response of the coalition organized to deal with it. Nonetheless, the Crimean War did not represent the same type of threat as that posed by the Germans in 1914. The Crimean War was part of the some 160 years of Eurasian sparring between Britain and Russia (and then the Soviet Union). It did not represent an attempt to establish European regional hegemony along the lines of a Philip, Louis XIV, Napoleon, or Hitler. Nor was it a full-fledged assault on the global order.

---

35. Martel, "The Meaning of Power," p. 682.

36. Similarly, French challenges (e.g., involving Belgium, Mohammed Ali, and Switzerland) in the first half of the nineteenth century always stopped short of going to war with Britain.

8. *Britain at its peak never equaled Rome.*[37]

Precisely. The analogy is completely wrong. For a time, Britain led the global system in long-distance commerce and advanced technological production. Rome was a regional land power and traditional imperial hegemon. It engaged in long-distance trade as a function of its wealth but it never specialized in it. It also ran into political-economic trouble once its territorial expansion had reached its technological limits. In contrast, Britain became the ruler of an extensive territorial empire only after it had specialized in trade—and in large part it became an imperial ruler to defend its trading prospects. Whether all or much of that extensive territorial empire facilitated British prosperity or became a drain on its resources remains a contested proposition.

9. *No great power, certainly including Britain, is or ever was omnipotent.*[38]

Without doubt this is true and no one ascribes omnipotence to Britain in the nineteenth century or to system leaders in general. While it seems true that system leaders have become increasingly powerful over the past few centuries, and that Britain was more powerful in its second term as system leader (the nineteenth century) than in its first term (the eighteenth century), omnipotence is never very likely in a system of multiple states.[39] One would first have to transform a system into a single state or empire along the intermittent succession of centralizing dynasties (Han, T'ang, Mongol, Ming) lines to attain some level of omnipotence. With the exception of the Mongol experience, such unification has only been successful at the regional level. The territorial unification of the global system is an awkward subject and, in any event, would involve an awesome, transregional undertaking that may have been contemplated from time to time, but only rarely attempted—and never so far by a system leader.[40]

10. *At the turn of the nineteenth and twentieth centuries, Britain retreated from the Americas and made new arrangements with Japan, France, and Russia to share its security burden. These developments cannot be attributed to British*

---

37. Martel, "The Meaning of Power," p. 681.

38. Ibid., p. 682.

39. Structural analysts do not agree on the existence of a British first term as system leader in the eighteenth century.

40. Some might be tempted to nominate Alexander, but while the Macedonian attempted to conquer a respectable proportion of his known trading world (or global system), the nature of the operation had a number of more traditional regional expansion aspects.

relative decline. Rather, they demonstrated British strength in international politics.[41]

British decision-makers are to be credited for unusually insightful deal-making in the period roughly between 1890 and 1910. Devising new grand strategies to meet new sources of threat is rarely accomplished smoothly or easily. If we knew more about the construction of grand strategies, it might even be possible to argue that devising new grand strategies to meet new sources of threat is rarely accomplished. Still, it is difficult to see how else we might interpret the need to pull back from extended positions that had been acquired in less threatening circumstances than as a function of relative decline. At one time, Britain was prepared to contain France within Europe, to contain Russia within Eurasia, to contain the United States within the Americas, and might have been prepared to also attempt to contain Japan within east Asia. The first three containment plans variably preoccupied the British throughout most of the nineteenth century. The French gradually became less of a perceived threat within the European theater although they still raised problems in Africa and Asia. The Russians remained a problem but were weakened severely by the Russo-Japanese War and domestic tensions, permitting a temporary détente in the Anglo-Russian cold war or Great Game. In the Americas, the British gradually yielded to the greater local capability of the United States during the second half of the nineteenth century.

Had the Japanese ascent begun much earlier in the nineteenth century, there probably would have been a British attempt to contain the expansion of Japan's regional influence. However, Japan had begun to become increasingly significant at a time when Britain was in the market for an Asian ally. That may not seem so remarkable except that Britain preferred to avoid alliances throughout the nineteenth century. Only when a combination of new threats and competitors had emerged and its own relative position had declined were British decision-makers prepared to change their way of doing things. They did not have to seek out alliances from a declining position, but alliances, accommodations, and military retrenchment were one option to pursue given the changing circumstances. British decision-makers might also have attempted to maintain their earlier containment strategies and simply add Germany to the list. This is precisely where relative decline enters the picture in the sense that decision-makers seemed to sense that they could no longer

---

41. Martel, "The Meaning of Power," pp. 683–684, 686; and Neilson, "'Greatly Exaggerated,'" pp. 698–704.

continue doing business as usual. Their relative resources were not up to the expansion in challenges, despite the fact that at least two of their longtime rivals' potential for generating threat had been curtailed in the first decade of the twentieth century.

11. *It was German policy and not German power that led Britain to identify Germany as a threatening adversary prior to World War I.*[42]

This statement constitutes another curious assertion. Threat equals capability multiplied by intentions. Yes, the British were agitated by perceived and real German intentions. But they would have been much less agitated by a Prussian state of the early nineteenth century funded by an agrarian economy. In the late nineteenth century, Germany was one of two states with the potential to overtake and surpass the British lead in technological innovation. That potential was very much a part of British threat perception[43]

12. *The emphasis on British relative decline in manufacturing and trade ignores the critical role played by Britain's leadership in providing investment capital and international finance, especially after 1870. In any event, wealth in Britain continued to be based on land ownership. For much of the nineteenth century Britain remained a preindustrial state, run by aristocrats, bureaucrats, and bankers, and not industrialists and merchants.*[44]

Without question, Britain remained the leading source of capital and investment even after (or especially after?) its relative economic foundation had begun to deteriorate. So had the Dutch before them. Some structural theories go so far as to argue that there is a lock-step order to economic preeminence: agro-industrial, commercial, and then financial.[45] And as the first two give way, financial preeminence lingers on. Be that as it may—and while it is clear that industrial and commercial preeminence can lead to financial preeminence, it is less clear that it must always

---

42. Martel, "The Meaning of Power," p. 685.

43. I advance a five-variable model differentiating violent challenges of system leaders from nonviolent challenges and apply it to the past thousand years. See William R. Thompson, "The Evolution of Political-Commercial Challenges in the Active Zone," *Review of International Political Economy*, Vol. 4, No. 2 (1997), pp. 286–318.

44. Martel, "The Meaning of Power," p. 686; Neilson, "'Greatly Exaggerated,'" p. 721; Ferris, "'The Greatest Power on Earth,'" p. 733; McKercher, "'Our Most Dangerous Enemy,'" p. 751; and Ingram's chapter in this volume.

45. See Wallerstein, *The Politics of the World-Economy*.

do so in the same way—it is also not clear how lingering financial preeminence challenges structural perspectives.

As for the assertion about land-based wealth, there may be something of an ecological fallacy (assuming that generalizations that hold at one level of analysis also hold at other levels) operating here. Wealth inequalities within Britain were and presumably remain to some extent linked to land holdings. Even wealth gained in technological endeavors might be exchanged for aristocratic titles and land. But, surely, the argument is not that Britain's spectacular international activities were predicated to whatever degree on the exploitation and mobilization of agrarian resources in England, Ireland, and Scotland?

The issue concerning the nature of ruling elites is an interesting one but it is not an issue that has been studied comparatively (across different system leaders). Shifts in ruling elites within system leaders have occurred in every case since the Sungs and usually after considerable lags. That is, fundamental changes in the nature of a system leader's predominant economic activities predate equally fundamental shifts in what sorts of elites have influence over decision-making. As a consequence, the national prioritization of interests and policies tends to change more slowly than one might otherwise expect. In what respects these transitional lags make systematic differences in foreign policy behavior deserves more study. But since no structuralist argument portrays British decision-makers as being former merchants or industrialists, it is also not clear exactly what the criticism is about.

13. *"Britain had the money, the technology, the industrial capacity and the will to maintain the underpinnings of deterrence [in 1914]."*[46]

Why then did World War I ensue? This is hardly the place to review the multiple causes of World War I, but one important element that has been neglected too often was the structural disarray. The international hierarchy was challengeable and in the process of being challenged. Britain was no more able to deter Germany in 1914 than it was in 1939. Nor had the British, the Dutch, or the Portuguese been successful in preventing the outbreak of war in 1792, 1688, or 1579–80. To the extent that one finds similar structural circumstances at play in these episodes, there would appear to be a generalizable phenomenon at work. Declining system leaders are less able to deter attempts at regional hegemony than are system leaders that have not yet begun to decline. The ultimate irony of deterrence in this context is that it is most likely to be successful when

---

46. Neilson, "'Greatly Exaggerated,'" p. 724.

it is least necessary and least likely to be successful when it is most necessary.[47]

14. *Britain and Germany twice found themselves fighting wars that neither expected or desired. Throughout the nineteenth and early twentieth centuries, Britain's challengers were France and Russia. At different times, Austria and Germany acted as Britain's continental allies to contain the threat of French and Russian expansion. Britain's decision to go to war in 1914 was thus not predicated on balancing against German expansion. Rather, it was based on a fear that a Franco-Russian victory would lead to their shared domination of Eurasia and a subsequent joint bid for global supremacy. Britain had no choice but to bandwagon with the side that was likely to win, in hopes of restraining their future appetites.*[48]

This is an interesting hypothesis that mixes some established facts and unverified conjecture. As a hypothesis, it cannot be ruled out as entirely implausible. Yet, so far, it lacks any supporting evidence. It would also seem even more plausible as an explanation for Britain's entering World Wars I and II on the side of Austria and Germany or not entering at all, and not, as it did, on the sides of France and Russia. If the motivating force was fear of a Franco-Russian victory, why contribute to its probability? Why not sit on the sidelines and hope for an outcome beneficial to Britain more or less as Britain did in 1861–65, 1870–71, and 1904–06?

Ingram is quite correct to point out that France and Russia were Britain's principal rivals and challengers throughout much of the nineteenth century. One could add the United States to this group of challengers as well.[49] It is also true as a general rule that system leaders, given their maritime capabilities, have needed continental allies in order to be successful in Eurasian politics and war. But something changed toward the end of the century as German capabilities and potential expanded from its earlier Prussian form. British decision-makers, accurately or inaccurately, ultimately chose to look upon Germany as Britain's principal foe and made separate arrangements with the United States, France,

---

47. William R. Thompson, "The Anglo-German Rivalry and the 1939 Failure-of-Deterrence," *Security Studies*, Vol. 7, No. 2 (1997/98), pp. 58–97.

48. See Ingram's chapter in this volume.

49. For more discussion of these rivalries, see Edward Ingram, "Great Britain and Russia," and William R. Thompson, "The Evolution of a Great Power Rivalry: The Anglo-American Case," in William R. Thompson, ed., *Great Power Rivalries* (Columbia: University of South Carolina Press, 1999).

Japan, and Russia to deescalate their traditional rivalries with Britain. German behavior after 1890, and especially after 1914, certainly contributed to this major power realignment of rivalries. It is possible that the realignment might have been a temporary expedience of great power politics, and in some respects it was. The British rivalries with Russia and Japan later resumed. But while Britain and France, and Britain and the United States, continued to compete and quarrel, they were increasingly less likely to go to war with one another after about 1904. The strategic nature of their nineteenth-century rivalries had come to an end.[50]

15. *Global relations do not determine relations in the system's core region (Europe between 1494 and 1945). Global relations are derived from relations in the system's core region. If global wars were fought only between states with global reach and about global relationships, they would have had little impact on the world's great power clashes.*[51]

The relationship between the global political economy and the system's core region is indeed an important one. One leadership long cycle argument is that between 1494 and 1945, power concentration tendencies in the global and European systems were dissynchronized.[52] When power was most highly concentrated in the global arena, power within the Western European region tended to be deconcentrated. As global concentration eroded, European power concentration increased. These tendencies were hardly coincidental. Global wars, for instance, accelerated global concentration while contributing to deconcentrating Western European power, especially as manifested in defeating a regional hegemonic aspirant. Moreover, the rise of regional hegemonic aspirants seems to have been encouraged to varying degrees by declining system leaders. Declining leaders are seen as weakening obstacles, increasingly vulnerable, and potentially capable of being supplanted. Thus, there is no argument that global or regional relations are autonomous. They are interdependent and tend to become highly fused in periods of crisis.

Global wars, in particular, represent periods of acute regional and global fusion. They are wars fought simultaneously over questions of regional and global governance. For instance, World War I could be said to represent the convergence of several ongoing rivalries. The Anglo-German rivalry was predominately global in nature. The Franco-German

---

50. The wartime ascendance of the junior partner has occurred before, as exemplified in the Dutch-British transition in the 1688–1713 fighting.

51. See Ingram's chapter in this volume.

52. See Rasler and Thompson, *The Great Powers and Global Struggle.*

and Austro-German–Russian rivalries were mainly regional (western and east-southeastern Europe) in nature. World War I was a global war, or more precisely, the first phase of the 1914–1945 global war, but its onset cannot be explained solely in terms of global relations (or the Anglo-German rivalry). Yet even though global wars constitute regional-global fusions and are brought about by multiple factors, they still play a crucial role in creating opportunities for the emergence of new global leadership—among other consequences. That is why, especially from a global perspective, World War I was inconclusive.[53] A new global leadership did not emerge fully until after the conclusion of World War II.

16. *World War I can only be seen as a triumph for Britain. In the twenty years following the war, Britain was as strong, if not stronger, than it had been in the preceding 150–200 years.*[54]

World War I was certainly a triumph for Britain and British coalition management, but the triumph hinged on the coalition's marshaling greater and more effective resources than were available to the Central Powers' coalition. It eventually did put together a superior resource base, but the outcome was not inevitable. Nor was the outcome attributable to a Britain that had maintained its preeminence up to and through 1914. Without U.S. intervention, a stalemate or worse had been conceivable in view of the Russian collapse. Britain survived World War I but not without a great deal of help from various quarters.

The assertion that Britain was stronger in the interwar years than at any time during the nineteenth century is peculiar. From either a British or imperial security perspective, there were few immediate external threats in the immediate aftermath of World War I. But that aftermath was an incredibly short-lived period. One does not even have to invoke short- versus long-term distinctions to point out that a postwar decade or less of relative strategic security is hardly an appropriate or compelling slice of time for evaluation. One could point out that this same period was characterized by various internal threats to the perseverance of the British empire and that former allies (Italy and Japan) soon became external threats. World War I also made a significant dent in British financial preeminence—both in capital lost directly to war purposes and

---

53. World War I was also inconclusive from a regional perspective as well. The Austro-Russian and Austro-Serbian rivalries ended in 1918 but others persisted.

54. Martel, "The Meaning of Power," pp. 657, 692; Ferris, "'The Greatest Power on Earth,'" pp. 733, 739–740; McKercher, "'Our Most Dangerous Enemy,'" pp. 751, 783; and Ingram, "The Wonderland of the Political Scientist," p. 59, and his chapter in this volume.

in the opportunity for competitors (most notably, the United States) to make headway in places such as Latin America that had once been British financial preserves.

Yet what is most striking about the statement of British relative strength in the interwar years is that it simply is not very accurate, in terms either of economic production—a point with which the antistruc-turalists would probably agree but not care—or of naval capability. As demonstrated in Table 9.3 and Figure 9.1, the British relative position between 1919 and 1939 was the poorest it had been over the preceding 150 years. Whatever else might be said about the war to end all wars, World War I did nothing significant to arrest or reverse the long-term, relative economic and naval decline of Britain. In terms of Britain's financial position and even the cohesion of the empire, World War I only accelerated the disintegration of the British position.

17. Britain was great because of its empire, not despite it. One interpretation is that the real British problem was its failure to create a tightly integrated empire in 1919 (or before) that could generate the resources necessary to compete effectively in international politics. If one counted the population and resources of the Empire, as opposed to those of the United Kingdom, one would construct a much different impression of the relative position for "Britain," as well as little evidence of relative decline. This failure of imperial integration was compounded by the losses experienced in World War II. But the real sources of the demise of the British Empire were colonial agitation for independence after World War II and the pernicious policies aiming at decolonization and the destruction of the Empire by Britain's ally, the United States.[55]

It is sometimes argued that Germany in the early part of the twentieth century was more concerned with keeping up with the Soviet Union and the United States than it was in succession to the British position as global system leader. Territorial expansion in Ukraine was supposedly the central European answer to the gigantic scale of the future superpowers. If so, the charge that the fundamental British strategic error was the failure to create a tightly integrated empire when it had the chance may belong in the same vein of thought. However, there are two problems with the argument. First, the British empire may not have been founded "in a fit of absence of mind," as Martel puts it, but it was not entirely premeditated either.[56] Much of the time territorial gains were resisted by British

55. Martel, "The Meaning of Power," p. 693; Ferris, "'The Greatest Power on Earth,'" p. 736; Ingram, "The Wonderland of the Political Scientist," pp. 56–57, 59; and In-gram's chapter in this volume.

56. Martel, "The Meaning of Power," p. 690.

Table 9.3. Britain's Decline in Naval Power and Leading Sector Production.

Year	Naval Power Share	Leading Sector Share
1780		0.292
1786	0.360	
1790		0.455
1796	0.363	
1800		0.534
1806	0.419	
1810		0.603
1816	0.660	
1820		0.549
1826	0.582	
1830		0.643
1836	0.482	
1840		0.583
1846	0.493	
1850		0.546
1856	0.505	
1860		0.500
1866	0.475	
1870		0.519
1876	0.434	
1880		0.430
1886	0.479	
1890		0.333
1896	0.467	
1900		0.245
1906	0.392	
1910		0.146
1916	0.424	
1920		0.100
1926	0.336	
1930		0.082
1936	0.273	
1940		0.075
1945	0.350	
1950		0.093
1960		0.087
1970		0.070
1980		0.039

Sources: The naval capability shares are taken from George Modelski and William R. Thompson, *Seapower and Global Politics, 1494–1993* (London: Macmillan, 1988); the leading sector shares are taken from William R. Thompson, *On Global War* (Columbia: University of South Carolina Press, 1988).

Figure 9.1. British Relative Decline.

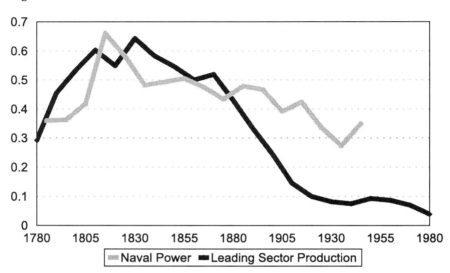

decision-makers, and while local agents of expansion may have known what they were doing, decision-makers in London often did not seem to know what to do with the scattered and intermittent faits accomplis on some distant border of the empire.[57]

One could criticize this ostensibly timid approach to empire building as a missed opportunity. Whether it was or was not, though, imperial expansion was never the primary goal of British foreign policy. Nor was expansion necessarily considered an indicator of foreign policy success. As long as one had an edge in producing valued industrial commodities and distributing valued commercial goods—and were not entirely precluded from competing for foreign markets—territorial possessions beyond the minimum necessary for a global network of support bases were more a liability than an asset. The British were hardly the first to grapple with this policy problem. Similar debates are found in the annals of the Venetians, the Portuguese, and the Dutch. The usual pattern was an initial avoidance of territorial acquisition followed by a gradual deviation from the avoidance policy. By the time an empire was fully established by a

57. See William R. Thompson and Gary Zuk, "World Power and the Strategic Trap of Territorial Commitments," *International Studies Quarterly*, Vol. 30, No. 3 (1986), pp. 249–267.

trading state, the state in question had already lost its competitive edge.[58] Then the question usually became whether to retreat behind the imperial tariffs and mercantilistic walls of the empire as opposed to continuing to compete at a growing disadvantage in more open markets.

A second angle on the full unification of the British empire was that significant parts of the empire were not interested in a more integrated union. It is an irony of considerable proportions, given the strong Canadian identity of the members of the historical antistructuralist school, that Canadians led the resistance to tighter union in the early twentieth century. The first British Empire and the first British stint as global system leader fell apart over a quarrel about how tightly the empire should be managed. There was also an element of British relative decline in the last quarter of the eighteenth century, which complicated its ability to hang onto its empire. It is doubtful whether the second British empire could have been reconsolidated after an extensive period of nineteenth-century relative decline. Too many of the constituent parts were eager to go their own way.

A third way to look at this imperial thesis, ironically, is provided by one of the antistructural critics. Edward Ingram argues that nineteenth-century Britain was a dual monarchy—one centered in the British Isles and the other centered on the large South Asian peninsula.[59] As such, "Britain" lacked the insularity usually associated with system leaders and customarily attributed to the Britain situated off the shore of Western Europe. The Asian part of the British Empire forced Britain to engage in Eurasian politics and to compete with Russia in southwest and central Asia for primacy.

Anglo-Russian relations and rivalry in the nineteenth century were certainly predicated in part on the need to defend Britain's position in, and the approaches to, India. However, Anglo-Russian rivalry actually began over Baltic commerce in the eighteenth century and was later extended further south to the struggle over the disposition of the Ottoman Empire and access to the Mediterranean and Indian Ocean. But Britain's position in south and southwest Asia, the Middle East, and North Africa were also subject to dispute with other rivals, such as France and Germany. Britain's Indian position did not uniquely privilege the

---

58. The exact institutional form of the elite actors is beside the point from a long cycle point of view. What is important are the roles that are played in global politics (i.e., world power, challenger, global power). In this respect, leadership long cycle analysis does not focus on, or differentiate between, nation-states or empires.

59. See Ingram's chapter in this volume.

Russians as Britain's principal rival. The identification of Britain's principal rival fluctuated between 1815 and 1914, depending on who was in power in Britain and what sort of foreign policy problems seemed most pressing.

In addition, Britain's imperial commitments in Africa and Eurasia expanded throughout the nineteenth century. In 1815, at the onset of the second British period of systemic leadership, British commitments to defend far-flung possessions were relatively limited. That strategic flexibility gradually vanished as Britain increasingly resembled Ingram's dual monarchy. It is precisely in this respect that Britain's imperial successes detracted from its ability to perform systemic leadership roles. But then the problems Britain encountered in the late nineteenth century were only partially related to its noninsularity in Asia.

As for the U.S. stab-in-the-back thesis, we have seen this sort of phenomenon emerge as a form of explanation in a variety of circumstances. Usually, it involves groups that have lost position and resources and prefer to blame some perfidious external or internal agent for their problems. If only they had not been so preoccupied or trusting, the losses might have been prevented by taking more forceful action against supposed allies or fellow countrymen. In this particular case, the problem seems to be that the incumbent global system leader organizes a successful coalition sometimes only to be supplanted by a former junior ally. England did this to the Netherlands in the 1688–1713 period and the United States did this to Britain in the 1914–1945 period.

If one denies the reality of relative decline, then perhaps the stab-in-the-back thesis is one way to make sense of the world. It is not a very accurate portrayal, however, of the way in which new global system leaders move aside old global leaders and their privileged arrangements. In the Anglo-U.S. case, as in the Anglo-Dutch case, the incumbent leader and its eventual successor had been strategic rivals before they coalesced to deal with a mutual threat. In the Anglo-U.S. case, the two states maintained a commercial rivalry after they had ended their strategic rivalry in the first decade of the twentieth century They continued to be commercial rivals after World War II, but the rivalry had become increasingly asymmetrical thanks to British decline and U.S. ascent. Hence, there is no question that U.S. policy contributed to the demise of the British Empire. The only question is why this should be viewed as a stab in the back after nearly 200 years of hot and cold rivalry? In the final analysis, perhaps it only betrays some antediluvian sentiments about the desirability of Anglo-Saxon solidarity or a wish to express some considerable disappointment about the payoffs of ostensible "special relationships." It would be interesting to compare these sentiments with what the Dutch, in particular Dutch authors with experience in Jakarta, China, or India, had to say about the British a generation or so after 1714.

The Debate Goes On

Is it possible to successfully rebut the antistructuralist assertions? My own answer, not surprisingly, is affirmative. That that is the case, no doubt, is due to my constructing the rebuttal, my own methedological propensities, and my version of social science biases. Readers will have to arrive at their own conclusions and, no doubt, the evaluations will need to proceed assertion by assertion. Whatever else is clear, it should be apparent that the British role in nineteenth- and twentieth-century world politics remains contested. One book chapter will not resolve the contest.

Is it possible to persuade the antistructuralists that they are wrong? Probably not, if the argument about analytical predispositions is accurate—but then hope springs eternal. There are some very real disagreements. Should economic and technological variables be given priority over the intangible skills of strategists? Can international hierarchies be measured, compared, and tracked over time? Did Britain possess the prerequisites for global leadership? Did Britain actually play a systemic leadership role, and when, and where? Did Britain experience relative decline? Does relative decline explain British behavior very well? All of these questions deserve more attention.

Yet there are also some disagreements that are wholly unnecessary. Structuralists make assertions about the long term. Antistructuralists tend to make counterassertions about the short term. Short-term antistructuralist interpretations have the potential for delimiting more sharply the assertions of structuralists about the capability-influence relationship. Similarly, structuralist interpretations have the potential for delimiting the assertions of antistructuralists about the capability-influence relationship. Whether Martians and Venusians can find an efficacious way to communicate productively between their two planets remains to be seen. Regrettably, the likelihood of such a meeting of the minds seems slim.[60] That does not seem to be the way cognitive dissonance operates in academia, or elsewhere.

Yet communication, persuasion, and conversion between and among different camps are not the sole goals of our collective endeavors. We are

---

60. While antistructuralists have their communication problems, so do structuralists. See, for example, William R. Thompson, "Interstate Wars, Global Wars, and the Cool Hand Luke Syndrome: A Reply to Chase-Dunn and Sokolovsky," *International Studies Quarterly*, Vol. 27, No. 3 (1983), pp. 369–374.

all trying to make sense of historical reality. That must remain the primary goal. If we choose radically different assumptions about how best to go about achieving that goal, so be it. If consumers of our attempts at grappling with explaining historical realities select only those products that have been constructed in accord with their own assumptions, so be that as well. Ultimately, we have no choice but to proceed along lines of inquiry that make the most sense to us as individual analysts. Still, it will not hurt to keep an eye out for what alternative approaches are doing. We all might learn something in the process.

Chapter 10

Postscript: When Did Britain Decline?

Richard Rosecrance

The papers by William Thompson and Edward Ingram offer opposite views of British decline (or the lack of it) in the nineteenth and twentieth centuries. They also depict with great clarity the difference between historical and international relations approaches to the study of diplomacy and world politics. William Thompson, a political scientist, searches for regularities in the data. He seeks to explain the pattern of hegemonic war, not the occurrence of individual wars. Edward Ingram, an imperial historian, is interested in particular phenomena and specific wars. Change, or the lack of it, is his focus. These papers mirror their own disciplines remarkably well. With the exceptions of Paul Kennedy and Arnold Toynbee, historians (and many consider Toynbee a sociologist) typically seek to explain particular turning points in international or domestic history such as the causes of the French Revolution, the origins of World Wars I or II, and the causes of the Cold War. Political scientists, on the other hand, generally look for regularities in international behavior: the causes of war in general terms. They explain deviations from the pattern on the basis of changes in one or more systemic elements, such as the movement from a multipolar to a bipolar international system. Political scientists expect to see a balance of power system at work at all times and places in international history. Some political scientists appear to believe that there is a kind of "conservation of conflict" within international relations in that among particular national units, the amount of cooperation cannot be limitlessly increased.[1] If two states reach agreement, it may drive a third farther away. Cooperation and conflict have a tendency to balance one another.

Yet differences of attention between the particular and the general do

---

1. Kenneth Waltz, *Man, the State, and War: A Theoretical Analysis* (New York: Columbia University Press, 1959).

not imply inherent variations in methodology between the two disciplines. Diplomatic historians can be as Hempelian as political scientists. Both are interested in generalizations that apply to social phenomena, though the canvas is typically smaller in the instance of historians.

Social researchers know that a series of points charting the value of two variables can be patterned in different ways. For example, a straight line can link the points in Figure 10.1, but so can a sine wave curve or a reverse sine wave curve. If each of these lines goes through the points, a decision as to which is most nearly right will depend upon collecting additional data. If point P is then found to exist, the straight line and the reverse sine wave can no longer explain the relationship. Of course, the points can be linked in an indefinite number of ways, yet both political scientists and historians continue to look for additional points (like P) that can help them to reject alternative hypotheses.

In the argument between Thompson and Ingram, each is seeking to find data points difficult for the other to interpret in terms of his theory and approach. Their fundamental disagreement concerns whether Britain declined in the nineteenth century, paving the way for the hegemonic World War I. Thompson believes that Britain did decline, Ingram believes that it did not. Thompson also offers a structural theory to explain that decline. In his view, economic growth precedes naval concentration and military expenditure. But advantages won through navies and armies (and the results of warfare) do not feed back into recharging economic batteries. Nonetheless, Thompson agrees with antistructuralists who contend that influence and empire do not decline as rapidly as economic growth. Thus, a rapidly deteriorating economic position need not spell political disaster in the short term. Britain was a strong financial power at the time of its economic decline.

In addition to economic growth, Thompson also emphasizes naval strength as the crucial constituent of international power. In Thompson's table of leading sector (production) shares, Britain declines rapidly after 1870. Britain's naval strength, however, holds up over a longer period. Relative to the armaments of potential opponents, Britain appears very strong in 1920. Germany has been defeated and provisionally disarmed. The Russian position has deteriorated with the Bolshevik Revolution and the onset of internal conflict. The United States has withdrawn from world politics with the rejection of the Treaties of Guarantee and Versailles. France has been grievously weakened by demographic losses in World War I. However, Thompson insists that British power has become a shell without substance because, relative to Germany, the United States, and potentially Russia, British industrial strength has declined. Germany passed Britain in the 1890s and by 1913, the U.S. economy equaled

Figure 10.1.

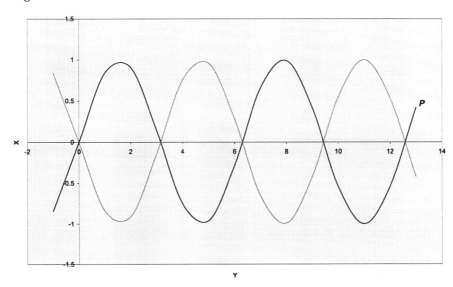

Britain's and Germany's combined. If the United States had not come into the war in 1917 (at the time when British gold and foreign currency reserves were running out), the United Kingdom would have lost the war. The possibility of defeat in World War I, moreover, was not remedied by imperial contributions from India, Australia, and New Zealand. They added first line troops, but not logistics and little industrial strength. The key contribution was made by American, not imperial, power. After the war, Thompson observes that "the British relative position between 1919 and 1939 was the poorest it had been over the preceding 150 years. In terms of Britain's financial position and even the cohesion of the empire, World War I only accelerated the disintegrating British position."

Nor was Britain aided greatly by the empire. It was not a federated decision-making unit. Joseph Chamberlain's attempts at imperial federation and tariff reform had failed at the turn of the century and had been rejected by both the Conservative-Unionists and the country as a whole. Free trade remained in place and the empire was not consolidated. After World War I, the Commonwealth prime ministers took an even more independent view of foreign policy, hampering British efforts to restrain Hitler.[2] The Commonwealth-Empire did not act as a coherent unit and could not simply be added to British power.

2. See Ritchie Ovendale, *"Appeasement" and the English-speaking World: Britain, the United States, the Dominions, and the Policy of "Appeasement"* (Cardiff: University of Wales Press, 1975).

Edward Ingram, the imperial historian, adopts an entirely different view. He raises the question of the proper definition of state or nation, global power or world leader. Essentially, he contends that a systemic leader consists of the metropole and its imperial territories. In the case of Britain's second period of world leadership (which obtained during the nineteenth century), its hegemony includes Great Britain and India. India added a very considerable sum to the United Kingdom's gross domestic product (GDP). In P.J. Cain and A.G. Hopkins's formulation, with which Ingram at least partly agrees, a state can have an "informal empire" as well as a constitutional one, making it bigger still.[3] The two imperial historians include much of Latin America (though not the United States) in the United Kingdom's informal total. There is a point at which this extension of the state into informal alignments may lose credibility; nevertheless, the argument is an interesting one.

Ingram seems to turn the conventional wisdom on its head. According to Ingram, "The 1850s and 1860s were not the apogee of Great Britain's power, the era of hegemony within the international system." Instead, Britain was more powerful in 1922. That was because Britain was willing to use power in the twentieth century, but hesitant to do so in the nineteenth. In the Indian Mutiny, the Crimean War, and the U.S. Civil War, Britain played an ignoble and indecisive role, certainly failing to demonstrate or fully to exert its power. In contrast, between 1915 and 1922, "Great Britain turned itself into the world's foremost military power." As opposed to Thompson, Ingram insists that it was Britain's land power and not sea power that was decisive. Britain's plans as a military power were laid down in 1905–07 and carried out in 1915–18. British power "undoubtedly decided the outcome of World War I." (So much for the "decisive" role of U.S. intervention!)

Ingram also disputes Thompson's notion that sea power is the critical element in national strength. Neither in 1805 nor in 1856 could Britain force a decision against French or Russian land armies with ships of the line. Britain's long-term strength was to be found on land, or at least in alliance with a substantial land power. The latter (the link with France) made possible an attempt at a third period of British hegemony (between World Wars I and II). Britain could then "counter the levers used by its

---

3. See P.J. Cain and A.G. Hopkins, *British Imperialism: Innovation and Expansion, 1688–1914* (London & New York: Longman, 1993); and P.J. Cain and A.J. Hopkins, *British Imperialism: Crisis and Deconstruction, 1914–1990* (London & New York: Longman, 1993).

challengers in the wider world," principally Japan and revolutionary Russia.

Did Britain decline in the nineteenth century, or was it merely a later victim of the all-engulfing embrace of the United States?[4] To answer this question, two fundamental issues need to be disentangled. First, how strong was the British metropole, independent of India? How formidable would it become if India and the empire were included? Second, is it true that British weakness in the nineteenth century (at least as judged by other states) was due to the failure to mobilize its power, and that British strength in 1922 was the product of such mobilization?

Does Empire Lead to Strength or Weakness?

In the nineteenth century, the verdict was favorable to empire. India appeared to increase British power and everybody was seeking to find a "new India" for themselves. That is why Rosebery pegged out colonial claims for the future and Salisbury could remain isolated in Europe. Yet, Grover Clark's work on *The Balance Sheets of Imperialism* offers little comfort to imperialists.[5] With the exception of Italy, according to Clark, all European powers including Britain put more into their empires than they received from them. Italy was a net beneficiary only because it invested so little. In 1913, for example, the United Kingdom had a deficit in the balance of trade with Australia, New Zealand, Canada, and South Africa (to say nothing of Germany and the United States). The only significant imperial unit with which Britain still maintained a surplus was India.[6] The rest of the empire did not help Britain.

In addition, Britain's relations with other powers suffered because London was always trying to protect the land or sea route to India. This led it to exclude France from Egypt in 1882, an issue that disturbed Anglo-French relations for the next forty years. Protecting the route to India also led to continual conflict with Russia in the Near East and in the "great game" over the control of Afghanistan. Ingram admits that the British link with India caused hostility from both France and Russia, and therefore required Britain either to find a counterweight or to "band-

---

4. Correlli Barnett, *The Collapse of British Power* (London: Eyre Methuen Limited, 1972).

5. See Grover Clark, *The Balance Sheets of Imperialism: Facts and Figures on Colonies* (New York: Columbia University Press, 1936).

6. Brian R. Mitchell and Phillis Deane, *Abstract of British Historical Statistics* (Cambridge: Cambridge University Press, 1971).

wagon" with them in 1914. One possible counterweight, Germany, rebuffed Britain's overtures in 1899–1901, and the Foreign Office then turned to Japan. But Japan could only restrain Russia, not France. In 1904, France and Britain negotiated an imperial entente over Morocco. Joining France became a partial substitute for an otherwise permanent tension in relations between the two countries. Britain certainly did not want war in 1914, but it could not disentangle her position from France's. What essentially happened is that colonial commitments came more and more to determine British policy in Europe. India did not help Britain solve this problem. It accentuated it. Without the tie to India, Britain would not have had to oppose Germany or to link with Paris and Moscow. The United Kingdom plus India may have totaled 117 on Ingram's power index, but the alignments required to protect India weakened Britain in the net, producing the polarization that led to World War I.

What about Mobilized vs. Reserved Power?

Power is an evanescent quantity. It is most present when least perceived.[7] When a country has to exercise power, it has already lost some part of it. The states with the greatest influence are always those with enormous potential, but with little need to actualize power. In medieval and premodern history, the king was stronger before the emergence of the doctrine of "divine right of kings." The latter arose only when the king's power had been challenged. British power was greatest when it did not have to exert it, as for example at the time of the Don Pacifico affair in 1850, when Britain agreed to protect a single British subject from Greek mobs in response to his claim: *civis romanus sum.* In the 1840s and early 1850s few other powers had navies and the British margin was at its peak. At the same time, British industrial power emerged triumphant at the Crystal Palace Exhibition in 1851. Britain was not only the first industrial nation, it was the only industrial nation. British electric motors, power plants, and textile machinery were the envy of the world.[8] By 1876, as shown by the Philadelphia Exposition, however, the United States had completely caught up.

It is not only perceived power that counts, however. In 1940–45, the United States produced a formidable array of military equipment. Its

---

7. Benedict Anderson, "The Idea of Power in Javenese Culture," in Benedict Anderson, *Language and Power* (Ithaca: Cornell University Press, 1990).

8. Barbara Rosecrance and Richard Rosecrance, "The Apogee of British Vitality," in Armand Clesse, ed., *The Vitality of Britain* (Luxembourg: Luxembourg Institute for European and International Studies, 1997).

rearmament was so swift and powerful that by the end of 1943, it was already thinking and planning for reconversion to a civilian economy. U.S. military production was easy and tolerable economically after 1938 because of the plentitude of unemployed resources owing to the Great Depression. In the 1930s, Britain faced the opposite problem: it could either rearm or it could use its metal fabrication industries for exports. By 1941 it was nearly forced to stop rearming in order to begin exporting again.[9] Only the U.S. Lend-Lease policy obviated that necessity. As a percentage of GDP, the British exported ten times that of the United States. The United States had a choice in economic-military strategy, but Britain did not. If it rearmed, it would become dependent upon a donor power, the United States. The mobilization of British power to fight two world wars completely undercut the British economy. Because of wartime inflation, British exports were priced out of their traditional markets after 1920 and again in 1947. The British balance of payments turned into deficits that could only be remedied by tariffs and the devaluation of the pound in 1931 and in 1949. About one-half of British overseas investments were sold to finance World War I. The rest disappeared in World War II. These extreme results and policies were a reflection of British weakness, not strength.

British financial power, nonetheless, was a great addition to its industrial strength. The last year in which Britain ran a trade surplus in the nineteenth century was 1822.[10] The British surplus on current account continued until 1914, but it was based on financial services, shipping, insurance, and income on foreign investments—invisible, not manufactured goods. Had the war not intervened, British economic strength and influence would have declined much more slowly. Ingram is wrong to regard nineteenth-century Britain as an agricultural economy. Following Arno Mayer, one can make a case that the old regime persisted in politics if not in economics.[11] Middle class industrialists did not rule Britain until after World War I. The city financiers always took precedence over North Country manufacturers in education as well as political clout. Britain invested too much abroad and too little at home.

In a particular sense, however, the record of nineteenth-century Britain shows strength, not weakness. Victorian Britain taught the world a

---

9. Richard Rosecrance and Zara Steiner, "British Grand Strategy and the Origins of World War II," in Richard Rosecrance and Arthur A. Stein, eds., *The Domestic Bases of Grand Strategy* (Ithaca: Cornell University Press, 1993).

10. See Mitchell and Deane, *Abstract of British Historical Statistics*.

11. See Arno J. Mayer, *The Persistence of the Old Regime: Europe to the Great War* (New York: Pantheon Books, 1981).

lesson about the power of international services—intangibles—that is only gradually becoming understood today. It was that intelligence (information) is critical to the success of any economy. Today, on a worldwide basis, the return on such services is growing much more rapidly and pervasively than is the return on manufacturing. American strength in the age of the Internet, new software, and in finance is founded on the more than 70 percent of U.S. gross domestic product that resides in services, not the 15 or so percent that still exists in manufacturing. In the age of the "virtual state," power has been redefined largely on precedents set by Victorian Great Britain.[12]

---

12.   See Richard Rosecrance, *The Rise of the Virtual State: Wealth and Power in the Coming Century* (New York: Basic Books, 1999).

Chapter 11

In Defense of Particular Generalization: Rewriting Cold War History, Rethinking International Relations Theory

John Lewis Gaddis

Historians tend to respond to theory as small children do to spinach: we don't much like it, but we rarely explain why. No other academic discipline so strongly resists the specification of assumptions and the explication of methods. "The majority of historians," one of them recently noted, "still belong to the Nike school—'Just do it!'—more often than not regarding what they do as self-evident."[1] There are several reasons for this attitude, some more defensible than others.

One has to do with aesthetic sensibilities. Historians work within a wide variety of styles, but we prefer, in all of them, that form conceal function.[2] We recoil from the notion that our writing should replicate, say, the design of the Pompidou Center in Paris, which proudly places its escalators, plumbing, wiring, and ductwork on the *outside* of the building, so that they are there for all to see. We do not question the need for such structures, only the impulse to exhibit them. Most theoretically based social science scholarship strikes us as unnecessarily displaying ductwork. We reject it because we find it inelegant; our taste runs to more traditional architecture.

A better reason for historians' distrust of theory is that we see our

---

Portions of this essay appeared in a slightly different form in John Lewis Gaddis, "History, Theory, and Common Ground," *International Security*, Vol. 22, No. 1 (Summer 1997), pp. 75–85.

---

1. John Brewer, "The Year of Writing Dangerously," *New Republic*, Vol. 219, No. 5 (August 3, 1998), p. 44. See also David Hackett Fischer, *Historians' Fallacies: Toward a Logic of Historical Thought* (New York: Harper and Row, 1970), p. xii.

2. This point is perceptively noted by Colin Elman and Miriam Fendius Elman in "Diplomatic History and International Relations: Respecting Difference and Crossing Boundaries," *International Security*, Vol. 22, No. 1 (Summer 1997), p. 13.

field having been there, done that—and failed. The quest for grand patterns in history extends as far back as Herodotus and as far forward as Toynbee, yet few if any of these schemes have held up in the light of further investigation.[3] One of them, that of Karl Marx and certain of his followers, defined much of twentieth-century history with devastating results.[4] Many historians, as a consequence, would endorse Geoffrey Elton's warning: "Preconceived notions are a much greater danger to historical truth than either a deficiency of evidence or error of detail."[5] We think it important to keep an open mind, and we see theory—at least theory that purports to *account for* history rather than simply *reflecting* history—as more often than not closing minds.

But the best reason for historians' distrust of theory is that we sense in it a lurking Catch-22: theorists seek to build universally applicable generalizations about necessarily simple matters; but if these matters were any more complicated their theories wouldn't be universally applicable. From our perspective, then, when theories are right they generally confirm the obvious. When they move beyond the obvious they're usually wrong. Historians proceed quite differently: we construct narratives in order to reconstruct complex events. In doing so we subvert as much as we facilitate generalization. Because life is complicated, so is history.

Theory, thus, isn't what most historians *think* they do. But I wonder if they're right about that, for what is "theory" in the first place? My dictionary defines it as "a coherent group of general propositions used as principles of explanation for a class of phenomena."[6] This seems harmless enough: few historians would deny the need for coherence, generalization, and explanation in the writing and teaching of their sub-

---

3. For some useful overviews, see Herbert Butterfield, *The Origins of History* (New York: Basic Books, 1981); Fritz Stern, ed., *The Varieties of History* (New York: Vintage, 1973); and William H. McNeill, *Arnold J. Toynbee: A Life* (New York: Oxford University Press, 1989).

4. One recent study, Stéphane Courtois et al., *The Black Book of Communism: Crimes, Terror, Repression* (Cambridge, Mass.: Harvard University Press, 1999), places the number of people killed by Marxist-Leninist regimes during the twentieth century at approximately 100 million. R.J. Rummel, *Death by Government* (New Brunswick, N.J.: Transaction, 1997), reaches similar conclusions. These figures may be exaggerated, but even if one were to discount them by a factor of *ten*, the number of victims would still exceed those of Hitler's Holocaust.

5. G.R. Elton, *The Practice of History* (New York: Crowell, 1967), p. 36.

6. *The Random House Dictionary of the English Language,* 2nd ed., unabridged (New York: Random House, 1987), p. 1967.

ject. To imagine the field without such qualities is to call up unsettling images of monkeys taking over computer keyboards, or of unalphabetized telephone books, or of historians' notecards blowing across bleak landscapes in no particular order. Not even postmodernists would admit to those methods of composition.

So like Moliere's bourgeois gentleman, it may be that historians have been doing a kind of theory all along without realizing it. I should like to explore this possibility, with a view to distinguishing the *implicit* theories historians use from the more *explicit* approaches of the other social sciences. I shall then focus on the uneasy relationship between historians and theorists of international relations, an area in which the gap between implicit and explicit methods seems particularly large. Along the way, I will try to illustrate what I say with some examples from my own recent reassessment of Cold War history, *We Now Know*.[7] For if historians are indeed closet theorists, my work ought to reflect that tendency. With apologies for the self-indulgence, therefore, this will also be an experiment in theoretical self-outing.

I.

Sigmund Freud once observed that "it is precisely communities with adjoining territories, and related to each other in other ways as well, who are engaged in constant feuds and in ridiculing each other." He called this "the narcissism of minor differences," explaining it as "a convenient and relatively harmless satisfaction of the inclination to aggression, by means of which cohesion between the members of the community is made easier."[8] Freud had nationalism in mind here, of course, not rivalries between historians and social scientists. But shoes may fit several pairs of feet.

Are we academic nationalists? We have been trained since graduate school to defend our turf against assaults from deans, dilettantes, and neighboring disciplines. We organize our journals, scholarly organizations, and university departments within precisely demarcated boundaries. We gesture vaguely in the direction of interdisciplinary cooperation, rather in the way sovereign states put in polite appearances at the United Nations; reality, however, falls far short of what we routinely promise.

---

7. John Lewis Gaddis, *We Now Know: Rethinking Cold War History* (New York: Oxford University Press, 1997).

8. Sigmund Freud, *Civilization and its Discontents*, trans. and ed. by James Strachey (New York: Norton, 1961), p. 72.

And we have been known, from time to time, to construct the intellectual equivalent of fortified trenches from which we fire artillery back and forth, dodging shrapnel even as we sink ever more deeply into mutual incomprehension.

We rarely ask, though: what is it that actually divides us? Like leaders of the Soviet Union and the United States during the Cold War, we often find it difficult to remember. "It's always been that way," we tell each other—but what if it hasn't? The world is full of what seem to be ancient patterns of behavior that are in fact relatively recent: real-world nationalism is one of them.[9] Another, as it happens, is disciplinary professionalization: historians and social scientists have not *always* thought of themselves as distinct communities.[10] Might there be a connection? Could we have allowed a "narcissism of minor differences," over the past several decades, to balkanize our minds?

II.

It might help, in thinking about this possibility, to set aside disciplinary boundaries for a moment to consider a simple question: can we, in investigating phenomena, replicate phenomena?

Certain fields do this all the time. They rely upon controlled reproducible experimentation. They are able to rerun sequences of events, varying conditions in such a way as to establish causes, correlations, and consequences. Mathematicians recalculate *pi* to millions of decimal places with absolute confidence that its value will remain what it has been for thousands of years. Physics and chemistry are only slightly less reliable, for although investigators cannot always be sure what is happening at subatomic levels, they do get similar results when they perform experiments under similar conditions, and they probably always will. Verification, within these disciplines, takes place by repeating actual processes. Time and space are compressed and manipulated; history itself is in effect rerun.

But not all sciences work this way. In astronomy, geology, and paleontology, for example, phenomena rarely fit within computers or laboratories. The time required to see results can exceed the life spans of those

---

9. E.J. Hobsbawm, *Nations and Nationalism Since 1780: Programme, Myth, and Reality* (Cambridge: Cambridge University Press, 1990); and Benedict Anderson, *Imagined Communities: Reflections on the Origins and Spread of Nationalism*, rev. ed. (New York: Verso, 1991).

10. Dorothy Ross, *The Origins of American Social Science* (New York: Cambridge University Press, 1991), shows how and when these differences began to emerge.

who seek them.[11] These disciplines depend instead upon thought experiments: practitioners rerun in their minds what their petri dishes, centrifuges, and electron microscopes cannot manage. They then look for evidence suggesting which of these mental exercises comes closest to explaining their real-time observations. Reproducibility exists only as a consensus that such correspondences seem plausible. The only way we can rerun this kind of history is to imagine it.[12]

Where would Einstein have been without an imagination so vivid that it allowed experiments with phenomena too large to fit not just his laboratory but his galaxy? Or Darwin without the ability to conceive a time scale extending hundreds of millions of years? Or Alfred Wegener without visualizing a globe on which whole continents could come together and drift apart? What is the reconstruction of dinosaurs and other ancient creatures from fossils, if not a fitting of imagined flesh to surviving bones and shells, or at least to impressions of them?[13]

Historians function in just this way, matching mental reconstructions of experiences they can never have with whatever "fossils" these may have left behind. "A historical fact is an inference from the relics," John Goldthorpe has argued. These may include bones and excrement, tools and weapons, great ideas and works of art, and documents that get deposited in archives: "However, none of this alters the situation that the relics themselves, in a physical sense . . . are finite, and are . . . probably only a quite small and unrepresentative selection, of all that could have survived. It must therefore be the case that. . . . [t]here are things about the past that never can be known simply because the relics that would have been essential to knowing them did not in fact survive." But the conclusions historians may draw from these materials, Goldthorpe adds, are by no means finite: "The 'facts' that the relics yield will tend to increase with the questions that historians put to them and, in turn, with

---

11. We do, however, now have limited real-time evidence for Darwin's theory of natural selection. See Jonathan Weiner, *The Beak and the Finch: A Story of Evolution in Our Time* (New York: Knopf, 1994).

12. Why, for example, does today's North American pronghorned antelope run twice as fast as any of its predators? Perhaps because "ghost" predators now extinct—cheetahs and hyenas—forced them to do so. There is no way to verify this hypothesis, though, apart from examining the fossil record to see whether antelope did indeed once live alongside speedier carnivores. See Carol Kaesuk Yoon, "Pronghorn's Speed May Be Legacy of Past Predators," *New York Times*, December 24, 1996.

13. Stephen Jay Gould, *Wonderful Life: The Burgess Shale and the Nature of History* (New York: Norton, 1989), provides one of the best explanations of how it is done.

the range of the problems they address and with the development of their techniques of inquiry."[14]

Like other practitioners of nonreplicable science, therefore, historians use their imagination to conduct thought experiments. They simulate realities to which they lack access. They do so through the use of narrative—at once the oldest and the most sophisticated form of simulation. They tell stories, and as Hayden White has observed, "what distinguishes 'historical' from 'fictional' stories is . . . their content, rather than their form."[15] A few brave historians have even begun relying upon what they have acknowledged to be fictional fragments to fill gaps in the archival record;[16] many others have no doubt done so without being quite so honest about it.

And what then of novels, plays, poems, and films? Do these not also reveal aspects of human behavior that would be difficult to document in any other way? Surely Shakespeare's contribution to our understanding of human nature was at least as great as Freud's—even if he did take liberties with the historical record at least as great as those of Oliver Stone.[17]

My point, then, is that whenever we set out to explain phenomena we cannot replicate—whether in paleontology or playwriting—the best we can expect to manage is to simulate it. We approximate reality, because that is the only way we can hope to understand reality. All the world's a stage; but without a stage upon which we can *represent* the world, we can hardly function within the world. Our minds require this representation—and representation, in turn, demands imagination.

---

14. John H. Goldthorpe, "The Uses of History in Sociology: Reflections on Some Recent Tendencies," *British Journal of Sociology*, Vol. 42, No. 2 (June 1991), pp. 213–214.

15. Hayden White, *The Content of the Form: Narrative Discourse and Historical Representation* (Baltimore: Johns Hopkins University Press, 1987), p. 27. See also Lawrence Stone, "The Revival of Narrative: Reflections on a New Old History," *Past and Present*, No. 85 (November 1979), pp. 3–24.

16. Simon Schama, *Dead Certainties: Unwarranted Speculations* (New York: Knopf, 1991); and John Demos, *The Unredeemed Captive: A Family Story from Early America* (New York: Random House, 1994).

17. Edmund S. Morgan discusses these issues in reviewing Arthur Miller's screenplay for the film version of *The Crucible* in the *New York Review of Books*, Vol. 44, No. 1 (January 9, 1997), pp. 4–6. For a fine novel that illustrates clearly the gap between what gets left behind in archives and what really happened, see A.S. Byatt, *Possession: A Romance* (New York: Random House, 1990).

III.

Let me illustrate what I mean by citing my own recent book, *We Now Know: Rethinking Cold War History.* I began it, I must confess, as a kind of liberation from theory, at least from theories of international relations.[18] I found it a relief to get back to doing "straight" history without having to worry too much about systems, units, dyads, defections, and matrices. The opportunity had arisen to retell an old story—the coming of the Cold War—from two new points of view.[19] A theatrical counterfactual will suggest what I had in mind.

Suppose all we'd had of *Hamlet,* for several hundred years, had been only a partial text, from which were missing both the central character's interior monologues and the final act. We would have known, from observing his behavior, what Hamlet did, but we wouldn't have a clue as to why. Nor could we have evaluated the consequences of his actions. We'd have been stuck in the position of those puzzled poseurs, Rosencrantz and Guildenstern, wondering what the hell was going on and how it was all going to come out.[20]

That's pretty much the situation Cold War historians confronted as they tried to write that conflict's history from only one side's sources and without knowing the outcome. But then, with the gradual release of Soviet, East European, and Chinese documents in the late 1980s and early 1990s, the missing lines began to appear. The end of the Cold War and the simultaneous collapse of the Soviet Union gave us, quite abruptly, the final act. A competition therefore ensued to mount new productions of

---

18. I had discussed these theories at great length in "Expanding the Data Base: Historians, Political Scientists, and the Enrichment of Security Studies," *International Security,* Vol. 12, No. 1 (Summer 1987), pp. 3–21; "International Relations Theory and the End of the Cold War," *International Security,* Vol. 17, No. 3 (Winter 1992/93), pp. 5–58; and "History, Science, and the Study of International Relations," in Ngaire Woods, ed., *Explaining International Relations Since 1945* (New York: Oxford University Press, 1996), pp. 32–48.

19. My earlier efforts at telling the story include *The United States and the Origins of the Cold War, 1941–1947* (New York: Columbia University Press, 1972); *Russia, the Soviet Union, and the United States: An Interpretive History* (New York: John Wiley, 1978), 2nd ed. (New York: McGraw Hill, 1990); *Strategies of Containment: A Critical Appraisal of Postwar American National Security Policy* (New York: Oxford University Press, 1982); and *The Long Peace: Inquiries Into the History of the Cold War* (New York: Oxford University Press, 1987).

20. Tom Stoppard's play, *Rosencrantz and Guildenstern Are Dead,* captures this perspective precisely. This and other theatrical analogies in this paper reflect the influence of Toni Dorfman, who has taught me a great deal about the relationship between history and theater.

the old play using this fresh material. *We Now Know* was one of them; and it's fair to say that it's opened to, well, mixed reviews.

I like this analogy to the theater because it makes my point that the writing of history is a representation of reality, not reality itself. It is, in one sense, truer than truth, in that it can reflect any number of simultaneous events not apparent at the time. Hence, I could show what was happening in Moscow, Washington, Beijing, Tokyo, Seoul, and Pyongyang during the weeks preceding the Korean War.[21] Like a Picasso painting, I could see the same event from several different perspectives at once, something participants in these events could never have done. But history is, in another sense, a falsification of truth, because even with the best sources historians can never know the precise combination of motives that led people to act as they did. Too few of Goldthorpe's "relics" tend to survive. However many perspectives Picasso picked up, his models must have found it difficult to recognize themselves on his canvases. The same would be true, I fear, if the statesmen about whom I wrote could come back now and read what I have written about them.

History therefore is also, inescapably, dramatization. Documents never speak for themselves; historians speak for them. Their histories, like plays, can reveal the ambiguities of human behavior as real life can never do. Depending upon how the story is told, it can accelerate or slow down time; it can compress or extend space; it can excite, appall, elucidate, infuriate; and—if done badly—it can bore an audience to tears. But it is, in the end, a *story*: it may approximate what happened, but it can never recapture all that happened.

It follows that stories and storytellers are inextricably linked. However much they may respect each other's work, no two theater directors will stage the same play in exactly the same way, and no two historians will write about the same event in exactly the same manner. They cannot help but bring their own distinctive viewpoints to the material with which they work. At times they will be explicit about this; at times they will not be; at times they may not even be aware of the extent to which circumstances of time, place, and personality have shaped their view of the past.

Contrary to what historians like to claim on their book jackets, then, *there is no such thing as a definitive account of any historical episode.* Revision in history is like restaging in theater: it is what the business is all about. And just what is the history business in the first place? It is certainly not one of piling up bricks upon which some grand edifice must permanently

---

21. See Gaddis, *We Now Know,* pp. 70–75.

rest. It involves instead the recurring reexamination of foundations, and all that they support.

IV.

If that's the case, though, how do we know when we're reading—or writing—good history? If historical research does not neatly cumulate, if this field contains no agreed-upon body of knowledge beyond basic facts, how are its products to be evaluated? Since historians so rarely answer this question, social scientists have every reason to wonder; and many of the misunderstandings that divide our communities arise as a result. There is, I believe, a functional theory of historical verification, but it is largely implicit. It is best seen indirectly: by looking first at how certain other professions "fit" representation to reality.

Return, for a moment, to the "reality" a paleontologist has to work with, which is chiefly bones, shells, and fossils. Representing the creatures that left these behind requires linking precise observation and description of what has survived with the ability to imagine what life must have been like hundreds of millions of years ago. More is involved, though, than just taxonomy and imagination. Paleontologists must also persuade their colleagues that their conclusions make sense. They cannot, for example, simply *assert* that the apatosaurus nurtured its young, or that the archaeopteryx is the ancestor of today's birds; they must also *convince*. Paleontologists, therefore, must "fit" together three things: first, what remains from original sources; second, what they themselves make of these remains; and third, what they can bring their professional colleagues to accept.

Another way of thinking about this is to imagine yourself as a tailor. Clothes make it possible for people to appear in public: tailors are the intermediaries between society and naked bodies. But unless you were working for, say, Mao Zedong, you wouldn't want to dress all your customers in exactly the same way. You would want to allow for their varying shapes and sizes. You would probably want to reflect their preferences as to fabric, style, and ornamentation. You would, in this sense, be *representing* them to a world in which they wouldn't want to be seen as they really are. But since you'd have a professional reputation to uphold, you would also be representing yourself: you wouldn't want to deck your clients out, these days, in bell-bottom trousers or polyester leisure suits. You might even want to try to shift current fashions a bit by coming up with a style others might emulate. Once again, though, the "fit" would have to extend across three levels: the body to be clothed, the design of the clothing, and the world of fashion, which will either embrace, reject, or ignore what results.

Or consider the making of maps. Cartographers represent realities they can't replicate and wouldn't want to: a truly accurate map of Connecticut, for example, would be an exact clone of Connecticut, and would therefore not easily fit within backpacks or briefcases. Maps vary scale and content according to need. A world map has a different purpose from one intended to identify bicycle paths or garbage dumps. Nor are maps free from preconceptions. There is always some prior reason for what is shown, and not shown.[22] We evaluate maps according to their usefulness: is the layout legible? is the representation credible? does the map extend our perceptions beyond what we ourselves can manage, so that it performs the practical task of getting us from here to there? As with the reconstruction of dinosaurs and the construction of fashions, though, there is again the reality to be represented, the representation itself, and its reception by those who use it.

I find these metaphors useful in explaining how historians work, for like paleontologists, tailors, and cartographers, we seek a good "fit" across three distinct levels of activity. In recounting an event, or a series of them, we begin with what is there—normally archives, the equivalent for us of bones, bodies, or terrain. We interpret these through our own distinctive viewpoints: that's why the writing of history resembles the production of plays, for imagination, indeed dramatization, is very much involved. Ultimately, though, the product must go before an audience, at which point one of several things may happen. The patrons may approve because what they see confirms their preconceptions. They may disapprove if it does not. Or—and this is what dramatists, paleontologists, tailors, cartographers as well as historians hope for—the product may move those who encounter it to revise their own view of the world so that a new basis for critical judgment emerges, perhaps even a new view of reality itself.

How do we know when a play succeeds? How do we judge a museum exhibit of an animal no living person has ever seen? How do we appreciate good fashion design? How do we decide what maps are useful to us? In the same way, I think, that we evaluate works of historical scholarship: they have to reflect what we already know of reality, they

---

22. Jeremy Black, *Maps and History: Constructing Images of the Past* (New Haven: Yale University Press, 1997), contains many examples. See also James C. Scott, *Seeing Like a State: How Certain Schemes to Improve the Human Condition Have Failed* (New Haven: Yale University Press, 1998), for an illuminating discussion of how states impose ideological grids upon landscapes.

have to reinterpret that reality in ways that cause us to reassess its meaning, and they have to command a consensus, among others who know the field, that they have indeed accomplished these tasks. "I'll know it when I see it," a judge once famously said in defining pornography. With the appropriate adjustment for subject matter, this is roughly how "knowing," among historians, takes place.

V.

Where, then, does theory come in? It is, I believe, the link between reality and our understanding of it. Operating as it does at the second of my three levels, theory is the process we use to make sense of a subject for those who need to know about it. It doesn't matter whether you're directing a play, depicting a dinosaur, designing a set of clothes, making a map, or writing a history: in each case you're reconstructing reality in order to explain it. You seek the best "fit" between what you're trying to characterize and the reception you expect your characterization to get. And you'd have a hard time doing that without "a coherent group of general propositions used as principles of explanation."

Not all disciplines use theory in just the same way, though, and here there is an important difference between historians and most social scientists. Historians generally embed theory within narrative. They seek to simulate some past sequence of events, and they subordinate theory to that end. They practice, therefore, *particular generalization*. Social scientists, in contrast, expect theory to encompass narrative: their principal objective is to confirm or refute a hypothesis, and they subordinate narrative to that purpose. Their task is *general particularization*.[23] This distinction between embedded and encompassing theory—between generalization lodged within time and generalization for all time—causes historians to function differently from their social science colleagues in several ways:

Historians work with limited, not universal, generalizations. We rarely claim applicability for our findings beyond specified times and places. Although I argued, in *We Now Know*, that the structure of the Stalinist

23. I am following, here, the central argument of Clayton Roberts, *The Logic of Historical Explanation* (University Park, Penn.: Pennsylvania State University Press, 1996). My thanks to Alexander George for recommending this excellent analysis of how historians function. But my argument also parallels Jack Levy's distinction between the "idiographic" and "nomothetic" uses of theory. See "Too Important to Leave to the Other: History and Political Science in the Study of International Relations," *International Security*, Vol. 22, No. 1 (Summer 1997), pp. 24–26, and his chapter in this volume.

dictatorship rendered it insensitive to the impact of its actions beyond its borders, that is not an assertion I would want to try to defend for *all* dictatorships. Nor, despite my claim that Stalin did just this, would I insist that dictators *always* project their domestic behavior onto the world at large.[24] These were theories, but they were drawn from, and limited to, particular sets of circumstances.

Such generalizations do not have to be universal, though, to have wide applicability.[25] Historians are perfectly prepared to acknowledge tendencies, or patterns: these may not be laws applying in all instances, but they are by no means useless. If we had to make all of our judgments about reality only on the basis of laws, we would be—because there are so few laws—quite out of touch with most of reality.

My generalization about Stalin might thus provide some basis for making comparisons to other dictatorships, or to democracies, or to still other forms of government. It certainly caused me to rethink a proposition I had absorbed long ago from the post–World War II realists: that democracies have greater difficulties than autocracies in aligning their policies with their interests.[26] But would that amended hypothesis then apply, say, to China in the post–Cold War era? Here I and most other historians would hedge, echoing Zhou Enlai on the French Revolution: "It's too soon to say."

Historians believe in contingent, not categorical, causation. "It all depends," we would continue, before holding forth on all that the future of China (or whatever else *it* may be) is likely to depend upon. Historians have a web-like, or ecological, sense of reality, in that we see everything as connected in some way to everything else.[27] For that reason, we do not find it useful, as social scientists do, to distinguish between independent and dependent variables. Trained to be sensitive both to timescape *and* landscape, we fail to see how any variable (apart from perhaps God) can be truly independent.

This does not mean, though, that we feel obliged to trace each causal

---

24. Gaddis, *We Now Know,* pp. 288–291.

25. See Roberts, *The Logic of Historical Explanation,* pp. 1–15.

26. The classic text is George F. Kennan, *American Diplomacy: 1900–1950* (Chicago: University of Chicago Press, 1951).

27. Robert Jervis, *System Effects: Complexity in Political and Social Life* (Princeton: Princeton University Press, 1997), pp. 10–27, provides one of the best discussions I've seen. I have also benefited here from the work of one of my Ohio University graduate students, Jeffrey Woods, "The Web Model of History," a 1994 paper prepared in the Contemporary History Institute.

chain back to the Big Bang (whether divinely arranged, or not). We differentiate between proximate and distant causation: if a man falls off a mountain, we place greater weight on the fact that he slipped than that tectonic processes uplifted the protuberance.[28] We separate out distinctive from routine links in causal relationships: in accounting for what happened at Hiroshima on August 6, 1945, we give greater emphasis to the fact that President Truman ordered the dropping of an atomic bomb than to the decision of the Army Air Force to carry out his orders.[29] We try to identify those points of "sensitive dependence on initial conditions," at which particular actions had larger consequences than one might have expected: hence the unintended importance of Red Army rapes in determining how Germans regarded their respective occupiers during the months that followed the end of World War II.[30]

Historians do not, however, accept the doctrine of immaculate causation, which seems to be implied in the idea that one can identify, without reference to all that has preceded it, such a thing as an independent variable. Causes always have antecedents. We may rank their relative significance, but we would think it irresponsible to seek to isolate (or, to use a favorite social science term, "tease out") single causes for complex events. We see history as proceeding rather from multiple causes and their intersections. Interconnections matter more to us than does the enshrinement of particular variables. It follows, then, that:

Historians prefer retrocasting to forecasting. Social scientists try to reduce the number of variables with which they deal because this facilitates calculation, which in turn simplifies the task of forecasting. But if events have complex causes, forecasting based on simple ones is likely to be wrong.[31] Knowing this, historians prefer to avoid forecasting altogether, which frees us to incorporate as many variables as we want into our "retrocasting." But there is a deeper issue here, which has to do with

---

28. The example comes from Marc Bloch, *The Historian's Craft*, trans. Peter Putnam (New York: Knopf, 1953), pp. 190–191.

29. See Roberts, *The Logic of Historical Explanation*, pp. 116–117.

30. See Gaddis, *We Now Know*, pp. 286–287; for sensitive dependence on initial conditions, see also James Gleick, *Chaos: Making a New Science* (New York: Viking, 1987), pp. 11–31.

31. For a good example, see Stephen G. Brooks, "Dueling Realisms," *International Organization*, Vol. 51, No. 3 (Summer 1997), pp. 465–466, which discusses John Mearsheimer's prediction—quite wrong, as it turned out—that the Ukrainians would never give up their nuclear weapons.

the fact that although the past is never completely knowable, it is more knowable than the future.

Recounting the past requires narrative—a simulation of what happened—but not necessarily modeling, which involves demonstrating the operation of a system. A simulation, as I am using the term, attempts to illustrate (not replicate) some specific set of past events. A model seeks to show how a system has worked in the past but also how it will work in the future. Simulations rarely forecast; models must. Because the future is less knowable than the past, though, the only way we can illuminate it is to project forward the attributes of known systems. That is where the need for parsimony arises, because when systems become complex, variables proliferate and projection becomes impossible: *systems themselves become entangled in events.*[32] Parsimony, therefore, is a life preserver for social scientists: it keeps them from sinking into complexity. Historians, who swim in that medium, have little need of it.

To illustrate my point, consider Alexis de Tocqueville's famous prophecy, cited at the beginning of *We Now Know*, that Russia and the United States would one day each dominate "the destinies of half the world."[33] Here was a forecast most theorists can only dream of: dating from 1835, it seemed quite implausible at the time, but by 1945 it had proven to be absolutely correct. When I looked at how Tocqueville made it, though—by calculating potential power in terms of geographical extent and high birth rates—it quickly became clear that his vision of the future bore little relation to the actual set of processes that produced two superpowers at the end of World War II. There were too many intervening variables.

There was the fact that, far from being antagonistic, the Russian-U.S. relationship through most of the nineteenth century was as amicable as any the United States had with a European power. There was the realization that when hostility developed, as it did before World War I, this happened as much over issues of human rights as of geopolitical rivalry. There was the unexpected emergence, in both countries at just the same time, of charismatic ideologues, Wilson and Lenin, both with blueprints—which did not match—for the future of the world. There was the surprising withdrawal of both the United States and the Soviet Union from European politics during the 1920s and 1930s, so that neither country had

---

32. Roberts, *The Logic of Historical Explanation*, pp. 105–108, has a helpful discussion of what an "event" is.

33. Alexis de Tocqueville, *Democracy in America*, ed. J.P. Mayer, trans. George Lawrence (Garden City, New York: Doubleday, 1969), p. 413. Cited on pp. 1–2 of Gaddis, *We Now Know.*

much to do, at least until the Nazi-Soviet Pact of 1939, with the outbreak of World War II. There was the sheer improbability of Adolf Hitler, a leader foolish enough to bring his adversaries together by declaring war on both in 1941. And there was the unexpected rapidity with which the coalition Hitler formed fell apart, in 1945, within months of his demise.

No model that I know—certainly not Tocqueville's—could have anticipated this *sequence* of events. If one had cited his 1835 prophecy as late as the winter of 1939–40, a point at which the Soviet Union was an ally of Nazi Germany and the United States had not even entered the war, it would have seemed wildly speculative. We can see, in retrospect, how the Soviet-U.S. global rivalry evolved: indeed we simulate it through the use of narrative, or "process tracing," or what Clayton Roberts calls "colligation."[34] The only *system* that could produce such an outcome, however, would be one of such complexity that one could never model it. One can only call it—history. Hence,

Historical explanation means tracing processes over time. When one works with multiple intersecting variables, one has to abandon any illusion that the "tape," if "replayed," would produce the same results. In such an environment, conditions that prevail at the beginning guarantee nothing about the end.[35] Historians concern themselves, therefore, as much with the evolution as the structure of phenomena. For us, indeed, *evolution is structure.* Objects exist in time as well as in space: the dimensions we worry about are of both a spatial and a temporal character.

This issue of dimensionality became, for me, an important one in writing *We Now Know.* Like many other students of international relations, I'd been greatly impressed by Kenneth Waltz's counterintuitive proposition (to me, at least) that bipolar systems are inherently more stable than multipolar systems.[36] The more I thought about this the more sense it made, and it was Waltz's insight that largely propelled me toward advancing a thesis of my own, that the Soviet-U.S. Cold War rivalry had

---

34.   Roberts, *The Logic of Historical Explanation*, pp. 16–37. For more on process tracing, see the chapter by Andrew Bennett and Alexander George in this volume.

35.   Parallels in paleontology appear throughout Gould's *Wonderful Life*, the theme of which is the role of contingency in natural selection. The analogy in economics is the phenomenon of "increasing returns," described well in M. Mitchell Waldrop, *Complexity: The Emerging Science at the Edge of Order and Chaos* (New York: Viking, 1992), pp. 15–98.

36.   Kenneth N. Waltz, *Theory of International Politics* (New York: Random House, 1979), pp. 161–193.

evolved into a "long peace."[37] This was, I can now see, an example of embedded theory: I used neorealism to explain a particular historical outcome. But I did not try to encompass the entire Cold War within a neorealist framework.

Waltz, however, did attempt that feat, and on the basis of it he made his own Tocqueville-like forecast, in 1979, of how the Cold War might end. Soviet-U.S. hostility would gradually diminish, he argued, but bipolarity would survive: "the barriers to entering the superpower club have never been higher and more numerous. The club will long remain the world's most exclusive one."[38] He was quickly proven wrong on both counts: distrust between Washington and Moscow reached dangerous new levels during the early 1980s; but by the end of that decade bipolarity had virtually disappeared.

The problem here was Waltz's focus on polarities rather than categories of power. Working on *We Now Know* convinced me that the single most significant pattern in Cold War history was one of asymmetrically evolving capabilities: that while both the United States and the Soviet Union began that conflict possessing power in multiple dimensions—military power to be sure, but also ideological, economic, and even moral power—only the United States and its allies retained that multidimensionality, and with it the capacity to compete in a shifting international environment. We need, therefore, a theory that will address kinds of power and the environments within which they manifest themselves.

Can we construct such a theory? I think we can, but only if we relax certain Waltzian rules: a definition of power that accords primacy to military capabilities; an insistence on making sharp distinctions between systems- and unit-level phenomena; and the aspiration to universality, which obscures the role the passage of time itself can play in determining the course of events. All of this led me in *We Now Know*, logically enough, back to dinosaurs:

To visualize what happened, imagine a troubled triceratops. From the outside, as rivals contemplated its sheer size, tough skin, bristling armament, and aggressive posturing, the beast looked sufficiently formidable that none dared tangle with it. Appearances deceived, though, for within its digestive, circulatory, and respiratory systems were slowly clogging up, and then shut-

---

37. See Gaddis, *The Long Peace*, esp. pp. 219–223.

38. Waltz, *Theory of International Politics*, p. 183. In fairness to Waltz, this prediction was not all that much more off target than my own: "that the point at which a great power perceives its decline to be beginning is a perilous one: behavior can become erratic, even desperate, well before physical strength itself has dissipated." See *The Long Peace*, p. 244.

ting down. There were few external signs of this until the day the creature was found with all four feet in the air, still awesome but now bloated, stiff, and quite dead. The moral of the fable is that armaments make impressive exoskeletons, but that a shell alone ensures the survival of no animal and no state.[39]

Obviously this is a metaphor, not a theory. But do not theories sometimes begin with metaphors? The political scientists I know speak often enough of billiard balls, dominos, bandwagons, rolling logs, prisoner's dilemmas, stag hunts, and chickens—a very eclectic metaphorical menagerie! Why, therefore, cannot a dead dinosaur provide a basis for a reconceptualization of theory drawn, this time, not from mathematics or physics, but from medicine?

The theory would be this: that the health and ultimate survival of states depend upon their maintaining a combination of life-support systems in balance with one another, and with their external environment. If any one of them gets out of whack and nothing is done, its collapse can affect all the others. Treatment may require specialists, to be sure, but no specialist will succeed without taking into account the entire organism, its case history, and its surrounding ecosystem. Physicians, in short, may offer us more than physicists in seeking to understand international systems and the states that function within them.[40]

But this is only to bring us back around, again, to narrative, for what do physicians do, in treating their patients, if not track multiple interrelated processes over time, recounting these for others so that all may ultimately benefit? Physicians generalize, but only on a limited basis, for they must allow for the particularities of their patients as well as those of the ills that beset them. No physician would want to treat the heart without considering what the effects might be on the blood vessels, the lungs, the kidneys, and the brain: even in an era of specialization, doctors must still maintain some sense of the patient as a whole. They would certainly not rely upon a monodimensional explanation for illness or health, nor would they want to have to depend upon a single remedy. Nor would they exclude the role of time, both as an enemy and as an ally in the art of healing.

Physicians deal, therefore, with the paradox of particular generalization all the time. So too do theater directors, paleontologists, tailors, cartographers—and, I would venture to say, most of the rest of us in most

---

39. Gaddis, *We Now Know*, p. 284.

40. Paul W. Schroeder makes a similar point in "History and International Relations Theory: Not Use or Abuse, but Fit or Misfit," *International Security*, Vol. 22, No. 1 (Summer 1997), p. 69.

aspects of everyday life. It's worth considering, therefore, where the push for generalized particularization in the social sciences comes from. Perhaps professionalization has pushed us into a Freudian "narcissism of minor differences": groups often define themselves in terms of what their neighbors aren't.[41] Perhaps it's a confusion of form with function: methodological purity sometimes takes precedence, in discussions of theory, over simple questions like "what is it for?"[42] Or perhaps it's a misunderstanding of how the "hard" sciences operate, for particular generalization abounds in many of these. I should like to pursue this possibility further, because I think it may get at the heart of the particular differences between historians and theorists of international relations.

VI.

If one were to visualize an axis extending, say, from Einstein at one end to Emily Dickinson at the other, the disciplines involved would have in common a reliance upon thought experiments, or simulations, or representations in theorizing about reality. They would lack the means—available to any laboratory science—of replicating reality itself, in short, of rerunning history. Since international relations theory concerns itself with the unavoidably complex actions of people operating in an inescapably temporal context, it has got to fit somewhere along this interdisciplinary spectrum. Or so one might think.

From this outsider's perspective, though, the field seems torn between the substance with which it deals—nonreplicable human affairs—and the methods many of its practitioners want to employ, which are those of the replicable laboratory sciences.[43] The disciplines deemed wor-

---

41. See, on this point, Samuel P. Huntington, *The Clash of Civilizations and the Remaking of World Order* (New York: Simon and Schuster, 1996), p. 20.

42. "There is no documented case," William C. Wohlforth has claimed, "of a noted scholar of international relations (IR) who has changed his or her view of any theory in response to fresh historical evidence." See "A Certain Idea of Science: How International Relations Theory Avoids the New Cold War History," *Journal of Cold War Studies*, Vol. 1, No. 2 (Spring 1999), p. 39.

43. For an expansion of this argument, see Gaddis, "History, Science, and the Study of International Relations," pp. 32–48; see also Christopher Shea, "Political Scientists Clash Over Value of Area Studies," *Chronicle of Higher Education*, Vol. 43, No. 2 (January 10, 1997), pp. A13–14. It is of course true that political scientists, like other social scientists, can in a manner of speaking replicate *current* phenomena by means of surveys and simulations. See, on this point, Goldthorpe, "The Uses of History in Sociology," pp. 214–215. Only through the use of imagination, though, can they apply such techniques to the study of past events in which the human subjects of their research did not directly participate.

thy of emulation are, curiously, mathematics, physics, and chemistry, fields in which generalizations are expected to encompass rather than be embedded within time and space. There is much less interest, as far as I can tell, in following the examples of such contingent and evolutionary sciences as geology, paleontology, and biology.[44] These preferences, in turn, give rise to procedures historians find it difficult to accept. Thus:

The quest for parsimony. Most international relations theorists appear to assume that simple mechanisms—the functional equivalents, say, of entropy or electromagnetism—drive human events, and that if we can only discover what they are, we can use them to forecast the future. Rigor requires reductionism: there is a search for what the physicist Steven Weinberg calls "final theory."[45] Historians would acknowledge some such universals: people grow old and die; reproduction requires sex; gravity keeps us from floating off into space. Reliable though these are, however, we regard them as insufficiently discriminating in their effects to provide much useful information beyond what most of us already know.

For international relations theorists to insist that all nations within an anarchic system practice self-help, therefore, strikes us as a little like saying that fish within water must learn to swim. It is neither untrue nor untrivial—just uninteresting. Anyone who knows the nature of fish, water, and states will have already figured it out. Such pronouncements only raise further questions: what is meant by "anarchy," "self-help," and "system"? But here the answers are much less clear because so much depends upon context. From a historian's viewpoint parsimony postpones more than it provides—except, perhaps, for the vicarious thrill of appearing to do physics.[46]

The belief in immaculate causation. By insisting on distinctions between independent and dependent variables, international relations theorists are, I think, following the example of chemistry, where one seeks to sort out active from inactive or partially active agents, thereby establishing

44. A prominent recent exception to this pattern is Jervis, *System Effects.*

45. Steven Weinberg, *Dreams of a Final Theory: The Search for the Fundamental Laws of Nature* (New York: Pantheon, 1992). Significantly, Kenneth Waltz criticizes reductionism in his classic *Theory of International Politics,* esp. chaps. 2 and 4. But he never repudiates it.

46. Several distinguished political scientists share the historians' skepticism about parsimony. See Alexander L. George, *Bridging the Gap: Theory and Practice in Foreign Policy* (Washington, D.C.: United States Institute of Peace, 1993), pp. 140–141; and Gary King, Robert O. Keohane, and Sidney Verba, *Designing Social Inquiry: Scientific Inference in Qualitative Research* (Princeton: Princeton University Press, 1994), p. 20.

causation. Why chemistry, though, when biology—a field much closer to the human experience—functions so very differently?

Biologists assume all organisms to have arisen from a long, complex, and often unpredictable chain of antecedents extending back hundreds of millions of years. The common roots of human beings, as of animals, plants, and whatever newly discovered organisms may lie in between, are taken for granted. But exogenous events—shifting continents, global warming or cooling, giant killer asteroids—ensure that any replay of evolution, were that somehow possible, would produce vastly different results.[47] That is why it is hard to find the independent variables for Neanderthals, kangaroos, or pumpkins.

How might one determine, for example, whether rattlesnakes are acting offensively or defensively when they strike their victims? It depends on your point of view, most people would say. An evolutionary biologist might add that nature doesn't make such neat and sharp distinctions. A historian might suggest that countries behave similarly: that to try to cram complex behavior into "offensive" and "defensive" pigeonholes is to oversimplify to the point of uselessness.[48] And yet, international relations theorists would probably complain about the "overdetermination" of such analyses—I think they mean indecisiveness—and demand the specification of independent and dependent variables.[49] Who, here, is being "scientific"?

Accounting for change. In this area, too, international relations theorists tilt toward the replicable sciences despite the nonreplicable character of the subjects with which they deal. Such sciences assume constancy: principles are expected to work in the same way across time and space. Hence concepts like "balancing," "bandwagoning," and "deterrence" are often assumed to have equivalent meanings across centuries and cultures.[50] But

---

47. Gould's *Wonderful Life* again provides the best overall discussion. But see also Colin Tudge, *The Time Before History: 5 Million Years of Human Impact* (New York: Simon and Schuster, 1996), pp. 84, 99–100.

48. For a wicked send-up of such false dichotomous reasoning, see Fischer, *Historians' Fallacies*, pp. 9–12.

49. The example is not completely hypothetical. See, in his chapter for this volume, Richard Ned Lebow's criticism of my account of the origins of the Cold War in *We Now Know*. For the same reason, I find it impossible to separate out Stalin's personality from his ideology, as Lebow wants me to do. Stalin was both the product of Marxism-Leninism and a redesigner of it. In short, a *symbiotic* relationship existed between the two.

50. Paul W. Schroeder makes this point about time in "Historical Reality vs. Neo-realist Theory," *International Security*, Vol. 19, No. 1 (Summer 1994), esp. pp. 116–124. For

as Robert Jervis has pointed out, "a strategy can succeed at one time and fail in another not because of any difference in the actor's resources or skill, but because others are behaving differently."[51] Historians know that every concept is embedded in a context, and that the only thing permanent about contexts is that they shift. We doubt, therefore, that even the most rigorous terminology fixes phenomena in quite the manner that amber freezes flies.

Nonreplicable sciences share our skepticism: biology, geology, paleontology, and astronomy concern themselves as much with change as with stability. So too does medicine, an applied science that combines a reliance on replication with an acknowledgment of evolution. Physicians seek verification by repeating phenomena, to be sure: that is what case histories are all about. But they find long-term prediction problematic. Particular treatments produce known results against certain diseases—for the moment. Viruses, however, can evolve means of defending themselves, so that what works today may not a decade hence.[52] Reproducible results, in this field, can make the difference between life and death. They guarantee less than one might think, though, about the future.

Do societies develop the equivalents of medical vulnerabilities and immunities? Can these change, so that what may hold up as a generalization about the past—for example, that democracies do not fight each other—may not for all time to come? Scientists used to think that proteins could not possibly be infectious agents. Now, with mad cows, it appears as though they can.[53] But that hardly means that *all* proteins are infectious—it only means that we need to qualify our generalizations.

Assuming commensurability. Replicable sciences work with commensurate standards of measurement: all who aspire to reproducible experimentation must share the same definitions of kilograms, voltages, and molecular weights. How close are we to agreement, though, on the meaning of terms like "power" or "hegemony" or "democracy"? Many international relations theorists see the "democratic peace" hypothesis as hinging precariously on whether imperial Germany was a democracy in

a similar argument about cultural space, see Shu Guang Zhang, *Deterrence and Strategic Culture: Chinese-American Confrontations, 1949–1958* (Ithaca: Cornell University Press, 1992).

51. Jervis, *System Effects,* pp. 77–78.

52. See, for example, Nicholas D. Kristof, "Malaria Makes a Comeback, and Is More Deadly Than Ever," *New York Times,* January 8, 1997.

53. John Lanchester, "A New Kind of Contagion," *New Yorker,* Vol. 72 (December 2, 1996), pp. 70–81.

1914. But historians who are in the best position to know, most inconveniently disagree on this point, just as observers at the time did.[54] The reason is that we have no universally accepted standard for what a democracy actually is.

Would historians then jettison the concept of a "democratic peace" if there should prove to be such a glaring exception to it? I think not, *precisely because we distrust* absolute standards. We would probably acknowledge the anomaly, speculate as to its causes, and yet insist that democracies really do not fight one another *most of the time.*[55] Like physicians seeking to understand how mad cows might infect those unlucky enough to have eaten them, we would *qualify* what we used to think— whether about proteins or politics—and then move on.

Historians' interpretations, like life, evolve. We live with shifting sands, and hence prefer explanatory tents to temples. Yet on the basis of what they *understand* us to have concluded, international relations theorists make categorical judgments about the past all the time, confidently incorporating them within their data bases.[56] No wonder historians stand in awe of their edifices, while finding it prudent not to enter them.

The possibility of objectivity. Thomas Kuhn showed years ago that even in the most rigorous sciences the temptation to see what one seeks can be overwhelming. Postmodernism has pushed the insight—probably further than Kuhn would have liked—into the social sciences and the fine arts.[57] Historians have long understood that they too have an "objectivity" problem: our solution has generally been to admit the difficulty and then get on with doing history as best we can, leaving it to our readers to determine which of our interpretations come closest to the truth.[58] The

---

54.   See, on this point, Ido Oren, "The Subjectivity of the 'Democratic' Peace: Changing U.S. Perceptions of Imperial Germany," *International Security*, Vol. 20, No. 2 (Fall 1995), pp. 147–184.

55.   Bruce Russett and Michael Doyle make this point in "Correspondence: The Democratic Peace," *International Security*, Vol. 19, No. 4 (Spring 1995), pp. 165–167, 182–183.

56.   The complaint is a familiar one, recently reiterated in Ian S. Lustick, "History, Historiography, and Political Science: Multiple Historical Records and the Problem of Selection Bias," *American Political Science Review*, Vol. 90 (September 1996), pp. 605–618.

57.   Thomas S. Kuhn, *The Structure of Scientific Revolutions*, 3rd ed. (Chicago: University of Chicago Press, 1996). The chemist Carl Djerassi's novel, *The Bourbaki Gambit* (New York: Penguin, 1994), illustrates the problem from a different viewpoint.

58.   See, for example, Joyce Appleby, Lynn Hunt, and Margaret Jacobs, *Telling the Truth About History* (New York: Norton, 1994), esp. pp. 271–309. Peter Novick, *That Noble Dream: The "Objectivity Question" and the American Historical Profession* (New York:

procedure resembles what happens in the "hard" sciences, where it is also possible to construct a consensus without agreeing upon all of the generalizations that make it up. Physicists who could not settle so fundamental an issue as whether light is a particle or a wave managed, nonetheless, to build an atomic bomb.[59]

Do international relations theorists think objectivity possible? I find this question surprisingly hard to answer. Vast amounts of time and energy go into perfecting methodologies whose purpose seems to be to remove any possibility of bias: the determination certainly exists, more than in history and perhaps even physics, to agree on the fundamentals before attempting generalization. And yet, it is striking how much work in this field begins with professions of belief, followed by the quotations from what would appear to be sacred texts. Dogmas are defended and heresies condemned, with the entirely predictable result (to a historian at least) that sects proliferate.[60] Whether we are really dealing with science or faith, therefore—or perhaps a science *bounded* by faith—remains unclear.

VII.

So what is to be done? Where, if at all, might historians and theorists of international relations find common ground? I would start by looking at the subjects with which we deal: we share a focus on people and the ways they organize their affairs, not on processes that take place inside laboratories. We concern ourselves inescapably, therefore, with nonreplicable phenomena; this by no means requires, however, that we do so unscientifically. There is a long and fruitful tradition within what we might call the "evolutionary" sciences for finding patterns in particularities that change over time.[61] Which of our two disciplines best reflects it is an interesting question.

Cambridge University Press, 1988), is the most thorough discussion of historians and objectivity. For an excellent introduction to the debate over postmodernism, see Lynn Hunt and Jacques Revel, eds., *Histories: French Constructions of the Past* (New York: New Press, 1995).

59. John Ziman, *Reliable Knowledge: An Exporation of the Grounds for Belief in Science* (Cambridge: Cambridge University Press, 1991), pp. 6–10.

60. A quick survey reveals that "realism" now exists at least in "classical," "neoclassical," "structural," "hegemonic," "strategic," "constitutional," "defensive," and "offensive" forms, each with its own distinctive set of assumptions. Possibly I have missed others.

61. One of the most prominent practitioners actually prefers the term "historical" science. See Gould, *Wonderful Life*, p. 279.

My preliminary conclusion is that the historians, without trying to be scientific, manage this task better than most of them realize; while the international relations theorists, by trying to be too scientific, accomplish less than they might. Historians are "evolutionary" by instinct if not formal training: were they to make their methods more explicit (as they certainly should do),[62] they would find more in common with other sciences than they might expect. International relations theorists, conversely, are explicit to a fault: their problem is that they cannot seem to decide what kind of science—replicable or nonreplicable—they want to do.

But is there really a choice? I detect, among some international relations theorists, a growing sense that there is not: that insurmountable difficulties arise when one tries to apply the methods of replicable science to the nonreplicable realm of human affairs.[63] This has led, among other things, to an interest in "process tracing" as a way of extracting generalities from unique sequences of events. How is this different, though, from the construction of narratives, which is what historians do? It is here, I think—in a careful comparison of what our two fields mean by "narrative" and "process tracing"—that the most promising opportunities for cooperation between historians and international relations theorists currently lie.[64]

Any historical narrative is a simulation, a highly artificial representation of what happened in the past involving the tracing of processes—as well as structures—over time. Such accounts cannot help but combine the general with the particular: revolutions, for example, have certain common characteristics, but the details of each one differ. Historians could hardly write about revolutions without some prior assumptions as to what these are and what we need to know about them: in this sense, they depend upon theory. They also, however, require facts—even

---

62. According to Raymond Martin, "After a full century of critical philosophy of history, we still do not know how historians do, or should, decide among competing historical interpretations." See Raymond Martin, "Objectivity and Meaning in Historical Studies: Toward a Post-Analytic View," *History and Theory*, Vol. 32, No. 1 (February 1993), p. 29.

63. "What is needed to rectify the situation is not utopian, but a simple recognition of IR's status as a historical science. We need to reconcile the propensities for generalization with the detailed kinds of historical data we routinely obtain about international events." See Wohlforth, "A Certain Idea of Science," p. 60.

64. Andrew Bennett and Alexander George have most thoroughly worked out these comparisons. See their chapter in this volume. The concept of "increasing returns" in economics also involves tracing processes over time. See Waldrop, *Complexity*, pp. 15–51.

awkward ones inconsistent with theories—for without these no link to the past could even exist. What results is a kind of tailoring: we seek the best "fit" given the materials at hand, without the slightest illusion that we are replicating whatever it is they cover, or that our handiwork will "wear well" for all time to come.

Nor can we function without imagination: like a good tailor, we try to see things from the perspective of our subjects and only then make alterations based upon our own. Implicit in all of this is some sense of what might have been: the assumption that history did not *have* to have happened in the way it did, and that many of our conclusions about what did happen involve an implicit consideration of paths not taken—which is of course fiction.[65] Are such methods "scientific"? Of course they are: "hard" scientists ponder alternative scenarios all the time, often on the basis of intuitive, even aesthetic, judgments.[66] Can international relations theorists live with such methods? If their rapidly developing interest in counterfactuals is any indication, they have already begun to do so.[67]

Our fields, therefore, may have more in common than their "narcissism of minor differences" has allowed them to acknowledge. Both disciplines fall squarely within the spectrum of *nonreplicable* sciences. Both trace processes over time. Both employ imagination. Both use counterfactual reasoning. But what about forecasting, or at least the specification of policy implications? Most historians shy away from these priorities like vampires confronted with crosses. Many international relations theorists embrace them enthusiastically. If common ground exists here, it may be hard to find.

VIII.

Return, though, to our initial distinction between replicable and nonreplicable sciences. The former assume that knowing the past will reveal the

---

65. This "tailoring" metaphor owes a lot to John Le Carre's novel *The Tailor of Panama* (New York: Knopf, 1996).

66. According to Weinberg, "The consensus in favor of physical theories has often been reached on the basis of aesthetic judgments before the experimental evidence for these theories became really compelling." See Weinberg, *Dreams of a Final Theory*, p. 130.

67. See Philip E. Tetlock and Aaron Belkin, eds., *Counterfactual Thought Experiments in World Politics: Logical, Methodological, and Psychological Perspectives* (Princeton: Princeton University Press, 1996). Niall Ferguson, ed., *Virtual History: Alternatives and Counterfactuals* (New York: Basic Books, 1999), provides the best recent defense of counterfactuals by historians.

future; the latter avoid such claims, but seek nonetheless to provide methods for coping with whatever is to come.

No one can be certain where or when the next great earthquake will occur. It is helpful to know, though, that such upheavals take place more frequently in California than in Kansas: that people who live along the San Andreas Fault should configure their houses against seismic shocks, not funnel clouds. Nobody would prudently bet, just yet, on who will play in next year's World Series. It seems safe enough to assume, though, that proficiency will determine which teams get there: achieving it, too, is a kind of configuring against contingencies.[68] Not even the most capable war planner can predict where the next war will occur, or what its outcome will be. But is it equally clear that war planning should therefore cease? The point, in all of these instances, is not so much to *predict* the future as to *prepare* for it.

Training is not forecasting. What it does do, though, is *expand ranges of experience,* both directly and vicariously, so that we can increase our skills, our stamina—and, if all goes well, our wisdom. The principle is much the same whether you're working out in a gym, flying a 747 simulator, or reading William H. McNeill: whatever the exercise, you come out of it better equipped to deal with the unexpected. Here too then there is, or could be, common ground for historians and theorists of international relations, as well as for the social sciences generally. The terrain upon which to train may be more accessible—and hospitable— than at first glance it might appear to be. It deserves, at a minimum, joint exploration.

---

68. For the importance of proficiency in baseball, see Stephen Jay Gould, *Full House: The Spread of Excellence from Plato to Darwin* (New York: Harmony Books, 1996), esp. pp. 77–135.

Chapter 12

Sources and Methods in Cold War History: The Need for a New Theory-Based Archival Approach

Deborah Welch Larson

Is there anything new to be said about the Cold War? Political scientists have generalized about deterrence, coercive diplomacy, crisis management, offensive military doctrines, and so on using cases from the Cold War. Foreign-policy making theorists have theorized about bureaucratic politics, psychological stress, motivated biases, and cognitive processes. These works rely on journalists' accounts of Cold War crises or secondary sources written by historians. Now that new archival sources are becoming available, as U.S. records from the later Cold War period are opened up and some former Soviet records are made available to researchers, political scientists can develop new insights, particularly if they do their own archival work instead of relying on secondary sources written by historians.[1]

In this chapter, I will argue that political scientists could benefit from doing their own archival research, rather than relying on secondary sources written by historians. Political scientists should look at primary sources in order to identify the causal mechanisms underlying foreign policy events. Documents allow the investigator to determine if potential causes such as domestic politics or economic interests actually influenced policy. Historical evidence is essential to assess the accuracy of psychological explanations of foreign policy decisions. Experiments provide useful hypotheses about cognitive and motivational influences on human decisions. But precisely because the laboratory is an artificial environment, such hypotheses need to be validated by real-world data. Since cognitive or motivational processes are not directly observable, the investigator must look for indirect indicators in the form of verbal statements,

---

1. Two political scientists, Richard Ned Lebow and Janice Gross Stein, have used new archival sources in *We All Lost the Cold War* (Princeton: Princeton University Press, 1994).

and so on. Memos, letters, and so forth written at the time are a valuable source of evidence of mental states.

In the first section, I argue that political scientists and historians should look for causal mechanisms underlying historical events. These causal mechanisms can best be uncovered by archival research. Counterfactuals, as I argue in the second section, are a means of assessing the relative importance of these causal mechanisms. The third section presents arguments and examples from my own research to make the case that political scientists interested in explaining decision-making should consult primary sources, and provides guidelines on how to use documents to make inferences about the author's mental state. In the fourth section, I show how newspapers can be used to establish the context of historical documents in order to interpret their meaning. I conclude with observations on how political scientists and historians can learn from each other.

The Need to Examine Causal Mechanisms

Historians typically describe the chain of events that led to a particular historical outcome. According to Andrew Bennett and Alexander George, historical narrative is one form of process tracing, a method which tries to identify the intervening causal process between an independent variable and the outcome of the dependent variable. Bennett and George advocate a more theoretically informed narrative, in which events are linked together by explicit, causal generalizations rather than the implicit covering laws favored by historians.

Instead of theoretical generalizations, the generalizations that historians use are typically inductive, summarized from their experience and research.[2] For example, historians have observed that the Russians throughout history tried to extend their control over neighboring states, whereas the United States intervened only reluctantly in Europe when the continent was about to come under the hegemony of a hostile power. After World War II, the United States did not come to the assistance of Western Europeans until they requested it, an "empire by invitation." The U.S. containment policy was a reaction to Soviet probes against Iran, Turkey, and Greece.

Most historians do not explicate the mechanisms responsible for these recurring patterns in history or uncover detailed cause-effect linkages.

---

2. Clayton Roberts, *The Logic of Historical Explanation* (University Park: Pennsylvania State University Press, 1996), p. 86.

For example, why has the United States been passive, intervening only at the last minute, rather than adopting a proactive policy? Were U.S. presidents constrained by U.S. isolationist attitudes, lulled by the relative geographic isolation of the United States, or offended by amoral *realpolitik?*

Historians generally identify underlying *conditions* responsible for an event rather than the *causes.* Stephen Pelz argues that historians describe conditions that make an event possible and changes in these conditions that make the event more probable, such as a shift in the balance of power. He suggests that human decisions are only the proximate causes of events, explaining mainly the timing and the form of historical outcomes.[3] For example, historians generally focus on nationalism and the arms race when explaining World War II instead of the assassination of Archduke Franz Ferdinand. Indeed, David Hackett Fischer goes so far as to state that "Sometimes the question of causality can be by-passed by an investigator. In my opinion, whenever it can be avoided, it should be."[4]

Cold War historians typically identify the conditions conducive to the occurrence of particular events such as the Truman Doctrine, the Berlin Blockade, and the Korean War, not the causes. Conditions identified as responsible for the Cold War include bipolarity, ideological differences, a U.S. public opinion conditioned by wartime rhetoric to expect democracy in Eastern Europe, a power vacuum in Europe brought about by the devastation of World War II and German occupation, and a Soviet economy geared to war. Vojtech Mastny attributes the Cold War to Soviet insecurity. Stalin's quest for absolute security bred East-West tensions, as the dictator used communism to extend his control over other countries, thereby arousing Western fears and provoking countermeasures. Soviet insecurity is a condition rather than a cause because it does not vary in Mastny's account, regardless of actions taken by the West. Nothing that the West could have done would have prevented a Cold War from developing. Mastny posits that the Soviet Union was insecure because the Bolsheviks recognized that they had seized power by coup d'etat

---

3. In referring to standing conditions as "causes," it seems that Pelz is conflating three dimensions: deciding which of several initial conditions is more important; tracing a sequence of events leading to a historical outcome; and trying to decide which of several factors is responsible for a large number of similar conditions. See Roberts, *Logic of Historical Explanation,* p. 90.

4. David Hackett Fischer, *Historian's Fallacies: Toward a Logic of Historical Thought* (New York: Harper Colophon Books, 1970), p. 169, cited in Roberts, *Logic of Historical Explanation,* pp. 32–33.

instead of popular revolution; Stalin was paranoid; and communist ideology portrayed the West as a threat.[5] While these factors could have caused the Soviet regime to be insecure, Mastny does not produce any supporting evidence. Soviet insecurity and expansionism could also have been caused by a history of invasions or by the longstanding Russian inferiority complex toward the West.

Causes differ from conditions in several respects. Causes are events. We are more likely to view the lighting of a match as the cause of a fire than the presence of flammable material. To be causal, these events should be intrusive, abnormal, or wrong. Thus, loss of blood was caused by the doctor's severing of an artery, not the heart's pumping action.[6] An accident was caused by the person who made a left turn, not the individual who drove straight ahead. By the same reasoning, Stalin's pressure against Iran and Turkey helped to cause the Cold War because it was surprising and contrary to norms of diplomatic discourse. While U.S. State Department officials expected the Soviets to exercise predominant influence over neighboring countries in Eastern Europe, they were shocked and disturbed by Stalin's attempts to move into the Near East.

Cold War historians include such critical events within their narratives, but do not highlight their causal significance or account for their impact on U.S. officials. Historians have not tried to illuminate how decisions were made—the beliefs, thoughts, and calculations of leaders. They have not tried to explain why leaders viewed the world as they did or why they chose a particular course of action over another. Historians do not engage in microanalysis of the psychological mechanisms by which foreign policy is made.[7] For example, when I began research on *Origins of Containment*, none of the voluminous literature on the origins of the Cold War investigated when and why individual U.S. officials adopted Cold War beliefs about the Soviet Union.[8] Instead, diplomatic historians were concerned with the origins of U.S. *policy*.

---

5. Vojtech Mastny, *The Cold War and Soviet Insecurity: The Stalin Years* (New York: Oxford University Press, 1996), pp. 11, 23, 29, 194.

6. J.L. Mackie, *The Cement of the Universe* (Oxford: Clarendon Press, 1974), p. 34.

7. Alexander L. George, "The Causal Nexus between 'Operational Code' Beliefs and Decision-Making Behavior: Problems of Theory and Methodology," in Lawrence Falkowski, ed., *Psychological Models and International Politics* (Boulder, Colo.: Westview Press, 1979), pp. 96–124; Alexander L. George and Timothy J. McKeown, "Case Studies and Theories of Organizational Decision Making," in Robert J. Coulam and Richard A. Smith, eds., *Advances in Information Processing in Organizations*, Vol. 2 (Greenwich, Conn.: JAI Press, 1985), pp. 26–27.

8. Deborah Welch Larson, *Origins of Containment: A Psychological Explanation* (Princeton: Princeton University Press, 1985), p. 14.

Insofar as historians do explain foreign-policy making, they adopt a rational calculus: they look at the actors' reasons and goals as an explanation for their actions in response to prevailing conditions. According to Paul W. Schroeder, "historians . . . conceive and explain historical change primarily or ultimately in terms of human conduct, that is, purposive acts of agency, not behavior."[9] Certainly historians recognize that official decision-makers may err or miscalculate the effects of their decisions on other states. But even mistakes are explained as purposive attempts to achieve certain goals given a set of beliefs about the world. In *Preponderance of Power*, Melvyn Leffler argued that U.S. officials had a grand design for the postwar world that would maintain U.S. control over resources, industrial infrastructure, skilled labor, and strategic bases. Washington did not want a cold war, but its pursuit of security through preponderant power aroused Soviet fears. When the Soviet Union took defensive measures, mistrust spiraled. The United States was not, however, merely reacting to Soviet policies. Washington seized upon a malevolent interpretation of Soviet actions to rationalize its preferred policies. Instead of trying to reassure the Soviet Union, U.S. leaders adopted a prudent foreign policy course of containment and deterrence.[10] While the Truman administration overestimated the probability that demoralized Western leaders would turn to communism and that indigenous communists would take their countries into the Soviet orbit, U.S. officials were "not irrational."[11] In his favorable review of *We Now Know*, political scientist Miroslav Nincic observes that Gaddis, "as do most diplomatic historians, accounts for both minor and major events almost exclusively in terms of human agency—things happen because of what important people wanted and how they acted."[12]

Whereas historians study human conduct, political scientists analyze behavior. Emphasis on behavior goes back to the professionalization of political science in the interwar period at the University of Chicago, where seminal theorists such as Harold Lasswell developed the new field of political psychology. The "behavioral revolution" after World War II disseminated these developments more widely. Political scientists turned

---

9. Paul W. Schroeder, "History and International Relations Theory: Not Use or Abuse, but Fit or Misfit," *International Security*, Vol. 22, No. 1 (Summer 1997), p. 66.

10. Melvyn P. Leffler, *Preponderance of Power: National Security, the Truman Administration, and the Cold War* (Stanford: Stanford University Press, 1992), pp. 3, 12, 55, 98–99, 100, 121.

11. Ibid., pp. 502–506, quotation on p. 506.

12. Review of *We Now Know: Rethinking Cold War History*, in *American Political Science Review*, Vol. 92, No. 2 (March 1998), p. 260.

away from the study of law, history, and philosophy to opinion polls, interviews, quantitative data, and so on to study behavior.[13] Behavior is not always aimed at an immediate or long-term goal; it may be reactive, emotional, expressive, consummatory, symbolic, or mindless. The assumption that policymakers consciously direct their actions to achieve larger goals is called into question by social psychological experiments showing that people frequently behave contrary to their professed beliefs; their convictions are often internally contradictory; and on many important issues they have no stable, preconceived notions whatsoever.[14] Certainly we need to consider what policymakers *thought* they were trying to achieve at the time. But we should as well recognize that officials make snap judgments using whatever information is at hand, and then later rationalize. Then, too, policymakers are generally unaware of how their actions will influence the calculations of others, resulting in unintended consequences as other states adjust their behavior to the new environment. For example, officials increased their defense spending to be more secure, without realizing that the adversary would take appropriate counteraction.[15] We should not overrationalize foreign policy by assuming that policymakers must have anticipated the results of their actions.

Psychological research suggests that many determinants of human decision lie outside the realm of consciousness. For example, in visual perception, the world is represented upside down on the retina. But we cannot access an upside-down image from our minds.[16] Information from the environment passes though a complex series of stages in which it is perceived, encoded, and stored in memory. Not all the information that we entertain in short-term memory for problem-solving is retained in long-term storage. Psychologists Richard Nisbett and Timothy Wilson present evidence that people are often unaware of why they do what they do.[17] More recently, researchers found that they could get shoppers to buy German or French wine by playing either German Bierkeller or

---

13. For a discussion, see Gabriel A. Almond, "Political Science: The History of the Discipline," in Robert E. Goodin and Hans-Dieter Klingemann, eds., *A New Handbook of Political Science* (Oxford: Oxford University Press, 1996), pp. 65–75.

14. Larson, *Origins of Containment*, p. 13.

15. Robert Jervis, *System Effects: Complexity in Political and Social Life* (Princeton: Princeton University Press, 1997), pp. 258–259.

16. Howard Rachlin, *Judgment, Decision, and Choice: A Cognitive/Behavioral Synthesis* (New York: W.H. Freeman, 1989), pp. 237–238, 240–241, 249–250.

17. Richard E. Nisbett and Timothy DeCamp Wilson, "Telling More than We Can Know: Verbal Reports on Mental Processes," *Psychological Review*, Vol. 84, No. 3 (March 1977), pp. 231–259.

French accordion music, even though shoppers generally prefer French wine. The German and French wines were matched by dryness and placement on the shelf. But none of the customers was aware of the music or realized that he had been manipulated. Psychologists hypothesized that the music activated higher-order knowledge structures about the countries.[18] Just as a trained therapist might understand a person better than he does himself, so a scholar knowledgeable about psychology and history might have a more veridical understanding of what U.S. policy-makers were doing than they themselves did at the time.

To explain events, according to realist philosophers of science, we need to uncover the causal mechanism.[19] A causal mechanism connects the causal event with the effect. The mechanism is what produces or generates the effect, just as natural selection brings about the survival of the fittest species or viruses induce symptoms of disease.[20] Although I referred to mechanism as singular, it may consist of a series of links or subevents.[21] Often causal mechanisms are at a lower level of analysis than the event that is explained—genes for population ecology, molecules for chemical reactions.[22]

Without knowledge of the causal mechanism, we have not really explained events.[23] For example, we have long known that smoking is associated with cancer. But until scientists identified the mechanism by which inhaled smoke produces cancerous cells, cigarette industry repre-

---

18. Adrian C. North, David J. Hargreaves, and Jennifer McKendrick, "In-store Music Affects Product Choice," *Nature,* Vol. 390, No. 6656 (November 1997), p. 132.

19. Andrew Sayer, *Method in Social Science: A Realist Approach* (London: Hutchison, 1984), p. 97.

20. R. Harré, *The Philosophies of Science: An Introductory Survey* (London: Oxford University Press, 1972), p. 118; Sayer, *Method in Social Science,* p. 95; and Jon Elster, *Nuts and Bolts for the Social Sciences* (Cambridge: Cambridge University Press, 1989), p. 3.

21. Elster, *Nuts and Bolts,* pp. 6–7; Daniel Little, *Varieties of Social Explanation: An Introduction to the Philosophy of Social Science* (Boulder, Colo.: Westview Press, 1991), p. 15.

22. Arthur Stinchcombe, "The Conditions of Fruitfulness of Theorizing About Mechanisms in Social Science," *Philosophy of the Social Sciences,* Vol. 21, No. 3 (September 1991), pp. 367, 371–372.

23. Harré, *Philosophies of Science,* pp. 118–119; Roy Bhaskar, *A Realist Theory of Science* (Leeds, U.K.: Leeds Books, 1975), pp. 46–47, 186–187; Sayer, *Method in Social Science,* pp. 104–105; Little, *Varieties of Social Explanation,* p. 159; John Ferejohn and Debra Satz, "Unification, Universalism, and Rational Choice Theory," *Critical Review,* Vol. 9, Nos. 1–2 (Winter–Spring 1995), p. 74; Elster, *Nuts and Bolts,* p. 4; Wesley Salmon, *Four Decades of Scientific Explanation* (Minneapolis: University of Minnesota Press, 1990), p. 156; and David Dessler, "Beyond Correlations: Toward a Causal Theory of War," *International Studies Quarterly,* Vol. 35, No. 3 (September 1991), p. 345.

sentatives could deny that cigarettes caused cancer.[24] Recent scientific advances identifying the mechanism afford proof of the causal link and show how smoking is merely one of a host of environmental factors that produce cancerous mutations in genes.[25] By uncovering the micro-connections between events, scientists open up the "black box."[26]

The first step toward identifying causal mechanisms is to look for patterns in the data. The second step is to "retroduce" what could be responsible for recurring events. Often the causal mechanisms identified by scientists have been unobservable entities such as molecules, viruses, or genes whose physical existence was later confirmed. Scientists may figure out the causal mechanism by analogy to some causal process with which they are more familiar. For example, Charles Darwin deduced that the natural selection of species was analogous to a farmer deciding which animals to breed, but not wishing to posit a supernatural breeder, he also drew on the theory of population pressure, developed by Malthus and later elaborated by Herbert Spencer as the "survival of the fittest," reasoning that animals, like people, compete for space, light, and food. The scientist tests the model by inferring additional consequences that may be assessed in new situations. For example, paleontologists could test Darwin's theory of natural selection by generating other hypotheses about the appearance of new species in the fossil record. Confirmation of these additional hypotheses suggests that the model may accurately represent the mechanisms underlying the events explained. If new instruments or evidence confirm the existence of the mechanism, then scientists may construct models of the inner workings of the mechanisms, and so on.[27]

In social science, we can test hypotheses about causal mechanisms by gathering data about the structures and processes intervening between causes and events. Philosophers of history and political scientists have given various names to the method, such as "microcolligation" or "theoretical process tracing," but it involves reducing the event to be explained to a lower level where the analyst can uncover detailed cause-effect

---

24. Harré, *Philosophies of Science*, p. 116; David Stout, "Direct Link Found Between Smoking and Lung Cancer," *New York Times*, October 18, 1996.

25. J. Madeleine Nash Chicago, "Stopping Cancer in its Tracks," *Time*, April 25, 1995, pp. 54–61.

26. Salmon, *Four Decades*, p. 182.

27. Harré, *Philosophies of Science*, pp. 171, 176; and Russell Keat and John Urry, *Social Theory as Science* (London: Routledge & Kegan Paul, 1975), p. 35.

linkages that can be explained by generalizations.[28] The investigator goes down the ladder of abstraction to uncover the connection between cause and effect. In political science, causal mechanisms can often be directly observed. If a foreign policy is shaped by interest group pressure, for example, scholars may be able to study association meetings, campaign contributions, presidential speeches to affected industries, and so forth.[29] To find out *why* democracies tend not to go to war against each other, scholars have studied the reasons given by leading democratic officials and politicians for not going to war against fellow democracies and the impact of public opinion.[30] At the decision-making level, the causal mechanisms include beliefs, explanations, calculations, deductions, predictions, motivations which have observable indicators such as memos, speeches, and the minutes of meetings. Thus, to argue as Jack Levy does, that political scientists seek to find theoretical generalizations, does not absolve them of the responsibility to elucidate the nature of the causal connection between events and hence to look for evidence at a lower level of generalization than the event to be explained, which may entail the use of documents.

Counterfactual Analyses

Counterfactual analyses are useful for assessing the relative importance of causal mechanisms and are strengthened by the use of primary sources. Historians sometimes engage in such contrary-to-fact speculation when they try to weigh the importance of factors such as Stalin's paranoia or Truman's tough rhetoric. If Stalin had not been in power, would the United States and Soviet Union have gotten into a Cold War?[31]

Now that the Cold War is over, analysts have some interest in speculating on whether there were missed opportunities to resolve some conflicts of interest between the superpowers. Scholars, journalists, and officials also conjecture whether tragedies such as the genocides in Rwanda, Bosnia, or Kosovo might have been prevented through more

28. Roberts, *Logic of Historical Explanation*, pp. 66, 125–129; and Bennett and George in this volume.

29. Sayer, *Method in Social Science*, p. 106.

30. Miriam Fendius Elman, "The Need for a Qualitative Test of the Democratic Peace Theory," p. 33, and case studies by Stephen Rock and Christopher Layne in Miriam Fendius Elman, ed., *Paths to Peace: Is Democracy the Answer?* (Cambridge, Mass.: MIT Press, 1997).

31. Gaddis, *We Now Know*, p. 294.

timely action. The identification of missed opportunities entails engaging in a mental experiment; how would varying an antecedent variable affect the outcome? If the cause that is varied was not necessary for the outcome, then removing it would have made no difference.[32]

To establish that there was a missed opportunity also entails showing how changes in a set of historical conditions *could* have led to a different outcome. Primary sources can strengthen counterfactual judgments by indicating whether policymakers considered alternative options that could have led to a better outcome. An opportunity was more likely missed if a different course of action was available at the time, and not only in hindsight.[33]

Historians often identify turning points in the path of historical development, whereby a different path might have altered an entire series of events, by placing the actors on a different trajectory. For example, historians debate whether the Truman Doctrine, the Marshall Plan, the Korean War, or the Vietnam conflicts were turning points in the Cold War. Making such assessments presupposes that analysts consider what might have happened if the event in question had not occurred.[34]

To make valid counterfactual statements, scholars should appeal to theoretical generalizations and undertake detailed historical analysis of particular cases. A theory is useful, because otherwise it is difficult to judge the validity of something that did not happen. The analyst must also have an informed understanding of the causes of a historical event in order to judge whether a change in some condition would alter the outcome.[35]

In *Anatomy of Mistrust*, I observed that most missed opportunities for cooperation during the Cold War entailed U.S. rejection of Soviet overtures. This is not to say that the Soviet Union always proposed arrangements that were equitable, but that the Soviets displayed greater interest in moving toward cooperative agreements. It was then important to address the causes of this asymmetry. The United States was more satisfied with the status quo than were the Soviets, who wanted greater

---

32. See, for example, Alexander L. George and Jane E. Holl, *The Warning-Response Problem and Missed Opportunities in Preventive Diplomacy* (New York: Carnegie Corporation of New York, May 1997).

33. George and Holl, *The Warning-Response Problem and Missed Opportunities in Preventive Diplomacy*, p. 19.

34. Raymond Martin, "Causes, Conditions, and Causal Importance," *History and Theory*, Vol. 2 (1982), p. 70.

35. Deborah Welch Larson, *Anatomy of Mistrust: U.S.-Soviet Relations During the Cold War* (Ithaca: Cornell University Press, 1997), p. 3.

prestige and relief from the economic burdens of the arms race. When both states wanted to resolve some of their conflicts or control the arms race, they found it difficult to get negotiations started. To propose diplomatic talks risked conveying an image of weakness. Accepting the enemy's offer to negotiate entailed the risk of being suckered, deceived, cheated, or locked into an inferior position. To get discussions underway, at least one side had to lower the barrier of mutual mistrust by making conciliatory gestures as proof of serious intent to negotiate. The U.S. president is constrained from making unilateral concessions because U.S. public opinion insists that relations should be reciprocal; the Soviet general secretary had greater freedom from domestic political restraints.[36] Thus, counterfactual analysis brought forth additional reasons why the Cold War lasted so long.

The Need for Primary Sources

History is necessarily selective; a full recounting of all the people and events leading up to a major foreign policy event such as the Truman Doctrine or the Marshall Plan would be impossible. Political scientists and historians have different criteria for selecting evidence, which makes it risky for political scientists to rely solely on secondary sources written by historians. Cold War historians winnow evidence based on intuitive theories such as the U.S. need for markets and raw materials, bipolarity, Stalin's paranoia, externalization of U.S. domestic problems,[37] historic Russian expansionism, and so forth. Political scientists, on the other hand, are more concerned with causal variables such as domestic public opinion, images of the opponent, beliefs and ideology, analogical reasoning, or trust.

Partly these differences reflect the histories of the two disciplines, and the field of history's membership in the humanities rather than the social

36. Ibid., pp. x, 17.

37. Works that argue for economic determinants of U.S. foreign policy include Gabriel Kolko, *The Politics of War* (New York: Random House, 1968); and Joyce and Gabriel Kolko, *The Limits of Power, 1945–1954* (New York: Harper & Row, 1972). Bipolarity is the focus of Norman A. Graebner, *Cold War Diplomacy: American Foreign Policy, 1945–1960* (Princeton: Van Nostrand, 1962); Louis J. Halle, *The Cold War as History* (New York: Harper & Row, 1967); and Martin F. Herz, *Beginnings of the Cold War* (Bloomington: Indiana University Press, 1966). Arthur Schlesinger, Jr., "Origins of the Cold War," *Foreign Affairs*, Vol. 46 (October 1967), pp. 22–52, emphasizes the role played by Stalin's paranoia, and William Appleman Williams, *The Tragedy of American Diplomacy*, 2nd ed., rev. and enl. (New York: Dell, Delta, 1972), looks at the externalization of U.S. domestic problems.

sciences. Historians accord more importance to events under human control, especially those having tragic or ironic consequences; their aim is to apportion moral responsibility.[38] Political scientists adopt a positivist value-neutrality; their aim is explanation, not blame-fixing. Cold War historians debate who bears more responsibility for the Cold War, the United States or the Soviet Union. Political scientists tend to view both sides as equally responsible in a causal if not moral sense, which makes questions of relative blame theoretically trivial.

Historians focus on actions that were under human control because if the behavior was unintentional or coerced, then the actors could not be held morally responsible.[39] Cognitive social psychologists, on the other hand, agree that people are often unaware of how their beliefs influence perception and judgment. If this research is valid, then historians should not take at face value the explanations that officials give for their past actions. Our inability to rely on retrospective reports or introspection means that it is not an easy task for a historian or political scientist to show that beliefs or ideology influenced the content of foreign policy. To show that a person's actions were generally consistent with his or her beliefs is not to prove that his actions were guided by these beliefs. The correlation could be spurious; both beliefs and behavior could be effects of some other external factor, such as bureaucratic pressures. Or a politician may be using ideological rhetoric to rationalize actions that were chosen for other reasons. Good historians recognize that self-reports are not always reliable, and consider, for example, that private remarks are more revealing than ghostwritten speeches; and diaries are more reliable than memoirs written many years later. But even then, historians assume that their subjects are acting purposively.[40]

Beginning in the 1930s, social psychologists tried to correlate attitudes with behavior, with highly disappointing results. People did not behave in a way that was consistent with their attitudes in different types of situations, prompting some to wonder if attitudes really existed. Since the mid-1960s, attitude theorists have achieved greater success in predicting behavior by identifying *when* attitudes guide behavior, in other words, the conditions under which people are guided by their beliefs and evaluations. According to psychologists, whether attitudes predict behavior

38. William H. Dray, *Laws and Explanation in History* (Oxford: Oxford University Press, 1957), pp. 98–99; and William H. Dray, "Concepts of Causation in A.J.P. Taylor's Account of the Origins of the Second World War," *History and Theory*, Vol. 17 (1978), p. 166.

39. Dray, *Laws and Explanation in History*, pp. 98–99.

40. Roberts, *Logic of Historical Explanation*, pp. 165–166, 170–171.

depends on the situation, personal experience, and the strength of the attitude. Newer approaches to attitude also look at *how* cognition influences behavior. In short, social psychologists have engaged in process tracing, uncovering the causal process by which the cause is related to the effect.[41]

Psychological hypotheses about how beliefs affect information-processing provide a way to infer these internal processes. If policymakers are influenced by their general beliefs about the world or other states, then those beliefs should affect their deliberations. We might see biases in an official's selection and interpretation of information, his definition of the situation, or his evaluation of policy alternatives.[42] If an individual has an enduring personality disposition or belief, then we should find continuities in his behavior over time and across different situations. John Lewis Gaddis applies such a test to decide whether Stalin had a disposition to wage cold wars, adducing numerous instances, despite changing circumstances, where Stalin demonstrated suspicion and mistrust of his allies in war, Churchill and Roosevelt. Gaddis concludes that the question of whether Stalin wanted a cold war is "a little like asking: 'does a fish seek water?' Suspicion, distrust, and an abiding cynicism were not only his preferred but his necessary environment; he could not function apart from it."[43]

Primary sources are essential for such fine-grained decision-making analyses. Through memos and letters, we can reconstruct the world as perceived by policymakers at the time, untainted by hindsight. We tend to assume after the fact that we knew what would happen all along.[44] Experiments show that information about the outcome of an event leads subjects to estimate the retrospective probability of the event as higher than they did at a prior occasion, an example of *hindsight bias* or the *knew-it-all-along* effect. Moreover, people are *unaware* of the distorting effects that outcome knowledge has on their memories; they are not

---

41. Susan T. Fiske and Shelley E. Taylor, *Social Cognition*, 2nd ed. (New York: McGraw-Hill, 1991), pp. 8–9, 465–466, 514–515.

42. For a model of how attitudes influence behavior, see Russell H. Fazio, "How Do Attitudes Guide Behavior?" in Richard M. Sorrentino and E. Tory Higgins, eds., *Handbook of Motivation and Cognition* (New York: Guildford Press, 1986), pp. 204–243.

43. John Lewis Gaddis, *We Now Know: Rethinking Cold War History* (Oxford: Oxford University Press, 1997), pp. 21–23, quotation on p. 25.

44. Baruch Fischhoff, "Hindsight ≠ Foresight: The Effect of Outcome Knowledge on Judgment under Uncertainty," *Journal of Experimental Psychology: Human Perception and Performance*, Vol. 104, No. 1 (August 1975), pp. 288–299; and Baruch Fischhoff and Ruth Beyth, "'I Knew It Would Happen': Remembered Probabilities of Once Future Things," *Organizational Behavior and Human Performance*, Vol. 13, No. 1 (1975), pp. 1–16.

consciously trying to put themselves in the best light by shading their recollections. People's judgments of what they knew about factual information, political events, and economic decisions have all been shown to be subject to hindsight bias.[45] Aware of how things turned out, we find it hard to recapture the perspective of decision-makers who could not predict what might happen next. In retrospect, the end of the Cold War seems inevitable, if not overdetermined, although no one predicted it. Through documents we can discover what information policymakers were exposed to and how they interpreted it. In light of the distorting effects of hindsight on memory, though, oral histories and memoirs should be used cautiously, preferably corroborated with documentary evidence.

Because they are working with a different set of questions than political scientists, historians often exclude evidence that would be relevant from a cognitive perspective. No one, for example, took note of Truman's frequent comparison of Stalin to Machine Boss Tom Pendergast, who gave the president his start in Missouri politics. After meeting with Stalin at Potsdam, for example, Truman told an aide that "Stalin is as near like Tom Pendergast as any man I know."[46] Yet, this analogy helps to explain why Truman placed so much emphasis on Stalin's keeping his word, and why he was reluctant to abandon Roosevelt's policy of cooperation despite Stalin's repressive occupation of Bulgaria, Rumania, and Poland. From his superficial resemblance to Pendergast, Truman inferred that Stalin had other characteristics associated with the stereotype of a political boss. In Truman's day, it was thought that a political boss always kept his word. In an interview with a reporter shortly before he died, Pendergast said: "I've never broken my word. Put this down: I've never broken my word to any living human being I gave it to. That is the key to success in politics or anything else." The "code of the politician" held that a man who failed to keep his word could never again be trusted. Truman himself subscribed to this code. It provided a test for him of his ability to work with Stalin.[47] The Pendergast schema helped to shape Truman's expectations about Soviet occupation of Eastern Europe. A

---

45. For reviews of this literature, see Jay J. Christensen-Szalanski and Cynthia F. Willham, "The Hindsight Bias: A Meta-analysis," *Organizational Behavior and Human Decision Processes*, Vol. 48, No. 1 (1991), pp. 147–168; and Scott A. Hawkins and Reid Hastie, "Hindsight: Biased Judgments of Past Events after the Outcomes are Known," *Psychological Bulletin*, Vol. 107, No. 3 (1990), pp. 311–327.

46. Eben Ayers's diary, October 18, 1947, Harry S. Truman Library [hereafter HSTL], cited in Larson, *Origins of Containment*, p. 192.

47. Larson, *Origins of Containment*, pp. 133–134.

machine boss ruled his bailiwick with a firm hand and carried out rigged elections. Indeed, Truman himself was elected to the Senate with "ghost" votes.

Alerted to Truman's use of the Pendergast schema to understand Stalin, I discovered a passage in Truman's diary where he indicated that he did not expect Stalin to conduct elections in Eastern Europe that were any freer than those held in the Tammany machine's jurisdiction in New York City. Truman held a meeting with Roosevelt's adviser Harry Hopkins before sending him to meet with Stalin to resolve U.S.-Soviet differences over Poland. Afterwards, he recorded a summary of his instructions to Hopkins:

He said he'd go, said he understood my position and that he'd make it clear to Uncle Joe Stalin that I knew what I wanted—and that I intended to get it—peace for the world for at least 90 years. That Poland, Rumania, Bulgaria, Czechoslovakia, Austria, Yugoslavia, Latvia, Lithuania, Estonia et al. made no difference to U.S. interests only so far as World Peace is concerned. That Poland ought to have a "free election," at least as free as Hague, Tom Pendergast, Joe Martin, or Taft would allow in their respective bailiwicks. That . . . Uncle Joe should make some sort of jesture [sic] whether he means it or not to keep it before our public that he intends to keep his word. Any smart political boss will do that.[48]

That Truman viewed Stalin as another Pendergast suggests other hypotheses: that political leaders tend to view international events in terms of preconceived patterns or schemas; and that politicians draw from their own domestic political experience in dealing with their foreign counterparts.[49] It may be true that the discipline of political science rewards scholars who come up with new theories, not researchers who uncover new facts. But new theories must come from somewhere, and a theorist can just as well get ideas from looking at the real world as from speculation.

When a theory does not work out, one should try a different argument. For example, my initial hunch that attribution theory from social psychology explained the origins of Cold War beliefs was wrong. I had conjectured that after World War II, U.S. officials were inclined to explain

---

48. Truman diary, May 23, 1945, Truman Papers, President's Secretary File: "Longhand Memos," HSTL, cited in Larson, *Origins of Containment*, p. 177.

49. The first hypothesis is proposed by Yuen Foong Khong, *Analogies at War: Korea, Munich, Dien Bien Phu, and the Vietnam Decisions of 1965* (Princeton: Princeton University Press, 1992); the second by James M. Goldgeier, *Leadership Style and Soviet Foreign Policy: Stalin, Khrushchev, Brezhnev, Gorbachev* (Baltimore: Johns Hopkins University Press, 1994).

Soviet actions in Eastern Europe in terms of dispositional qualities such as ideological expansionism or Russian insecurity while overlooking situational pressures and circumstances such as Soviet diplomatic isolation and the experience of the recent invasion by Germany. What ruled out this interpretation was the timing of the change in Truman's image of the Soviet Union: he did not adopt Cold War beliefs about the Soviet Union until some time *after* he made the Truman Doctrine speech.

That Truman changed his policy before altering relevant beliefs was very disturbing to me because we normally think of beliefs as causing behavior rather than the reverse. I had to go back to social psychological theories of attitude change to find out why Truman could have changed U.S. policy toward the Soviet Union, then adopted supporting beliefs later. Self-perception theory holds that people often either do not have firm beliefs on a particular issue or do not know what their beliefs are. For such issues, people may try to reconstruct what they believe by remembering how they have acted in the past. Thus, someone might try to infer her beliefs on global warming by recalling whether she donated money to the Sierra Club or signed a petition favoring greater conservation. Thus, according to self-perception theory, people use their behavior as a guide to what they really believe. When an individual has no strong preexisting beliefs but acts anyway, largely in response to external pressures or social cues, she may later form beliefs that explain and justify her behavior. After Truman made the Truman Doctrine speech, he had to rationalize his use of ideological rhetoric for what was really an attempt to preserve the balance of power. He adopted an image of the Soviet Union that supported his shift to a policy of containment.[50] Other puzzling aspects of Truman's behavior were also consistent with self-perception theory—his inconsistency, propensity to say things off the top of his head, and waffling. Thus, self-perception theory helped to make sense out of behavior that was anomalous from the standpoint of other social psychological theories that assume that people have a need for consistency and try to preserve their beliefs in the face of discrepant information.

Political scientists who consign historical analyses to the category of anecdote complain that case studies are unscientific because history can say anything you want. Without examining the documents on which historical arguments are built, it *is* difficult to know which interpretation seems to accord best with available evidence. Some well-established political science theories may be based on erroneous or outdated histo-

---

50.   Larson, *Origins of Containment*, pp. 318–319, 342–343.

ries. By checking out the documents for themselves, political scientists could discriminate between competing explanations of the same event.[51]

In sum, historians try to uncover the background conditions underlying complex historical events, the purposive acts of historical figures trying to make the best of the situation, and the moral consequences of those actions. Because historians and political scientists approach their topics with different sets of questions, it is all the more incumbent on political scientists to carry out their *own* historical research. Standard historical accounts probably will not contain the kind of data that political scientists need to test a theoretical hypothesis.

But there is no guidebook for political scientists on how to use primary sources. In addition to advice from my dissertation adviser Alexander George and from Barton Bernstein, I studied books such as John Lewis Gaddis's *The United States and the Origins of the Cold War, 1941–1947* to figure out how historians constructed their narratives using primary sources. Below, I discuss some lessons that I drew.[52]

Documents in Context

Political scientists try to find generalizations across time and space, a quest that makes us insensitive to differences in the meaning of language across historical eras or even situations within the same era. It is important to interpret documents within their historic, situational, and communication contexts. We need to understand the purpose of a document and the events leading up to it in order to interpret its meaning correctly. In his book on propaganda analysis, George recommends applying the formula: *who* said *what* to *whom* under *what circumstances* and with *what purpose?*[53] Careful attention to the goals of the communicator and the

---

51. Ian S. Lustick discusses the dangers of using secondary sources reflecting historians' "selection biases," but argues that political scientists can guard against error by highlighting differences between competing historiographical schools, justifying the choice of one school over another, and selecting points of convergence between schools. Lustick does not, however, explain how a political scientist is to judge between competing claims of different schools. Nor does he deal with the problem of missing data, when historians have not found evidence on subjects of interest to political scientists. See "History, Historiography, and Political Science: Multiple Historical Records and the Problem of Selection Bias," *American Political Science Review*, Vol. 90, No. 3 (September 1996), pp. 605–618.

52. John Lewis Gaddis, *The United States and the Origins of the Cold War, 1941–1947* (New York: Columbia University Press, 1972).

53. Alexander L. George, *Propaganda Analysis* (Westport, Conn.: Greenwood Press, 1973), pp. 37–44.

situation should address Richard Ned Lebow's concerns that historical subjects might plant erroneous documents for the record or keep their private preferences secret.

The author of a memorandum or speaker at a meeting may be trying to ingratiate himself with superiors, create a favorable impression of himself, put himself on the record in case of leaks, or persuade others to adopt her preferred policy. Whatever her goals, we cannot directly infer the communicator's state of mind from her arguments without considering her immediate aims. We must consider what anyone in that situation would say, given those objectives. For example, Truman gave a speech in Central Park on Navy Day on October 27, 1945, in a setting that dramatized U.S. military power. Forty-seven fighting ships were anchored along the Hudson River. As he cruised up the river, all forty-seven gave him a twenty-one-gun salute. Overhead, 1,200 planes flew. Truman was trying to get the Congress to approve universal military training, at a time when everyone was anxious to "bring the boys home." Thus, it is not surprising that Truman emphasized U.S. military power and the need for strong armed forces. Truman announced that the United States would not share the information needed to manufacture the atomic bomb with the Soviet Union; armed strength was the only guarantee of U.S. security; and the United States in its foreign policy would not approve "any compromise with evil."[54] The speech did not indicate that Truman was beginning the arms race or had abandoned the policy of cooperating with the Soviet Union. In the same speech, Truman reminded the public that in the past, alliances had disintegrated when the common enemy was defeated. He declared that the former allies must take control of history and mold it in the direction of continued cooperation. Truman asserted there were no conflicts among the great powers that could not be resolved.[55] If Truman had *not* spoken about the importance of military power on Navy Day, if he had instead called for cuts in defense spending or reliance on diplomacy, his address would have been considered an affront to the military.

Public pressures or role demands can help us to infer whether a politician is expressing his true beliefs or trying to please a constituency. For example, Truman succeeded to the presidency because of the sudden, unexpected death of Roosevelt, the man who had led the nation out of the Depression and to victory in World War II, a master politician who had been popularly elected four times. Having little preparation, Truman's insecurity was manifest. He compensated for his feelings of inade-

---

54. Larson, *Origins of Containment*, p. 230.

55. Ibid., p. 231.

quacy by quickly agreeing with State Department officials who, fed up with the difficulties of cooperating with a suspicious Soviet ally, recommended that Truman "get tough with the Russians." But when Truman realized that such a policy might bring on another war, he quickly shifted course and sent Roosevelt's trusted adviser Harry Hopkins to work out a deal with Stalin on Eastern Europe.[56] Lack of preparation and pressure to make decisions led Truman to follow others' recommendations.

That officials may use statements for instrumental purposes means that we should not view one document as conclusive proof; it should be part of a pattern. Political scientists should not follow the bad example of revisionists who wave a single document as proof of a radical new interpretation. One or two documents do not stand alone as evidence. If a document is construed as evidence of an official's beliefs or outlook, there should be more than one expression of such sentiments. The president may have been indulging himself with a flight of fancy, thinking aloud, expressing his frustration, or testing out a new idea. A memo may not be representative of policy at the time. A disgruntled lower-level official might have written it, without the knowledge of his superior. Military officials write contingency plans. During and immediately after World War II, officials wrote contingency plans for war against the Soviet Union. These planning exercises do not prove that U.S. officials considered starting a war. Before concluding that we have found a "smoking gun," we need to see whether a document is part of a larger pattern.

The Role of Newspapers

Newspapers are essential for establishing context. News accounts can help to establish the atmosphere of the times, the purpose of speeches or statements, or the public reaction to a statement. Newspapers help to show what information a policymaker had and provide clues about what events they regarded as important. Policymakers often rely more on the *New York Times* for information about what is happening abroad than they do on classified intelligence reports, which are often delayed as they pass up through the bureaucracy. In this way, newspapers help us to recapture the perspective of officials at the time. For example, the *New York Times* reported the essence of the "secret" spheres of influence agreement between Churchill and Stalin in October 1944. Walter Lippmann applauded President Roosevelt for sending an observer to the Churchill-Stalin talks, rather than assert an interest in an area where the United States was not

---

56. Ibid., pp. 147–148, 157–158, 176–177.

willing to guarantee a settlement. "Of course there are spheres of influence," Lippmann wrote. "Is anyone going to argue that the influence of the United States is not greater in the Caribbean Sea than it is in the Baltic, the Black Sea, or the eastern Mediterranean? Or is anyone going to argue that the Soviet influence should be equally great in Central America and in Central Europe?"[57] The *New York Times* story occasioned no protest over Soviet dominance of Eastern Europe, suggesting that U.S. citizens did not object to classic spheres of influence.

Immediate events affect the beliefs that policymakers express. Politicians like Truman are often ambivalent; they may have several contradictory beliefs, and the belief that is evoked depends on what is salient to them at the time. They may say different things on different occasions depending on what is on their minds. For example, in October 1945, Soviet troop movements seemed aimed at intimidating Iran and Turkey. In mid-October, Truman told his staff that during the Potsdam conference, Churchill had warned Stalin that the Pope was concerned about Poland. "How many divisions does the Pope have?" Stalin retorted. Yet, the incident probably never happened. The minutes of the Potsdam Conference contain no record of this exchange. On October 26, however, Truman told his cabinet that "we were not going to let the public know the extent to which the Russians had tried our patience but that we were going to find some way to get along with the Russians."[58]

By helping us to reconstruct the environment in which a document was written, newspapers can help the investigator to infer the actor's goals. Why did Truman invite Stalin to visit the United States in the middle of the Iranian Crisis in March 1946? Democratic Senator Tom Connally made a speech in which he called for resumption of meetings of the Big Three heads of state. Influential columnists such as Anne O'Hare McCormick and Walter Lippmann urged that the great powers hold another meeting to avert the collapse of the Grand Alliance. Truman wrote Stalin reminding him of his invitation to the Soviet leader to visit the United States: "You were kind enough to say that you would like to do that. Why can you not arrange to come at this time. I certainly would be delighted to have you do so." On March 22, 1946, in answer to

---

57. Pertinax, "Balkan 'Spheres' Decided in Moscow," *New York Times*, October 27, 1944; and Walter Lippmann, "Today and Tomorrow," *Washington Post*, October 19, 1944.

58. Ayers diary, October 16, 1945, HSTL; Henry Wallace diary, October 26, 1945, in John Blum, ed., *The Price of Vision: The Diary of Henry Wallace, 1942–1946* (Boston: Houghton Mifflin, 1973), pp. 501–502, quoted in Larson, *Origins of Containment*, pp. 226, 229.

questions submitted to him by an Associated Press correspondent, Stalin said that he "attached great importance" to the United Nations, although the Security Council was considering the Iranian complaint against the Soviet Union for refusing to withdraw its troops from Iran as it had promised. That same day, Truman told the U.S. ambassador to the Soviet Union, Walter Bedell Smith, to "tell Stalin I had always held him to be a man to keep his word. Troops in Iran after March 2 upset that theory. Also told him to urge Stalin to come to U.S.A."[59] Stalin's statement gave Truman hope that the Soviet leader favored maintaining the policy of U.S.-Soviet cooperation and suggested that another high-level meeting between Truman and Stalin could improve their two countries' relations.

Journalistic analyses and interpretations of speeches provide a code book by which to decipher the meaning of a document. Newspaper columnists' accounts suggest that "tough" speeches made by Secretary of State James Byrnes and Truman in 1946 were a continuation of a policy of cooperation with the Soviet Union, not the beginnings of containment. For example, in his February 28, 1946, speech to the Overseas Press Club, Secretary Byrnes criticized Soviet occupation practices when he said that no country had the right to maintain troops in other states without their consent; to help itself to enemy properties before a reparations settlement; or to conduct a war of nerves to achieve strategic ends. But Byrnes's reproach, while unprecedented, did not indicate that he was changing U.S. policy toward the Soviet Union. James Reston reported that "the general feeling among those who know the habits of Mr. Byrnes, his colleagues at the State Department, the pressure of work on him in many areas, and his political approach to national and international problems is that the pronouncement . . . was something in between a speech and a policy." While Byrnes's address might "result in a firmer policy," the general conclusion was that "the speech preceded the policy and not vice versa." New York Times columnist Edwin L. James agreed that "it is too early to say that this country has worked out an all-embracing policy vis-a-vis the vigorous foreign policy of the USSR."[60] In his speech to the opening session of the United Nations General Assembly in October 1946, Truman admitted that there were differences among the Allies. But he insisted that it was not necessary to exaggerate these disagreements, and

59. New York Times, March 13, 1946; Walter Lippmann, Washington Post, March 14, 1946; Truman to Stalin, March 19, 1946, Truman Papers, President's Secretary File (PSF): "Russia: Stalin," HSTL; Daily Sheets, March 23, 1946, Truman Papers, PSF: Presidential Appointment File, HSTL, quoted in Larson, Origins of Containment, pp. 268–269, 272.

60. New York Times, March 3, 1946, quoted in Larson, Origins of Containment, p. 260.

that no differences of interest stood in the way of settling their problems. According to a *New York Times* editorial, Truman "expressed the firm belief of our Government that despite all the disappointments which have accompanied the business of making peace, this is still One World, compact and indivisible."[61]

Newspapers enable researchers to develop a chronology of important events that is unbiased by hindsight or interpretation. Once we know how an event turned out, we automatically update our mental stories, selecting certain evidence, leaving out extraneous details, so that the ending is immanent in the details.[62] Conventional historical narratives come to emphasize particular events while omitting other happenings that were perhaps more consequential at the time. It is important to establish an accurate chronology because the sequence of events tells us *who* was responding to *what*. We tend to assume that the other state's behavior is internally generated, and overlook evidence that it could be responding to our moves. For example, in December 1957, Soviet Premier Nikolai Bulganin sent a public letter to Eisenhower calling for a test ban and a nuclear-free zone in Central Europe, just days before the North Atlantic Treaty Organization (NATO) heads of state met to discuss putting intermediate range ballistic missiles in Europe. The timing of the Soviets' offer suggests that they were worried that West Germany might gain access to U.S. nuclear weapons. From January through April 1958, Khrushchev sent more public letters proposing disarmament measures including a nuclear-free zone, test ban, and disengagement of U.S. and Soviet forces in Europe. He backed up his proposals by unilaterally reducing Soviet conventional forces by 300,000. Through a variety of channels, Khrushchev indicated that he wanted a summit meeting with Eisenhower to discuss such issues as a nuclear-free zone in East and West Germany, Poland, and Czechoslovakia and a ban on nuclear testing. At Secretary of State John Foster Dulles's insistence, however, Eisenhower maintained that there must be preliminary agreement at lower levels before he would meet with Khrushchev. Since Dulles did not intend to reach any agreements with the Soviet Union, Eisenhower's condition ruled out a summit meeting. In November 1958, Khrushchev initiated the Berlin Crisis by threatening to turn over access routes to the East Germans unless the United States agreed to make West Berlin a free city. But the

---

61.   Thomas J. Hamilton, *New York Times*, October 24, 1946; *New York Times* editorial, October 24, 1946, quoted in Larson, *Origins of Containment*, p. 299.

62.   Hawkins and Hastie, "Hindsight," pp. 323–324.

Soviet leader hinted at his willingness to withdraw the deadline if the United States would *begin* negotiations.[63]

Unless one knows the background of Khrushchev's attempts to meet with Eisenhower and to obtain some agreement that the Germans would not be allowed to have nuclear weapons, the Soviet ultimatum appears puzzling. George Kennan did not find it surprising that the Soviets would want to prevent the West Germans from obtaining nuclear weapons. Kennan later observed that "We might well have foreseen that Moscow would be likely to reactivate [the Berlin] question following the North Atlantic Treaty Organization decision to introduce nuclear weapons and missiles into the continental NATO defense, and particularly into the armed forces establishment of Western Germany."[64] The timing of Khrushchev's ultimatum in light of the Soviets' failure to obtain some assurances that West Germany would not be allowed to acquire nuclear weapons suggests that Khrushchev was using Berlin as a lever to get the United States to promise not to share nuclear weapons with the Germans. But standard historical accounts of the Berlin crisis typically omit Khrushchev's prior peace efforts. Historians are not typically interested in non-events—the peace proposal that was not discussed, the offer that was not considered. Such non-events are critical for analyzing missed opportunities.

Similarly, the events leading up to the Cuban missile crisis—the breakdown of negotiations over Berlin, Khrushchev's humiliating withdrawal of his second Berlin ultimatum, his plans to visit Kennedy in November and make an address at the United Nations—all suggest that Khrushchev intended to use the missiles in Cuba as a bargaining chip for changes in the status of West Berlin.[65] Recent archival research has tended to confirm this hypothesis.[66]

Toward Complementary Efforts

Using primary sources to test theory can contribute both to our understanding of the causes of the Cold War and to general knowledge about foreign policy. Diplomatic historians can formulate more scientific expla-

---

63. Larson, *Anatomy of Mistrust,* pp. 75–79, 87.

64. George F. Kennan, "Proposal for Western Survival," *New Leader,* November 16, 1959, p. 10, cited in Larson, *Anatomy of Mistrust,* p. 88.

65. Larson, *Anatomy of Mistrust,* pp. 143–144.

66. Ernest R. May and Philip D. Zelikow, *The Kennedy Tapes: Inside the White House During the Cuban Missile Crisis* (Cambridge, Mass.: Harvard University Press, 1997), pp. 679–680, 691.

nations of the Cold War by searching for the mechanisms that produce events rather than background conditions. By uncovering the causal mechanisms underlying decisions, history can illuminate how policymakers might learn from the past, take control of foreign policy, and avert unwanted outcomes in the future.

Political scientists can also contribute by using primary sources to uncover the causal connections between events. Often, social psychology can illuminate how policymakers' beliefs influenced their decisions by making more specific predictions about each stage of their mental operations, from definition of the situation, and selection of relevant information, to the adoption of belief-consistent behavior. The causes of foreign policy decisions may not always lie in the beliefs or cognitive processes of policymakers. Sometimes foreign policy can be explained by domestic politics or organizational processes. Quite possibly, leaders selected a policy on the basis of cost-benefit analysis. But in order to make such judgments, political scientists need to open up the black box and reveal the mechanisms underlying foreign policy behavior. By looking at the world the way decision-makers did and trying to reconstruct their calculations, political scientists can understand better how and when public opinion, Congress, and ideology influence the formation of foreign policy.

Political scientists can use theory for disciplined imagination of what might have happened if a particular cause had been different. Such counterfactual statements can help us to identify turning points in the Cold War, where the history of the relations between the superpowers might have taken a different path. Explaining these critical turning points will then contribute not only to better theory, but to lessons for policymakers.

Chapter 13

Postscript: Historical Science and Cold War Scholarship

William C. Wohlforth

The Cold War is a tough test for scholarship. Its importance was so obvious that both political scientists and historians overcame disciplinary prejudices (against studying singular events, or doing current history) to study it intensively for four decades. The record of scholarly claims concerning the Cold War is open for all to examine. It ended suddenly and in a manner no one expected. Its ending produced a rapid outflow of new evidence. Much can be learned about what scholars do (as opposed to what they claim to do) by answering a few basic questions concerning this series of events: To what extent is new learning about the event based on knowing its outcome as opposed to the cumulation of new evidence? How do scholars relate their old arguments and explanations to new evidence?

Three major points emerge from the chapters by Deborah Welch Larson and John Lewis Gaddis that relate directly to the subject of this volume. First, historians and political scientists who study international relations are frequently in competition with each other. The comforting notion that somehow we are doing completely different things and need not reconcile our contrasting practices is belied by the example of Gaddis and Larson, who are both obviously trying to explain the Cold War. Second, the two disciplines often differ so deeply in their approaches to their subjects that they talk past each other, as Gaddis and Larson often do here. Third, however, there are few members of either discipline willing to defend the proposition that scholarship cannot improve; that the way things have been done is the best possible approach to the subject matter; and that there is no need for new thinking of any kind. Both Gaddis and Larson agree that scholarship on the Cold War is not as good as it can be. My main criticism of their chapters is that they say too little about why or how international relations scholars and historians should improve their work. I shall end by arguing that the questions I posed about the Cold War's end and the sudden advent of new evidence help to complete the criticisms begun by Larson and Gaddis.

I.

Unlike many of their colleagues, Larson and Gaddis understand that historians and political scientists do compete with each other. They both try to explain complex historical events. Larson does not take refuge in the notion that political scientists' interest in generalization somehow absolves them of the need to explain specific events. Her chapter, like her books, is chock full of explanatory claims about specific episodes in the Cold War. Testing a theory requires coding cases, and the placement of any case in any particular box presupposes an explanation of that case. One can argue this point on methodological grounds, but the argument ends the moment you show an international historian your list of cases.[1] He or she will quickly show you how the coding of cases depends on an explanation of them—an explanation that is and always will be contested among historians. For example, in her recent book, Larson finds that missed opportunities for cooperation in the Cold War were the result of certain general tendencies explained by social psychology and rational-choice theory.[2] Unlike some of her colleagues in political science, she recognizes that this finding hinges on quintessentially historical claims: the contention that there really were missed opportunities, and that they were caused by the pathologies she identifies. Those claims are, and will likely always be, contested by historians.

Moreover, as Gaddis asks, what is theory *for*, if not to help us understand complex historical events? Most scholars of international relations think that good theory should inform policy choices. From 1945 to 1989, the Cold War *was* policy. Why should theory stop making strong claims about a policy problem the moment it becomes history? Obscured in the comforting "different strokes for different folks" argument is the fact that if social scientists' aspiration for general theories were ever achieved, the

---

1. Political scientists who favor testing across large numbers of cases frequently seek coding rules that do not depend on contestable historical interpretations of actors' preferences and motivations. In addition, they argue that robust empirical results across large numbers of cases outweigh any uncertainty caused by questionable coding validity. See, for an example, Paul Huth and Bruce M. Russett, "Testing Deterrence Theory: Rigor Makes a Difference," *World Politics*, Vol. 42, No. 4 (July 1990), pp. 466–501. But note that notwithstanding their theoretical rigor, Huth and Russett still must reach judgments on critical cases by evaluating standard historical evidence.

2. Deborah Welch Larson, *Anatomy of Mistrust: U.S.-Soviet Relations During the Cold War* (Ithaca: Cornell University Press, 1997).

result would be superior (because scientific) explanations of complex historical events. The theories social scientists seek would explain laws; and those laws would explain events by subsumption. If the event were appreciably complex, it would be broken down into parts that could be explained by subsuming them under covering laws, much as the operation of a complex machine might be explained scientifically by showing how known physical laws govern the functioning of its many parts.[3]

Who would make such a claim? Read Larson: "a scholar knowledgeable about psychology and history might have a more veridical understanding of what U. S. policymakers were doing than they themselves did at the time." If you buy this claim, the explanation based on this theory is simply better than what historians can offer. No archival digging, no historian's insight can beat what Larson promises for this theory. In short, the goal of social-scientific international relations scholarship is profoundly competitive with most historians' understanding of their craft. Success in theory-building would not, as some argue, leave historians the job of explaining specific events. If international relations became a successful social science, the historian's job would be relegated to telling good stories and probing history for morality lessons.

The other side of this coin is illuminated by Gaddis. He accepts the standard "different strokes" idea that historians are interested mainly in explaining particular events. But unlike many, he recognizes the full implications of this fact: the historian's interest in particular generalization is based on a reasoned judgment that this is the only way to study world politics. Historians' practice is a rejection of the very idea that events can be neatly coded as cases to test theories. So historians cannot be neutral toward social science practice. If they believe in the rightness of their methods, they must consciously reject the social science approach of many international relations scholars, including Larson. If general theories explaining nontrivial regularities of world politics were possible, they would be powerful tools of historical explanation that historians could not ignore. The fact that historians by and large no longer join the quest for these theories is, in Gaddis's view, a considered judgment based on historians' centuries of experience with the complex, nonreplicable subject matter of world politics. Thus, Gaddis makes the case that the "different strokes" argument sidesteps: if their approach to their subject is defensible, then historians are not only theorists of international relations, they are actually better theorists than most political scientists, whose approach to international relations violates its true nature.

---

3. This is the standard positivist response to the problem of complex events. See Carl G. Hempel, *Aspects of Scientific Explanation* (New York: Free Press, 1965), chap. 12.

II.

So, these chapters argue with each other. But their arguments often pass each other by, for the way each treats the other's discipline is bound to vex rather than persuade. Larson's chapter will infuriate historians because its main point is that political scientists are better at explaining historical events than historians are. According to Larson, to the extent that they are even concerned with the dispassionate explanation of events, historians are hamstrung by their aversion to social science theory. As a result, historians "have not tried to explain why leaders viewed the world as they did or why they chose a particular course of action over another." If that statement surprises me, it's bound to be news to historians. What would historians gain by mastering basic social psychology? They would know that "people frequently behave contrary to their professed beliefs; their convictions are often internally contradictory; and on many important issues they have no stable, preconceived notions whatsoever." Moreover, "officials make snap judgments using whatever information is at hand, and then later rationalize." Theory tells us that policymakers may not know "how their actions will influence the calculations of others, resulting in unintended consequences." It is difficult to imagine that insights such as these will convince historians of the utility of social science theory.

The underlying problem with Larson's argument is that there are no generally accepted theories that make nontrivial predictions (or "retrodictions") about decision-making. Obscured in her chapter is the fact that the very psychological theories for which she makes such bold claims are themselves matters of contention among social scientists. Political psychologists aren't the only political scientists who think they can out-explain historians. Game theorists sometimes make such claims as well, and they build their models on the same rationality assumptions that Larson questions.[4] Indeed, it is striking that Larson criticizes *historians* for adopting rationalistic models of explanation, since that basic model is by far the dominant one in political science today. The veracity of psychological or rational choice models of decision-making is contested among inter-

---

4. See Robert H. Bates et al., *Analytic Narratives* (Princeton: Princeton University Press, 1998). Many exponents of game theory in international relations, by contrast, are strong believers in the "different strokes" idea, and share with postmodernists a deep skepticism about the possibility of traditional historical explanation—that is, obtaining true explanations of complex events through the careful analysis of historical evidence.

national relations scholars. Why should historians favor one over the other?

Gaddis's chapter will similarly be irksome to scholars of international relations, mainly because it never discusses the kinds of theories most of them think they are trying to build. His main target seems to be Waltz—a foil he shares with 98 percent of international relations scholars. All Gaddis's talk of physics envy, paleontology, and biology is going to have little effect on scholars like Larson, who use psychology, or on those who use game theory. Perhaps Gaddis has good reasons for why historians should reject these theories—written, after all, explicitly to explain human choice under uncertainty, and presumably therefore more relevant to explaining the Cold War than paleontology—but he does not spell them out here.[5] Moreover, Gaddis never discusses the one activity that is, love it or leave it, the mark of science: *testing* conjectures. Much of what Gaddis criticizes about the work of international relations scholars concerns things they think they're doing to make their arguments vulnerable to refutation by testing. For example, Gaddis argues that "by insisting on distinctions between independent and dependent variables, international relations scholars are . . . following the example of chemistry." Actually, they are trying to use the methods of statistics (never mentioned by Gaddis), a basic tool of hypothesis-testing in almost all the social sciences, as well as biology, paleontology, medicine, and other favorites of Gaddis.

Do historians' narratives presuppose causal arguments? My sense is that they very often do—that, in fact, historians often want to have their cake and eat it too by making arguments that presuppose some concrete and testable relationship among variables while insisting that "everything matters" and that any effort to translate the argument into a test somehow violates the "essence of history." The narrative in Gaddis's *We Now Know*, for example, is driven by the difference between the democratic United States, and its resultant full portfolio of "hard" and "soft" power, and the authoritarian Soviet Union, whose international position ultimately rested solely on its military power. Because of this difference, one superpower's bloc was largely consensual and the other's mainly coercive. "The resulting asymmetry," Gaddis argues, "would account, more than anything else, for the origins, escalation, and ultimate outcome

---

5. In an e-mail exchange with Bruce Bueno de Mesquita, Gaddis was quite favorably impressed by the ability of Bueno de Mesquita's rational choice model to simulate the course and end of the Cold War in a way that seemed consistent with how historians think. See James Lee Ray and Bruce Russett, "The Future as Arbiter of Theoretical Controversies: Predictions, Explanations and the End of the Cold War," *British Journal of Political Science*, Vol. 26 (October 1996), pp. 454–455, n. 59.

of the Cold War."[6] Is it just my political scientist's training, or do others detect here a robust causal claim based on independent and dependent variables?

III.

Despite their differences, the two chapters agree on one proposition: things could be better in their respective disciplines. Larson argues that international relations scholars need to use primary historical sources in their research. And Gaddis argues (in one throwaway line, to be sure) that historians ought to come out of the closet and make their implicit theories and methods more explicit. But this agreement undercuts their arguments on behalf of their respective disciplines. Larson's contention that social science theories hold the key to historical explanation is hurt by her acknowledgment that these theories are written by people with little or no experience with primary historical sources. How good can theories be, if they are insensitive to the kinds of data that are available? And Gaddis's argument that historians are the better scientists of world politics is certainly wounded by his admission that they are evasive or ambiguous about their methods. How confident can we be that historians have really adopted their methods to the subject at hand if they never clarify them, vary them, and monitor the results? For all we know, historians have arrived at their current approach to their subject not because these methods are best, but because the discipline is intellectually lazy or hidebound.

Taken together, then, the two preceding chapters amount to a simple criticism of our two fields that has been made before but clearly bears repeating: Political scientists who study international relations expend immense intellectual effort to adopt some laudable scientific practices—logical rigor, clarity, falsifiability—but often with little regard for the nature and limits of historical evidence. Diplomatic historians immerse themselves in the particular details of empirical research, but often with little regard for those same scientific practices. The result is missed opportunities for learning.

Consider the problem with which I began this commentary: the Cold War ended and significant new information suddenly became available. What has been the response of our two fields? In general, the ending of the Cold War has arguably *increased* the gap between history and political science. As noted, as long as the Cold War was policy, international

---

6. John Lewis Gaddis, *We Now Know: Rethinking Cold War History* (Oxford: Clarendon, 1997), p. 17.

relations scholars had a legitimate interest in focusing on it, and they could happily work alongside those few historians bold (or foolhardy) enough to tackle the explanation of an ongoing superpower rivalry. Historians, meanwhile, faced a shortage of archival materials, and, perhaps, a resulting incentive to look to theory to aid inquiry. The Cold War's demise undermined this intellectual alliance. The historians have gained archival data—and the chance to do "real" history, just like their colleagues. The political scientists have lost the Cold War as a policy problem, and gained in its stead another set of historical "cases" of interest only as particular instances of general tendencies.

How are the two fields assimilating the new data on Cold War decision-making? Within the political science subfield of international relations, it is hard to detect any reaction to the new data. The reason is simple: these scholars do not see a clear connection between explaining the Cold War and the veracity of the theories they care about.[7] And the reason they don't is precisely the one Larson identifies. Since political scientists are not accustomed to thinking of international relations as a historical science, they do not write theories or fashion tests that are sensitive to the cumulation of historical data. If political scientists thought that historical data about the Cold War might alter the fate of influential theories, surely they would look forward to new releases with some nervous or eager anticipation. Because international relations theories are not written with an eye toward their evaluation against historical materials—which, after all, account for most of the data on world politics—the sudden appearance of a large new data set on a major international rivalry apparently has no diagnostic utility for contending theories of international politics.

Among historians, there is intense interest in the new evidence, but a confused free-for-all when it comes to connecting the evidence to the larger debates that framed research for so long. In addition to an argument over the probative value of the new evidence, four things are going on simultaneously (often in the same book or article): revisiting old debates with new evidence; revisiting those debates based on knowledge of the outcome; reformulating the debates in response to new evidence; and reformulating based on knowing the outcome. Doubtless an outsider's bias is at work here, but it is hard to read this literature without thinking that it would be much more fruitful if it kept these four activities distinct. What is striking is how rarely historians perform the boring but

---

7. I develop this argument at greater length in "A Certain Idea of Science: How International Relations Theory Avoids the New Cold War History," *Journal of Cold War Studies*, Vol. 1, No. 2 (Winter 2000), pp. 39–60.

instructive exercise of stating exactly what kinds of evidence in which archives would serve to undermine or advance a particular narrative explanation or a larger interpretive school.

Nowadays almost no one believes that evidence alone drives scientific progress, but most acknowledge that there are better and worse ways of clarifying and evaluating conjectures about the world. Few international relations scholars and historians are probably willing to defend the proposition that their respective fields cannot be improved. A clear-eyed look at how the two fields responded to the Cold War's end and the outpouring of new evidence almost certainly would convince die-hard conservatives that we can do better. The idea that international relations theorists need to be more sensitive to the requirements of historical research and historians need to be more self-conscious about theory and method is hardly utopian. The barriers are probably best captured by Stephen Jay Gould's phrase "historical science." To many historians and international relations scholars, these two words are mutually contradictory. They might be right, but there is no way to know until we try to unite the two in new ways.

Chapter 14

Reflections on the History and Theory of Military Innovation and Diffusion

John A. Lynn

The study of rapid and radical military change currently enjoys a vogue among historians, social scientists, and even national security types. Scholarly discussions of transformations in martial practice and technology have produced volumes of narrative and theory, works that might at first glance offer a useful way to explore the relationship between history and political science, perhaps even serving as a bridge between the two. But unfortunately, such expectations are not justified. Nonetheless, even if it does not bridge that gap, the attempt to understand the phenomenon of military revolution takes us toward a better appreciation of the historical discipline per se. This chapter employs the literature on this subject to explore the differing way in which historians treat theory, the unique character of military history within the historical discipline, and the limitations imposed upon inquiry by the structure of the subdiscipline.

The reader should beware that any essay entitled "reflections" is almost certainly doomed to be a collection of personal impressions, and this is no exception to that rule. These pages flow from three decades of experience struggling with the subject of military change, most notably with various assertions that one or another form of military revolution transformed institutions and warfare in Europe. So this is not the normal academic survey of the literature in either military history or, even less, political science. Given the personal nature of this piece, my chosen field, military history, stands at center stage, with social science playing a supporting role.

Military history, despite its advanced age, has yet to achieve maturity, but remains in a permanent state of adolescence. A characteristic of this immaturity is the relative lack of fundamental debate that transcends the level of refighting past wars; and this paucity is one of the central reasons why there still exists no body of general theory on military change. In contrast, political science can boast more theoretical sophistication, yet it has not really confronted military change for its own sake, but simply as one element in discussions of such greater phenomena as state formation and arms competition. Social science consideration of military change has yet to match the complex, many-layered theories that try to describe and predict international behavior. Thus, despite a number of works that take military innovation and transformation as their theme, both military history and political science provide too thin a body of literature to justify the elevated consideration lavished in this volume on international relations. Of course there are many books and a good many more articles on the Military Revolution (however that is defined) of early modern Europe and on the very fashionable topic of the Revolution in Military Affairs (RMA), that is, the impact of high-tech weaponry, communications, and computers on warfare today. But this does not form a coherent whole, and it remains theory-poor.

Cultural Wars in the Discipline of History and the Place of Theory

So much of the discussion contrasting history and political science deals with a perceived difference in their relationship to theory—basically that historians are averse to employing theory, while it is the bread and butter of political science. Even those who deny or want to nuance this generalization seem to take for granted that it is the starting point of any argument. However, the entire premise misses the fact that the discipline of history today has a Janus-faced relationship to theory. To make the complex simple, one can distinguish between a now dominant avant-garde and a more traditional school of historical inquiry. To be sure, in reality, historical opinion lies on a continuum, not simply at two poles, yet the avant-garde/traditional dichotomy says something valid, important, and intensely disturbing about the academic study of history.

In contradiction to the usual social science comments on historians' reluctance to operate on a theoretical level, the avant-garde embraces its version of theory with such passion that it excludes as unworthy anyone and any work that does not. However, the kind of theory that matters so much to the avant-garde is not a type that international relations specialists would feel comfortable with. The avant-garde is most concerned with importing theory generated in philosophy, literary criticism, and anthropology.[1] In general, this kind of theory concerns the perception of reality

---

1. For a condemnation of the avant-garde, see Keith Windschuttle, *The Killing of History: How Literary Critics and Social Theorists Are Murdering Our Past* (New York: Free Press, 1997). This book is, to be sure, alarmist and extreme, but it also provides a very useful handbook concerning the kinds of theory being imported into history.

more than objective conditions. At its most intense this becomes the "linguistic turn," which cut to its essentials argues that an observer's understanding of his or her world is trapped within the "structure" of language. The words we use confine and direct our perception and expression because those words contain prepackaged conclusions and biases. Thus, to uncover the full meaning of a statement, including its hidden biases, its language must be "deconstructed." "Language" here should be broadly defined to include not only words but other "signs" and "representations," which are conceived of as "texts."

Applying these postmodernist theories to historical studies has proved to be corrosive, eating away at necessary props of reasonability and reason that support the study of history. The emphasis on the power of language to shape or even dictate understanding leads to two problems in history: 1) skepticism toward the value of sources, and 2) denial that a historian can convey the story of the past with any accuracy. Following this argument, a document from the past tells us little or nothing about the actual past, because the text is determined by the language and biases of the author. All we can really know from a document is something about the individual who wrote it. Devotees to this point of view sum up assumptions and values that express and determine attitudes and actions in the term "discourse," a term that again emphasizes the function of language. The fact that historians are trapped in the same way as their subjects by their own contemporary "discourses" means that their works are also not really about the past but about themselves. And this pushed to extremes argues that there is little difference between fiction and nonfiction, and it is only honest for a historian to see his or her work as fiction and to adopt a freer, some would say cavalier, use of evidence.

At this point, I must offer some disclaimer, because my colleagues who are excited about language, signs, and texts do not usually pursue them over the edge of the cliff, but stop while they are still supported by solid ground. Certainly, there is something artificial about ascribing philosophical purity to the historical profession in the United States as a whole or even to its avant-garde. In fact, I am less concerned with the extreme version of all of this than I am with the aspects that have found wide circulation, such as concern over the power of language broadly defined. The avant-garde applies its new theoretical bent to the subjects that most concern it: perception and "representation" more than reality itself (which may be unknowable), and the study of the marginalized and downtrodden of history, often portrayed as the "other."

Avant-garde and traditional practitioners are not hermetically sealed into certain specialties of history, although they predominate in different subdisciplines of history. Particularly modish varieties of history where the avant-garde exerts its dominance include women and gender, various forms of ethnic history, post-colonial studies, and the new cultural history, a highly theoretical consideration of popular culture.

Of particular relevance in gauging the present place of theory is the fact that the avant-garde, with its theoretical bent, has come to control the historical profession. Now-unfashionable historical subdisciplines, which include political, economic, diplomatic, and military, have practically become endangered species, at least on university campuses. The most obvious case is military history, as I demonstrated in an article published in 1997.[2] The flagship journal of the discipline, the *American Historical Review* (AHR), provides quantifiable evidence of tastes and tendencies. It has remained firmly in the grasp of the avant-garde over the past two decades, and to put it mildly, military history did not fare well in the hundred issues that appeared from 1977 to 1996. The *AHR* failed to publish a single research article focused on the conduct of the Hundred Years' War, the Thirty Years' War, the Wars of Louis XIV, the War of American Independence, the Revolutionary and Napoleonic Wars, World War I, or World War II; neither did it consider any research article on the Korean War or the Vietnam conflict to be fit for its pages, although it printed three group book reviews on those struggles.

Quite independent of my inquiry, Stephen Haber, David Kennedy, and Stephen Krasner published an article in *International Security* at the same time that mine appeared. It too used the *AHR* as evidence to lament the fate of the history of international relations. They delved deeper, using a forty-year sample from 1955 to 1995 to show the slipping presentation of diplomatic history, which the authors claim fell from an average of 10 percent of the articles published in the *AHR* from 1955 to 1969 down to 0 percent in the decade 1985 to 1995.[3] The *AHR*, that important reflection of, and powerful influence upon, historiographical taste has essentially banished the history of international relations and military history.

When political scientists comment upon the untheoretical nature of the way in which historians deal with the past, they are a bit behind the

---

2. John A. Lynn, "The Embattled Future of Academic Military History," *Journal of Military History*, Vol. 61, No. 4 (October 1997), pp. 777–789.

3. Stephen H. Haber, David M. Kennedy, and Stephen D. Krasner, "Brothers Under the Skin: Diplomatic History and International Relations," *International Security*, Vol. 22, No. 1 (Summer 1997), Table 1, p. 41. The authors, who conclude that diplomatic history has "all but disappeared" from the *AHR*, actually missed a group of four articles on the nature of balance of power in the June 1992 issue, but their point remains.

curve; however, this is understandable, because the historical works they most often employ are products of the traditional wing of the profession. In regard to this traditional wing, there is some truth to the old stereotype that historians are embedded in their case studies and usually reluctant to generalize.[4] The defining characteristic of historians may not be their dedication to the past in general, but their immersion in a *particular* past. By innate inclination followed by intense training and careful screening, historians are experts in one here and now—or one there and then, to be correct. Few historians are historians of it all. Historians almost always specialize in time and place, and by staying in one spot—as opposed to the roaming social scientist—they simply see more there. They are required to master a very broad horizontal sample; thus, the historian of international relations in mid-eighteenth-century Europe must also know a good deal about aristocratic values, Enlightenment philosophy, Baroque music, and Rococo architecture, to say nothing of gender roles and the emerging public sphere. That investment in a particular place and time naturally reveals more layers and draws connections between them. The historian, then, creates more complex models and is reluctant to apply them to other cases, because the more layered and complex a model the more it is anchored in one setting and likely to be unique. Complexity is the enemy of transportability, but general theory must have transportable models. Therefore, in the real world, the oft-noted tendency of historians to favor complex descriptions and explanations, while social scientists prefer examples with a more streamlined form, still rings true.

Popular, Practical, and Academic Military History

Although military history stands soundly on the traditional wing, it is more willing to trim its material and more open to generalizing across boundaries of time and space than are other specialties in the traditional spectrum of history. This results from the peculiar fact that military history has three manifestations: popular, practical, and academic.

Popular military history addresses the great appeal that stories of

---

4. In the symposium published by *International Security,* Vol. 22, No. 1 (Summer 1997), which gave birth to this volume, several contributors argue that it is superficial to state that historians are interested in evidence as opposed to theory, or to point out that historians prefer complex explanations as opposed to the parsimony favored in the social sciences. Several contributors also condemn as shallow any insistence that, as opposed to social scientists, historians are dedicated to the past for its own sake. However, these sophisticated critiques are, I believe, too subtle by half. The more common statement that historians are wedded to their individual cases cuts closer to the bone.

daring-do in combat have always enjoyed ever since cavemen first huddled around a fire, and there is no sign of this interest flagging. This genre is more about entertainment than enlightenment, the male equivalent of the romance novel with its exciting and escapist promise of allowing the reader to fantasize about putting himself in the plot. Too much complexity just confuses the reader, so this literature tends to portray all battles as decisive and all commanders as brilliant or dastardly. While some of this genre is good, much is not, or is at least very limited in context and unsophisticated in argument. It is frustrating to me to be found guilty for what my university colleagues find weak in popular military history.

Practical military history contrasts with the popular genre; it is military history as sponsored, employed, and practiced by the military. It is about business not pleasure, hard reality not fantasy. Whether practical military history is better, worse, or just different depends on the particular piece of work you are discussing. The practical genre has many demonstrable values, but there are undeniable pressures when working for the Department of Defense to serve Mars before Clio. Understandably, the military has its own agenda, entirely proper to its purposes, but which restricts the range of historical studies. War college history is directed toward learning the lessons of past experience, usually quite recent, and directing these toward current problems and future conflicts. However, the search for useful lessons learned can lead historians to focus rather narrowly, or to leave out inconvenient or distracting detail. This sort of history tends to assign value by how good a historian is at carving the past into a shape meaningful to the present-minded military.

Academic military history differs from popular and practical varieties in standards, foci, and goals. In contrast to popular history, scholarly inquiry requires an exhaustive use of evidence and a consideration of the full historical context. It also evidences interest in a broader range of influences, consequences, and periods as it emphasizes warfare and military institutions as historical subjects worthy of study for their own sakes. More importantly, the primary purpose of academic military history is not practical in any immediate sense; rather it is to achieve, or at least to strive for, an understanding of the past as a value unto itself—a goal shared with the entire historical profession. In my unquestionably prejudiced opinion it is the most demanding but also the freest form.

A certain amount of overlap links these different varieties, and the same individual might be capable in all three genres. How well he or she does so without distortion is a case-by-case matter of integrity and intelligence, but there is a temptation to try to please the crowd, and the flesh is weak. But beyond this important issue of quality, the mixture of approaches exerts another influence, an influence that to an early modernist like myself is also detrimental. Academic military history is all too often concerned with the recent past, as opposed to more distant eras, and this results from, or at the very least is reinforced by, the needs and rewards of practical military history. As a general rule, the more one specializes on the last war, or last wars, the more the defense community is likely to take you seriously. Twentieth-century specialists abound and receive the perks, payments, and appearance of influence that the military provides. The recent interest in the RMA has given some of us who study the Military Revolution fleeting attention, but this will not last. The fact is that those who study remote eras enjoy less cachet, even among academic military historians, than those whose expertise is more "front-loaded."

Another problem that seems to be more rampant among military historians than those who pursue other subdisciplines is the search for the quick and easy answer. You will find this everywhere, but there is good reason to see it at work among the chroniclers of conflict. We study a world of apparent victory and defeat, winners and losers, geniuses and fools. The search for decisive battles infects both generals and historians.[5] One reads a good deal of malarkey, particularly in popular military history, of how the fate of battle may rest on that one horseshoe nail. Military history can become the land of the reductionist par excellence. It need not be, but it often is. Again, this means that while historians as a rule like complex models, military historians are often willing to produce far more simple ones.

This tendency to cut and trim is far from universal among military historians, but it is certainly a factor. It can be clumsy and simplistic at times. While at an unnamed conference some time ago, the brilliant and demanding Jon Sumida and I steamed at what at the moment struck us as a misuse of history by a panel of social scientists. They were quoting the past record, bringing forward some simplistic analysis provided by a convenient military historian. At this point, Jon fumed, "Political scientists get the military historians they deserve!" The fact is that military historians are willing to be on the "deserved" list all too often, and some very odd stuff wins praise.[6]

---

5. See, for example, Russell Weigley, *The Age of Battles: The Quest for Decisive Warfare from Breitenfeld to Waterloo* (Bloomington: Indiana University Press, 1991). In fact, I think the concern for decisive battle is a Napoleonic legacy accepted by military historians. In contrast, consider the hesitance of Louis XIV and other early modern commanders to engage in battle. See John A. Lynn, *The Wars of Louis XIV, 1667–1714* (London: Longman, 1999), particularly chap. 8 on "war-as-process."

6. For a discussion of an example of weak history which has won great approval, see John A. Lynn, "The History of Logistics and *Supplying War*," in John A. Lynn, ed.,

At this same conference Jon uttered another quotable judgment about a political scientist at the podium who seemed cavalier in his use of historical detail: "What they don't realize is that if they get the facts a little wrong, they do not get the results a little wrong, they get them all wrong." This is no place to get into a discussion of inputs into complex systems and chaos theory, but it is worth stressing the need for extreme care in choosing examples. But again this needs to be a warning for both social scientists and military historians.

The Poverty of Theory and Knowledge

Despite the willingness of military historians to trim and generalize, they have not displayed any great ability to postulate theory. To qualify as a theory, a statement about people, institutions, processes, and events must be systematic and broad, that is, covering a variety of individual cases; it can be descriptive, but necessarily in a general sense; and it is preferably analytical, claiming validity over a wide range of time and circumstance. It need not predict—there is something bizarre about predicting the past—but it must claim to explain in a fairly universal sense. In contrast, particular hypotheses deal with unique situations; such hypotheses are extremely common, in fact they are essential to any interpretation, and they are not our concern here. In military history, particular hypotheses abound, but general theories are rare.

The discussion of military change by historians and social scientists bears poor comparison with the other matters covered in this volume. The fields of diplomatic history and international relations theory have produced abundant literatures, and their richness allows for sophisticated and rewarding discussions of differing assumptions and methodologies and of the way in which the two fields can benefit by cross-pollination. In contrast, the theoretical literature on military change is neither broad nor deep.

There are some exceptions to the general superficiality of comparative literature in military history. One could except the large number of intriguing and intelligent works on Clausewitz from this general condemnation. Unquestionably, references to *On War* constitute the greatest conscious application of theory within the field of military history. Also, it might be claimed that the study of soldiers' motivations has produced a challenging literature, from S.L.A. Marshall to Omar Bartov and James McPherson. In addition, there is the varied and valuable outpouring of

---

Feeding Mars: Logistics in Western Warfare from the Middle Ages to the Present (Boulder, Colo.: Westview Press, 1993).

scholarly efforts lavished today on the Military Revolution of early modern Europe, the most relevant discussion for our purposes. This will be dealt with shortly. Despite such notable efforts, military history is not blessed by a high level of scholarly debate on important subjects. Of course there is a cottage industry refighting past wars and second-guessing strategists, but this is not our concern here. Part of the lack of debate can be ascribed to the fact that academic military history suffers a dearth of practitioners. It has always been something of a pariah field, and the current dominance of the avant-garde has simply made a bad situation worse. Thus, military history has not attracted a large assembly of first-rate scholars, although its small crew includes some great intellects. Therefore, academic military history has but rarely attained critical mass. Large areas remain uncultivated or are so sparsely populated that they do not find a number of toilers working the same plot of land. In particular, there simply is no definable body of literature dealing with *general* phenomena of military change to compare with the theoretical literature on international relations. Granted, scholars can be, and have been, asked to focus on the issue of military revolutions for a particular conference or a special project, often driven today by the military's concern with the RMA.[7] But these interesting examples of scholarly entrepreneurship are no substitute for a self-generating tradition of research and discussion.

There is not much more on the social science side of the equation. The most impressive political science literature weighing military change as a key variable is that addressing state formation and civil-military relations.[8] Again, concern with, and funding for, considerations of the RMA have kick-started some interest in the general phenomenon, but whether it will bear fruit in the long run is still unclear. The political science literature on war and state formation is itself relatively thin, and

7. Some examples include the conferences "Historical Revolutions in Military Affairs," Marine Corps University, Quantico, Va., April 11–12, 1996; "Considerations on the Revolution in Military Affairs," Monterey, Calif., August 26–29, 1997, sponsored by the Joint Center for International and Security Studies of the University of California-Davis and the Naval Post-Graduate School; and "Defense and Security and the Dawn of the 21st Century: Toward a Revolution in Military Affairs?" sponsored by several universities and the Collège militaire royal du Canada.

8. See, for example, Brian M. Downing, *The Military Revolution and Political Change in Early Modern Europe* (Princeton: Princeton University Press, 1992); Kalevi J. Holsti, *The State, War, and the State of War* (Cambridge: Cambridge University Press, 1996); Bruce Porter, *War and the Rise of the State: The Foundations of Modern Politics* (New York: Free Press, 1994); Karen Rasler and William Thompson, *War and State Making: The Shaping of the Global Powers* (Boston: Unwin Hyman, 1989); and Charles Tilly, *Coercion, Capital, and the Rise of the State* (Cambridge, Mass.: Basil Blackwell, 1990).

has yet to gel into competing schools; the works are simply too idiosyncratic as yet. The theories proposed are interesting, and as a whole do not play too fast and loose with the historical record they have received. With the exception of *War and State Making* by William R. Thompson and Karen A. Rasler and *Coercion, Capital, and the Rise of the State* by Charles Tilly, the volumes are not intensely theoretical. So it is at least premature to explore the divergence or conflict between history and theory in this case. The problem of arms competition during the Cold War also spawned a literature on innovation and diffusion.[9] Such works attempt to explain the process of developing new weapons technology and the way in which competing states attempted to duplicate or counter their foe's advantages. Some of this literature deals specifically with the arms race between the United States and the Soviet Union, and to that extent it is dated; other work examines the process of military innovation across a broader spectrum during the entire twentieth century. In any case, the focus is limited to a very recent timeframe and thus does not lead to an overarching theory of military change through the centuries.

Sheer ignorance has crippled attempts to create substantial theory on military change over broad periods of time, because the underpopulated field has not produced a body of work across a broad range of historical experience that would provide a solid data base for historians and social scientists. Take something as basic as useful quantitative data; explorations of war and great states depend on counts of total army size, battle strengths, and casualties, but these are often taken from weak sources, because, frankly, historians do not really know. Considerations of state formation are particularly hampered by the lack of reliable studies. For example, they usually assume that coercion played a central role and that standing armies were the key to compulsion.[10] The France of Louis XIV, my own bailiwick, is often presented as an example, and as notable a historian as William McNeill justifies the case: "[Louis XIV's] standing army was initially designed to assure the king's superiority over any and every challenge to his authority within France, and only secondarily

9. For example, see Michael Armacost, *The Politics of Weapons Innovation: The Thor-Jupiter Controversy* (New York: Columbia University Press, 1969); Matthew Evangelista, *Innovation and the Arms Race: How the United States and Soviet Union Develop New Military Technologies* (Ithaca: Cornell University Press, 1988); Donald A. MacKenzie, *Inventing Accuracy: A Historical Sociology of Nuclear Missile Guidance* (Cambridge, Mass.: MIT Press, 1990); and Stephen Peter Rosen, *Winning the Next War: Innovation and the Modern Military* (Ithaca: Cornell University Press, 1991).

10. Consider the "coercion-extraction" cycle in Samuel E. Finer, "State- and Nation-Building in Europe: The Role of the Military," in Charles Tilly, ed., *The Formation of National States in Europe* (Princeton: Princeton University Press, 1975).

intended for foreign adventure."[11] My research suggests that this assertion distorts the relationship between the international threat, the creation
of permanent professional military forces, and the role of local militias in
repressing uprisings, to say nothing about the importance of consensus
in the entire process. But the fact is that we simply did not know better
when McNeill wrote; as David Kaiser complained in 1990, "we lack any
really systematic studies of [Louis XIV's] armies."[12] Until the appearance
of *Giant of the Grand Siècle* in 1997, there was no volume in any language
devoted to a consideration of French military institutions throughout the
entire course of the seventeenth century.[13] In contrast, such could hardly
be said of the well populated and more prestigious subdiscipline of
diplomatic history during the reign of Louis XIV. With the historical
literature on war and military institutions often weak, it may be unfair
to condemn the political scientists for misusing it.

The Military Revolution, the RMA, and Military Revolutions

Luckily for students of military change, the debate concerning the "Military Revolution" is the most active and currently productive scholarly
discussion among military historians. And not only has it enjoyed unprecedented scholarly attention, but because of its promised parallels
with the RMA, it is currently "hot" among the policy community. The
discussion began with the publication of an inaugural lecture by Michael
Roberts in 1956, "The Military Revolution, 1560–1660" and has been
revivified over the past decade thanks to the publication in 1988 of
Geoffrey Parker's *The Military Revolution: Military Innovation and the Rise
of the West, 1500–1800*.[14] Theories of a Military Revolution posit a radical

---

11. William McNeill, *Pursuit of Power* (Chicago: University of Chicago Press, 1982), p. 125.

12. David Kaiser, *Politics and War* (Cambridge, Mass.: Harvard University Press, 1990), p. 153.

13. John A. Lynn, *Giant of the Grand Siècle: The French Army, 1610–1715* (New York: Cambridge University Press, 1997). It is worth noting that the last published volume covering the wars of Louis XIV in their entirety appeared over 270 years ago. This gap in modern scholarship was only redressed by the appearance of my *The Wars of Louis XIV*.

14. Important works on the Military Revolution include the following: Michael Roberts, *The Military Revolution, 1560–1660* (Belfast: Queen's University, 1956); George Clark, *War and Society in the Seventeenth Century* (Cambridge: Cambridge University Press, 1958); Geoffrey Parker, "The 'Military Revolution' 1560–1660—a Myth?" *Journal of Modern History*, Vol. 48, No. 2 (June 1976), pp. 195–214; and Geoffrey Parker, *The Military Revolution: Military Innovation and the Rise of the West, 1500–1800*, 2nd. ed.

change, or a series of radical changes, of a technological and technical nature that then had far-reaching effects. Michael Roberts particularly emphasized tactical and operational innovations made by Maurice of Nassau and Gustavus Adolphus. Geoffrey Parker stresses advances in artillery and their sixteenth-century spin-offs in military architecture that yielded the new, low-lying, *trace italienne* fortress designed to withstand cannon fire. He has also drawn attention to the rise of the broadside-firing sailing ship during the same century.[15] The consequences of this "Revolution" have been extended to include not only a transformation of warfare, but also the rise of modern bureaucratic government and the spread of European dominion around the globe. The Military Revolution debate has provided the study of military institutions and war with an intellectual boost that has not only helped early modernists, but, one hopes, has provided an example of the value of such exploration and controversy.

Those involved in the debate dispute the period defined as the Military Revolution and the nature of its driving forces—be they technological, tactical, institutional, or cultural. Things are still unsettled. It is reasonable to argue that to qualify as a revolution, something must bring about great change in a short time. To be sure, the more monumental the change, the larger time it may consume and still be considered revolutionary. So we speak of the Industrial Revolution without expecting that it move at the speed of the French Revolution of 1789. Michael Roberts gave his Military Revolution a century, 1560–1660, which is long enough, but Geoffrey Parker assigns it three hundred years, 1500–1800. Who would doubt that three centuries will bring considerable change, but is not that period too long to be described as a single revolution? Jeremy Black, and others, deny a revolution before 1660 and argue that if one occurred it came later, and its technological totem was the flintlock musket and bayonet, not the *trace italienne*. Another common response has been to break the one great revolution into a series of smaller revolutions, an infantry revolution, a gun-powder revolution, a fortress revolution,

---

(Cambridge: Cambridge University Press, 1996). For criticisms of the Roberts and Parker formulations of the theory, see Jeremy Black, *A Military Revolution? Military Change and European Society, 1550–1800* (Atlantic Highlands, N.J.: Humanities Press, 1991) and *European Warfare, 1660–1815* (New Haven, Conn.: Yale University Press, 1994); Clifford Rogers, ed., *The Military Revolution Debate: Readings on the Military Transformation of Early Modern Europe* (Boulder, Colo.: Westview Press, 1995); and Lynn, *Giant of the Grand Siècle.*

15. For the first complete statement of the important role of new naval and artillery technology, see Carlo M. Cipolla, *Guns, Sails and Empires: Technological Innovation and the Early Phases of European Expansion, 1400–1700* (New York: Minerva Press, 1965).

etc. However, a series of such mini-revolutions fits better into a general theory of evolution than revolution. The drama of the word "revolution" tempts us away from the greater, and probably truer, evolutionary tale.

The greatest reward from the debate over the Military Revolution in early modern Europe has not been a resolution of the question at hand but the stimulation of a great body of research and writing that has appeared over the past decade concerning war and military institutions in the period from the late middle ages through the French Revolution. Certainly Roberts gave the Military Revolution thesis its first expression, but that impetus had largely subsided when, thirty years later, Geoffrey Parker refashioned and bolstered the argument in such a powerful manner that he engaged the scholarly community to a degree that Roberts never had. Parker deserves a good deal of the credit even for works that have taken exception to some details of his thesis, because without his resurrection of this important subject, those works and the new information they provide would not have appeared. However, even this, the most sophisticated debate in the entire field of military history, has rarely produced anything approaching a general theory, but rather a series of particular hypotheses about this or that military revolution claimed for this or that time and place.

Also a subject of current debate, the RMA is a different kind of animal from the Military Revolution. Discussion of the Military Revolution originated in pure historical scholarship, whereas concern with an RMA came out of Cold War defense analysis. About the same time that Roberts proposed his Military Revolution, Soviets labeled the new strategic environment of nuclear weapons and ballistic missiles as a revolution in military affairs. Later they talked of a military-technical revolution, again to define the way in which military technology was transforming warfare at an unprecedented pace. U.S. success in the high-tech Gulf War stimulated strong interest in our defense community with the phenomenon of rapid military change, particularly looking forward to the ultra-high-tech possibilities promised in the near future. The terminology of the Revolution in Military Affairs resurfaced in a broader context to identify radical military change initiated by technological progress but going beyond that. One commentator, Benjamin Frankel, stated that the RMA contains four elements: new technologies; organizational changes; political, sociological, and cultural changes; and changes in international power distribution and relationships.[16] This more inclusive look at change, however, still views the introduction of new technologies as critical, particularly those

16. Ben Frankel in his instructions to participants in the August 1996 conference, "Considerations on the Revolution in Military Affairs."

of precision-guided munitions, stealth, computerization, and communications. So while the RMA discussion is intricate and wide-ranging, it still is wrapped up more with the F-117A fighter and the B-2 bomber than it is with society and politics.

The labels alone practically beg us to conflate the Military Revolution with the Revolution in Military Affairs, but that would be a grave error. The Military Revolution took a long time; if we accept Parker's chronology it is best considered as an entire epoch of three centuries. The RMA has just come upon us and is a high-speed phenomenon. The wellspring of the Military Revolution may or may not have been technological—that is still a matter of debate—but its impact went far beyond the realm of combat operations, and that makes it most interesting. The RMA, despite all attempts to cast it in more inclusive terms, remains essentially the product of rapid and recent advances in technology, and its implications outside the security realm are, as yet, mainly just speculation. And the RMA is considered in wholly military terms, which have supposedly transformed the conduct of operations, but not struck society and government as a whole.

The different natures of the debates have not deterred those in search of new perspectives on the RMA from seeking parallels in the Military Revolution, or in a series of military revolutions to be discovered in the past. The entire concept of the Military Revolution of early modern Europe invites comparison with other military revolutions from other epochs. The policy community simply asks historians to find analogous situations demonstrating how military institutions have dealt with periods of rapid change in the past. The task can actually be quite simple and not particularly intellectually challenging; it falls short of the complex and rewarding controversies concerning international relations. International relations types deal with sophisticated theoretical debates and a rich historiography on diplomacy; military historians search a rather sparse literature for questionable analogies. Whether those who instigated the attempt to mine history for analogies intended this result, the greatest benefit to be had from bringing the past into play has been to demonstrate the importance of factors beyond technology in the process of change. In other words, history provides a cautionary tale to those who would see the propulsion of all progress and the source of all solutions in technology. That, at least, is a good, if only partial, result of the effort.

The attempt to call upon past military revolutions to inform us concerning the present RMA characteristically results in the lists-and-lessons approach. Many have walked this road, but a prime example is the Andrew F. Krepinevich article "Cavalry to Computer: The Pattern of

Military Revolutions."[17] There he supplies ten military revolutions, and the number can go higher than that.[18] From ten examples he generates seven lessons, and then tries to apply these to the RMA. It is entirely within the tradition of military history to make such lists; the recently published *Reader's Companion to Military History* is replete with several lists of the ten best or the ten worst, such as "Ten Greatest Generals" or "The Ten Greatest Military Disasters."[19]

There is nothing inherently wrong with the lists-and-lessons approach; it can be rewarding, and at times it has been raised to a very sophisticated level when the "list" becomes a series of first-rate case studies by prominent scholars. The collaboration of Allan Millett and Williamson Murray has provided the finest military examples of this genre to date.[20] With support from the Office of Net Assessment at the Department of Defense and the Mershon Center at the Ohio State University, they assembled teams of highly qualified scholars, drafted appropriate questions for these scholars to ask within the parameters of their expertise, and then used the resultant case studies as a basis upon which to form general conclusions. The works they have produced are excellent and demonstrate the full potential of this methodology, which reins in the inherent idiosyncrasy of most historical research. Murray and MacGregor Knox are putting together another collection of case studies on the subject of military revolutions, which promises to be a valuable work on the subject.[21]

However, even when pursued on the highest level, the lists-and-les-

---

17. Andrew F. Krepinevich, "Cavalry to Computer: The Pattern of Military Revolutions," *The National Interest*, No. 37 (Fall 1994), pp. 30–42.

18. Williamson Murray, "Thinking About Revolutions in Military Affairs," *Joint Force Quarterly*, Vol. 16 (Summer 1997), lists over twenty RMAs.

19. Robert Cowley and Geoffrey Parker, eds., *The Reader's Companion to Military History* (Boston: Houghton Mifflin, 1996).

20. Allan R. Millett and Williamson Murray, eds., *Military Effectiveness*, 3 vols. (Boston: Allen and Unwin, 1988); Williamson Murray and Allan R. Millett, eds., *Calculations: Net Assessment and the Coming of World War II* (New York: Free Press, 1992); Williamson Murray, MacGregor Knox, and Alvin Bernstein, eds., *The Making of Strategy: Rulers, States, and War* (Cambridge: Cambridge University Press, 1994); and Williamson Murray and Allan R. Millett, eds., *Military Innovation in the Interwar Period* (Cambridge: Cambridge University Press, 1996). Obviously, Knox and Bernstein worked on one of these volumes, but the volume was still part of the Murray and Millett string of projects.

21. This work, to be entitled *The Historical Parameters of Revolutions in Military Affairs*, is based on a conference held at the Marine Corps University in 1996.

sons approach does not amount to theory. Comparisons and analogies cannot substitute for theory. To be sure, if one gathers enough analogies and case studies they can form the basis for theory, but historians seem perpetually happy to remain in the hunting and gathering stage. Of course, a Millett or a Murray might reply that their approach produces more valuable information, and they may well be right. Theory might impose a regularity on reality that does not actually exist. But that is not the point here, because in this chapter the issue is methodology, not practical value.

And the fact is that there have been precious few attempts to formulate a theory of military change, or even a narrative on the subject, on either side of the social science divide. It is interesting to note that military historians have been the most likely to produce what general gambits there are—more evidence of the military historian's willingness to cut and trim, perhaps. Cliff Rogers has made a stab at it, suggesting the use of a variant of punctuated equilibrium theory advanced by evolutionary biologist Stephen J. Gould.[22] Gould's notion that evolution is not a smooth process, but moves by a series of rapid jumps followed by periods of relative stability, has been imported into the social sciences as well.[23] As yet this punctuated equilibrium hypothesis has yet to receive the full development it deserves, but it seems promising. On a different tack, there is also my work on the military evolution of army style, to be discussed at greater length in the following section. Perhaps one should also put in the hopper current claims for a "Western way of war" first formulated by Victor Hanson, extended to the breaking point by John Keegan, and then given a more sophisticated twist by Geoffrey Parker.[24] However, whether one accepts the thesis or not, it only encompasses a contrast between the West and the non-West, and not a comprehensive view of military change. So one is left with the conclusion that the most complete discussion of past military innovation has been generated by

---

22. Clifford Rogers broached this theory before an audience at a roundtable during the annual meeting of the Society for Military History in 1991; he then presented a paper, "The Evolution of Might: A Punctuated Equilibrium Model of Military Innovation, 1300–1800," at the 1994 meeting.

23. See, for example, reference to punctuated equilibrium in Thompson and Rasler, *War and State Making*, pp. 15–16. Note that this predates Rogers's use of the concept.

24. Victory Davis Hanson, *The Western Way of War: Infantry Battle in Classical Greece* (New York: Knopf, 1989); John Keegan, *A History of Warfare* (New York: Knopf, 1993); and Geoffrey Parker, *The Cambridge Illustrated History of Warfare* (Cambridge: Cambridge University Press, 1995), pp. 2–9. He includes five factors in his catalog of advantages in the Western Way: technology, discipline, aggressive military tradition, military innovation, and war finance.

proponents of a Military Revolution in early modern Europe, but that is too focused in time and place for a general theory, and besides it has generated a series of descriptions and particular hypotheses rather than an all-encompassing statement about military change.

Toward a Grand Theoretical Narrative of Military Change?

Beyond any other factors mentioned thus far, the lack of a satisfactory theory of military change results from the great magnitude and multifaceted character of the issue. The debate over the Military Revolution has revealed just how difficult it is to produce a clear and accepted narrative of military transformation in one era and, primarily, in one cultural context. To the extent that the problem of change ever receives the theoretical attention it deserves, these temporal and cultural limits must expand, with all the complexity that implies. The task may well be too great for any single overarching theoretical explanation, and it is probably unrealistic to expect one to develop.

Perhaps the reader will permit a relevant digression concerning my own work. Frustration with the Military Revolution debate led me to broaden the context in "Evolution of Army Style in the Modern West, 800–2000."[25] This article self-consciously limits its discussion to the institutional development of armies in Christian Europe, at least until the analysis expands to consider the United States from the mid-nineteenth century. Explicitly accepting these boundaries made the project more manageable. "Evolution of Army Style" argues for a core-periphery approach and stresses the role of paradigm armies in defining an army style that is then emulated by other forces. The theory rejects a single or a series of revolutionary changes for a seven-staged evolution in which the elements of earlier stages endure into later ones, and novel elements that will define later phases of evolution first appear in earlier phases.

While I felt reasonably happy with the breadth of conception in this piece, a recent thoughtful essay by Jeremy Black attacks it for being too narrow.[26] On the one hand it excludes navies, and on the other hand it is definitely Eurocentric. Models developed to explain European development do not say much about a non-Western environment, and, Black

---

25. John A. Lynn, "The Evolution of Army Style in the Modern West, 800–2000," *International History Review*, Vol. 18, No. 3 (August 1996), pp. 505–545.

26. Jeremy Black, "Military Organizations and Military Change in Historical Perspective," *Journal of Military History*, Vol. 62, No. 4 (October 1998), pp. 871–893. Despite his objections to my approach, Jeremy was kind enough to judge it "the most valuable and sustained analysis of the development of military organization," p. 873.

insists, experience outside Europe not only defined military action in non-Western settings, but influenced the great European powers. He points to the obvious case of the Ottomans. He also points out that any exclusively Western analysis has a tendency to "primitivize" the non-West.[27] Black provides valuable caution. Another critic coming at the subject from a very different angle might also express alarm that the questions that pop up most often concerning military innovation involve the role of technology, and my work very consciously did not address that issue head on. My initial reaction to Black's commentary was defensive, to point out that the article ranged more widely and was more theoretical than any other attempt, and that without its self-conscious limits it would have been an ungainly project; it is, after all, an article and not a book. But a more fundamental problem underlies Black's critique. There is simply so very much to consider, so many factors to weigh for such long periods of time, that no one theoretical approach can cover it all. Thus, the wish for a single overarching theory may be expecting the impossible. This is not to deny the value of more focused theoretical efforts, but they will always be open to the criticism that they are too narrow and limited.

The most obvious way around the kind of objections raised by Black would be to pursue a much grander scheme, a theoretical narrative that would combine the story of change over time on a global scale with a series of interlocking theoretical explanations organizing the information. However, such a grand meta-narrative may be too huge a project to ever appear. The most that one could expect at this point would be a sort of menu of necessary topics. An ideal view of military development would have to consider a range of aspects: technology, training, tactics, operations, and strategy to be sure, but also military values, force size and composition, leadership, and organization. This list could be composed differently and extend to cover the relationship of the military to the economy, society, and government; the point here is that ideally a number of factors would be interwoven. Naval forces require consideration in addition to land forces; this is one of the strengths of Parker's work. Navies are more than wet forms of armies; they operate on different technological, economic, and social levels, to say nothing of the different political implications of navies and armies.[28] Of course, a theory that encompasses the twentieth century as well must deal with air forces too.

---

27. This is even truer of the "Western Way of Warfare" approach—a kind of "orientalism" for military historians.

28. For fascinating insights on the differing parameters and contexts of armies and navies, compare Jean-Paul Bertaud, *The Army of the French Revolution: From Citizen-*

As to the process itself, at least three phases of change demand attention: innovation, primary diffusion, and secondary diffusion. Innovation brings the introduction or substantial refinement of weaponry or practices to a particular military at a particular time. Here one examines the comparative roles of technological advance, political environment, social structure, cultural context, and other factors that drove initial change. Primary diffusion deals with the first spread of new weaponry and practices to neighbors. This process concerns states, or entities, that approach one another in terms of technology, government, society, and culture, such as the states of the European heartland. Yet even here, imitation certainly has its limits, because no two states share the exact same circumstances, but there are fewer barriers to emulation in primary diffusion than in the next phase, secondary diffusion. In the latter, military innovations made in the context of one culture are transported into another. This has obviously been a considerable factor in world history since at least the seventeenth century, when western European military arms, techniques, and organization were exported around the world on a large scale. In earlier epochs, military innovation spread not from west to east, but from east to west. In secondary diffusion, the interplay between imported military practice and indigenous culture complicates adoption. In certain circumstances, the need to adapt forms to new environments then feeds back to alter the original, as in the case of the British army in its colonial role.

A grand theoretical narrative would subsume the Military Revolution debate, appropriate the lists-and-lessons works on periods of rapid military change, and put the discussion of a RMA in necessary perspective. While we are a long way from seeing such a global interpretation worked out, it is possible to hazard a commentary on some of its probable themes.

Obviously a theory must consider the impact of technological innovation upon military practice; that is a given and clearly essential to modern concerns about an RMA. At least two sorts of technological innovations must be dealt with: those of a specifically military character and those generated for general societal use, but which then affected the conduct of war. In the first category, none seem more fundamental than the advances in artillery after 1420. Much improved metallurgy and powder created an artillery that transformed siege warfare, redefined warfare at sea, and established itself as a substantial force in land battle. It would be hard to overestimate the impact of this new military technol-

Soldiers to Instrument of Power, trans. R.R. Palmer (Princeton: Princeton University Press, 1988); and William S. Cormack, *Revolution and Political Conflict in the French Navy, 1789–1794* (Cambridge: Cambridge University Press, 1995).

ogy. Artillery also made it easier for monarchs to quell the resistance of their nobility by voiding the capacity of their personal fortifications to shield them from royal power. Mounted on the new ships that came out of the middle ages, cannons allowed Europeans to establish colonial footholds around the world. Even those other great military technologies, atomic and thermonuclear weapons, have not transformed the world so much—and we can only hope they never do.

The technology that has altered warfare has not always been specifically military. Railroads were not developed in the mid-nineteenth century to alter the face of warfare, but they did. With transport and logistics depending now on the iron horse instead of the flesh and bone variety, armies could be moved faster and farther than before. Railroads made possible the mass reserve armies of the second half of the century. In the twentieth century, the internal combustion engine, powering airplanes and, above all, trucks, again rewrote transport and logistics.

Although the impact of technological progress seems to dominate the concerns of the contemporary military, a grand theoretical narrative would undoubtedly have to qualify the influence of technology. While it clearly sets the parameters of warfare, it rarely dictates military practice; rather, it tends to present menus of possibilities. The choices made among technological options are probably more important than the hardware itself. For example, given essentially equal technology the Germans and French made very different choices in tank design before World War II. Guided by ideas of mobile, decisive warfare, the Germans opted for speed, coordination, and communication, while the French clung to notions of the "methodical battle" and chose firepower and defensive armor above all. Therefore, from a single technological menu, the two created very different armored forces, which although of similar size, were organized very differently and integrated into very different operational concepts. Similar arguments would be made concerning capital ships in the late nineteenth and early twentieth centuries and aircraft design in the Cold War. This makes the role of conceptual factors more intriguing, and in important ways more influential than sheer technology.

Many important changes were not based upon hardware, and any comprehensive narrative or theory of military revolutions must integrate these as well. Organizational and institutional innovations have been critical to the practice of warfare. The emergence of a new style of army in the mid-seventeenth century, one I have called the state commission army, exemplifies the way in which military institutions profoundly affected warfare.[29] This new army was no longer a temporary aggregation

---

29. Lynn, "Evolution of Army Style."

of hired mercenary bands or forces raised privately by great nobles, but was created by the ruling individual or institution of the state from standardized units, regiments, raised and maintained on a permanent basis. Rulers exerted far greater control over this kind of army and provided it with more support than ever furnished before. And for a variety of reasons these armies grew rapidly; the French army doubled in size during the Thirty Years' War, expanding from previous wartime highs of perhaps 60,000–80,000 to 125,000 in the 1630s. This force later surpassed 400,000 on paper, and attained 350,000 in reality during the mid-1690s. In the same period, peacetime levels rose from 10,000 men around 1600 to 150,000 men by 1680.[30] It is entirely reasonable to credit both the power of this army and its immense appetite for resources as driving forces in early modern state formation. There is, as yet, no convincing argument that this critical transformation was simply a by-product of technological innovation. It is best to see it as just what it appears to be, an organizational and political change with great implications for the history of war, politics, and society.

Fundamental transformations in government and society, as occur during great revolutions, can also bring profound military change. No case of this is clearer than that associated with the French Revolution of 1789–99. Some historians want to talk of a Napoleonic military revolution, but the truly revolutionary steps were taken before Napoleon assumed power in 1799. A government now thought to represent the people could mobilize the people at arms in defense of French territory and its new revolutionary society. New and potent tactical combinations became possible with soldiers who could be depended upon to harbor commitment and employ personal initiative.[31] Army size again swelled, making necessary the creation of divisions and then corps to manage such large forces. Napoleon's operational genius multiplied the effect of this innovation on the battlefield; however, it is important to distinguish the system from its use by one of the great military practitioners of history.

The spread of new military technologies and practices from their country or region of origin to another provides an entirely distinct subject of great intrinsic interest. Within Europe, for example, the life-and-death nature of military struggle promoted imitation as the most common form

---

30. My figures are available in several places, for example, John A. Lynn, "Recalculating French Army Growth During the *Grand Siècle, 1610–1715*," *French Historical Studies*, Vol. 18, No. 4 (Fall 1994), pp. 881–906, an article reproduced in Rogers, *The Military Revolution Debate*, pp. 117–147.

31. John A. Lynn, *The Bayonets of the Republic: Motivation and Tactics in the Army of Revolutionary France, 1791–94*, rev. ed. (Boulder, Colo.: Westview Press, 1996).

of primary diffusion. By this logic, frequent wars fostered rapid diffusion, improvements generated in different environments generalized, and military forces came to resemble one another. Although even in such a relatively homogeneous area as western Europe, emulation almost always required alteration, as imported practices had to be tailored to fit new circumstances. The process of innovation and emulation can be complicated by a tendency for militaries to try to fit new technologies and practices into old patterns of warfare, a problem that creates a deadly gap between perception and reality. But it was not only by copying that one military responded to potent innovation by its foe. When the sociopolitical infrastructure of a state blocked imitation, it might respond by innovation. So, when the aristocratic Prussians were unable to duplicate French practices of selecting and promoting officers according to skill and without regard to birth—the Revolutionary ideal of "careers open to talent"—the Prussians responded by developing a special meritocracy, the General Staff, which could guarantee performance without overthrowing social privilege.

Even more intriguing than the transmission of military change within a given culture is transmission between cultures, what is labeled here secondary emulation. Military change cannot be transported whole across cultural frontiers. Secondary diffusion is probably less amenable to being encapsulated in general theory, because it would always depend on the particular alchemy of the exporting and the importing cultures. This has been studied in a number of different examples, but the best comparison of case studies remains that by David Ralston.[32] Perhaps the most compelling instance comes from Japan, where the Meiji Restoration recreated from whole cloth a European-style military system after 1868. Of course it is clear that this imported system greatly changed Japan, but it is essential to recognize that the system was also transformed by being transplanted there. Its weaponry may have been European, but its values would remain Japanese. It is worth noting that the "code" of Bushido post-dated the Meiji Restoration, so the Japanese codified tradition just as they adopted new techniques of warfare.

My own interests lead me to be more concerned with the transportation of French and British military styles to South Asia in the mid-eighteenth century. There, the key institutional transplant, the regiment, took on a specifically South Asian character far different from its European parallel. For secondary diffusion to succeed, there must be at least a symbiosis between the imported practice and indigenous values. Most

---

32. David Ralston, *Importing the European Army* (Chicago: University of Chicago Press, 1990).

amazing, the introduction of European regimental culture into South Asia produced not merely compatibility, but a true synergy between innovation and tradition that mobilized native military values more effectively than had earlier Indian military institutions.

It is also worth noting, as Ralston demonstrates, that the successful diffusion of European military practice involved bringing a great deal beyond the narrowly military sphere, from Western styles of dress, to educational practices, to industrial production. When cultural gulfs separate innovation from its imitation, then only a resolute borrowing of supporting institutions and practices can successfully import military change. Thus, secondary diffusion can be a Trojan horse for alien cultural influence.

Conclusion

The call for a grand theoretical narrative, be it revolutionary or evolutionary, may simply be a counsel of perfection, a demand for the impossibly erudite and complete. Its greatest value may be simply to demonstrate that the only conceptualizations that are realistically possible are by necessity partial, and, thus, partial is probably as good as it gets concerning the immensely complex issue of global military change and diffusion across the millennia of human history.

Should a global theory of military change appear, either generated by a military historian or by a social scientist, it would have to be based upon a large body of volumes on specific military development generated by specialists in the field. And were such a library available, it would require astounding erudition to master the military literature, put it all in a variety of cultural contexts, and then reconstitute it into a single narrative. But that ideal library does not yet exist. Even in the European case, that which has been most closely examined, the historiography is far from complete, and non-Western cases, with the possible exception of Japan, are extremely thin. This comes back to something said earlier in this chapter; despite the immense acceptance of popular military history, the academic version remains an understaffed pariah field. And not only is the subdiscipline underpopulated, but its pronounced front-loading limits its range of expertise. Current fashion in historical studies only threatens to make the situation worse, as military history and the history of international relations adhere to subject matter and methodologies regarded as wrong-headed or obsolete. Without the necessary bricks, it will be impossible to build the wall.

If this logic holds, then our praise must go not to the perfection that will probably never come but to those presentations that advance the state of knowledge on this important subject, even though they do not provide a comprehensive theory. This leads us back to the most sophisticated of all the historical discussions of military change, that surrounding the Military Revolution. Here the contribution of Geoffrey Parker appears all the more noteworthy, for whether or not his particular narrative of military change in the early modern world survives intact, there is no question that he has spread and advanced our knowledge, and, of even greater value, he has caused many others to do so as well. The history and theory of military change illustrate what is so often true in scholarship: the pursuit of knowledge is a race to be run, not a race to be won, a relay in which the most one can do is advance the baton, rather than break the tape.

Part III
Conclusions

Chapter 15

International History and International Politics: Why Are They Studied Differently?

Robert Jervis

When I was an undergraduate, an assignment in my Introduction to Religion class was to make a list of the characteristics that differentiated human beings from other animals. At first the task seemed easy, but difficulties became apparent as soon as my classmates and I got more deeply into the exercise. I find it as least as difficult to understand the differences between the approaches of political scientists and diplomatic historians. Part of the problem is that some of the differences within each group are as great as those between them; part is that it is hard to discriminate style from substance and the superficial from the fundamental.

But even if they are difficult to describe, the differences between political scientists and diplomatic historians pass Potter Stewart's test for pornography: "I know it when I see it." As one reads the chapters in this volume (and most books and articles in the field), it is easy to guess the author's disciplinary affiliation.[1] Deborah Welch Larson uses archives and John Lewis Gaddis theorizes, but they are clearly a political scientist and a historian, respectively. Robert Gilpin and Paul Kennedy both study the rise and fall of states and empires and reach similar conclusions, but again only someone who wanted to criticize their works, if not insult their authors, would refer to *War and Change in World Politics* as a work of history and *The Rise and Fall of the Great Powers* as political science.

---

1. Of course there are exceptions: for example, Richard Ullman's three-volume study of *Anglo-Soviet Relations, 1917–1921* (Princeton: Princeton University Press, 1961–1972); and Christopher Thorne, *The Limits of Foreign Policy: The West, the League, and the Far Eastern Crisis of 1931–1933* (New York: Putnam, 1973).

What the Differences Are Not

The chapters in this book make clear what some of the differences are *not*. While William R. Thompson and Edward Ingram disagree at least in part about whether Britain declined in the late nineteenth and early twentieth centuries, it is not the case that political scientists always—or even usually—adopt a structural explanation and historians do not. Similarly, while the contrast between Randall L. Schweller's chapter and Gerhard L. Weinberg's is in part between an analysis of the structure of the international system (in a somewhat different sense than Thompson's) and an argument for the importance of the nature of an individual regime and its leader, there are enormous differences between Schweller's approach and Thompson's and between Weinberg's and Ingram's. In fact, a great deal of political science shares with Weinberg the focus on what can be too crudely labeled as the domestic sources of foreign policy and insists, with him, that states differ in their international behavior in large part because they differ internally. Similarly, the argument that different kinds of states have very different foreign policy goals, motives, and intentions is not only common among scholars of international politics, but is consistent with Schweller's analysis here and has been strongly articulated by him elsewhere.[2]

I also reject the more widely held view that a key difference is that political scientists are more policy-oriented, or more influenced by current policy concerns, in large part because they want to discern if not influence future events. Ingram argues that "being political scientists, [Thompson and Modelski] ask the dead to show us the way to the future."[3] I doubt whether this is the case for Thompson and George Modelski and I know it is not true for many of my colleagues, who care about understanding the past in its own terms and who doubt their ability to predict the future and lack the stomach for trying to influence it. It is simply not the case that most political scientists wish to whisper in the ear of policymakers, let alone take their place. This marks a change from forty or fifty years ago, when the connections between the study and the practice of politics were much closer. But as the discipline has sought to become more scientific, both the people recruited into it and

---

2. See, for example, Randal L. Schweller, "Bandwagoning for Profit: Bringing the Revisionist State Back In," *International Security*, Vol. 19, No. 1 (Summer 1994), pp. 72–107; and Randall L. Schweller, *Deadly Imbalances: Tripolarity and Hitler's Strategy of World Conquest* (New York: Columbia University Press, 1998).

3. See Ingram's chapter in this volume; also see Edward Ingram, "The Wonderland of the Political Scientist," *International Security*, Vol. 22, No. 1 (Summer 1997), p. 54.

the patterns of socialization have changed. This is not to say that political scientists are uninfluenced by current international politics or their own political outlooks. But this is at least as true for historians: as Jerald Combs has shown, interpretations of past events in U.S. foreign policy were strongly influenced by what was happening when scholars were writing.[4]

A Tale of Two Disciplines

The nature of our academic disciplines and the outlooks of the individuals who populate them mutually affect one another and co-evolve over time. I think an observer from Mars would be puzzled at how our disciplines carve up—and create—areas of knowledge. It would be easy if different disciplines studied different phenomena, even if the edges blurred. But it will not do to say that sociology studies societies, political science studies politics, and history studies the past. If we could start all over, we might do a better job of advancing knowledge by redrawing disciplinary lines, or abolishing them. But of course we cannot, and each of us reacts to the different mores and incentives of our discipline.

One noteworthy difference is that the study of international politics from the perspective of political science is almost exclusively an enterprise of the United States, or at least one of the English-speaking world.[5] There is much less international politics studied elsewhere, and most U.S. scholars are almost completely ignorant of what there is, in part because of language barriers. The community of historians, especially those who study the history of world politics, is much more international. I believe that it is this fact rather than the concern for the future that leads the analyses of Thompson, Modelski, and many other scholars to seem to Edward Ingram to be so marked by their North American origins and interests.

Even more important, I believe, were the different responses of the two disciplines to the major upheavals of the war in Vietnam and the campus protests. I suspect that opposition to the war was a major factor in the move of history to the left in its politics, to the marginalization of

---

4. Jerald Combs, *American Foreign Policy* (Berkeley: University of California Press, 1983).

5. Interesting discussions can be found in Ole Waever, "The Sociology of a Not So International Discipline: American and European Developments in International Relations," *International Organization*, Vol. 52, No. 4 (Autumn 1998), pp. 687–727; and Knud Erik Jorgensen, "Continental IR Theory: The Best Kept Secret," *European Journal of International Relations*, Vol. 6, No. 1 (March 2000), pp. 9–42.

international, political, and military history, and to the growth of the study of non-elites and an antipositivist methodology. These trends themselves fit together, but do not form an inevitable package. That is, it was certainly imaginable—and indeed was my expectation twenty-five years ago—that while the field would move to the left, it would retain a heavy focus on political history. One can also imagine the dominance of social and even cultural history coupled with the maintenance of history's deep roots in tangible evidence and a commitment to the search for objectivity. One could even see these subjects analyzed with mathematical techniques: much of sociology consists of studying non-elites with quantitative methods, and it too is generally critical of capitalism.

It is particularly noteworthy that history resisted the onslaughts of the cliometricians. The strengths and weaknesses of this approach—or rather this family of approaches—is not relevant here. In any event, I do not think we can account for the success or failure of alternative approaches by how well they explain previously agreed upon evidence.[6] Twenty years ago, an economist and I served on a university committee called to judge the proposed appointment of a mathematical sociologist. When I admitted to my colleague not only my inability to follow much of the material, but my skepticism about whether it could answer the questions that were posed, he replied: "Bob, I can't tell you whether he is right or wrong, but I've watched this methodology in economics and it is like a steamroller: it will flatten everything in its path." Well, in history it did not. Part of the reason is that such methods were seen as flattening the material whose meaning history was supposed to convey. But its rejection may also have been linked to politics. Civil rights was the major domestic issue of the 1960s and 1970s and while it did not divide the academy as the war in Vietnam did, it was a deep moral commitment. The key book that developed and applied statistical and economic methods to history was *Time on the Cross*, which among other things argued that the experience and effects of slavery may not have been quite as dreadful as was previously believed.[7] I wonder if a different conclusion would have gained more adherents for the approach.

The political and methodological trends in political science were quite different. Politically, the central tendency in the discipline remained relatively unchanged, with liberal Democrats remaining the strong majority. Although the popularity of economic models has been coupled with

---

6. Of course this raises the question of how I would go about trying to confirm this proposition.

7. Robert Fogel and Stanley Engerman, *Time on the Cross: The Economics of American Negro Slavery* (Boston: Little, Brown, 1974).

some increase in libertarian politics and faith in free markets, movement has not been great. Marxism grew rapidly in the 1960s but did not thrive. Some argue that its conceptual framework was wrong and that the analyses it produced were badly flawed. Others reply that Marxists were discriminated against and excluded from the profession. (My centrist view is that both these explanations capture a measure of the truth.) At the same time, the discipline became more strongly engaged in analysis of quantitative data and the application of formal models borrowed from economics.[8] These approaches were slower to catch on in international politics than in some of the other subfields of the discipline but in recent years have become much more popular, with modeling now perhaps the most prestigious although far from the most common technique. What is relevant here is that these techniques grew in political science at just the time that history was moving in the opposite direction, thus widening the gap between the two fields. Indeed, the nonquantitative but evidence-based approaches represented by the chapters in this volume may have more in common with each other than they do with most of the work in their home disciplines.

Intellectual Differences

Significant intellectual differences between the fields remain, and it is to them that I now want to turn. Edward Ingram and Paul W. Schroeder have stressed that the conventional wisdom is wrong: one should not associate political science with theories and generalizations and history with description and treatments of each event as unique.[9] They are correct that one should not exaggerate, but, with John A. Lynn, I do not think the conventional view is entirely wrong. Both political scientists and diplomatic historians seek to explain events, and, in a sense, explanations must always involve general theories and particular cases, but they go about the task characteristically differently. The field of political science places priority on generalizations and explicit, parsimonious theorizing. These values are not shared by historians. To call a work of history nuanced and subtle is to pay it a compliment; for political scientists, these adjectives, if not supplemented by others, have a critical undertone. Too

---

8. People outside the discipline tend to see these two tendencies as the same. They are not, and their proponents argue bitterly with each other.

9. Ingram, "The Wonderland of the Political Scientist"; and Paul W. Schroeder, "History and International Relations: Not Use or Abuse, but Fit or Misfit," *International Security*, Vol. 22, No. 1 (Summer 1997), pp. 64–74.

much subtlety, too many nuances, mean that the theoretical edge is likely to be lost.

PARSIMONY

Parsimony is extremely important for most political scientists. This does not have to mean monocausality or even simplicity, although sometimes it does. Rather, it refers to a favorable ratio between the explanatory factors deployed and the range of behavior explained. Parsimony is necessary for theory-building, discussed further below, and this is why political scientists are willing to forego a complete account of any individual event in order to seek explanations that apply to behavior that occurs in very different times and circumstances. It is particularly impressive to construct an explanation that helps unravel behavior that previously seemed very different. One attraction of collective goods theory, for example, is that it explains—or purports to explain—significant phenomena in alliance politics, tariffs, interest group behavior, the internal organization of legislatures, political leadership, internal group maintenance, and budgeting practices, to give just an incomplete list. This sort of "theoretical robustness" is highly prized both because it allows us to understand a lot with a little and because the range of phenomena being accounted for (a phrase that sets off alarm bells among historians) indicates that the posited cause is indeed potent.

There are two basic and quite different sources of the drive for parsimony. The first is convenience—Occam's Razor. Simpler is better because it makes handling explanations easier: things should not be complicated unnecessarily. Of course the world is more complicated than our theories; that is the reason we need them. The second justification for parsimony is more interesting because it constitutes a claim about the world, not about the pragmatic foundations of research strategy: parsimonious theories are more likely to be correct because the world is actually built around a manageably small number of important factors. This belief is particularly strong in physics.[10] Thus during the 1960s, many physicists were deeply disturbed by the discovery of one new "fundamental" particle after another. Rather than being overjoyed at these discoveries and claiming that they brought new understanding, most physicists felt that they indicated crippling flaws in the prevailing theories. Nature simply could not be built out of forty or fifty fundamental particles. The search for smaller and more basic particles out of which others were constituted was driven in large part by the belief that parsi-

---

10. As Einstein said, "When I am evaluating a theory, I ask myself, if I were God, would I have made the universe in that way?"

mony was a law of nature. Although political scientists rarely explicate a parallel claim, my sense is that many of them, but only few historians, do believe it.

This implies that some but not all subjects are appropriate for theorizing and that, relatedly, we should not confuse theorizing with monocausality. Thus Kenneth Waltz, perhaps the most influential contemporary theorist of international politics, stresses that the theory of structural realism that explains how the search for security in an anarchic world plays out differently under bipolarity than under multipolarity applies only to international politics, not to foreign policy.[11] While the general patterns of international politics can be understood in terms of parsimonious theory because the systemic pressures and interactions induce common results despite differences in state attributes, this approach cannot be applied to individual foreign policies because their sources are so many and can form so many combinations. Interestingly enough, some historians do see a single cause as dominating at least some states' foreign policies. Thus the New Left believes that the key to U.S. foreign relations is the economic interest of the ruling class, a conviction that produces both intriguing insights and bizarre interpretations. As in theory-driven political science, the story is told in a way that makes it fit the single posited motivating force.[12]

Even when parsimony is correctly applied, however, it does not come cheaply. At a minimum, it means that individual cases will not be fully explained and that some of them will have to be pushed and pulled to fit at all. Most historians are unwilling to pay this price. To them, the point is to understand the past and if this means that different events have to be explained quite differently, so be it. To develop incomplete or, even worse, distorted explanations for particular events in order to construct some grand overall view has the whole exercise backwards: we develop mental constructs to fit the world; we do not—or should not—present a picture of the world for the purpose of showing its fit with theories.

A related difference in approach, taste, or sensibility was brought

---

11. Kenneth N. Waltz, *Theory of International Politics* (Reading, Mass.: Addison-Wesley, 1979); Waltz, "Realist Thought and Neorealist Theory," in Robert Rothstein, ed., *The Evolution of Theory in International Relations* (Columbia: University of South Carolina Press, 1991), pp. 21–38. The issues are brought our clearly in the exchange between Colin Elman and Waltz in *Security Studies*, Vol. 6, No. 1 (Autumn 1996), pp. 7–61.

12. See, for example, Gabriel Kolko and Joyce Kolko, *The Limits of Power: The World and United States Foreign Policy* (New York: Random House, 1968); and Robert Buzzanco, "What Happened to the New Left? Toward a Radical Reading of American Foreign Relations," *Diplomatic History*, Vol. 23, No. 4 (Fall 1999), pp. 575–607.

home to me when a colleague who disapproved of the pressures for greater "science" in the study of international politics said to me, "Thank God, you don't have a theory." I was a bit taken aback, but he was contrasting my work, favorably in his eyes, to that of others who sought to explain a wide range of cases with a "powerful" argument that saw one or two factors as dominant in quite different circumstances. As an example of parsimonious theory let me take Jack Snyder's analysis of overexpansion, although one could argue that Paul Kennedy's work on this subject also fits this description. In *Myths of Empire,* Snyder argues that in many cases states seek to expand past the point at which they are able to do so successfully because of a domestic political system that is built around log-rolling coalitions in which each faction gets what it cares most about at the expense of the overall national interest.[13] The behavior of Wilhelmine Germany resembles that of Khrushchev's Soviet Union because both were characterized by cartelized politics that required policies that engendered widespread foreign opposition. These and other cases, while different in particulars, fit the same general pattern and the number of explanatory factors was quite small. A critique by a historian would presumably argue that each case requires an individual and richer explanation; a critique by a political scientist would be quite different, arguing that an alternative theory could encompass not only the cases Snyder studied, but others as well, that his theory would not explain other cases of overexpansion, or that the factors he singled out were present in cases in which the state followed a more moderate foreign policy.

For political scientists, individual cases are just that—cases of *something,* and the task of the scholar is to determine exactly what they are cases of. While the cases need to be understood, they are also in service of developing an explanation of a wider range of phenomena, and, reciprocally, can only be understood in light of what happened elsewhere. For historians, to talk of "a case" is to assume generality that is not likely to be present and to downplay if not deny what is central to their concerns, which is to understand why things happened as they did in that instance.

I think this is why historians are less troubled than political scientists by multiple sufficient causation—i.e., the possibility that the same outcome or behavior can be produced by different causes and through quite different pathways. For political science, this is a real problem because it constitutes a menace to one of its prime methodologies. Returning to the

---

13. Jack Snyder, *Myths of Empire: Domestic Politics and International Ambition* (Ithaca: Cornell University Press, 1991).

example used earlier, assume that someone looks at other cases of over-expansion and finds that, contrary to what Snyder would expect, domestic politics was not characterized by log-rolling coalitions. On one level, this does not disturb Snyder's explanation. He did not say that this kind of domestic politics was necessary in order to produce overexpansion, only that in at least some cases it did have this effect. But political scientists will be disturbed and will seek more fundamental factors at work in both sets of cases. At a minimum, they will be unsettled unless and until they can determine what distinguishes the two kinds of cases. Historians are not likely to be upset because they do not expect this sort of parsimony. Indeed, I suspect that they would regard as a delight rather than an inconvenience a finding that radically different kinds of explanations are needed for apparently similar behavior in different periods of time or different geographic areas. They are ready to accept the notion that the causes of a war, peace, an alliance, deteriorating relations, and anything else of interest can be quite different from one case to the next. They also believe that they can understand the story by examining how all the factors fit together (see the chapters by Ingram and Gaddis) and by studying the progression of internal discussions and events by methods that are akin to process tracing as described by Andrew Bennett and Alexander George. Many political scientists are somewhat skeptical about these approaches and feel more comfortable when they can compare several cases in which the suspected independent variable in fact varies to determine whether the outcome changes as well, even though this cannot eliminate the possibility of multiple sufficient causation.

THEORY-BUILDING

Political scientists place a high priority on theory-building. This means developing, elaborating, and criticizing constructs at a fairly high level of abstraction, which is one reason for the interminable debates that strike outsiders—and many insiders—as akin to theology. The stress on theories also leads to the search for new, different, and additional implications of existing arguments. Although the ultimate test of these theories is their ability to explain, a great many scholarly points are given for elegance and the ability to produce new and unexpected propositions.[14] If these are wildly at variance with accepted beliefs about the historical evidence,

---

14. Of course how theories explain or even exactly what "explanation" and "theory" mean is subject to dispute: see, for example, the *American Political Science Review*, "Forum," Vol. 91, No. 4 (December 1997), pp. 899–935, with contributions by John Vasquez, Kenneth Waltz, Thomas Christensen and Jack Snyder, Colin Elman and Miriam Fendius Elman, Randall Schweller, and Stephen Walt.

the general claims will be treated with skepticism. But if the match comes at all close, the arguments will be taken as at least "productive," "interesting," and "worthy of further detailed exploration."

Let me illustrate some of the differences between the stances of political science and history toward explicit theorizing by comparing my own work on two subjects with that of John Gaddis in one case and Ernest May in another. Both these historians are much more analytical and closer to the style of political science than is true for most of their colleagues, yet the relevant differences still appear. Gaddis and I reach similar conclusions about the role of nuclear weapons in maintaining peace during the Cold War.[15] Gaddis proceeds by examining the history and showing how the individual pieces of behavior and self-reports of statesmen fit together to reveal a stabilizing role for nuclear weapons. Although I reached some of my conclusions by thought processes that are not terribly dissimilar from those of Gaddis's narratives, my presentation and method of argument was quite different. I first laid out the theory of the "nuclear revolution," then argued that if this theory were correct the historical record should reveal a number of patterns: not only should the United States and Soviet Union abstain from fighting, but crises should be less frequent, especially after the attainment of mutual second strike capability; the status quo should be preserved; credibility should be particularly important; estimates of resolve should be a crucial part of national calculations; and both sides should be willing to make concessions in order to end dangerous crises. I then argued that these inferences from the theory were borne out by the evidence. My argument was phrased in terms of testing, or at least probing, the validity of the theory and pointing to implications of mutual retaliatory capability that I believed had been missed before. I thus sought to gain theoretical power by linking sorts of behaviors that, although known previously, had not been closely related to a theory of nuclear weapons and showing that it required only a few assumptions about capabilities and states' calculations to yield propositions that matched actual behavior.

A prime purpose of this method of exposition (the "hypothetico-deductive method") is to take the theory seriously, to deduce what the world would look like if it were true. This inevitably produces some flattening of the historical record in order to gain analytical rigor and parsimony. It also produces ways of judging the validity and utility of

---

15. John Lewis Gaddis, *The Long Peace* (New York: Oxford University Press, 1987); and Robert Jervis, *The Illogic of American Nuclear Strategy* (Ithaca: Cornell University Press, 1984); and Jervis, *The Meaning of the Nuclear Revolution* (Ithaca: Cornell University Press, 1989).

the theory. This is brought out by the differences between the way Ernest May and I studied how decision-makers learn from history.[16] Both of us argued that statesmen tend to see situations in terms of historical analogies, and we both supported our claim by showing that statesmen make explicit references to past situations when diagnosing current ones and adopt policies that they believe would have worked in previous cases. But a greater concern with testing these propositions led me to see whether I could eliminate competing explanations for this pattern, particularly the possibility that the analogies might have been post-hoc rationalizations for preferences arrived at on other grounds and the role of third factors in influencing both the lessons that were drawn about the past and the preferences for current policies (a problem of "spurious correlation"). Thus I tried to see whether the lessons of the past case were established *before* the arrival of the problem to which they were then applied, and I also looked to see whether people with different interests and outlooks drew the same lessons from historical events. For most historians these excursions are irrelevant if not confusing; for political scientists, they are crucial for establishing the causal role of historical learning. May, on the other hand, explored his cases in much more depth, thereby both telling a full story that has value aside from the analytical point and bolstering the conclusion by the detailed narrative. For historians this keeps the focus on the events, where it belongs; for political scientists it fails to meet the central requirement for establishing causation.

Their stress on asking what one would expect to happen if the theory is correct leads to what political scientists consider to be the crucial step of looking for "dogs that do not bark," to take the line from a Sherlock Holmes story. In "The Hound of the Baskervilles," Watson did not see why Holmes thought it was significant that the dog did not bark the evening its master was murdered; for Holmes, this was crucial because it showed that the killer gave the dog no reason for alarm and so must have been known to his victim. Thus political scientists keep an eye out for events that did not occur, but that a plausible theory indicates should have. Turning this around, they try to avoid "searching on the dependent variable," that is, looking only at cases in which a particular kind of outcome occurred (e.g., the outbreak of war, the formation of an alliance, successful deterrence). If one looks only at those cases, there is no way

---

16. Ernest May, *"Lessons" of the Past: The Use and Abuse of History in American Foreign Policy* (New York: Oxford University Press, 1973); and Robert Jervis, *Perception and Misperception in International Politics* (Princeton: Princeton University Press, 1976), chap. 6.

to tell whether the factors that the scholar believes to be causal were also present when the outcome was very different. If they were, they could not be the whole story because they would not discriminate cases in which the outcome was of one type from those which turned out quite differently.[17] The reply from historians is that this method, although not without its virtues, takes things out of context. It is possible—indeed likely—for one "factor" to have a very different outcome depending on several other factors. Thus showing that a particular historical lesson led to one kind of behavior in one instance but not in another would not show that it was unimportant in either, but just that the historical explanations deployed by statesmen, like those of historians, are inevitably multifaceted and involve the interaction of many considerations.

Because of their stress on theory, the distance between description and explanation in the discipline of political science is greater and more explicitly demarcated than in history. It is not that the latter is atheoretical, but that the explanation is more deeply embedded in the description. For a political scientist, a sharp division between the description and the explanation is a badge of honor; for a historian, it would be nonsensical. When political scientists read works of history, they are often annoyed that the discussion of what happened is entangled with an analysis of why it happened. By contrast, many international relations monographs consist of an introductory chapter that sets out several possible theories, a second chapter that develops the author's own proposed argument, a number of case studies, and a concluding chapter. In the empirical chapters the author frequently pauses to point out how the evidence fits or does not fit with various theories. A reader who is in a hurry, who trusts the author's judgment, or who is uninterested in history can skip these chapters. This would be unthinkable in a book of history. Indeed, many of the latter contain only brief introductions and conclusions. It would be pointless, indeed a violation of the historian's craft, to present an explanation for the history, let alone an analysis that might be applied to several cases, divorced from a discussion of the events to be explained.

Relatedly, political scientists often implicitly assume that people and states behave quite consistently. This does not mean that the behavior is constant, but that the changes are responses to alterations in incentives and, secondarily, in beliefs about how desired goals can be reached. As I noted earlier, theories gain credibility by being able to account for behavior across widely disparate realms. But what if people and states are

---

17. This does not mean that these factors are unimportant—indeed, they might be necessary conditions for the outcome to occur.

moved by one set of impulses in one area or in one instance and by another set for other issues or at other times? Can a single explanation fit the U.S. policy toward the Kurdish "terrorists" and the Kosovo "liberation movement"? If not, how is political science to proceed? Taken to an extreme, the behavior could be patternless and not amenable to a general explanation. Although it would still be caused, determining what the causes were will be very difficult. So it is not surprising that people in general and political scientists in particular not only search for consistency in national and individual behavior, but go to great lengths to find it. Thus Deborah Welch Larson has shown that students of U.S. foreign policy in the late 1940s were led astray by their expectation that the path from conciliating the Soviet Union to containing it would be smooth and glossed over the considerable evidence that Truman and his colleagues vacillated and contradicted themselves for a considerable period of time.[18]

Political scientists would have even more difficulty with the notoriously erratic behavior of Kaiser Wilhelm. Behavior that seems to be self-defeating, that varies greatly over time, and that at any point contains elements that pull in opposite directions cannot be readily fit into standard political science categories. Furthermore, political scientists, following the hypothetico-deductive approach outlined earlier, often ask "if my theory or general argument about what was motivating this state is correct, what behavior would I expect to find in circumstances A, B, C. . . . ?" But this implies a sort of consistency which may be absent. The fact that the expected behavior is not found at points B, D, and E would usually be taken as casting doubt on the explanation for A and C. But the motive may have been present in those cases, and the absence of the expected behavior at other times may indicate that the actor was not as consistent as the theory.

It remains unclear how consistent human behavior is. When serial murderers are finally caught, their neighbors are often stunned: "But he seemed like such a nice man; he always looked after my cats when I was away." Most of us instinctively expect quite a bit of consistency in the world. People who are humane in one sphere of life are expected to display this characteristic in others. Psychologists have found that in explaining individual behavior we usually place excessive weight on personal predispositions, underestimate the power of the situation the person is in and, as a result, incorrectly project behavior in one instance

---

18. Deborah Welch Larson, *Origins of Containment: A Psychological Explanation* (Princeton: Princeton University Press, 1985).

on to a wide range of realms and into the future.[19] This not only corresponds to the Western sense of individual responsibility (the psychological studies have not been replicated in other cultures) but also makes our world seem manageable by leading us to expect people and states to act in one set of circumstances as they have acted in others. We deploy implicit assumptions about consistency all the time. To cast doubt on the charge that President Clinton had made an unwanted sexual advance toward Kathleen Willey, his defenders released copies of letters she had written after the incident in which she praised him, offered her support, and sought employment in the White House.[20] The implication is that such behavior would have been inconsistent with her later account of the incident.

Scholars make arguments about motives on the assumption of consistency all the time. For example, Gar Alperovitz and Kai Bird argue that one reason for doubting that the Soviet Union seriously contemplated invading Western Europe after World War II is that it tore up railroad tracks in East Europe, thereby gaining war booty but making a move West much more difficult.[21] This assumes that the Soviet state or its decisionmakers were consistent, which is the sort of move that political scientists often make but that historians resist. Drawing on the work of Norman Naimark on Soviet behavior in East Germany, John Gaddis argues that the Soviet Union as a country and Stalin as an individual acted in contradictory and self-defeating ways, on the one hand hoping and even expecting popular support and on the other hand allowing their occupation troops to continue to rape and pillage.[22] Similarly, Odd Arne Westad concludes that Soviet foreign policy in the early Cold War years was not so much "inexplicable in its parts as incoherent in its whole."[23] To take another example, in 1914 many German leaders appear to have preferred a limited war against Serbia to one that involved Russia, yet only the latter clash held out hope of diminishing if not destroying Russian mili-

---

19. For a summary, see Lee Ross and Richard Nisbett, *The Person and the Situation: Perspectives of Social Psychology* (New York: McGraw-Hill, 1991).

20. Jill Abramson and Don Van Atta, Jr., "White House Attacks Credibility of Aide Who Accused Clinton," *New York Times,* March 17, 1998, p. 1.

21. Gar Alperovitz and Kai Bird, "The Centrality of the Bomb," *Foreign Policy,* No. 94 (Spring 1994), p. 12.

22. Norman Naimark, *The Russians in Germany: A History of the Soviet Zone of Occupation* (Cambridge, Mass.: Harvard University Press, 1995); and John Lewis Gaddis, *We Now Know: Rethinking Cold War History* (New York: Oxford University Press, 1997).

23. Odd Arne Westad, *Cold War and Revolution: Soviet-American Rivalry and the Origins of the Chinese Civil War* (New York: Columbia University Press, 1993), p. 55.

tary power, whose expected growth was what the Germans most feared. Even a diplomatic victory that divided Russia from her allies was not likely to do more than postpone the day of reckoning. But if German policy did not follow the dictates of what can be seen in retrospect as clear logic, this does not mean either that its leaders did not in fact prefer to keep Russia out of the war or that they were not driven by the belief that Russia would dominate if its military programs continued unabated. This is not an isolated case. Under the Kaiser, German attitudes toward Great Britain were complex to the point of inconsistency in their tortured combination of envy, resentment, fear, and scorn. In July 1914 German leaders sought British neutrality, which their military plans not only made unlikely because Belgium was to be invaded, but also unnecessary because British opposition would make little difference in the short war that was expected. Here too all the beliefs are important parts of the story even if they do not easily fit together.

My sense is that historians accept these inconsistencies and contradictions as facts of life. But how are political scientists to construct explanations that move a respectable distance beyond description in cases like these? Historians may feel that Westad has explained each bit of Soviet behavior, but political scientists are uneasy with seeing each incident as different if not unique because this does not allow them to use comparisons to test these accounts against alternatives. Relatedly, the inconsistencies are deeply troublesome because such behavior cannot be easily accommodated within a hypothetico-deductive framework. The statement that "if Germany expected a short war, then it should not have feared British entry" is correct, but nevertheless German leaders simultaneously thought the war would be short and dreaded British participation.

MORAL CONCERNS

Another difference in sensibility is less often remarked upon. I think historians are more influenced by moral concerns and are quicker to make moral judgments than are political scientists.[24] While the latter put their theories up front and disguise or bury their conclusions about the appropriateness of the actors' behavior, historians do the reverse. Many political scientists want to be scientific and believe that evaluations of the actors, especially on moral dimensions, have no place in such an enterprise. The other side of this coin is that many historians, but fewer political scientists, feel a responsibility to educate the public. A leading

24. For another perspective on this question, see Paul W. Schroeder's chapter in this volume.

diplomatic historian ends an exchange with a colleague with these words: "the test of one's scholarly credentials and ethical values is. . . . whether one is committed to history as a way of learning about how to preserve a more decent and humane world."[25] I think that few historians would have trouble accepting this standard; most political scientists would, arguing instead that the test is to understand the world, not to change it. I think this explains much of Vietnam's impact on many historians. Although in fact U.S. policy cannot be explained by Marxism and economic interests, its apparent pointlessness and futility not only opened space for non-orthodox accounts, but generated moral revulsion that animated a condemnation of U.S. motives and behavior throughout its history.

Political scientists often decline to discuss whether the actors behaved wisely, let alone morally. Partly because they are studying not actors but people, historians do not shy away from such judgments. Indeed, in some cases making them seems to be the point of the enterprise. Thus in discussing his role as a witness in the trial of a Vichy official accused of war crimes, the noted historian of France Robert Paxon said: "Historians don't decide the guilt or innocence of an individual with respect to the penal code. . . . But you certainly do judge—this person did well, that person didn't do well."[26]

The non-evaluative stance of political scientists may be linked to an avoidance of the role of emotion in human affairs and a rejection of accounts that involve ego dynamics and Freudian analysis. Like ethical judgments, these may be too "hot" to handle, either because they seem unscientific or because the people who have been drawn to political science in the past generation have been attracted by a flattened view of human behavior without affective, unconscious, and moral dimensions. Although psycho-history is not particularly popular in their discipline either, historians are readier to see national leaders as individuals who differ from one another and who are influenced by their deepest emotions, which they often do not understand. Perhaps it is their greater interest in people that also leads historians to venture assessments of the wisdom and the morality of those they are studying.

---

25. Melvyn Leffler, "Ideology and American Foreign Policy," *SHAFR Newsletter*, Vol. 28, No. 3 (September 1997), p. 38.

26. Quoted in Elisabeth Bumiller, "A Historian Defends His Leap From Past to Present," *New York Times*, January 31, 1998, p. B7; also see Buzzanco's peroration in "What Happened to the New Left?" p. 607.

TIME

Although in his chapter Ingram denies that chronology is necessary for narrative, most historians do build their stories by tracing beliefs, national behavior, and international interactions through time. The point is to show how one thing leads to another, often in ways that few individuals anticipated. What comes after is as it is in part because of what went before. Not all history is constructed in this way: comparative history often is not. But the latter is relatively rare and not accepted by the entire discipline. For political scientists, on the other hand, comparisons among cases are primary, either studied quantitatively with large numbers of cases being coded according to specified rules or qualitatively with a more thorough examination of a few cases. While the latter approach is closer to that employed by historians in its scrutiny of detail and its less structured approach to the material, it usually involves looking at each case as a discrete entity without asking how or whether the course and outcome of one case influences others. Thus, for example, a political scientist might examine a series of confrontations during the Cold War to determine the circumstances under which nuclear threats were used. But typically she would not be alert to the possibility that the use or avoidance of a threat in one case was a major part of the explanation of what happened in subsequent instances, a form of causation that confounds the standard comparative method in both its quantitative and qualitative forms.

Without the element of time, history loses the narrative thread that produces coherence and intellectual satisfaction. Comparisons over time are possible, but they are closely linked to the changes that are produced as the interaction proceeds. This means that the point at which the analyst starts her investigation can be crucial. Although historians are usually quicker to note this than are political scientists, it is Larson who provides a clear example: the Berlin crisis of 1958–62 looks very different if one begins it with Khrushchev's ultimatum than it does if one notices that the Soviet leader acted only after he was rebuffed in his diplomatic efforts to ensure that West Germany would not gain access to nuclear weapons.[27] Time may be a variable for political scientists and they are not unaware

---

27. See Deborah Welch Larson's chapter in this volume. Even if Khrushchev's diplomacy had been better crafted Eisenhower would not have responded because he was committed to withdrawing American troops from Europe, and this required that West Germany control nuclear weapons. See Marc Trachtenberg, *A Constructed Peace: The Making of the European Settlement, 1945–1963* (Princeton: Princeton University Press, 1999), chap. 5.

of change, but for few of them is it central. For historians it provides the thread with which they weave their tapestries.

Differences: Productive, Continuing, and Inevitable

I read almost as much history as I do political science and enjoy and learn from each discipline in roughly equal measure as well. But I could never imagine myself becoming a historian. Even if I had the necessary linguistic skills, I doubt if I could learn to present a complex story the way historians do. I could phrase the impulses that made me a political scientist in terms of a preference for understanding the world through fairly abstract generalizations and models, but I never consciously chose one method of understanding over another. It is more accurate, I believe, to see my choice—and I assume others' as well—as less intellectual than aesthetic, perhaps even instinctive. It goes to the way I see the world and what I find to be not only a satisfactory but a satisfying explanation.

Communication might be easier if we all approached questions in the same way. But this is not only unlikely, it would also represent a great loss of diversity. Our collective understanding of the world would be much poorer if political scientists or historians were to convert the other to their way of seeing the world. A dialogue in which neither party would benefit by converting the other is a bit odd, but it provides the basis for a constructive conversation, and one without an end.

Chapter 16

International History: Why Historians Do It Differently than Political Scientists

Paul W. Schroeder

This title is chosen not to indicate a dispute but to acknowledge a debt. It conveys first what this essay represents: unabashed piggybacking on Robert Jervis's essay, including its title. I have concluded that an attempt on my part to comment on all the previous essays or to discuss the general topic of the book independently would serve little purpose, but that something worthwhile and germane may be contributed by commenting on Jervis's arguments from a historian's point of view. These are comments, I emphasize, not basic disagreements or attempts at refutation. I largely agree with what Jervis says; the demurrers generally amount to saying "Yes, but." My purpose is to develop some points he makes further, and to respond to questions he raises and possible answers he suggests with some of my own from a historian's point of view.

This essay will therefore follow his topics fairly closely. To his initial arguments on what the differences are *not* between the international historian's and the political scientist's respective approaches to international politics, I have nothing to add or object; the analysis seems to me correct and pertinent. The same holds generally for most of his discussion of historians' and political scientists' environments, with only this marginal comment: I wish that his remark about American international historians being more international in outlook and conversant with scholarship being done in the rest of the world than American political scientists are were strictly and universally true. My impression is that it usually holds for international historians doing European or world international history, but less so for those who work on U.S. foreign policy.[1]

---

1. This was illustrated by a recent interchange on the internet site H-Diplo (H-DIPLO@H-NET.MSU.EDU), whose contributors are primarily historians of U.S. foreign policy, in which various scholars who usually disagreed on other issues agreed

A more important demurrer, though still a mild one, concerns Jervis's explanation of the leftward shift in recent decades in the study of history which has generally led, he says, "to the marginalization of international, political, and military history, and to the growth of the study of non-elites and an antipositivist methodology." Jervis attributes much of this to the impact of the Vietnam War and campus protests. I accept his description of the phenomenon and agree that these events played a role in it, but see more powerful causes in two areas: first, certain sociological changes in the country as a whole, in universities and colleges generally, and in the social makeup of the historical "profession;" and second, the very nature of the historical enterprise, the kinds of material it uses, and its conception of its central task. On the sociological side, the rise of the feminist movement and similar movements among disadvantaged or marginalized groups in the country as a whole (gays and lesbians, various ethnic groups, etc.), combined with organized pressure on the universities to promote cultural and ethnic diversity, plus the greater entrance of women and members of ethnic and racial minorities into a profession previously dominated by white males, mainly accounts for this leftward trend. The impact of the Vietnam War and the campus protests, initially important, has since receded.

More important still in accounting for these developments are certain features inherent in history as a discipline. First, the materials with which it works are almost infinite in their scope and variety and very widely, though not infinitely, malleable in terms of their possible treatment, approach, and interpretation, so that new approaches are always possible and alluring. Second, it has always been the nature of history since it became a serious scholarly discipline in the nineteenth century not to content itself with new discoveries and interpretations in historical fields as traditionally conceived and practiced, but constantly to try to discover (some would say, invent) new fields. Thus an essential task of history as it is now practiced is to show that areas of human life hitherto seen as timeless, permanent, and unchanging—part of "nature," so to speak—actually have a history and help shape history as a whole. It is this quest which mainly accounts for the ongoing splintering of the historical profession into dozens of specialties, many of them new, and for the emergence in recent decades of such broad fields as psychohistory, gender history, history of everyday life, the history of memory, discourse, and representation, and even postmodernism and deconstruction.

Except for the very last, I consider all these on balance to have been

---

that the study of foreign languages and foreign language materials was sadly neglected in American historiography.

valuable developments. For various reasons, however, some good, some bad, all normal, they have had the unfortunate side effect here in the United States (not everywhere and certainly not in some other parts of the Western world) of promoting the marginalization of more traditional fields of history such as the international history of Europe and the wider world. One can deplore this and see it as a serious loss without despairing of the future; these fields, I am confident, will eventually regain their due status and importance also in the United States (where U.S. diplomatic history has always flourished); I think the beginnings of a recovery are now visible. In the meantime, to be sure, considerable short-range damage to them and imbalances within the discipline of history in the United States have occurred, and measures of fire-fighting and damage control are badly needed.

In regard to parsimony, again I agree with Jervis's identification of this as a prime source of difference between historians and political scientists, and with his remarks on the inclination of the latter to seek and prize parsimony and of historians to be suspicious of it. His observations on how many historians conceive of the search for parsimony and react to it strike me as accurate. My contention, however, is that the view commonly encountered among historians, that the quest for parsimony is per se inappropriate for history because its true nature and genius lies in its complexity and richness of detail, and that the historian therefore should eschew parsimonious explanations for richer, more complex, and ambiguous ones, is fundamentally wrong, a misunderstanding of history's task. In fact, history as actually practiced and presented by good professional historians is full of parsimonious explanation, if not theory, and historians should be as interested in achieving parsimony in their way and for their purposes as political scientists are in theirs.

How so? Every broad summary judgment, every conclusion of a major work that tries to sum up what the story finally amounts to, every insight or argument that says, "Here is the nub of the question, here lies the real answer," constitutes a parsimonious explanation. Works of history, especially good, important ones, are full of these.

To illustrate, one could point to the many widely used collections of excerpts from the writings of historians designed to introduce students to major controversies and historical debates, often with titles like, "The Nazi Revolution: Germany's Guilt and Germany's Fate?" or "Britain and Appeasement: Guilty Men or Terrible Times?" These collections could, to be sure, be dismissed as mere pedagogical tools rather than serious history, whose intent and effect, moreover, by introducing students to the richness, indeterminacy, and ambiguity of the historical literature, and by presumably getting them to read more deeply on their own, is to bring them to the realization that parsimonious explanations are impossible. One must simply understand that all important developments have multiple causes or factors, that these often contradict or work against each other, and that no formula or thesis can do justice to this rich complexity. This may be what many historians would say—but again, they would be wrong. The very fact that these collections exist shows that good historians do offer explanations that are parsimonious, though not monocausal. They do say, "This in the final analysis is the central factor," or "This is the best way to understand this whole development and phenomenon, and to understand its component elements." Moreover, the competition and clash between such attempts at parsimonious explanations, far from being illegitimate and from distorting historical inquiry, drives it forward. Consider, for example, how much valuable research has been engendered by the clash in German historiography between the intentionalist and the functionalist views of the Nazi regime and its policies, including central ones like its foreign policy and the Holocaust. The fact that both broad views cannot be equally sound and true does not mean that either is necessarily false or useless, and still less that no parsimonious explanations are possible at all. For every James Joll, who in his classic study of the origins of World War I examines the major parsimonious explanations and finds them all wanting, there is an Ian Kershaw on Nazi Germany or a Michael Marrus on the Holocaust who on reviewing and analyzing the literature comes to his or her own relatively parsimonious formulation of the best answer.[2]

The reason for insisting on this point is not to contradict what Jervis says on this score, but to prevent it from inadvertently strengthening a common stereotype: that historians are mainly or solely interested in telling stories, recounting developments in all their rich and fascinating detail, and that political scientists are interested instead in explaining developments, categorizing them into classes, determining their causes. Historians are just as much interested in the latter pursuits and engage in them as much as political scientists—or at least they should be.

Why then do the differences Jervis points out on the score of parsimony arise? Partly, as he says, they arise from the different subjects we

2. The works are James Joll, *The Origins of the First World War,* 2nd ed. (New York: Longman, 1992); Ian Kershaw, *The Nazi Dictatorship. Problems and Perpectives of Interpretation,* 2nd ed. (London: Edward Arnold, 1989); and Michael Marrus, *The Holocaust in History* (Hanover, N.H.: University Press of New England, 1987). Joll's conclusion is not that no overall parsimonious explanation is possible—only that he finds no fully satisfying one among those he presents, and offers none himself.

typically address. Political scientists typically, though not always, attempt to explain classes of phenomena (wars, revolutions, international crises, foreign policy decision-making in general, etc.). A normal, necessary question in political science is, "Of what general phenomenon, development, pattern of behavior, etc., is this particular action an instance?" Historians more often (though again far from always) propose to explain particular instances of these same classes of phenomena, and are not satisfied to treat them simply or mainly as examples of some general law or pattern. Partly they occur, as Jervis again says, because the respective parsimonious explanations are arrived at by different routes—the political scientist's ideally by the hypothetico-deductive method, the historian's by a more inductive method of process tracing. But on a third aspect, what Jervis says is, I think, not wrong but needs further development: his remarks on how political scientists are uncomfortable with the phenomenon of inconsistency and apparent irrationality in behavior, and dislike leaving cases of such apparent inconsistency (e.g., in Soviet behavior in the early Cold War, one of the examples he mentions) unresolved and unexplained, while historians on the other hand are apt actually to delight in the perverse, unpredictable nature of human conduct and are comfortable with the bedrock fact of constant inconsistency. Perceptive as his observations are, they do not quite get to the heart of the matter, especially on the historian's side. The question has to do, I think, with why, despite the fact that both groups prize parsimony, or should, historians in fact are more suspicious of the parsimonious explanations actually arrived at by political scientists; and most important, what each side tends to regard as satisfactory explanation by cause.

Neither political scientists nor historians value parsimony for its own sake, as a good desirable in and of itself. Both desire it, as Jervis notes of political scientists, for the sake of robustness, explanatory power, effectiveness in explaining as many phenomena as far as possible with as few explanatory elements as possible. Historians, I insist again, are as much engaged in the business of providing robust explanations as political scientists and should recognize parsimony as one element or feature of it. They have no business ignoring Occam's razor and multiplying either entities or causes beyond necessity. The trouble is that the historian's experience often forces him or her to the conclusion that particular parsimonious explanations and theories, including those of political scientists, are not robust, do not integrate and accommodate the pertinent evidence but ignore or distort it. James Joll, to refer to the instance previously mentioned, did not reject all the parsimonious explanations of the origins of World War I out of a desire to see the phenomenon in the round and picture it in its richness of detail and great interest; he did so because he found them all not sufficiently robust, leaving too much relevant evidence unexplained or explained in an unacceptable way.

Both this reason for the historian's frequent skepticism about social scientific theories in his field—not their parsimony but their lack of effective explanatory power—and the historian's greater willingness to accept and live with inconsistency in human affairs, including international politics, point also to a major difference between historians and political scientists: how they conceive of causes in human affairs and deal with them. Presumptuous though it is of me as a historian to discuss the mindsets and assumptions of political and social scientists, my impression is that without being rigid about it they try to conform as closely as possible to a Humean concept of cause: an antecedent condition or set of conditions that regularly and predictably produces a particular result. Historians, without thinking much about the question (less than they should, in fact), almost automatically or unconsciously use the term "cause" in the far richer, more varied, but entirely legitimate human understanding of the term, learned from inside through life itself and merely refined and developed by many scholarly disciplines, scientific and humanist. In this definition, "cause" is anything that effectively prompts or influences human beings to do certain things, and therefore varies almost indefinitely in kind and is unpredictable in precise effect and outcome. Instinct, learning, socialization, custom, habit, rational conviction, irrational or nonrational belief, emotion, impulse, example, need, persuasion, influence of others, etc., all can and do serve as "causes" for the historian, just as they are recognized by each of us as possible "causes" in our own lives and those of others. I would agree, even insist, that historians generally should be more aware of how they conceive of causality, more careful in how they use the term "cause" and its many synonyms, and more explicit in defining what they mean by it in particular instances. Doing this would at least help reduce the fog and smoke surrounding many historical controversies. I cannot agree, however, that history should forfeit its birthright by abandoning this wider, richer, and deeper concept of cause, with all its variety and the confusion it unquestionably introduces into every discussion, in exchange for the dubious pottage of social science rigor.

A further observation: Historians are less enamored of parsimony and more comfortable with inconsistency than political scientists in part because of a still more basic difference in their approaches: the tendency of political scientists to treat the common subject matter, international politics, as behavior, while historians insist on treating it as human conduct. This connects with observations by Jervis which I found intriguing, but also in need of further development—those on morality. Here my contribution can be more substantial and less parasitic than elsewhere. It consists of offering reasons why historians not only are more inclined to make moral judgments than political scientists, but why they must and should do so—why moral judgments are not superfluous and harmful addenda to historical investigation or mere appendages of it, but embedded, inescapable ingredients in it.

First, a mild objection to one of Jervis's propositions. Quoting Melvyn Leffler to the effect that the historian's scholarship and ethical values are closely tied to a commitment to history as a means to help achieve a more decent and humane world, Jervis writes: "I think that few historians would have trouble accepting this standard; most political scientists would, arguing instead that the test is to understand the world, not to change it." On this score, many if not most historians, including me, would agree with the political scientists, on precisely the same grounds. Scholarly history has traditionally conceived its task and goal predominantly in a Rankean sense, as that of portraying the past "*wie es eigentlich gewesen,*" rather than the Marxian one of understanding the world in order to change it. There are, of course, serious scholars who consciously attempt to make history an instrument of social change. A good example is the program of doing history as critical historical science (*kritische Geschichtswissenschaft*) directed toward emancipation and social progress, practiced by Hans-Ulrich Wehler and others in Germany, especially at the University of Bielefeld. These efforts, however, represent controversial protest movements against the mainstream, and the historical criticism they regularly face on evidential grounds often forces them in practice to subordinate their emancipationist-reformist goals to the general canons of historical investigation.[3] Moreover, while many historians, perhaps most, would deny that Ranke's ideal of an objective historical account corresponding to past reality is attainable (thereby incidentally misinterpreting what Ranke meant and intended by his aphorism), the claim that objective historical truth cannot be attained, which has now become the

---

3. An excellent example of this is Dietrich Geyer's *Der russische Imperialismus* (Göttingen: Vandenhoeck and Ruprecht, 1977), translated into English as *Russian Imperialism: The Interaction of Domestic and Foreign Policy, 1860–1914* (New Haven, Conn.: Yale University Press, 1987). Geyer, a student of Hans-Ulrich Wehler, set out to test and substantiate Wehler's theory of imperialism as secondary integration. He did not end up rejecting or disproving it, but being a very good historian he did show that the interaction between domestic and foreign policy was more nuanced and complex than any theory of the primacy of domestic politics would allow—a finding which, while it made much sense historically, largely rendered the book useless for emancipationist-reformist purposes.

conventional wisdom, is not a denial that the proper goal of history is to improve our understanding of the historic past. The argument I will make here is that while a historian's scholarship and ethical values do involve a moral commitment and task, it is not the task of changing the world or providing the means for doing so. Instead, moral values and purposes are firmly embedded within the historian's task of understanding the past and are inseparable from it.

The first reason why doing history inescapably involves making moral judgments is the easiest to understand: the unavoidable moral content and dimension involved in the very language required if we wish, even in strictly Rankean terms, to describe historical actions, to state what really happened. The subject matter of history is, as traditionally stated, all that humankind has done and suffered (suffered in the sense of experienced, gone through). One cannot tell this story, or any substantial part of it, in value-free language devoid of reference to its moral dimension. One is forced, simply in order to give any sort of coherent narrative and analysis, to use adjectives such as good, bad, rational, irrational, harmful, beneficial, selfish, unselfish; verbs like kill, injure, massacre, slaughter, insult, wound, help, console, save, rescue, heal; nouns like courage, cowardice, honesty, lies, loyalty, betrayal, honor, dishonor, strength, weakness—etc. ad infinitum. Every attempt to construct an "objective" value-free language to tell the story of what human beings have done and suffered not only breaks down and denatures the narrative and analysis alike, but does so without really avoiding moral judgments, instead masking, blurring, and fudging them. To try, for example, to construct an objective, nonmoral standard for judging the German attacks on Poland in 1939 and on Russia in 1941 in terms of their motives, actions, and immediate and long-range consequences—to do so, say, in terms purely of their success or failure to advance Nazi goals, concluding that in the strictly immanent terms of Nazi aims the former was a success and the latter a failure, and to leave it there—would not merely be extremely morally insensitive, but unhistorical, a failure to come to grips with the real, main story of what happened, what human beings here did and suffered. Apply this same sort of procedure to the Holocaust and it becomes wholly inhuman, obscene. The language of history, used to tell and analyze it, is inescapably moral in one of its essential dimensions, as is that of everyday life. That language can be used well or badly, sensitively or insensitively, subtly and by implication or crudely and by imprecation, but it cannot be morally neutered without neutering history itself.

The second main reason why historians (as well as other social scientists, I believe) cannot escape making moral judgments is a bit less obvious: that any important theory or large-scale explanation as to why things happen in human affairs inevitably carries with it large-scale moral implications as well. Take, for example, the substantial literature, including most recently David Landes's magnum opus on *The Wealth and Poverty of Nations*,[4] which argues that the main factors leading to prosperity or poverty are and always have been education and the development of human capital. An obvious implication of this theory or explanation is that if one wishes to promote economic well-being, one must not allow religious or ideological commitments and systems that stand in the way of education and the development of human capital to prevail. Similarly, if the theory of the democratic peace is sound, the implication that one ought to promote liberal democracy and a market system for the sake of peace is unmistakable. One can leave these judgments implicit and unstated, or put them conditionally ("if you want peace or prefer prosperity, then combat religious fundamentalism and promote democracy," etc.), but this makes no difference; they remain implicit in the theory and explanation. Similarly, the fact that the moral implications may be unclear, contested, and ambiguous, and involve a clash of incompatible values (e.g., "Is it right to destroy a traditional society and its culture for the sake of a highly unequal, consumption-oriented prosperity?") does not eliminate this moral dimension, but helps delineate it. To recognize moral ambiguity is to make a moral judgment.

There are even ways in which, in order to explain major events and to develop and test fairly broad theories or interpretations, one must make moral judgments on the nature of the actions involved. Let me illustrate this first from my own experience. Some years ago, in response to an important study of international crises by Richard Ned Lebow, I wrote an essay arguing that a major category of international crises was overlooked in his and other analyses in international relations theory, which I labeled the "failed bargain crisis."[5] My core argument was that many crises are caused by international bargains which fail after they have been successfully negotiated between the contending parties themselves, and that they principally fail because other parties not involved in the original bargain work deliberately or unwittingly to make them fail. I took as a major example of such a failed bargain crisis the Bosnian Crisis in 1908–09, principally involving Austria-Hungary and Russia. My

---

4. David S. Landes, *The Wealth and Poverty of Nations* (New York: W.W. Norton, 1998).

5. Richard Ned Lebow, *From Peace to War: The Nature of International Crisis* (Baltimore: Johns Hopkins University Press, 1981); and Paul W. Schroeder, "Failed Bargain Crises, Deterrence, and the International System," in Paul C. Stern et al., eds., *Perspectives on Deterrence* (New York: Oxford University Press, 1989), pp. 67–83.

interpretation was that a bargain had been made in good faith in September 1908 between the two foreign ministers, Baron Aehrenthal of Austria-Hungary and Count Izvolski of Russia, and that their bargain broke down when other leaders within the Russian government and among Russia's friends, France and Britain, acted to frustrate it. The British historian F. Roy Bridge later pointed out to me, however, that this explanation would not work and that the Bosnian Crisis could not be classed a failed bargain crisis because, according to Austrian and Russian documents he had discovered and published, there never had been a real good-faith bargain between Aehrenthal and Izvolski. Instead, the latter had always intended not to fulfill his end of the bargain, but instead to exploit Austria's actual annexation of Bosnia-Herzegovina, to which he had agreed, for purposes of embarrassing Austria, winning a diplomatic victory over it, and restoring Russia's sunken prestige in the Balkans.[6]

What does this have to do with the question of moral judgments in history? Simply this: I was forced to reclassify this crisis, removing it from the category of a failed bargain crisis, not simply because I learned facts hitherto unknown to me about the hidden agenda Izvolski had pursued in the negotiations. Statesmen almost always have a hidden agenda, especially in foreign policy; prevailing conventions in diplomacy expect and allow for it.[7] Diplomats are supposed to conceal their own government's hidden purposes and to try to ferret out those of their counterparts. What compelled me to change my interpretation and categorization of this crisis was the meaning and significance of these facts, a meaning inescapably bound up with and deriving from a moral judgment—that Izvolski, unlike Aehrenthal, had gone over the line, broken the conventions of good-faith bargaining. The fact that he had not simply concealed his hidden purposes and tacitly deceived Aehrenthal, but had flatly lied and intended to betray the bargain, changed the whole character of the transaction and the explanation of the origins of the crisis, compelling me to blame Izvolski more and his Russian colleagues and British and French leaders less for it. (The story also illustrates one reason why historians may be less enamored of theory-building than political scientists—not necessarily because they have less interest in large-scale, idealized and

---

6. F.R. Bridge, "Izvolsky, Aehrenthal, and the End of the Austro-Russian Entente, 1906–8," *Mitteilungen des Oesterreichischen Staatsarchivs, Sonderdruck*, Vol. 29 (1976), pp. 316–362.

7. There are many anecdotes which illustrate this tendency of diplomats to see a hidden purpose behind everything their opponents do. My favorite is a remark attributed to Prince Metternich of Austria when he learned that an old rival, the Russian diplomat Pozzo di Borgo, had died: "Now why do you suppose he did that?"

stylized, more or less abstract explanations, but because they have repeatedly learned how easily such explanations, however neat and convincing, can be upset by inconvenient facts.)

This process by which moral judgments enter integrally into the explanation and categorization of major developments has wide application in international history. Repeatedly historians are compelled, in order to state what a statesman or country was doing, to judge the action or purpose morally in terms of the prevailing rules and norms of international politics, and thus to say what game was being played, and whether this actor or that was playing the game or wrecking it. Playing this "blame game" is not necessarily a needless distraction from the historian's real task of stating what the actors did, though it can become this; it is often an integral, necessary part of telling what they did and explaining it. For example, a key question in seventeenth-century international history concerns how to interpret the policy of Cardinal Richelieu of France. Virtually all scholars have abandoned the old view (still held by Henry Kissinger) of Richelieu as the founder of a new, rational, secular, egoistic politics of *raison d'etat*.[8] All would now agree, as Matthew Anderson says, that Richelieu did not distinguish between the needs of his king, Louis XIII, the French state, and those of the Catholic church and Christendom generally.[9] But major disagreement arises over how he conceived those interlocking interests and ends and tried to advance them, and the dispute involves differing judgments, essentially moral in character, made as to what Richelieu was really doing. Some leading historians (Fritz Dickmann, Emanuel Thau, William F. Church, Hermann Weber, Karl Otmar von Aretin, and Klaus Malettke) have argued that Richelieu's real goal was not conquest, expansion, and French domination of Europe, but rather the erection of a collective security system for lasting peace in Europe, led by France. According to this view, his successor Mazarin followed Richelieu's policy in its externals but without its European spirit, and Louis XIV distorted it into a quest for French domination, conquest, and glory. Others, however, notably Johannes Burkhardt and Derek Croxton, argue that Richelieu's actions in allegedly pursuing a French-led collective security system in Europe differed little in terms of tactics, claims, and strategies from the actions of Mazarin and Louis XIV later. Hence regardless of Richelieu's claimed motives and intentions, this was in effect the same policy of expansion and domination as that of his successors. Note that this is not a dispute about the moral character

---

8. *Diplomacy* (New York: Simon and Schuster, 1994), pp. 58–67.

9. M.S. Anderson, *The Rise of Modern European Diplomacy 1450–1919* (London: Longman, 1993), p. 161.

of Richelieu himself, or about the aims of his policy. It is a dispute essentially about the character, at once moral and practical, of his actions. The factual judgment as to what he was doing and how his policy should be understood cannot be separated from the moral one. Similar cases arise frequently.

The last reason (at least the last I will develop here) for the historian's being necessarily involved with moral judgments is the subtlest and trickiest to explain, but also (to me at least) the most central. It originated with the famous historian of the Renaissance Garrett Mattingly, was further developed by the historian of seventeenth-century England J. H. Hexter, and is here given a slight further twist by me.[10] It involves a proposition first stated by Mattingly: that the historian has the moral obligation to do justice to the past, not for the sake of the past but for his own. It is easy enough, I think, to say what the first part of this means, to do justice to the past. It means essentially the obligation to treat the whole past fairly and with integrity—to understand it on its own terms and not anachronistically, to let the other side be heard, to be sensitive to the unheard or neglected voices, not to employ an ethics of success but give a due respect and attention to lost causes, and the like. It may not be easy to give a precise, categorical, practical definition of "doing justice to the past," but the concept passes the Potter Stewart test on pornography—we recognize it when we see it or fail to see it, or at least are convinced that we do. Nor is it at all difficult to show that this desire to do justice to the past plays a large role in the actual investigation and writing of history, and a vital, beneficial one. It is impossible, for example, to imagine so distinguished a historian as J.H. Elliott spending great time and energy in researching the career of so unsympathetic a character as the seventeenth-century Spanish statesman the Count-Duke of Olivares had he not been convinced, as he tells us, that however unlikeable Olivares was and however disastrous his policies turned out to be, history had not dealt justly with him.[11] Not only are a great many individual works of history powerfully influenced by this feeling, but it also helps account for the emergence of new fields and emphases in history. The history of women, gender history, the history of everyday life, history from below, the history of various ignored or suppressed groups, and other such fields have arisen not just because their practitioners had

---

10. See the discussion of Mattingly in J.H. Hexter, *Doing History* (Bloomington: Indiana University Press, 1974).

11. J.H. Elliott, *The Count-Duke of Olivares: The Statesman in an Age of Decline* (New Haven, Conn.: Yale University Press, 1986). See also his *Richelieu and Olivares* (Cambridge: Cambridge University Press, 1984).

career ambitions to pursue or ideological axes to grind, but because of a widespread conviction, often justified, that in these areas justice had not been done to the past.

It is harder to explain just what the second half of the axiom means: "not for the sake of the past, but for our own." The meaning of "not for the sake of the past" is clear enough: The past is not a sacred object of worship or veneration. Those in the past are beyond caring whether they receive justice from historians or not. But the second part, "for our own sake," admits of different meanings. Mattingly seems to have meant by it "our own sake as professional historians, in recognition of the high scholarly standards we have to live up to and the kind of history we want to deliver to our generation and future ones." Hexter takes it a bit further: "our own sake as moral persons, recognizing that we owe the same fair treatment to historic personages as we do to living ones, and should accord them justice in response to the same general moral obligation."[12] Admitting both these as true and important, I would go one step further: "our own sake as human beings seeking self-knowledge." By doing justice to the past we go further and deeper in finding out important truths about ourselves as human beings. The most apt description of the historian's attitude toward his or her subject and work is, it seems to me, the statement of the Roman writer Quintilian (though I am told he meant it ironically): "To consider nothing human alien to myself." In doing justice to the past, we approach those goals which history has always acknowledged, if not always served—to make the strange familiar and the familiar strange, to expand the range and increase the depth of our understanding of what it means to be a human being.

This understanding of the Mattingly-Hexter formulation of the moral task of history appeals to me also as a further demonstration of how moral judgments in history are inescapable because they are embedded in it. The task of doing history does not merely contain a moral aspect or dimension but is intrinsically a moral pursuit, belonging to one of humankind's supreme moral obligations, "Know thyself." I am of course not saying or hinting that history is the only discipline with this lofty purpose and function. All the liberal arts and the sciences, including the social sciences, share it. Nor am I hinting that social scientists in abstaining from making moral judgments in order to achieve their purposes become thereby less moral or truth-seeking or profound than historians, and offer less self-knowledge. But I would say that a difference between the two fields and approaches stems from the same source as their

---

12. These are my formulations of Mattingly's and Hexter's positions, not quotations from them.

different meanings and uses of cause and causality, namely, the difference between treating human actions mainly as behavior or mainly as conduct. It is the latter emphasis which I think makes history especially valuable for self-knowledge, and it is a reluctance to abstract from it and the moral dimension it contains that makes me sure that I could never be a political scientist. However, as Jervis says, this is no reason why we cannot be friends and, in some cases, allies.

Contributors

Andrew Bennett is Associate Professor of Government at Georgetown University and author of *Condemned to Repetition? The Rise, Fall, and Reprise of Soviet-Russian Military Interventionism 1973–1996* (1999). Together with Alexander George, he is the author of *Case Studies and Theory Development*, forthcoming from the BCSIA Studies in International Security and The MIT Press.

Colin Elman is Assistant Professor of Political Science at Arizona State University and was an International Security Fellow at the Belfer Center for Science and International Affairs, Harvard University from 1998 to 2000. He has published in the *American Political Science Review, International Security,* and *Security Studies* and is currently Secretary-Treasurer of the Interdisciplinary Approaches to International History and Politics section of the American Political Science Association, as well as the Executive Director of the Inter-University Faculty Consortium on Qualitative Research Methods.

Miriam Fendius Elman is Assistant Professor of Political Science at Arizona State University and was an International Security Fellow at the Belfer Center for Science and International Affairs, Harvard University from 1998 to 2000. She is the editor of *Paths to Peace: Is Democracy the Answer?* (1997) and her work appears in the *American Political Science Review,* the *British Journal of Political Science, International Security,* the *International History Review, Security Studies* and a variety of other scholarly journals.

Carole K. Fink is Professor of European International History at the Ohio State University. Her most recent publications include two edited volumes, *1968: The World Transformed* (1998) and *The Establishment of Frontiers in Europe after the Two World Wars* (1996), as well as a new paperback edition of *The Genoa Conference: European Diplomacy, 1921–22* (1984, 1993) which was awarded the George Louis Beer prize of the American Historical Association.

John Lewis Gaddis is Robert A. Lovett Professor of History at Yale University, a Senior Fellow of the Hoover Institution, and Oxford University's George Eastman Visiting Professor during 2000–2001. His books include: *The United States and the Origins of the Cold War, 1941–1947* (1972); *The Long Peace: Inquiries into the History of the Cold War* (1987); and *We Now Know: Rethinking Cold War History* (1997). Professor Gaddis is on the advisory board of the Cold War International History Project, served as a consultant on the CNN television documentary "Cold War," and is currently working on a biography of George F. Kennan.

Alexander L. George held the Graham H. Stuart Professorship in Political Science at Stanford University, and he is a leading expert on foreign and security policy, presidential decision-making, and political psychology. He is currently co-authoring a book with Andrew Bennett, *Case Studies and Theory Development*, which is forthcoming from the BCSIA Studies in International Security and The MIT Press.

Edward Ingram is Editor of *The International History Review* and Professor of Imperial History at Simon Fraser University. His most recent work is *Empire-building and Empire-builders* (1995).

Robert Jervis is Adlai E. Stevenson Professor of International Politics at Columbia University, and is President-elect of the American Political Science Association. His most recent book is *System Effects: Complexity in Political Life* (1997).

Deborah Welch Larson is Professor of Political Science at the University of California, Los Angeles. Her research draws on cognitive social psychology to explain foreign policy decision-making, as in *Origins of Containment: A Psychological Explanation* (1989). She is the author most recently of *Anatomy of Mistrust: U.S.-Soviet Relations During the Cold War* (1997), which uses social psychology to explain missed opportunities to mitigate U.S.-Soviet rivalry. She is currently working on a study of intuition and analysis in American foreign policy as well as the problem of "bringing Russia into the club" of Western developed states.

Richard Ned Lebow is director of the Mershon Center and Professor of History, Political Science and Psychology at the Ohio State University. He is the author, co-author or co-editor of numerous books and articles, including *We All Lost the Cold War* (1994), *The Art of Bargaining* (1996), *Unmaking the West* (forthcoming) and *Theory and Evidence in Comparative Politics and International Relations* (forthcoming).

Jack S. Levy is Board of Governors' Professor of Political Science at Rutgers University. His research interests concern the causes of war and foreign policy decision-making, and his current research projects include economic interdependence and war, the militarization of commercial rivalries, diversionary theory and politically-motivated opposition to war, the conditions under which democracies fight "preventive wars," the conditions under which states engage in balancing behavior, applications of prospect theory to foreign policy and international relations, and the criteria for evaluating progress in social science research programs.

John A. Lynn is Professor of History at the University of Illinois at Urbana-Champaign and Adjunct Professor at the Ohio State University. He concentrates on the military history of early modern Europe, eras of military transformation, and war and culture. His most recent volumes are *Giant of the Grand Siecle: The French Army, 1610–1715* (1997) and *The Wars of Louis XIV, 1667–1714* (1999).

Stephen Pelz is Professor of History at the University of Massachusetts, Amherst. He is the author of *Race to Pearl Harbor: The Failure of the Second London Naval Conference and the Onset of World War II* (1974) and "The Case for Limiting NATO Enlargement: A Realist Proposal for a Stable Division of Europe," *National Security Studies Quarterly*, Vol. 3, No. 3 (Summer 1997), pp. 59–72.

Richard Rosecrance is Director of the Burkle Center for International Relations and Professor of Political Science at UCLA. He previously held Full Professorships at Berkeley and Cornell and served in the Policy Planning Council of the U.S. Department of State. He has won Guggenheim, Fulbright, Rockefeller, Ford, and Carnegie Fellowships. He has written or edited more than a dozen books, including *The Rise of the Trading State* (1986); *America's Economic Resurgence* (1990) and most recently *The Rise of the Virtual State: Wealth and Power in the Coming Century* (1999).

Paul W. Schroeder is Professor Emeritus of History and Political Science at the University of Illinois at Urbana-Champaign. He is the author of four books and many articles on the history of international relations; his latest book is *The Transformation of European Politics, 1763–1848* (1994, 1996).

Randall L. Schweller is Associate Professor of Political Science at the Ohio State University. He is the author of *Deadly Imbalances: Tripolarity and Hitler's Strategy of World Conquest* (1998) and has published articles in various journals, including the *American Political Science Review, American Journal of Political Science, World Politics, International Studies Quarterly, International Security,* and *Security Studies*. In 1993, he received a John M. Olin Post-Doctoral Fellowship in National Security at the Center for International Affairs, Harvard University.

William R. Thompson is Professor of Political Science at Indiana University. His most recent publications include *Great Power Rivalries* (1999), an edited volume in which half of the chapters are written by historians and half by political scientists; and *The Emergence of the Global Political Economy* (2000), which focuses primarily on the past 500 years. His current research interests include strategic rivalries, North-South IPE, evolutionary approaches to IR theory, and modeling ancient world system dynamics.

Gerhard L. Weinberg is William Rand Kenan, Jr., Professor Emeritus of the University of North Carolina at Chapel Hill. He is the author of numerous books and articles on the origins and course of World War II.

William C. Wohlforth is Associate Professor of Government at Dartmouth College, and author of *The Elusive Balance: Power and Perceptions During the Cold War* (1993).

Index

BCSIA Studies in International Security

Published by The MIT Press

Sean M. Lynn-Jones and Steven E. Miller, series editors
Karen Motley, executive editor
Belfer Center for Science and International Affairs (BCSIA)
John F. Kennedy School of Government, Harvard University

Allison, Graham T., Owen R. Coté, Jr., Richard A. Falkenrath, and Steven E. Miller, *Avoiding Nuclear Anarchy: Containing the Threat of Loose Russian Nuclear Weapons and Fissile Material* (1996)

Allison, Graham T., and Kalypso Nicolaïdis, eds., *The Greek Paradox: Promise vs. Performance* (1996)

Arbatov, Alexei, Abram Chayes, Antonia Handler Chayes, and Lara Olson, eds., *Managing Conflict in the Former Soviet Union: Russian and American Perspectives* (1997)

Bennett, Andrew, *Condemned to Repetition? The Rise, Fall, and Reprise of Soviet-Russian Military Interventionism, 1973–1996* (1999)

Blackwill, Robert D., and Paul Dibb, eds., *America's Asian Alliances* (2000)

Blackwill, Robert D., and Michael Stürmer, eds., *Allies Divided: Transatlantic Policies for the Greater Middle East* (1997)

Brom, Shlomo, and Yiftah Shapir, eds., *The Middle East Military Balance 1999–2000* (2000)

Brown, Michael E., ed., *The International Dimensions of Internal Conflict* (1996)

Brown, Michael E., and Šumit Ganguly, eds., *Government Policies and Ethnic Relations in Asia and the Pacific* (1997)

Elman, Miriam Fendius, ed., *Paths to Peace: Is Democracy the Answer?* (1997)

Falkenrath, Richard A., *Shaping Europe's Military Order: The Origins and Consequences of the CFE Treaty* (1994)

Falkenrath, Richard A., Robert D. Newman, and Bradley A. Thayer, *America's Achilles' Heel: Nuclear, Biological, and Chemical Terrorism and Covert Attack* (1998)

Feldman, Shai, *Nuclear Weapons and Arms Control in the Middle East* (1996)

Forsberg, Randall, ed., *The Arms Production Dilemma: Contraction and Restraint in the World Combat Aircraft Industry* (1994)

Hagerty, Devin T., *The Consequences of Nuclear Proliferation: Lessons from South Asia* (1998)

Heymann, Philip B., *Terrorism and America: A Commonsense Strategy for a Democratic Society* (1998)

Kokoshin, Andrei A., *Soviet Strategic Thought, 1917–91* (1998)

Lederberg, Joshua, *Biological Weapons: Limiting the Threat* (1999)

Shields, John M., and William C. Potter, eds., *Dismantling the Cold War: U.S. and NIS Perspectives on the Nunn-Lugar Cooperative Threat Reduction Program* (1997)

Tucker, Jonathan B., ed., *Toxic Terror: Assessing Terrorist Use of Chemical and Biological Weapons* (2000)

Utgoff, Victor A., ed., *The Coming Crisis: Nuclear Proliferation, U.S. Interests, and World Order* (2000)

The Robert and Renée Belfer Center for Science and International Affairs

Graham T. Allison, Director
John F. Kennedy School of Government
Harvard University
79 JFK Street, Cambridge, MA 02138
(617) 495-1400

The Belfer Center for Science and International Affairs (BCSIA) is the hub of research, teaching, and training in international security affairs, environmental and resource issues, and science and technology policy at Harvard's John F. Kennedy School of Government. The Center's mission is to provide leadership in advancing policy-relevant knowledge about the most important challenges of international security and other critical issues where science, technology, and international affairs intersect.

BCSIA's leadership begins with the recognition of science and technology as driving forces transforming international affairs. The Center integrates insights of social scientists, natural scientists, technologists, and practitioners with experience in government, diplomacy, the military, and business to address these challenges. The Center pursues its mission in four complementary research programs:

- The International Security Program (ISP) addresses the most pressing threats to U.S. national interests and international security.

- The Environment and Natural Resources Program (ENRP) is the locus of Harvard's interdisciplinary research on resource and environmental problems and policy responses.

- The Science, Technology, and Public Policy (STPP) program analyzes ways in which science and technology policy influence international security, resources, environment, and development, and such cross-cutting issues as technological innovation and information infrastructure.

- The Strengthening Democratic Institutions (SDI) project catalyzes support for three great transformations in Russia, Ukraine, and the other republics of the former Soviet Union—to sustainable democracies, free market economies, and cooperative international relations.

The heart of the Center is its resident research community of more than one hundred scholars: Harvard faculty, analysts, practitioners, and each year a new, interdisciplinary group of research fellows. BCSIA sponsors frequent seminars, workshops, and conferences, many open to the public; maintains a substantial specialized library; and publishes books, monographs, and discussion papers. The Center's International Security Program, directed by Steven E. Miller, publishes the BCSIA Studies in International Security, and sponsors and edits the quarterly journal *International Security*.

The Center is supported by an endowment established with funds from Robert and Renée Belfer, the Ford Foundation, and Harvard University, by foundation grants, by individual gifts, and by occasional government contracts.